JA954.0

D0421468

SOAS LIBRARY WITHDRAWN

SOAS, University of London

18 0832623 5

Querying the Medieval

Querying the Medieval

TEXTS AND THE HISTORY OF PRACTICES IN SOUTH ASIA

Ronald Inden
Jonathan Walters
Daud Ali

SOAS LIBRARY
WITHDRAWN

OXFORD
UNIVERSITY PRESS
2000

OXFORD
UNIVERSITY PRESS

Oxford New York
Athens Auckland Bangkok Bogotá Buenos Aires Calcutta
Cape Town Chennai Dar es Salaam Delhi Florence Hong Kong Istanbul
Karachi Kuala Lumpur Madrid Melbourne Mexico City Mumbai
Nairobi Paris São Paulo Singapore Taipei Tokyo Toronto Warsaw

and associated companies in
Berlin Ibadan

Copyright © 2000 by Oxford University Press, Inc.

Published by Oxford University Press, Inc.
198 Madison Avenue, New York, New York 10016

Oxford is a registered trademark of Oxford University Press

All rights reserved. No part of this publication may be reproduced, stored in a retrieval system, or transmitted, in any form or by any means, electronic, mechanical, photocopying, recording, or otherwise, without the prior permission of Oxford University Press.

Library of Congress Cataloging-in-Publication Data
Querying the medieval : texts and the history of practices in
South Asia / Ronald Inden, Jonathan Walters, Daud Ali
p. cm.
Includes index.
ISBN 0-19-512430-8
1. South Asia—Civilization. I. Inden, Ronald B.
II. Walters, Jonathan S. III. Ali, Daud.
DS339.Q44 2000
954.02—dc21 99-10675

1 3 5 7 9 8 6 4 2

Printed in the United States of America
on acid-free paper

SOAS LIBRARY

Contents

Querying the Medieval

1

Introduction

From Philological to Dialogical Texts

Ronald Inden

South Asia has been one of the focal points for rethinking the forms that Western knowledge of non-Western civilizations has taken. The "scientific" study of "traditional" South Asian texts, beginning with the Vedas—once thought to be the oldest extant texts in an Indo-European language—has been central to the colonial construction of India as a civilization and to the nationalist project of making India, Pakistan, Sri Lanka, Bangladesh, and Nepal into "modern" independent nations. These texts figure prominently in South Asian fundamentalist, regionalist, and secular nationalist movements today. Strangely enough, postcolonial scholarship seems to have reinscribed a major divide in colonialist discourse, the divide between the traditional or medieval and the modern. The essays in this volume are concerned with the reevaluation of the approaches to these texts that have formed the basis of that discursive divide and of the constructions of the medieval and modern. The texts at issue here are the Sanskrit Purāṇas, crucial for the representation of an ancient and medieval Hindu civilization; the Pāli Vaṃsas, which have been the major sources for the writing of a history of an original Buddhism and for fashioning the history of the island kingdom and nation of Sri Lanka; and, finally, the royal genealogical eulogies inscribed on metal and stone, the "hard" empirical sources that modern historians have used to construct a chronologically accurate history of ancient and early medieval South Asia. The three essays in this book are the result of work in which several of us at Chicago and elsewhere have been engaged for close to twenty years. After a great deal of separate reading and criticism, and one-on-one discussion with colleagues and students, we decided in 1983 to formalize our questioning. We began a colloquium, "Texts and Knowledge of South Asia" that has met on the campus of the University of Chicago irregularly ever since.

Our position, after ten years, is this: we wish to see texts as participating in ongoing debates about how the human world should be ordered, and we wish to think of the traditions of which they are parts as something belonging to the living present and not as mere monuments of a dead past. We want to think of texts as works enmeshed in the circumstances in which people have made and used them, and we want to see them both as articulating the world in which they are situated and as articulated by it, that is, as integral to the makeup of one another. And because circumstances continually impinge on people's life-wishes and dislocate the orders people are trying to build, we also want to see texts and the world (context) as remaking or reworking one another. We reject the heavily criticized view that conceives of texts as merely or even uniquely expressive of something that lies beyond them.

This position has emerged from a prolonged questioning of scholarship on South Asia, combined with some widely dispersed and often critical reading of theoretical works. To some extent our work parallels that done by the "new historicists." It also relies on some of the work of "poststructuralists," especially Foucault and Derrida, and, from a different angle, Laclau and Mouffe. The predominant position here, though, follows on a reading of the post-Hegelian R. G. Collingwood and of the heterodox Marxists, Vološinov/Bakhtin, and Antonio Gramsci.

We address both textual scholars and historians in this collection of essays. It has become fashionable for historians to look to textual scholars (especially, in the United States, to critics in English departments with whom the Force now resides) for solutions to their problems, and for textual scholars to look to history. There are good reasons for this. If we give up the notion of a universal truth grounded either in theology or in scientific knowledge, if we no longer think of the state of affairs in the world as God's plan or nature's design, then the object of our inquiry shifts. We no longer concern ourselves with trying to know God or one of his reborn substitutes—human nature, reason, creative genius, modes of production, and the like—but turn to the causes of the human world: transitory human agents and their actions. Of special concern are the practices, persistent and consciously ordered activities, in which people engage because these, more than other activities, have to do with ordering the world and disrupting orders. Among these practices, the ones having to do with texts and with the use of texts take on an importance they did not have before. Our knowledge of the human world beyond the reach of our immediate experience comes to us through texts, if we construe this category as embracing stories told from memory, TV news, pulp fiction, computer databases, home videos, and magazines as well as the Bible and the humanist works of a high culture taught in universities. If texts and the practices in which their making and use are embedded are no longer merely the vehicles for knowledge that resides elsewhere—in God or Nature—then knowledge of textual practices becomes of paramount importance. History also becomes crucial because the direct, predictive knowledge we can have of the human world through disciplines modeled on the older natural sciences becomes less privileged. Knowledge becomes retrospective and critical, and concerned with the reconstruction of the past, of the practices in which people made knowledges—which is to say, historical.

History is also important in another sense. Critical, retrospective knowledge is not only vital in an intellectual project that privileges the actions of transitory human actors. It has always been important for any community that tries to make itself a polity, a complex agent capable of shaping itself and its world. That many of those specially charged with this activity have tried to erase and falsify or otherwise manipulate the past, and attribute past actions to gods and heroes or sages or, in our own time, to market forces or late capitalism, simply underlines the importance of this activity. To strip a community of this capacity to textualize its past or deny that they possess it, as in the case of India, is to strip those people of the knowledge to articulate themselves as polities. We call this colonialism. Our approach will also show that the makers and users of texts in India did indeed "have history" and were agents of their own world despite the double handicap of being in India and of being medieval. At the same time, we also wish to argue that the history denied in India either did not exist in the West until recently or is not, by our criteria, the thoroughgoing history we would like every polity to have.

Our problems would be solved if we could take the methods textual scholars and historians each have to offer and gratefully combine them. This, however, would not be desirable. Both textual and historical scholarship are beset with problems, and this is especially so for the ancient and medieval texts of South Asia.

Textualizing History

What, then, are the problems we face? Many South Asianists might suppose that the main problem we face in the postcolonial period is "orientalism." Certainly this is important, though by no means can we say that some easily identifiable orientalism is to be found uniformly at work in every treatment of a South Asian text. Scholars of South Asia have approached texts with a variety of assumptions. More importantly, orientalism cannot be isolated from the more general problems that textual scholars confront. It is, rather, an inflection of the existing approaches. The main problem we wish to address is what Vološinov calls the construal of the text as a monological utterance.[1] This holds that a text, for example the *Mahābhārata*, is a closed, isolated entity, one that has an identifiable essence, a permanent core of meanings, which is what its readers are supposed to obtain when they read it. There has been a long-standing debate about what the essence of a text consists of and where it is to be located. One side, dominated by aesthetics, assumes that the essence of the text is psychic and the property of discrete individuals or subjects. I shall refer to it as authorism.[2] The other, dominated by philology, assumes textual essences are material and belong to the objective linguistic (phonological, grammatical, lexical) structures (and by extension to social, economic, or cultural structures) that impinge on individual authors from outside.[3] I shall call this position contextualism. Scholars have oscillated between these two positions/trends in their study of texts. Since most of the scholars who have studied ancient and medieval India have combined their training in philology with an interest in literary esthetics, political history, or religion and mythology it is usual to find both of these trends at work in their writings.

The major position inherited by the post-World War II generation of scholars in the disciplines that study the texts of the West was estheticist.[4] It holds that a

[1]V. N. Vološinov, *Marxism and the Philosophy of Language*, translated by Ladislav Matejka and R. Titunik (Cambridge: Harvard University Press, 1973), p. 72.

[2]Vološinov refers to this position as "individualistic subjectivism," pp. 45–52.

[3]According to Vološinov, "abstract objectivism," pp. 52–63.

[4]Benedetto Croce works this out in *The Aesthetic as the Science of Expression and of the Linguistic in General*, translated from Italian by C. Lyas ([1900] Cambridge: Cambridge University Press, 1992).

text is the unique expression of a mortal (but perhaps divinely inspired) man and hence a monological utterance.[5] The "higher truths" in a text may be eternal, but their concrete expression in the text is based on the "experience" of the author and is confined, therefore, to a finite time and place. Once the author has inscribed his intent in a text, the work is complete and should, henceforth, be treated as the expression—one might as well say the property—of a unique individual.[6] The problem of how such authors are themselves constituted does not arise, for it is assumed that individual greatness is everywhere the same and will somehow manifest itself.[7]

On first sight, authorists seem to focus on historically transitory actors as the agents of their texts, but there is a strong tendency to turn authors into the instruments of what Collingwood calls a substantialized agent, a term by which he designates an agent which, although it underlies the actions of transitory historical agents, stands outside the flow of history and remains unaffected by the acts of those agents. The substantialized agent onto which authorists tend to displace agency is some supposedly universal expressive or creative genius, equated with either the spiritual essence of humanity or God himself.[8] It is a close relative of the ideas of human nature in free-market economics, though some would claim that it transcends the material and selfish urges of the marketplace.

Cultural and literary histories here privilege the authors of texts over their readers and, because authors precede readers in time, tend also to elevate the past over the present. Their narratives proceed by talking about the "influences" that earlier authors have on later ones. Indeed, they assume that the main job of the historian is to document these influences.[9] Combined with the notion of authorism (and expressive realism) is also the idea of a a high or elite culture, a great tradition that is the opposite of a low folk or mass culture, a little tradition. It doubles the author as the site of the unique expression of reality. Just as the author captures the essence of the human world around him, so the high culture (reducible to its authors) contains, represents, and expresses the values of the entire culture or civilization in question, be it Western or Eastern.

Most orientalists approached their texts with this authorist notion perhaps uppermost in their minds, but alas their project was to come to an understanding of texts that did not easily meet the criteria of the authorist and aestheticist concerns of their colleagues in English and Germanic or Romance language and literature departments. It appeared that many of India's "sacred" texts—Vedas, Epics, Purāṇas, and Sūtras—like that notorious text, the Bible (upon which tex-

---

[5]Vološinov, *Marxism*, p. 84.

[6]One literary critic refers to some of the major problems under the rubric of expressive realism: Catherine Belsey, *Critical Practice* (London: Methuen, 1980), pp. 7–14.

[7]Michel Foucault, "What Is an Author?" in his *Language, Counter-Memory, Practice: Selected Essays and Interviews*, edited by Donald F. Bouchard (Ithaca: Cornell University Press, 1977), pp. 124–25; Roland Barthes, "The Death of the Author" in *Image-Music-Text*, translated by Stephen Heath (Glasgow: Fontana, 1977), pp. 142–48.

[8]Croce, *Aesthetic*, pp. 15–16.

[9]Dominick Lacapra, "Reading Intellectual History and Reading Texts" in his *Rethinking Intellectual History* (Ithaca: Cornell University Press, 1983), pp. 23–71.

tual criticism as a discipline began)—are themselves not internally coherent works of the same "author." Much work has gone into making critical editions, trying to create discrete texts out of the mass of manuscripts accumulated by colonial scholars. The assumption behind this Indolological project is that once texts have been disentangled and attributed to discrete authors, then we can determine what reality they express, convey, or mirror. That is, authorist concerns would have to be deferred in favor of philological needs. To a very large extent, the philological project, for reasons given below, was antithetical to the aesthetic project. Nonetheless, Indologists claimed some success in this direction. The most famous Indian literary author to emerge from the process of philological scrutiny was the poet and dramatist, Kālidāsa, construed as a "genius" at expressing the Indian natural world (the tropics) in general and the life and times of the "classical" or Gupta age, the high point of Indian civilization as Brahmanical or Hindu, in particular. Here is A. B. Keith speaking of that playwright's *Raghuvaṃśa*:

> In the description of Raghu's conquests we need not seek for parallelism in detail with the achievements of Samudragupta and Chandragupta, but we have in it the poetic reflex of the achievements of these great Emperors; as ever Kālidāsa effects his aim not by direct means but by suggestion; just as Virgil glorifies Rome and incidentally the imperial dynasty by his *Aeneid*, so Kālidāsa extols the sway of the Guptas and the Brahmanical restoration by reminding his audience of the glories of the far gone days of the solar race.[10]

Even here, where some unity of authorship is assumed, an orientalist construct of the Indian mind as dominated by the *imagination* has permitted scholars to assume that South Asian texts have only the most tenuous connection with external reality. Whereas language in the Western text provides transparent access to its object, language in India, being either too elliptic or too ornate—and Kālidāsa is the least of the offenders on this score—conceals or obscures its object. Recently, literary markets and critics have reinscribed this notion of the imagination, but this time it is positively and highly valued under the rubric of magic realism. Salman Rushdie thus falls heir to Kālidāsa.[11]

Structuralists and cultural or symbolic anthropologists have been among the most prominent critics of the aestheticist form of authorism in the past four decades. They emphasize the importance of relations among units—meanings, themes, classes of objects—in cultural or social systems that stand as total objects outside of or between "individuals" arguing that these be given primacy in textual analysis over the individual properties that constitute authors and texts. Structuralism, however, cannot be said to have displaced philology in the study of India's ancient and medieval texts. Structuralism is, furthermore, only one form of contextualism. Taken more loosely, it is a trend that insists on the priority of context, the

[10]A. Berriedale Keith, *Classical Sanskrit Literature* ([1923; rev. ed. 1927] Calcutta: YMCA Publishing House, 1958), p. 35. Note here how the reflection that Kālidāsa mirrors to his reader is, like Virgil's, "oblique."

[11]Aijaz Ahmed has questioned this neo-orientalist treatment of the literatures of India and other decolonized countries on the part of poststructuralists and others in "'Third World Literature' and the Nationalist Ideology," *Journal of Arts and Ideas* 17–18 (June 1989), 117–35.

setting, system, or structure in which the text is embedded, over its author. From the standpoint of agency, the problem is this: the contextualist tends to displace agency from transitory agents onto the generality of what the text expresses—industrial society, the bourgeois family, the Greek polis, Roman imperialism, Christendom—because it is there that the essence of the text lies. History, as many critics have pointed out, is largely irrelevant for structuralists. At best we are concerned with histories of the sort that Braudel has made famous under the rubric of the longue durée.

Indologists have certainly treated texts in a contextualist manner. The Purāṇas are taken to be expressions of a classical Hinduism or a caste society or the interaction between Aryan and Dravidian races. The Vaṃsas are considered the expressions of an early, authentic Buddhism; and the land-grant inscriptions are made to reveal an Asiatic or feudal mode of production. Once again, Keith provides a good instance when he interprets an historical poem about Kashmir for his reader: the author, Kalhaṇa, is clearly not expressing the reality of Kashmir's political life for us on his own. He is the instrument of that higher author, the peculiarly ineffectual form of oriental despotism that many of the British imagined to exist as the essence of Indian politics. Though his "characterization in the main...lacks depth," Kalhaṇa

> knows well the types which thronged the petty principalities of his day, the rival ministers, the greedy soldiers, the intriguing priests, the teachers only too proficient in immorality, the untamed barons of the country, the frail ladies from the temples, and the royal *entourage* divided into hostile factions. He is a master of the petty politics of Kashmir and its treachery, massacres, intrigue, murder, suicide, strife of son against father, of brother against brother, its worthless debauchees of kings, its intriguing queens like the bloodthirsty and lascivious Diddā (A.D. 980–1003), who put her own grandson to death in order to rule alone. (p. 55)

Keith, like most of his colleagues, was not in any explicit sense a structuralist. But there is a stronger sense in which Indology has been structuralist.

Philology has and still does dominate the study of South Asian texts. Philology is no one thing historically. Germans in their industrious making of dictionaries have been more positivist than have French philologists. Still, I think it is possible, following Vološinov, to see structuralists as the descendants of the earlier French philologists and linguists, continuing to engage in a sort of orientalist practice.[12] According to Vološinov, the philologist was interested in languages that were not only dead but—and here one may see many of the philologists as orientalists—alien. The philologist could have treated his texts as dialogic utterances, but because they were not part of a living tradition for him, not part of a flow of utterances in which he had to make his way, the philologist construed them as monological. "The philologist-linguist," argues Vološinov, "tears the monument out of that real domain and views it as if it were a self-sufficient entity. He brings to bear on it not an

[12]The connecting link, of course, is the work of Georges Dumézil and those who follow him.

active ideological understanding but a completely passive kind of understanding, in which there is not a flicker of response, as there would be in any authentic kind of understanding."[13] The idea of a monological utterance that mirrors a static, dead tradition, passively reflected in the scholarship of the Indologist is, thus, grounded in the scientific discipline central to orientalism, philology.

It has its continuation in the structuralists' notion of a closed system of signs.[14] Anthropologists' theories of society and culture, I am afraid, are collateral kin of of the philologists' (especially if we think of Claude Lévi-Strauss and, for India, Louis Dumont). Indeed, anthropologists have provided the museums in which the philologists display their monuments.[15] Just as the texts reconstructed by philologists are abstract objects that noone historically used, so the tripartite structures of Georges Dumézil and the hierarchy of Dumont are themselves abstract objects, texts reconstructed from other actually existing texts.

Yet roughly the same problem, I contend, remains from the standpoint of the history of practices we want to undertake: the structuralists tend to treat their objective structures or systems as pregiven, in much the same way that the individualists do their authors (and readers). Those systems are, furthermore, as Vološinov shows (in relation to language) highly reductive abstractions from the real flow of utterances.[16] They take our attention away from situated textual practices and direct it to the abstraction which itself tends to become the subject of the narratives one constructs. Nor do the structuralists escape the dichotomy of a high and low culture, though they do tend to privilege the low or common over the high, or simply to conflate the two.

Beginning some twenty-five years ago, critics who have come to be called poststructuralists (Roland Barthes and especially Michel Foucault and Jacques Derrida) have criticized the presuppositions of unity, systematicity, and rationality in their structuralist predecessors.[17] Of particular importance in resolving some of

---

[13]Vološinov, *Marxism*, p. 73.

[14]According to Vološinov, "In reifying the system of language and in viewing living language as if it were dead and alien, abstract objectivism makes language something external to the stream of verbal communication" (p. 81).

[15]Unaccustomed to studying literate societies or "civilizations," the anthropologists Robert Redfield and Milton Singer attempted to recreate their object by making a distinction between great and little traditions. Singer used text to appropriate products of the great tradition and context in order to reposition ethnography; see "Text and Context in the Study of Contemporary Hinduism" and "Search for a Great Tradition in Cultural Performances," in his *When a Great Tradition Modernizes: An Anthropological Approach to Indian Civilization* (New York: Prager, 1972), pp. 39–52, 67–80. For him, a cultural performance was the site where the two came together. If the texts out of which scholars have written about Indian civilization or its supposedly distinctive religion, Hinduism, were abstracted ideals, then they would have to give way to the context of a cultural performance. Thus, at the end of the analysis, text is subsumed in context, returning the favor the Indologists had done the anthropologist by subsuming an entire civilization in a corpus of "classical" texts.

[16]Vološinov, *Marxism*, pp. 52–61.

[17]Above all, they have taken them to task for the primacy they place on binary opposition as the fundamental ordering principle of language and culture. Foucault has shown that the disciplinary practices assumed as rational can be seen as endowed with conflicting and shifting logics, and has demonstrated how an assumed opposition of power and knowledge works to manipulate our understanding of modernist practices. His emphasis on discourses as specific language practices articulative of the human

the difficulties of authorship and readership is Derrida's idea of supplementarity, which prevents the grounding of a text, the transcendence of its "outside." No text is, thus, complete unto itself.[18] People inevitably read a text through supplementation, through commentaries or representations of a text's significance in a tradition that postdates the text's supposed closure and keeps its eternal truth or universal insight up to date.

The poststructuralist opposition to monolithic structure equips us with some tools for the deconstruction of essentialism but does not provide the "space" or equipment for an alternative approach. Indeed, we are faced with the notion of text as infinite play of signifiers which Laclau has rightly called the "discourse of the psychotic."[19] This position comes dangerously close to the authorist approach with its emphasis on the text as a unique creation, but with the difference that "intertextuality," the interconnectedness of texts to which poststructuralists rightly point, extends to infinity the body of the text.

Each of these positions has something to offer. Authorists ask us to focus on creation of a specific text and its authorship, and they raise the problem of taste and evaluation, a problem that does not disappear in studies of the popular just by dismissing it. To the extent that contextualists, and especially the structuralists and poststructuralists, alert us to the importance of "systematicity" in cultural products, point to the social or collective and sometimes unconscious dimensions of textual production, and blur the dichotomy between the author and text and the realities they are supposed to express, their sociological and objectivist views are a desirable corrective to the individualist and subjectivist view that has tended to predominate in the Anglo-Saxon world. Yet there are major problems with both of these trends.

world is an important turn away from the universalism in structuralism (whether in the form of an unconscious savage mind or the practices of the unitary modern society) in Durkheimean sociology and the study of mentalité, and in classical Marxism; many of us have taken up this part of Foucault's approach. Derrida has shown how structuralism and earlier Western metaphysics both use opposition, and yet produce unity in their conceptions of the text, society, and the state by subsuming one of the elements of an opposition in the other, or by negating its existence altogether. Unfortunately, scholars of ancient and medieval South Asia have made little use of these criticisms. One example is that of text and context. Derrida's notion of undecidability is helpful in "deconstructing" such oppositions. Is, for example, the author of a text part of the text or of the context? Is that notoriously shadowy alter ego of the ethnographer, the informant, text or context? Where do we place the commentaries on a text, whether written or oral? And what is the status of the received wisdom of anthropology, carefully inscribed or printed and stored in libraries? More often than not, when my colleagues in anthropology call for context they seem to be asking for a detached, potentially feral, textual practice to be converted into an expression of or, at best, a commentary on this anthropological text.

[18]Michael Ryan, *Marxism and Deconstruction: A Critical Articulation* (Baltimore: Johns Hopkins University Press, 1982), pp. 10–11.

[19]Ernesto Laclau, *New Reflections on the Revolution of Our Time* (London: Verso, 1990), p. 90.

The authorist approach displaces our attention from the text onto its essence—the creative or expressive genius of the author and ultimately onto the psychic nature that underlies genius. The contextualist approach displaces our attention from specific texts onto an ur-text (or onto text fragments) that nobody used in the case of philology; or, in the case of structuralism or other structural approaches, it displaces agency onto the structure, system, or type that it supposedly expresses. We are thus left with a dichotomy between author and context (synonymous with the dichotomies of individual and society or agency and structure) and the problem of essence or substantialized agency.

To make matters worse, the very project of textual study has constituted itself as very much a part of the project of making and sustaining a European preeminence over the rest of the world. South Asian texts with all their "problems" were the underside of the European Self's construction of its own texts and tradition as the homogeneous, centered, and transcendent products of unitary authors. That work—the production of a unique canon of texts that would lead to or legitimate the rise of the West to world dominance—could only be carried out successfully if the same scholarship in its more "exotic" departments could show that the texts of the Other either lacked the qualities of their European counterparts, as in the case of sacred and epic texts, or, in the case of philosophical and literary texts, possessed them only in an inchoate ("underdeveloped") form.

In order to overcome this dichotomy of author and context and its attendant problem of essence, and make possible an alternative approach, we have turned to two connected notions, "complex agency" and "scale of texts." We have taken these notions from the English philosopher R. G. Collingwood, and extend them here.[20] His discussion of agency in connection with historical knowledge seems to offer a way both of criticizing current intellectual practices and of formulating an attractive alternative to the individualist and structuralist, as well as the antistructuralist, approaches in cultural history. We also draw out interesting parallels and convergences with the work of Vološinov.

Rather than thinking of the authors and readers (including listeners, reciters, performers, and so on.) of texts as either individual or collective, which is what scholars normally do, we want to think of the people and institutions concerned with texts as relatively simple (the "individual") or complex (the "nation-state") and more or less unitary or dispersed. The author might consist of a preceptor, himself the adherent of a particular disciplinary order and his royal pupil, of monks and nuns, of royal poets and key persons in a royal court. Authors, however, are complex in the sense that their composition consists of responses to other authors.

A text is a more or less composed utterance that is objectified in a practice involving some combination of writing, reading, reciting, performing, memorizing, teaching, and learning. Like utterances at large, texts are "dialogical" moments in the relations that agents, relatively simple or complex, have with themselves

[20] R. G. Collingwood, *The Idea of History*, rev. ed., with lectures 1926–1928, edited by Jan van der Dussen ([1946] Oxford: Clarendon Press, 1993). I read this in the light of his other works, following the example of Louis Mink, *Mind, History, and Dialectic: The Philosophy of R. G. Collingwood* (Middletown, Conn.: Wesleyan University Press, 1969).

and with other agents (both in their capacity as the agents of their actions and as the instruments and patients of them). It is important to distinguish two aspects of dialogue, the "dialectical" and the "eristical." An agent's practice of writing or reading a text is dialectical insofar as he or she starts from a position of nonagreement with another agent or agents, and comes through a process of argumentation to agreement. It is eristical to the extent that one agent attempts to gain victory over another with whom he or she disagrees. No act of speaking, writing, or reading is, however, purely dialectical or eristical.[21] Many texts in India (like Plato's Dialogues) are explicitly dialectical in their ordering, consisting of questions and answers.

To some degree or other and in varying ways, texts are discursive and narrative. Agents compose texts so that they may use them in their encounters to make arguments and to tell stories. Among the activities in which agents engage when they make and use texts is to determine what is rational in discursive practice and what counts as a plausible story. That is, there are no universal criteria that stand outside the practices of the agents concerned.

The arguments that agents are making, the stories they are telling in their ongoing utterances, are heterogeneous. The very practice of textualizing has as one of its purposes the reduction of heterogenity to homogeneities tailored to specified situations or organized around specific issues or wishes. A particular text is itself one momentary effect or result of the textual practices in which agents engage. It belongs to a tradition conceived of not as something dead and complete, or as the unfolding of an original unitary idea, but conceived of, after Collingwood, as a scale of texts. Later agents and their texts overlap with those of their predecessors and contemporaries and, by engaging in a process of criticism, appropriation, repetition, refutation, amplification, abbreviation, and so on, position themselves in relation to them. Vološinov, continuing with his treatment of the book as a dialogical form, confirms the notion of looking at tradition as a scale of utterances in Collingwood's sense.

> Moreover, a verbal performance of this kind also inevitably orients itself with respect to previous performances in the same sphere, both those by the same author and those by other authors. It inevitably takes its point of departure from some particular state of affairs involving a scientific problem or a literary style. Thus the printed verbal performance engages, as it were, in ideological colloquy of large scale: it responds to something, objects to something, affirms

[21]The term "dialectical" carries a great burden. Often when Hegelians or Marxists have used the term they have given it the opposite meaning of eristical. That is, the different modes of production are inherently antagonistic to one another and a later mode must gain victory through force over its predecessor. Some have also tried to make a dialectic process embrace natural as well as human phenomena and, as one might expect, have also tried to see it as determinate, to discover the laws of the dialectic. Following Collingwood, I use the term, as defined above, to designate relations among human agents and distinguish dialectical from eristical aspects. To eliminate the eristical aspects of agents' relations, some have opted for the term "dialoguing," but the extrusion of antagonism is just as reductive as is its privileging. (Following Vološinov, some have used the term "dialogic" in roughly the same way that Collingwood uses the term "dialectical").

> something, anticipates possible responses and objections, seeks support, and so on. (Vološinov, *Marxism*, p. 95)

Once we begin to look at texts in this discursive and dialogical fashion, our notion of text itself, of course, also changes. We begin to question the idea of "textuality," the notion of texts as inherently expressing the preset or unique mind of an author or, further, representing or participating in an essentialized great tradition, whether Judeo-Christian or Brahmanical. Texts and their authors and users are for us immanent in the world of practices and intertextualities. We would wish to take as texts many documents or utterances that students of great traditions would ignore—films and film scores, large-circulation magazines, political pamphlets, official pronouncements, the discourses of professions such as medicine and law, and even everyday dialogue. On the other hand, we do not wish to concede that "classical" or "canonical" works—the *Dharmaśāstra* of Manu, the *Bhagavadgītā*, Kālidāsa's *Śakuntalā*, or the *Caitanyacaritāmṛta* of Kṛṣṇadāsa, to name but a few—should be left to the traditional methods of Indologists or historians of religion.

The idea of a scale of texts allows us to avoid the "equal-and-opposite" reaction to the static, monolithic notion of culture or tradition, the notion of an infinitude of significations, the endless play of signifiers. People do make canons, they do order the texts they use. That people and scholars may misrecognize this process both in India and in the West does not require us to abandon any idea of ordering. At the very least, such a move tends to remove the using of texts from public places where wills encounter one another, and to situate their use in a private, personal space—a process I refer to as the novelization of texts.

We wish to emphasize that once texts are seen as participating in the making and remaking of a living, changing scale of texts, we become aware of their political and polemical dimension. Every text, no matter what claims its authors or users may make about its transcendence, is *articulative* with respect to specific actors and situations.[22] It is not merely a "source" that passively records events, but an intervention on the part of an agent in the world. It calls on its readers as they read the text not only to engage in (or refrain from) textual activity but to engage, to some degree, in other acts as well. The very composition (and reiteration) of a text, the placement of it in relation to other texts, is itself an assertion of relative power. The political effects of a text, however, are not uniform. Although the knowledges in South Asian texts may strengthen the will of some people to act in the world and in certain ways, they may also weaken the will of others, that is, they may have a disarticulative or dislocating effect on the world in which they intervene.

---

[22]One tendency has been to talk about texts as "constructing" or "constituting" the past. We prefer, following Laclau, to avoid these terms because they involve too much of a reaction to the essentialist position of which their users are critical. The essentialist saw texts as the expression of an author or context; the constructionist tends to see texts as "producing" tradition or history almost, as it were, ex nihilo. Instead we talk about "articulation." Laclau adumbrates a post-Marxist and poststructuralist notion of articulation in his discussion of the dislocation of structures. The articulation of a structure in his rendering is contingent and political; it is not given by "objective laws" of the structure and of its history or development; *New Reflections*, p. 50.

To the extent that one reads a text as discursive and polemical, one should be prepared to look for indirect statements or silences about its author or commentators and their rivals. In reading a document as a living text, we also want to be sensitive to tone, to the possibility that certain readers or commentators would have read some statements or characterizations as ironic or parodic. This is to say that we have to engage in informed speculation. We have to step away from the positivist notion that we should confine our task to understanding only that which is positively inscribed in the text (as if that were fully possible).

Not all texts are merely articulative. Some, we would argue, are comprehensively so. They are transformative, calling on their readers to make major changes in the world in which people compose and use them. Given the importance of ontological and theological issues in certain broad historical periods, it is perhaps uncontroversial to claim that texts such as the Epics, Purāṇas, and Dharmaśāstras, or the Maṅgalakāvyas of Bengal, and Vaṃsas of Sri Lanka are transformative. Yet we would not want to argue that literary texts are merely expressive of, say, the emotions, and not articulative or even transformative of them. Whichever they may be, we want to give up the notion of a text as passive and reflective. Having done so, we can begin to detect in many South Asian texts the signs both of hegemonic and counter-hegemonic practices ("resistance"). We can talk about agents, instruments, and patients deploying complex strategies of persuasion, parody, and criticism directed at themselves as well as others.

Texts do not, however, act on their own, however "great" or "seminal." Texts can only be articulative or transformative insofar as people use them, and the use of a text after its supposed moment of composition always involves supplementation, as Derrida has argued. That is, people read texts of the past through the later commentaries that frame, them and especially through those of their own present. Most of these commentaries in India were the oral commentaries of the texts' teachers. Some teachers formalized and inscribed their commentaries or glosses (almost invariably leaving out what we in the present would most like to know). We do not want, however, to suggest either that these supplements were either violent appropriations or the unfolding of an original author's intention. Rather, we wish to see the relationship between text and supplement as problematic. There is always some gap between them. The ongoing reality of daily life, with its smaller and larger disruptions, sooner or later transcends the capacity of an existing scale of texts to account for the world. The reader is, thus, always confronting a discourse in the text (including its earlier commentaries) that differs from his or her own discursive position.

To conclude, we wish to establish a dialogical or interdiscursive relationship with the texts we study. Instead of looking at them as dead monuments, as mere sources of factual information or the expression of a creative and exotic genius that we can only appreciate in itself for itself, or as the accidental expression/sedimentation of some larger structure or context, we want to see them as living arguments both in their historic usages and by virtue of our reenactment of their arguments, in our own present. We want to see what we can learn from these texts that pertains to our own time and its problems.

To approach texts as the dialogical utterances of complex authors in a shifting scale of texts would go far to help those who have been trained as philologists and historians. Let me turn now to the other half of our problem, that of situating texts historically, a problem often referred to as that of context.

Historicizing Texts

If the knowledge in texts is specific to situations and not universal, and if it is dialogical rather than monological, then it is important to historicize texts and to determine how the knowledges in them relate to one another. Authors and textual practices themselves are imbricated in other practices—the liturgical practices of monasteries and temples, the agricultural practices of villagers, and the political and military practices of royal courts. Formal, internal analysis of texts is no longer sufficient to reconstruct the relations among these practices. Historians, however, have not been exempt from the discursive practices that produced monological texts authored by substantialized agents. On the contrary, they have composed monological texts of their own, the master narratives of a nation's or civilization's history.

Historians of the nation use two principles to order their master narratives. First, they map people, institutions, and events, as if they were discrete objects, onto a homogeneous time-space grid. This is the empiricist or positivist phase embedded in a history text. This has mostly taken the form of reconstructing a "political" chronology that will constitute the "backbone" of history. The text the scientific historian creates also tends to be monological because, as Collingwood puts it, "He regards history as a mere spectacle, something consisting of facts observed and recorded by the historian, phenomena presented externally to his gaze, not experiences into which he must enter and which he must make his own" (p. 163). As Jonathan Walters and Daud Ali both show in this volume, the colonial and nationalist historians of South Asia have spent much of their energy producing dynastic histories of just this sort.[23]

Second, historians overlay their absolute time and space grid by ordering their narrative into the periods or epochs of a "universal" or totalizing philosophy of history, which that of the nation exemplifies or from which it deviates.[24] Those epochs are conceived of as teleologically connected (in Christian histories of salvation,

---

[23]Croce contends that, recognizing the shallowness of this history, historians sought the remedy "in turning the historical inquiry on to other sides of life, and in collating the various new histories thus discovered with the political-military history by means of a series of parallel chapters on letters, the arts, sciences, religions, morals, customs, agriculture, commerce, and so on. Even in our day this kind of historical treatment, though it has been satirized as 'pigeon-hole history,' is still cultivated because it is pleasing to unadventurous minds who, having panoramically arranged events of history, then think that they have fused them in the fire of thought and reduced them to unity:" *[1941] History as the Story of Liberty* (Chicago: Henry Regnery, 1970), pp. 171–72. Taking its cue from the *Cambridge History of India*, the nationalist multi-authored *History and Culture of the Indian People* (*HCIP*) epitomizes this approach.

[24]An intellectual practice that came to prevail in early Christian Europe; Collingwood, *Idea of History*, pp. 49–52.

Kantian and Hegelian histories of freedom, or Marxian historical materialism), and as brought into existence by an apocalyptic event: the birth of Christ, the discovery of the new world, the French or Russian (or Industrial or Green) revolutions, the Arab conquest of the Middle East. Some schemes also employ cyclical notions (such as those of Spengler and Toynbee) while others (such as Ranke) claim to treat of each epoch as self-contained.[25]

Partly shadowing the master narratives of European and world history, but with an orientalist twist, the historians of India divide its history into that most widely normalized scheme of periods—ancient (or classical), medieval, and modern. Whatever labels they give to them, historians have tended to equate ancient with Hindu, medieval with Muslim, and modern with Christian, British, or Western.[26] How are events related to one another within these periods and, more importantly, how are these periods related to one another? Historians use notions of repetition, influence, development or growth, and the unique, apocalyptic event to move their narratives along. Historians of South Asia have been fond of the apocalyptic event, in the form of invasion or conquest, as marking the shift from one period to the next.[27] That is, the narrative is a story of the conquest of one civilization by another, where each civilization is assumed to be a monolith.

The single "hero" of this history is the potentially or actually unitary national and imperial state, which more often than not, in the colonialist histories of India, turns out to be the instrument or patient of a substantialized agent—caste or Hinduism, or the imagination-dominated Indian mind. Historians have not invented these agents. They have taken them, often unwittingly, from one philosophy of history or the other, sometimes through the mediation of sociology or anthropology. There is, consequently, little room in these narratives for contingency, especially when it comes to the major events that separate periods. The successes enjoyed or the failures endured by the nation almost always have a single and necessary cause underlying them.

The three essays in this book all deal with texts from the eighth to twelfth centuries, an "early medieval" period in many of these master narratives. Let me, therefore, look at what we do in our three essays against scholar's representations of the medieval period in India. That period, as in Europe, follows a decline from a "golden age" in a classical or more generally ancient period, the age of the Guptas (c. 320–550) in India, that of Rome in the West. That decline eventuated in the invasion of the civilization by barbarians, the Germans in Europe and the Hūṇas in India. As a result of these disturbances, populations decreased and became impoverished, and polities became fragmented. The threat of a newly risen Islamic

[25] Croce used the term "historicism" to denote the relativist history of a Ranke; more recently, Popper uses it to label the universalist history of a Hegel or Marx. Collingwood argues, too dismissively, that these schemes are capricious and adhered to for "religious" reasons, to arouse the emotions for some political movement (pp. 263–66).

[26] U. N. Ghoshal, "Periods in Indian History," in his *Studies in Indian History and Culture* (Bombay: Orient Longmans, 1965), pp. 171–78.

[27] Martin Thom discusses the "metaphysics of invasion:" in "Tribes within Nations: The Ancient Germans and the History of Modern France," in *Nation and Narration*, edited by Homi K. Bhabha (London: Routledge, 1990), pp. 23–43.

civilization is also defining in both places, though in different ways. Finally, the sign of the medieval in both places was the prevalence of "faith" over "reason" and, within religion, of the more "emotional" or "devotional" forms over the more "ritual."

The Indian medieval period, as inflected by orientalism, is, of course, worse than the European.[28] It begins, according to the hegemonic text of the colonialist historian of premodern India, Vincent Smith, at about the same time in India as in Europe, after the death of Harṣa in 647, giving India a prolonged decline under the Rājputs (descendants of the Hūṇas) before the Muslim conquest around 1200.[29]

Other colonialist historians, consistently with the idea that the medieval period is essentially Islamic, signal its beginning with the Arab conquest of Sind in 712.[30] Some Hindu nationalist historians have attempted to recuperate the first two centuries of this period for the ancient period, compressing the decline into the later two centuries (or even less).[31] The point is nonetheless the same: whereas Western Europeans were able to repel Islam, in India that civilization triumphed. The apocalyptic moment, the Turkish Muslim conquest of the feuding Rājputs of north India, took place in the last decade of the twelfth century and culminated in the establishment of a sultanate at Delhi.

Most historians, surprisingly, agree on the decline that caused the Muslim Turkish conquest.[32] According to one of the most important "secular" nationalist historians of medieval India, the Muslims succeeded in their conquest of India because of the

> superiority of their social organisation. The Hindu social system had no coherence or unity. The Hindus were one only in name. They were divided into numerous religious sects, and therefore, did not form a single religious community. Not even did the members of a particular sect act as a solid group, because religion was more a personal matter than an affair of the community. There was no common worship. Again, Hindu society was divided into numerous sections and among them there was no sense of social oneness. There

---

[28]Romantic, progressivist historians came to revise the earlier Enlightenment view of the middle ages in Europe as a "dark age," and that rehabilitation has continued.

[29]Textual production also declined in this period, an age of poetics (Udbhaṭa, Rudraṭa, Ānandavardhana) rather than poetry, of commentaries and digests rather than original texts in law (Medhātithi, Vijñāneśvara, Lakṣmīdhara), philosophy (Vācaspati, Śaṃkara, and Bhāskara), and theology (Yādavaprakāśa, Rāmānuja). According to one aestheticist representation, "the literary productions are all stereotyped and laboured; they lack vigour, inspiration, and originality. They are merely mechanical reproductions of earlier models, without their vitality and living touch. It is an age of scholastic elaboration and systematic analysis, of technical skill and learning, of commentaries and sub-commentaries, and of manuals and sub-manuals"; M. A. Mehendale and A. D. Pusalker, "Language and Literature," *HCIP* 5 (1957), 297.

[30]Stanley Lane-Poole, *Mediaeval India under Mohammedan Rule (A.D. 712–1764)* (London: T. Fisher Unwin, 1903), and J. S. Grewal, *Medieval India: History and Historians* (Amritsar: Guru Nanak University, 1975), pp. 133–40.

[31]"In the fateful year A.D. 997, Abū-l-Qāsim Mahmūd, son of Sabuktigīn, captured Ghaznī, developed a marvellous striking power and turned his attention to India.... Ancient India ended. Medieval India began"; K. M. Munshi, "Foreword," *HCIP* 4 (Bombay: Bharatiya Vidya Bhavan, 1955), xxiii.

[32]U. N. Ghoshal provides an older empiricist summary in "Factors of Downfall of Ancient Indian Political Civilisation," in *Studies*, pp. 352–73.

> were numerous principalities which were perpetually hostile to one another, and which took no interest in the humiliation of their neighbours at the hands of foreigners. In fact there was no sentiment of nationality, and no hostility against an alien because he was an alien.[33]

The older colonial historians had emphasized the fanatical faith and greed of the Muslims.[34] The more conciliatory secular nationalists opted instead for the metaphor of civilizations as men at different stages of growth and decay.[35] The main point, though, was that India was about to enter an age of faith rather than reason, one in which the imagination or emotion dominated the mind.

Historians have depicted the late medieval period, the medieval period proper, as one in which two incompatible civilizations, Islam and Hinduism, remained fundamentally hostile to one another, a conflict that hindered development.[36] Or they have represented the Muslims, in secular nationalist discourse, as making efforts at rapprochement with the Hindus.[37] Either way, the salient fact is the rise to prominence all over the subcontinent of an intense devotionalism. Among Muslims, according to one well-known history, this took the form of Sūfism and the adoration of saints called *pīrs*. Among Hindus, it took the form of "the doctrine of *bhakti*, or salvation by Grace and Love," expressed in the poetic texts of the vernacular or regional languages.[38] Earlier scholars, directly or indirectly prompted by a Christian desire to see a predisposition to Christianity in the Indian people (their leaders having rebuffed Christian urgings to convert), tried to find Christian origins for these medieval sects. Within the Iberian imperial formation that the British and French had supplanted, the assumption prevailed that all people were, in essence, Christian—and if not, they were in league with the devil. The displacement of this ontology by a scientific materialist one did not cause Christians to give up

[33]Tara Chand, *A Short History of the Indian People from the Earliest Times to the Present Day*, 2nd ed. (Calcutta: Macmillan, 1944), p. 131. His chapter, "The Middle Age A.D. 700–1818" is divided into three periods: 700–1200 Rajputs; 1200–1526 Turks; 1526–1818 Mughals.

[34]"The Muslims, inspired by the spirit of adventure, of militant propaganda, of spreading the Kingdom of God upon earth, as well as seizing the goods of this world, had every advantage over the native Hindus, and when the invaders were led by kings who embodied these masterful qualities their triumph was assured"; Lane-Poole, *Mediaeval India*, pp. 63–64.

[35]"The war between the two peoples was really a struggle between two different social systems, the one, old and decadent, and the other, full of youthful vigour and enterprise"; Ishwari Prasad, *A Short History of Muslim Rule in India from the Advent of Islam to the Death of Aurangzeb* ([1939] Allahabad: Indian Press, 1965), p. 104.

[36]R. C. Majumdar, "Preface," *HCIP* 6 (Bombay: Bharatiya Vidya Bhavan, 1960), xxiii–iv.

[37]The earlier ecumenical poet-saint Kabir (c. 1425–1500) is made to exemplify this at the "popular level," whereas the later Mughal emperor Akbar (1556–1605) is seen as doing this work at the "state level."

[38]Conflating the Reformation with the High Middle Ages, one narrative asserts that "the effect of the literature produced during the fifteenth and sixteenth centuries may justly be compared to that of the Bible in the life of England—for the common people the one great accessible source of inspiration as of consolation"; W. H. Moreland and Atul Chandra Chatterjee, *A Short History of India* ([1936] New York: David McKay Co., 1957), pp. 192–94. The authors continue in their silently Christianizing way: "The peasant may still follow scrupulously the ancient ritual appropriate to the worship of this deity or that; but in his mind, or rather in his heart, there is the idea of something larger and more universal, and when his feelings find expression, it is in an appeal to Parameshar, the one Supreme Being, whom he has been led by this literature to know and love" (p. 194).

their quest to find proto-Christians among those their governments colonized. It did, however, shift the Christian project of textual study from one of looking for signs prefiguring the one true faith (or indicating the presence of its evil opposite) to an authorist concern with historical "influences." It is fair to say that many of the medieval religious texts edited and translated in the nineteenth and twentieth centuries are imbricated in this search.[39]

As highly as many Christian colonialists, Hindu and Muslim nationalists, and egalitarian secularists valued these devotional movements (albeit for different reasons), there remained a fundamental contrast with the West. Whereas, for them, Europe embodied a rationality that was able to reassert control over its civilization, the civilization of India lacked this internal capacity for positive change.[40] Left on its own, the substantialized agent of Indian civilization, whether its imaginational mind, caste, race, religion, or a peculiarly Indian feudal mode of production, was itself incapable of true autonomy. So the slow process by which a progressing, expanding, increasingly rational and scientific civilization reappeared in Europe in a renaissance of the fifteenth and sixteenth centuries (or as early as the twelfth century, according to revisionists) did not occur in the Indian subcontinent. A renaissance did not take place there until the early nineteenth century, when Bengal responded to the impact of the colonial presence of the West.

One part of the Western reason at work in these master narratives is historical consciousness. The society dominated by imagination or emotion cannot see its own past or its own destiny. So the idea that Indians lacked a historical consciousness is but another way of saying in the absence of the West it lacked the reason to order its affairs and progress.[41] All three essays in this volume, Ali's

---

[39]Tara Chand in his master narrative for medieval India, *Influence of Islam on Indian Culture* (Allahabad: Indian Press, 1936), completed in 1922, was probably the first to divert this project and direct attention instead to Islam and the nationalist project. Later scholars have criticized and abandoned many of his hypotheses on empirical grounds. Although Sūfis and *bhaktas* were similar in outlook, "They were unconcerned with the idea of achieving any form of union between the two religions and instead tended to work within their respective religious communities for an understanding of the spiritual and social values of each other"; Saiyid Athar Abbas Rizvi, *A History of Sufism in India* (New Delhi: Munshiram Manoharlal, 1978), 1: 399.

[40]A clear recent example of the global, unicausal historical writing that sees India as a defective mirror image of Europe is Satish Saberwal, *India: The Roots of Crisis* (Delhi: Oxford University Press, 1986). Taking a "world historical view" (p. 1) reminiscent of Braudel's longue durée, Saberwal concludes in a chapter, "Medieval Political Traditions" (pp. 36–57) after summarizing studies of Rājputs, the Delhi Sultanate, Mughals, and south India, that "Overall, then, organized officialdom was virtually missing in Rajasthan (except later under Mughal tutelage) and in south Indian polities" (p. 54). It was "more salient" in the Mughal state, "suggesting the seeds of bureaucracy," but because of dynastic succession struggles became parochialized. "Overall, therefore, the political domain in India remained host to cyclical processes of the rise and fall of dynasties, and often it took only a few brief generations to complete the cycle" (p. 55). The key to the difference between European and Indian history was a lack—the Roman Catholic Church: "Briefly, it was largely the Church that enabled Western Europe to grow out of cyclical political processes into others, facilitating the endogenic evolution of *political* and other institutions over the long term" (p. 55).

[41]Marc Aurel Stein, editor and translator of Kalhaṇa, quotes Alberūnī on his (and other Indians') limited historical horizon: "Unfortunately the Hindus do not pay much attention to the historical order of things, they are very careless in relating the chronological succession of their kings, and when they are pressed for information and are at a loss, not knowing what to say, they invariably take to tale-

especially, reexamine this long-standing notion. It is obviously the case that Indians did not, before the advent of colonial rule, practice the professional discipline of history that people established in Europe in the nineteenth century and that scholars practice now almost everywhere. It is, however, not as easy to sustain the claim that although Indians (both Hindu and Muslim, but differently) had "traditions of chronicling" the past and of producing "mythographies," they lacked a "modern and secular sense of history."[42] This dichotomy, which reinscribes that between the medieval or traditional and the modern, makes too sharp a contrast between different practices. What is "history" in such generalizations? Is it empiricist or positivist history (which Walters discusses in this volume)? On the empiricist front, the idea that modern academic history rests on three foundations—a "sense of anachronism," "rules of evidence," and "causality as a major means of explanation"—simply fails to distinguish what Kalhaṇa claims to have done with his material prior to fashioning his poetic narrative (see Inden below). It is also difficult, I fear, to assume that the histories of the nation—India or any other—rest exclusively on these foundations. Chakrabarty himself seems keenly aware of the tendency in those histories to naturalize the nation that amounts, from his point of view, to the systematic anachronizing of its values and institutions.[43] In other words, chronizing and anachronizing are integral components of any view of the past, although people use them on different materials. Need I say anything about the vexed question of causation?

Or is the history at stake in the master narratives that compare India and the West more a philosophy of history, Christian, Hegelian, or Marxist than a method? Certainly, to the extent that these latter presuppose substantialized agents—God, World Spirit, Feudalism and Capitalism, or Caste and the Hindu Mind—and reduce transitory humans and their institutions to the status of instruments or patients which it moves toward a final destiny, they can hardly be said to constitute the secular history that Collingwood advocates.[44] Indeed, I think I would be prepared to argue that whereas Theists in medieval India presupposed substantialized agents, Viṣṇu and Śiva, they positioned humans more as their coagents than as their instruments. When it comes to the Theravādin Buddhism of Walter's essay, the situation is more complicated. There, I think, one can perhaps talk about representations of the Buddha (textual and practical as well as pictorial and sculptural) as signaling and causing a way of life that is active in the world, but I would hardly want to characterize the Buddha in any form as a substantialized agent. So, in these respects one can argue that some medieval Indians and Sinhalese were more historical-minded than have been many modern thinkers in the West.

---

telling." See M. A. Stein, tr., *Kalhaṇa's Rājataraṅgiṇī, a Chronicle of the Kings of Kaśmīr* (Westminster: Archibald Constable, 1900; reprint Delhi: Motilal Banarsidass, 1979), 1: 31–32.

[42]Dipesh Chakrabarty, "The Death of History? Historical Consciousness and the Culture of Late Capitalism," *Public Culture* 4.2 (Spring, 1992), 50.

[43]Dipesh Chakrabarty, "Trafficking in History and Theory: Subaltern Studies," in *Beyond the Disciplines: The New Humanities*, edited by K. K. Ruthven (Canberra: The Australian Academy of Humanities, 1992).

[44]Surely Chakrabarty would agree that the history which suffers death or end, as in Fukuyama's postmodern world, is this philosophical variety and not the empirical.

We wish, then, to challenge the historical contextualization of texts that historians and textual scholars engage in when they insert them into a master narrative, a universal or civilizational narrative that has a single subject and goal—in this case, a unified secular (or Hindu) Indian nation (and the responses to that, separate Muslim and Buddhist nations). We especially wish to displace the chapter of this narrative that represents Europe's Indian Other in its "medieval" history as devoid of reason and history because the West (in one of its many incarnations—Reformation or Counter-Reformation Christian, Enlightenment absolutism, Burkean conservatism, historical materialism, free-market liberalism) has not yet come to be the major presence in their lives.[45]

Criticisms of the medieval notion in European studies seem to fall on either side of the old Enlightenment-Romantic faultline. David Aers voices the position of the former when he criticizes many of his colleagues' work for viewing medieval society as unproblematically hierarchic. He also questions the uniformity attributed to it.[46] It is possible to find parallel positions in the scholarship on South Asia.[47] The problem, however, is not solved by moving the medieval-modern divide back or forth a few centuries or reducing the tripartite scheme to the still more simplistic bipartite scheme of traditional-modern. Nor do we solve the problems of agency and text interpretation by changing our evaluation of the medieval without changing the way we think about it. Our own position is that any historical account is underdetermined by its evidence. It is always possible for two or more plausible accounts to be written using the same evidence. If different questions are asked and different evidence is brought to bear on a historical event, then the number and variety of the plausible accounts multiplies. The problem is rather that of doing away with the notion of a master historical narrative and its division of history into teleologically connected (or self-contained) epochs brought into existence by apocalyptic events.

As Lee Patterson points out, a "postmodernist" stance toward the past can exaggerate the strong antihistorical tendency of modernist discourses, or it can radically historicize it.[48] But what does "historicize" involve here? It could mean, as is often the case with those who work under the rubric of the "new historicism," not just a destabilization and fragmentation of the universal, master narratives of modernism, but a radical pluralization and particularization of history, one that lapses into an empiricist atomization of topics, or an anthropology of incommensurable cultures isolated in space-time from one another; or the infinite interplay

---

[45]One could include fundamentalism here, for it is, I would argue, as much a reworking of these other modernist positions as it is the recuperation of an earlier one.

[46]David Aers, "Rewriting the Middle Ages: Some Suggestions," *Journal of Medieval and Renaissance Studies* 18.2 (1988), 221–40.

[47]Ideas of the "village republic," an organic caste society, and "homo hierarchicus" have appealed to the more conservative in Europe, but have not been predominant among nationalists or socialists in the Indian subcontinent.

[48]Lee Patterson, "On the Margin: Postmodernism, Ironic History, and Medieval Studies," *Speculum* 65 (1990), 87–108.

of poststructuralist signifiers.[49] As I have already said, these responses are overreactions to the monoliths of modernism. These oppositional stances reinscribe the antihistoricist tendency of modernism, but in reverse: the human past is so diverse that no one can make more than a momentary, fragmentary sense of it.

The alternative to these oppositional stances is a historicization that theorizes human actions as dialogical and articulative of the human world. We are particularly concerned to focus on practices because, as we see it, practices were the activities most involved in making and articulating the agents and things of the human world. We think of the agents of history as more or less complex, ranging from persons to the ruling societies—royal or imperial courts—of polities through the so-called intermediate institutions of "civil society." For "medieval" India these included families, the ruling societies of villages and districts, associations of merchants and soldiers, and associations of Brāhmaṇ householder liturgists, Buddhist monasteries, and associations of Vaiṣṇava and Śaiva devotees. We would, thus, collapse the dichotomy between society and the individual thought of as pregiven wholes. We see the question of order and unity as empirical ones and not as inherently given or guaranteed. On what occasions and with what practices did people order their world? To what extent can we say that some people were successful and others not so? We wish also to emphasize that no order is complete or all-embracing, despite any claims its creators might make.

As one step in the direction of rethinking alternatives to the predominant images of a traditional India, and of medieval India in particular, we self-consciously change five discursive practices. First, we will use the expression "way of life" instead of "religion" both in its sense as belief or creed and as practice or institution (church).[50] We use that expression in order to embrace phenomena such as Buddhism and, for that matter, certain so-called Brahmanical practices that were not theocentric, as well as those that by some definition are or have been. We also use it to indicate modernist movements—liberalism, socialism, humanism, conservatism, and so on—both their "ideologies" and their parties, so as to place them and "religions" and their churches on the same playing field. We also use the expression "life-transforming practices" instead of the term "ritual" to point to those practices distinctively associated with a way of life, those that people have taken as most implicated in the making and articulating of the human world. We do not imply with this expression that the practices involved were life-affirming or completing. This quality differed both in degree and in kind among different associations claiming to adhere to the same way of life, and differed even more among those adhering to different ways of life. Some practices emphasized radical transformations, doing away with life and, in the case of Buddhism, the denial that the essential bearer of life, a "soul," even existed. In order to emphasize the compulsory aspect of these acts and avoid the irrationalist and obscurantist connotations of the term "cult," we will use the term "liturgy" to describe them.

---

[49] Brook Thomas, *The New Historicism and Other Old-Fashioned Topics* (Princeton: Princeton University Press, 1991), pp. 39–48.

[50] The various ideas of religion that scholars have used have a complicated and contested history, which we will bypass here.

Second, we will use the term "Theist" to denote the Vaiṣṇavas and Śaivas.[51] We do not use the term Hindu to refer to the Vaiṣṇavas and Śaivas of the eighth century. As is well known, this term was Persian, and used at first simply to describe the inhabitants of the subcontinent. Later, perhaps as early as the thirteenth century, certainly by the fifteenth, both the followers of Muḥammad and the devotees of Viṣṇu and Śiva (and, arguably, Śakti), use the terms Hindu and Muslim. Before this time, Vaiṣṇavas and Śaivas used the term *āstika*, the term we translate as Theist (despite its Christian connotations) to describe those who considered a god to exist. Perhaps more frequently, they used the negative of this term, *nāstika*, to tag those who did not. That is, the major division in the period I deal with was over theism and not over whether a way of life was barbarian or not. If anything, there was a tendency to associate atheism, Buddhism, and barbarians. Of course, the matter is further complicated because people also used these abstract terms in situated, shifting ways to denote varying configurations of "schools" or "sects," and not to denote an objectively constant thing, a "religion." If, for example, one took the term to mean that the Veda exists as the authorless ground of existence—as did some adherents of the Vedic sacrificial way of life—that would exclude those Vaiṣṇavas and Śaivas who believed that Viṣṇu or Śiva was the author of the Vedas. If, as some Vaiṣṇavas did, one considered the Buddha a manifestation of Viṣṇu, then one could count the Buddhist "monastic society" (*saṃgha*) as Theist.

Third, we will use the expression "disciplinary order" (which we can take as a translation in part of such terms as *caraṇa*, *vidhāna*, and *kalpa*, or such terms as *paramparā* or *sampradāya*, and, among Buddhists, *nikāya*), to denote both the societies of adepts who have taken some particular name and the life-transforming practices in which they engage. We avoid the terms "sect" and "school" used by most previous scholars to designate these societies and their practices. By emphasizing the disiplinary practices of these societies, we do not mean to deny that many of them did have moments of dissent or sectarian opposition. We do not think, however, that these moments should be made into their essences (unless that is what an order did). Each of the three essays is concerned in different ways with a disciplinary order. Inden focuses on the Pāñcarātra order of Vaiṣṇavas, Walters on the order of Theravādins at the Mahāvihāra ("great monastery") of Sri Lanka, and Ali, more indirectly, on the Śaiva Siddhāntins and Kālāmukhas of south India, some of whom were the recipients of royal grants of land.

Fourth, we will use such expressions as life-wish, royal wish, imperial wish, world wish, life-account, world account, and world vision in place of such conceptually overloaded terms as myth, ideology, and worldview to denote the effects of certain activities that people carried out in the course of their lives, activities that were crucial to the ways of life they pursued. The transformation of heterogeneous life- and world wishes into more coherent and stable world accounts and, in some cases, visions, was crucial to the practices of the disciplinary orders. It is the ac-

[51] There is no evidence we would judge reliable to justify talking about Śāktas, those who take the female principle (*śakti*) as the absolute and engage in Tantric practices, in this period. My own guess is that disciplinary orders constructed around these practices were post-Islamic, and constituted one sort of response to a situation in which an Islamic way of life was hegemonic.

tivity we see in the texts that they composed for fashioning or ordering the lives of their adepts and for addressing would-be followers and transforming their lives.

Finally, instead of dividing history into periods defined by apocalyptic events, the conquest of one civilization by another in a battle or war, we prefer to divide our history into successive "imperial formations." The idea of an imperial formation is one Inden first used to theorize India as a complex polity consisting of a hegemonic empire and other subjected, allied and rival kingdoms and allied, and rival empires. We do this in order to provide an alternative notion of order to the idea of India and the Indian empire as an administrative, centralized state or as the opposite of that, an inherently divisive congeries of feudal or segmentary states at best only "ritually" or "symbolically" united. Our alternative sees polities and other societies and communities as dialogically related, as more or less complex agents positioning themselves in relation to one another. Just as authors articulate themselves and their texts in this way as scales of forms, so, too, do the larger polities to which those authors belong. Finally, we consider one imperial formation as dialogically emerging from another. The many agents involved in making an imperial formation, more or less consciously and on occasion self-deceptively, evaluate what they and others have done in the past and make decisions about what to do in their present. That is, the ruling societies of imperial formations necessarily used ideas about the past and how it connected to a present and future.

The accounts of these imperial formations are, we assume, underdetermined by the evidence on which those accounts would be based. So historians can reconstruct different political histories for every imperial formation: the history of the hegemonic empire in that formation, that of its major rivals, and those of the polities whose rulers were either underlords of the imperial polities or their allies. The histories of those societies whom the ruling societies of these polities ruled are also possible, as are those of the different ways of life and disciplinary orders of which they were composed.

Textual scholars tend to dichotomize text and context and then privilege one over the other, as we have seen. Similarly, within larger histories there is a tendency to dichotomize the economic/political and the religious/ideological, and privilege one over the other. We see the idea of an imperial formation as overcoming this dichotomy of power and knowledge. Every imperial formation had an intimate and complex relation to the disciplinary orders of the ways of life within it, as the Inden and Walters essays both show. Hegemony within an imperial formation was not a simple matter of domination exercised within an essentially separate political and economic sphere but a question of both will and force, with adepts of disciplinary orders and ruling societies of polities closely involved in the articulation of one another's spheres of action and their life-, imperial, and world wishes. We wish to emphasize in this regard the strategic aspects of their acts, the situatedness of the agents of those acts, and the momentariness of the hegemony that a polity and its associated disciplinary order achieved.

So far as "early medieval" India is concerned, I tried in *Imagining India* to destabilize the existing images of a medieval India. I argued there that there is no evidence of overall population decline. It is plausible to argue for a relative political decline in north India—the middle Gangetic plains—but there is no need to deduce from that an overall decline of "Hindu" civilization. Rather, there was a shift of its hegemonic center southward, after Harṣa, to the Cāḷukyas in the Deccan, challenged by the Pallavas to their south. The Rāṣṭrakūṭas dominated its imperial formation from around 750, contested by the Pālas of eastern India and the Pratihāras of north India. Then, after 975, the Cōḻas emerged at the center of an imperial formation still further south, in Tamil Nadu. Before the rise of the Cōḻas to preeminence, an imperial polity centered on Kashmir and Gandhāra, a zone of Indo-Iranic cultural activity, appears to have stretched more or less continuously to the north and east from Kashmir along the Indus (Gilgit, Baltistan, Ladakh) and the Satlej (Spiti, Cīna, and Suvarṇagotra or Guge) and, further north, into Kashgaria around the northern and southern edges of the Takla Makan Desert. The successes of the Arab and then Turkish Muslim, Tang Chinese, and Tibetan Buddhist empires had the effect, eventually, of separating these Indo-Iranic centers from India. Islamic practices became the cosmopolitan way of life in much of central as well as southwest Asia. The eventual establishment of a Turkish empire at Delhi left Buddhist practices divided into its so-called Northern and Southern varieties. Meanwhile, the relations of the Indian kingdoms and Sri Lanka with kingdoms in Southeast Asia seem to have intensified in this period. So the idea of seeing the Cōḻas as the center of a predominantly Theist Indic world and of Sri Lanka as the decentered focal point of a largely Theravādin Buddhist world makes sense.

There is, finally, a major political point to be made about the tripartite division of history into ancient and modern eras that resemble one another and are separated by a medieval era of little value. It has shifted people's attention away from the practices and institutions of the past before the advent of colonialism, and onto a fanciful remote past that seems to have little to do with their everyday life—the primordial world of a heroic Rāma; the rational, secular, bureaucratic world of Aśokan India; or the world of a unified nonsectarian classical Hinduism of the Guptas. This tends to limit the agency of people in the present, for the only way they can explain their present lowly condition is by some apocalyptic event such as a conquest, and the only way they can get to a utopian future is, again, by some apocalyptic leap—a five-year plan that will lead to socialism or a Free Market that will lead to a consumerist paradise. What they cannot see is that their more immediate ancestors remade the world they inherited again and again through their own efforts. And if they cannot see what people like themselves have done in a past that is recognizably theirs, their own horizons for action become very limited. We hope that these essays will help to focus attention on a past that moves away from this tripartite division. We wish to advance a view of history that sees Indians as thinking, critical agents of their own traditions, and not just as its instruments or patients, one that is skeptical of master political narratives whose authors have tried to impose a single plot on divergent lives.

The three essays that follow have emerged from the "Texts and Knowledge" colloquium. They are an attempt to make some headway in carving out a space for articulative approaches to the study of South Asian texts. These essays concern themselves with three genres of texts that have been crucial to the Indological project of creating a history and civilization of South Asia—the Purāṇas, Sanskrit "encyclopedias" of Hindu cosmology and mythology; Pali "chronicles" of the Buddhist kings of Sri Lanka (formerly Ceylon); and Sanskrit and Tamil copper-plate "inscriptions" containing royal genealogies and recording land grants.

Scholars have viewed the Purāṇas, "originary accounts" (of the divine ordering of the world), as central to their attempts to recover the history of India, an attempt rendered extremely difficult because of these texts' refusal to reveal their "actual" authorship and provenance. To begin with, Europeans attempted to revive an early, "epic" stage in that history. Later, Indians endeavored to extract "social" history from them. Others have labored to distill the "mythology" of a "classic" Hinduism from these texts. Inden labels the first of these efforts "empiricist" and the second "idealist," and criticizes both for dehistoricizing the texts by treating them as "sources" or as expressions of an underlying "text," Hinduism itself. Instead, Inden argues, these texts can be read as discursive and narrative texts that can be historically situated.

His own account focuses on the *Viṣṇudharmottarapurāṇa* (*VDhP*), a text mined for its "facts" on iconography, kingship, and astronomy. On the basis of an analysis of textual precedents and innovations and of the text's organization and self-representations, Inden is able to show that the *VDhP* was composed in three "sessions" by a "complex author" that consisted of a world-conquering monarch and members of his court, as well as adepts of the disciplinary order of Pāñcarātra Vaiṣṇavas to which the king also belonged.

He argues that the *VDhP* positions itself as a supplement that claims to order all preexisting knowledges. Together with the texts it supplements, the text forms, argues Inden, a "scale of texts." Crucial in this scale are texts of the Vedic disciplinary order most closely associated with Kashmir, texts of the Pāñcarātrins called Āgamas or Saṃhitās, and another Purāṇā, the *Nīlamata*, a text explicitly about Kashmir but as reticent as the *VDhP* to disclose its date.

The vale of Kashmir, whose people are now almost wholly Muslim, is today largely a victim of India's and Pakistan's nation-making projects. The Kashmir of the eighth century was, however, the coagent of a new imperial formation, one in which Theism gained over both Vedism and Buddhism. The approach to texts Inden uses helps us to reconstruct this history.

Considering the evidence that points to the eighth-century kingdom of Kashmir as the site where the *VDhP* was composed, Inden suggests that the complex agent that authored this text probably included the two Kārkoṭa Nāga kings of Kashmir, Candrāpīḍa Vajrāditya and Muktāpīḍa Lalitāditya. Having made this connection, Inden is able to demonstrate that the life-wish of the *VDhP*—the institution of a kingdom embracing the entire earth in which the Viṣṇu of the Pāñcarātrins received recognition as overlord of the cosmos—and the circumstances faced by the Kashmiri imperial court were mutually articulative. The "conquest of the quarters" that Muktāpīḍa undertook was informed by the narrative and discursive contents of the *VDhP*, whereas the vision of the text was itself tailored to the situation. This can be seen most clearly in the temple-building activities (as documented in archeological traces and Kalhaṇa's history, *Rājataraṅgiṇī*) with which a paramount king was supposed to celebrate his triumph.

The *VDhP* was, Inden concludes, one of the major texts involved in the rise to hegemony of "temple Hinduism" at the expense of both the Vedic sacrificial liturgy and Buddhist monasticism. The *Nīlamata* as a text envisions Kashmir as a polity in which Pāñcarātra Vaiṣṇavism is recognized as the highest way of life. According to Inden's intertextual reading of the *Nīlamata*, that text is itself a dialectical reworking of an earlier Śaiva vision of Kashmir, which in turn reworked a still older Buddhist vision.

Scholars of ancient India, Sri Lanka, and Theravādin Buddhism have relied for the better part of two centuries on three texts of the Vaṃsa genre, the *Dīpavaṃsa* and *Mahāvaṃsa*, and a commentary on the latter, the *Vaṃsātthappakkāsinī*, to provide an absolute chronology of history not only for Sri Lanka but for ancient India, as well. Colonial historians claimed that the Sri Lankan Vaṃsas, along with Kalhaṇa's *Rājataraṅgiṇī* from Kashmir, formed the only works in premodern South Asia that approximated the practice of modern objective history. Challenging the empiricist and positivist underpinning of this colonialist notion of history, Walters shows how scholars have rather naively turned the claims of these texts into ahistorical essences that the texts are said simply to "express." The effect of this approach has been to turn medieval Sri Lankan agents into the "patients" of a world that they themselves created. Taking an articulative approach to the Vaṃsas, Walters is able to rethink completely some of the most basic presumptions in the historiography of ancient and medieval Buddhism, Sri Lanka, and even India itself.

Walters begins by showing how the "mythological" concerns of the Vaṃsas, bracketed out by positivist historians, actually framed the dynastic narratives within the larger project of creating an imperial Sri Lankan Buddhist notion of time, whereby, through the effects of their actions in previous lives, the Buddha (as Bodhisattva) and his disciples would be reborn together in successive ages. The Vaṃsas are, thus, better rendered as "successions of the Buddha's presence" than as chronicles. Walters locates the birth of this conception in earlier strands of Buddhist literature, and traces its uptake in the Vaṃsa texts, culminating with its formulation in the *Vaṃsātthappakkāsinī*, which fully enunciated an imperial Buddhist world vision with the Theravādin Hinayāna monks at the Mahāvihāra monastery and the Okkāka kings of Anurādhapura as its principal agents and "hearers." This history would eventuate in a polity where the Bodhisattva would be born as an Okkāka king and would lead his polity to *nibbāna*—a world wish that was sought after and even achieved momentarily in medieval Sri Lanka. In locating these texts so precisely in history while also making clear their claims about history, Walters not only helps us to rethink the political and intellectual history of medieval Sri Lanka and India but also opens up the possiblity of seeing other texts, like the Theist Purāṇas and "dynastic" eulogies, in a new light.

Despite the fact that colonial historians saw the *Rājataraṅgiṇī* and the Vaṃsas as indications of an "objective" historical impulse in premodern South Asia, they eventually gave pride of place to stone and copper-plate inscriptions as the most important tools for historians of South Asia. Ali's essay argues that the "inscriptions" of medieval India or, more precisely, the "royal eulogies" (*praśastis*) with which these inscriptions begin, should be seen as historical texts and not simply as primary sources for the reconstruction of a political history. The inscription on which he focuses, the "Order of Rājendra Cōḻa" (1012–1044), issued in year six of his reign, is a remarkable document consisting of thirty-one copper plates bound, in the manner of an Indian manuscript, by a ring. The Cōḻas, a dynasty of south India, made themselves the paramount rulers of all India in the twelfth century. Ali explores the claims about the present and the past that formed a crucial part of the Cōḻa paramount lordship. To be sure, Ali concedes, the eulogies contained in these "royal orders" do not form self-contained, free-standing histories of the sort to which we have become accustomed. Nonetheless, he argues, these royal eulogies, if read intertextually, can be seen as situated moments in a living historical text. He thus reads the royal eulogy in conjunction with other inscriptions and with those texts that long provided the metanarratives of history for Theists, the Purāṇas. The royal eulogies extend the notions of time and polity provided in the Purāṇas into their own present, both fulfilling and remaking Purāṇic time, and in conjunction with a range of other practices, attempt to complete a Theist way of life.

Each of the essays has an appendix in which the reader who wishes it will find a critical history of orientalist approaches to the text and tradition in question.

2

Imperial Purāṇas

Kashmir as Vaiṣṇava Center of the World

Ronald Inden

Opening an Indian Text

For more than fifteen years I have been at work on a text called the *Viṣṇudharmottara-purāṇa* (*VDhP*). When I first opened the printed version of this text, I had no intimation of the trouble we would cause each other. As a result of the dialogue I have had with this text and its authors, most of my views about the issues of texts, authors, genres, contexts, and cultural history have undergone a radical transformation. Most Indologists have considered the Purāṇas, the large genre of texts to which the *VDhP* belongs, to be of great importance. Present-day Hindus are supposed to accord them a respect second only to that given the Vedas, their oldest "sacred" texts, and the two Epics, the *Mahābhārata* and the *Rāmāyaṇa*. Indologists have told us that the Purāṇas, like the Epics, are worth investigating because they contain information on the ancestor of contemporary Hinduism, an "orthodox" religion of ancient India, a "classical" Brahmanism or Hinduism. Most scholars have taken this to mean a unitary nonsectarian religion of "devotion" dominated by Brāhmaṇ priests that flowered (at the expense of the "heterodox" religions, Buddhism and Jainism) under the Gupta emperors, in India's classical period (fourth to seventh centuries). In the same breath, however, they also tell us that these texts contain "medieval" and "sectarian" additions, usually failing to note that these are not odd interpolations here and there but constitute the overwhelming bulk of most extant manuscripts of the Purāṇas.To a very large extent, the study of the Purāṇas as a genre has consisted of various attempts to suture the texts, at the expense of their medieval contents, to a classical Hinduism as its genuine, original author.

Indologists generally translate the term that labels this genre of texts, *purāṇa*, by the term "ancient" or "old" in the sense of referring to cosmogonies, histories of a legendary past, or timeless myths. As we shall see, it has always been more than a little unclear what constitutes these texts as a genre. The only unity that seems to underlie analyses of these texts is the assumption that they consist of representations of a world based more on imagination than on observation. I originally wanted to find out from the *VDhP* about "medieval Hindu" ideas of kingship and their connections with "ritual," ideas that I could somehow deploy historically. There was no shortage of such material in the *VDhP*. The problem was this: the more I read the more I could see that kings and rites seemed to be inextricably bound up with the theology of the Pāñcarātra "sect" of Vaiṣṇavas, on the one hand, and with what seemed to me an imperial political agenda, on the other. That is, I seemed to be finding that the "religious" contents of the text were closely tied to purposive acts that were about the world. Was it possible that a purpose was inscribed here? Was this a text whose presumed author situated its argument in response to other textualized projects? If so, the text seemed to be at odds with the assumptions made by scholars about these texts.

This essay on that text is an exemplification of the agentive and articulative approach as well as a contribution to a new history of practices in South Asia. I first take up the question of authorship, and suggest that the idea of complex authorship provides a way around authorism, the notion of the unitary author (whether personal or collective) or his (*sic*!) absence. The person who took the lead in composing the *VDhP* was both a chronologer ("astrologer") and a Pāñcarātra preceptor of an imperial king, but others, through a process of dialogue, also took part. I then take up the problem of intertextuality, and present the possibility of looking at the *VDhP* as supplementing and articulating a scale of texts. The *VDhP* was, I argue, a text that claimed to rework Indian traditions from a Pāñcarātra Vaiṣṇava perspective, that of the emergent Āgamas, whose authors accepted the Vedas but supplanted the liturgy and the liturgical texts—the Kalpasūtras—that claimed to be based on the Vedas.

After that I show that the *VDhP* can be seen to have both a narrative and discursive aspect. The purpose of the complex author of the *VDhP*, as I have reconstructed it from the text, was to persuade an imperial king, a "king of kings," of the truth of its particular wish for and account of the world, that of the Pāñcarātra Vaiṣṇavas. Their ontology was a theist and activist one, as was that of their rivals, the Pāśupata Śaivas. It called on the king and his court to perform an ensemble of devotional works and other practices (such as vows) given in the text, the successful completion of which would eventually lead them to union with Viṣṇu. The grandest of these works would have the king of kings build a large, commanding Pāñcarātra temple after he had "conquered the quarters" and made himself the paramount king in an imperial formation that embraced all of India. That Pāñcarātra temple, together with its elaborate liturgy of image-honoring, would displace the Vedic sacrificial liturgy as the capstone of what I call the imperial formation of India in its own age. It would articulate India as a complex "chain of being," a Pāñcarātra theophany that included all life forms.

The final section deals with the historical situatedness of the text. I argue that the content of the text was in part articulated by the circumstances in which its complex author was situated, and that that author and text also rearticulated the world in accord with its contents. The *VDhP* was, I contend, the product of and producer of events in seventh- and eighth-century Kashmir. On the one hand, the authors of the text augmented their claims to paramountcy as the possibility of making Kashmir the center of an all-Indian imperial polity increased; on the other, the kings of Kashmir realized more of what the text foretold in its narrative and called for in its didactic, prescriptive chapters as they succeeded in extending their rule. Closely implicated in this process was the *Nīlamata*, a Sanskrit Purāṇa explicitly about Kashmir that antedates the *VDhP*. The use of another important Sanskrit text, Kalhaṇa's *Rājataraṅgiṇī*, "River of Kings," completed in A.D. 1150, makes this historical reconstruction possible. The appendix to this chapter gives a brief critical history of the major assumptions and presuppositions involved in Indological studies of the Purāṇas in general and of the *VDhP* in particular.

As I point out in the Introduction, the idea of a religion dominated by "devotion," the translation of the term *bhakti*, has been central to the notion of a medieval India, distinguishing it both from an ancient or classical period and from the modern. I wish to problematize the notion of *bhakti* as "devotion." Scholars often point out that the basic or original meaning of the term is "participation," but then go on to ignore the implication, as if devotion were something almost completely separate. I would like to argue that the idea of participation in the life of a lord, be he a "god" (*deva*, as in Theism) or "great man" (*mahāpuruṣa*, as in Buddhism) remains basic to many if not all of the forms of *bhakti*. Certainly it is central to the idea of *bhakti* in the *VDhP*. There have been many different *bhaktis* historically, which is why the efforts at a single definition are bound to fail. A devotee could participate in the life of a lord by honoring him as a guest, as the servant of a great king, as the acolyte of a great teacher, as a paramour, or as a slave, to list some of the practices of devoted participation articulated in different disciplinary orders. Certainly an emotion of affect, attraction, or love is integral to this participation. The general term for this emotion in the discourse of the *VDhP* is *rāga*, from the root *rañj*, meaning to color, especially to redden. The major synonym for *bhakti* is *anurāga*, a term used for someone who is attracted to—pleased by, attached to, in love with—a higher personage, a master or lord. Yet it would be a mistake to treat this emotion as sentimentality, as a prefiguring of Christian love, or as a superstructural feature of feudalism.

The shift to devoted participation in the Theist ways of life entailed broad changes throughout the human world of those who did so. The older Vedic narrative of the human world constructed disciplinary orders that proceeded by a principle of exclusion. The discourse of the *VDhP* instead emphasizes that all can participate, but also stresses that the capacities to do so are graded. As a reminder of this participatory aspect, I shall generally render *bhakti* as "devoted participation."[1]

Text, Author, Intertext

Adherents of a linguistic contextualism, Indologists have approached the texts of ancient or medieval India on the basis of an analogy: just as utterances are reducible to the normative system of a language, so texts are reducible to their genres, each of which is defined by an essence, a stable distinguishing feature or features. Relying on Indian "tradition," Indologists tell us that a Purāṇa has five distinguishing characteristics (*pañcalakṣaṇa*): cosmogony (*sarga*), the "emission"

[1] Krishna Sharma criticizes the representations of *bhakti* as a type of religion or as a mere adjunct of a fedual society in *Bhakti and the Bhakti Movement: A New Perspective; A Study in the History of Ideas* (New Delhi: Munshiram Manoharlal, 1987).

of the cosmos at the beginning of a grand cosmic formation (*mahākalpa*) from the body of a cosmic overlord; regeneration (*pratisarga*) of the cosmos at the beginning of the present cosmic formation (*kalpa*); the successive generation and population (*vaṃśa*) of the world with its various beings; accounts of the epochs of Manu (*manvantarāni*), fourteen of which made up a Cosmic Formation; and the genealogical succession of kings (*vaṃśānucarita*) of the Solar and Lunar dynasties of the present epoch of Manu and cycle of four ages (*caturyuga*). Here, then, we seem to have the essence of the Purāṇa as a genre: it is an account of the divine origin and ordering of the world.

Most surveys are careful to point out, however, that virtually none of the extant texts confines itself to these topics. Unlike the Vedas (including the Brāhmaṇas, Āraṇyakas, and Upaniṣads), the Purāṇas and the Epics have undergone numerous modifications over the centuries. They have come to contain "later' material on "customs" and "rituals" added by priests with "sectarian" interests. Distinguishing the Purāṇas from the Vedas, E. J. Rapson, an empiricist, asserted that "the Purāṇas have adapted themselves to the changes which have taken place in the social and religious life of the people, and their text has been perverted by generations of editors and transcribers."[2] Here the Purāṇas seem to impinge on other genres of texts: the earlier Kalpasūtras, on "ritual," and the later Dharmaśāstras, texts supposed to be about religious law; and the Āgamas, sectarian ritual texts of the Vaiṣṇavas, Śaivas, and Śāktas.[3] This is so much the case that many scholars consider the Purāṇas to be in actuality religious texts and not primarily histories.

The *VDhP* is typical of the Purāṇic genre. It is obviously a text "influenced" by the Pāñcarātra sect of Vaiṣṇavas. Art historians cite it because it contains important "early" material on Hindu iconography and temples. It would appear, therefore, to poach on the turf of another genre of texts, the Śilpaśāstras and Vāstuśāstras, having art and architecture, respectively, as their proper topics. I myself had turned to it not so much for this or for its account of cosmology or early history as for the information on Hindu kingship, one of the topics of Dharmaśāstra that comprises the entire second part of this text.

To make matters worse, the Hindu tradition speaks of eighteen of the Purāṇas as *mahā* or "great," and any number of others as *upa* or "lesser." The *VDhP* is nowadays classed as an Upapurāṇa (though there is no evidence of this distinction in the text itself). A close examination of some of the manuscripts has revealed that the contents of these texts overlap. Different names are applied to the same text, and the same name is applied to differing texts. As we shall see, the *VDhP* is also pesky in this regard, giving rise to considerable confusion over its name and contents. The apparent heterogeneity and volatility of this genre of texts have led Indologists

[2]E. J. Rapson, "The Purāṇas" in *Cambridge History of India* (Cambridge: Cambridge University Press, 1921), 1: 266.

[3]P. V. Kane, *History of Dharmaśāstra (Ancient and Mediaeval Religious and Civil Law in India)* (*HD*) ([1930–1962] Poona: Bhandarkar Oriental Research Institute) (1962–75) in 5 volumes; 1 (1968–75), 408–21; 5 (1962–74), 815–1002. Jan Gonda, "Medieval Religious Literature in Sanskrit" in *Epics and Sanskrit Religious Literature*, vol. 2.1 of *A History of Indian Literature*, edited by Jan Gonda (Wiesbaden: Otto Harrassowitz, 1977), pp. 114–15.

again and again to speak of them as "encyclopedic" and as "storehouses" of Hindu lore. Once again, the *VDhP* is more than typical, incorporating condensations or paraphrases of texts on everything from archery and medicine to astronomy and divination. Since many scholars have found this material attractive, they have tried to date it to India's "golden age," that of the Guptas.

Composite Authorship

Surprisingly little is said in scholarship on the Purāṇas about their authors. Scholars characterize them as the texts of "popular" Hinduism, and assume that they were more or less unconsciously and almost accidentally congealed collections of genealogies, myths, and legends, which originally belonged to an oral tradition and were the property of bards (see Appendix). Without saying much about what sort of persons in what positions and under which historical circumstances would have composed, learned, recited, and heard these texts, Indologists continue to assert that the Purāṇas were used to educate the "common" man and even to unify the diverse populations of the subcontinent. Many of these scholars simply assume that a unitary Brāhmaṇ priesthood has been the instrument for the conversion of these texts of the mass mentality into works of a "great" or Sanskritic tradition and has either to serve its own self-interests or to popularize the radical monism of Advaita Vedānta, made interpolations of rituals and other extraneous material into them in the process. R. C. Hazra's view is fairly typical.[4]

Now, there can be little doubt that Purāṇas have been differently situated in India's successive imperial formations (the complex polities consisting of a hegemonic empire and other allied and rival kingdoms), and within the same formation (see Introduction). One could, furthermore, make the case that the rise of a Hindu bourgeoisie in the nineteenth century and the use of the printing press may have brought about a certain "democratization" of the Purāṇas. But there is no reason to assume that an elite and mass dichotomy that was brought into existence in nineteenth-century India, as it was in Europe, is an essential feature of a civilization at all times. Nor is there any reason to substitute the Brāhmaṇs—thought of as a group version of the abstract individual of political economy, a unitary class with its own insatiable desires for wealth—for the uniquely inspired author of the European text. On the contrary, I think it is important to distinguish in broad terms the uses that Vedists made of Purāṇas redacted in polities where Buddhist monastic orders predominated from the uses that Theists made of the Purāṇas they redacted in polities where their ways of life held sway. And I would want to distinguish these, in turn, from the uses that Theists as Hindus made of the Purāṇas redacted or dispersed over digests in polities of the thirteenth to the eighteenth centuries where some configuration of Islamic orders was hegemonic.[5] Precisely because differing

[4]Hazra, "The Purāṇas," in *The Cultural Heritage of India* (Calcutta: The Ramakrishna Mission Institute of Culture, 1958–86), 2: 268–69.

[5]Nor should we fail to consider the uses that Islamic scholars and aristocrats made of texts like the Upaniṣads and *Mahābhārata* (*MBh*) or the use that Alberūnī made of the *VDhP* itself (see appendix to this chapter).

societies formed by disciplinary orders and lordly courts considered Purāṇas as authoritative sites for world accounts, they saw them as media for the articulation of themselves as complex agents, as coagents of the splendid and mighty beings described in the Purāṇas that could work their will in the world.

The argument I make here is that the *VDhP* was produced by and for a complex agent consisting of Pāñcarātra adepts and an imperial king and his court. That complex agent was synonymous with the disciplinary order of the Pāñcarātrins in the course of making itself paramount by combining its will with that of the ruling society of Kashmir, the king of kings and other dignitaries of the imperial court. The crucial part in this process was played by the royal preceptor and chronologer. This complex author should not, however, be seen as pregiven, as is often the case in studies using an unexamined notion of "patronage."[6] The very process of articulating the text, that is, of transforming preexisting and new textual elements into the *VDhP*, was also articulative of its author—the disciplinary order and imperial court. Let me begin with the way in which the *VDhP* situates itself.

The form taken by a Purāṇa is that of a "dialogue" or "colloquy" (*saṃvāda*) between a master and pupil, in which the former imparts an "account of the ancient past" (*purāṇa*) to the latter in response to his repeated questions or assertions of doubt. The knowledge imparted in this way may box within itself still earlier dialogues between other masters and pupils. The master of our text is the ancient sage (*ṛṣi*), Mārkaṇḍeya, a savant of the Brāhmaṇ or priestly estate. His pupil and interlocutor is Vajra, a king of the Kṣatriya or warrior estate. Mārkaṇḍeya, son of Mṛkaṇḍa and a man of the Bhṛgu clan, the foremost clan of sages and priests, was, it may be inferred, a master not only of the Veda but also of the Pāñcarātra.

This latter was the name of the major "order" or "rule" (*vidhi, vidhāna*) of Vaiṣṇavas in "early medieval" India, that is, in the eighth to twelfth centuries. The Śrīvaiṣṇavas or Rāmānujīyas of south India in the "late medieval" period and down to the present are a transformation of the earlier Pāñcarātrins. The other, lesser order of Vaiṣṇavas of which we have evidence from early medieval India was that of the Vaikhānasas.[7] The referent of the term Pāñcarātra, which literally means "relating to the five nights," has been a source of speculation for Indologists.[8] The *VDhP* gives no definition, but it is probable that authors of that text would have pointed to the two five-day festivals that mark the beginning and end of the four-month sleep of Viṣṇu's image (II.153). The reason for reticence is that the early Pāñcarātrins

[6]Nor should we think that single persons as authors are, by contrast, unitary. They are, if not complex to the extent possible in the case of a joint author, at least composite entities.

[7]Jan Gonda, "Religious Thought and Practice in Vaikhanasa Visnuism," *School of Oriental and African Studies Bulletin* 40 (1977), 550–71.

[8]See J. A. B. Van Buitenen, "The Name Pāñcarātra," *History of Religions* 1.2 (1962), 291–99; V. Raghavan, "The Name Pāñcarātra: With an Analysis of the Sanatkumāra-saṃhitā in manuscript," *Journal of the American Oriental Society* 85.1 (1965), 73–79; H. Daniel Smith, "A Typological Survey of Definitions: The Name 'Pāñcarātra'," *Journal of Oriental Research* 34–35 (1964–66), 102–17, according to whom (p. 104) some Pāñcarātra texts of the Śrīvaiṣṇavas refer to a sage as receiving the knowledge of the Pāñcarātrāgama in a session of five nights; p. 116, contemporary Pāñcarātrins (i.e., Śrīvaiṣṇavas of south India) use the term to mean the gift of god in five forms, and especially in the fifth, that of the image (*arcā*). See also Kane, *HD* 5 (1962–74), 954 n. 1546; and Gonda, *Medieval Religious Literature*, pp. 43–47.

probably used the term to refer to a Vedic sacrifice that this later liturgy of image-honoring had displaced.[9]

Both the Pāñcarātrins and the Vaikhānasas seem originally to have been orders of forest-dwellers only and not the advocates of costly temple liturgies. The term Bhāgavata, meaning "devotee of the Lord (*bhagavān*)," was used to designate any Vaiṣṇava, but appears also to have been used to denote householder Vaiṣṇavas (as in the *Bhagavadgītā*) who adhered to the Vedic sacrificial liturgy. For at least two or three centuries before the time of the *VDhP* it would seem that the Pāñcarātrins and Bhāgavatas were content to maintain this relationship of complementarity. So it would be wrong to assume that the Pāñcarātrins had always intended to descend onto the plains of India and establish the preeminence of their way of life and disciplinary order. Indeed, one might argue on the basis of the ambiguous position of the *Nārāyaṇīya*, the earliest extant text of the Pāñcarātrins in the *MBh*, that they were fortunate to have gained recognition at all.

Vajra, the royal listener of the *VDhP*, was himself the great-grandson of Vāsudeva Kṛṣṇa, the manifestation of Viṣṇu, the cosmic overlord, who descended to earth to impel the Pāṇḍavas, the protagonists of the *MBh*, on to victory over their senior cousins and rivals, the Kauravas. The only Yādava left on earth after the events of the Epic drew to a close, Vajra was made king at Indraprastha (near Delhi), the Pāṇḍava headquarters and cadet capital of the Kuru kingdom, by Yudhiṣṭhira, the eldest of the Pāṇḍavas.[10]

---

[9]The *Śatapatha Brāhmaṇa*, edited by Chinnaswami Sastri and Pattabhirama Sastri (Varanasi: Caukhamba, 1984) XIII.6.1 uses the term Pāñcarātra to refer to a Vedic sacrificial session (*sattra*) of five nights conceived by Puruṣa Nārāyaṇa, by the performance of which one could attain superiority over all beings. It equates that sacrifice (XII.3.4) with the sacrifice of Puruṣa in the Puruṣa-sūkta, the Vedic hymn that the Pāñcarātrins considered the most important hymn of the Veda, one that in their eyes established a cosmic Personality, equated with the Pāñcarātra godhead, Nārāyaṇa, as the absolute. See F. Otto Schrader, *Introduction to the Pāñcarātra and the Ahirbudhnya Saṃhitā* ([1916] Madras: Adyar Library, 1973), 28–29.

[10]He did this after he bathed Parikṣit (grandson of Arjuna, third of the Pāṇḍava brothers, and of Subhadrā, Kṛṣṇa's sister), who was to be the only Pāṇḍava to remain on earth, into kingship. Yudhiṣṭhira installed him at Hāstinapura, the senior capital of the Kuru kingdom, bestowing on him the paramount overlordship (*rājyaṃ sarvam*) of India; *MBh*, edited by V. S. Sukthankar and others (Poona: Bhandarkar Oriental Research Institute, 1927–66.) XVII.1.6–9. Afterward, he and his brothers and their wife, Draupadī, left Parikṣit and Vajra to rule the earth and set forth on a "great departure" (*mahāprasthāna*), a march into the Himalayas, where they died and ascended to heaven.

The Kauravas had earlier given the Pāṇḍavas the city of Khāṇḍavaprastha and half of the Kuru kingdom, after the latter agreed to give up the kingship as a whole. The Pāṇḍavas rebuilt this city, transforming it into a paradise, and renamed it Indraprastha, after the king of the gods, Indra, whose city, we are told, it rivaled. A demon, Maya, constructed for them a fabulous jeweled hall of pillars, attached to their new palace. Once the pillared assembly hall at Indraprastha had been completed and Yudhiṣṭhira had occupied his throne there, Nārada, greatest of the Vaiṣṇava sages, had visited his court and urged him to undertake the events narrated in the *MBh*.

On the advice of that sage, Yudhiṣṭhira dispatched his four younger brothers to Magadha, where they overpowered Jarāsandha, king of that country and wrongful paramount overlord of India. Meanwhile he prepared to perform the royal installation (*rājasūya*) to mark his rise as a "king of kings." Then, while he ruled from his throne in the glittering hall at Indraprastha, his four brothers set forth again, this time to conquer the "four quarters" of the "entire earth" and make good Yudhiṣṭhira's claim. The pillared hall at Indraprastha had thus been made into the meeting place of the paramount king of all India and his tributary kings, including the Kauravas themselves. It was the imperial capital of the earth. After

At the beginning of the very first chapter of the *VDhP*, the reciter of the text, who in the liturgical practices of the text is called just that (*vācaka*), takes the position of an unnamed person, presumably of the premier narrator, Sūta Lomaharṣaṇa (he who causes the hair, *loma*, to bristle, *harṣaṇa*).[11] The first thing he recites is the salutation at the head of the text. That first names Gaṇeśa, the god charged with removing the obstacles to an undertaking. Without the cooperation of this deity, the hypostatization of the circumstances of an action, the recitation will not even take place. Next the reciter names Nārāyaṇa, Viṣṇu in his transcendent form. The reciter then reads: "Now, then, the undertaking of the Viṣṇudharmottara." He then again names the overlord of the cosmos, Nārāyaṇa, and then that same god split into pupil and master, Nara and Nārāyaṇa, premier listener and author of the text. Next he names the goddess Sarasvatī, spouse of Brahmā, hypostatization of knowing as something to be mastered, followed by Vyāsa. The sage Vyāsa ("arranger"), also known as Kṛṣṇa or Viṣṇu Dvaipāyana, was the expert compiler of the Veda, the *MBh*, and the Purāṇa.[12]

What we can already see as one part of a complex author, its dramatic narrative voice, next describes the arrival of Mārkaṇḍeya at Indraprastha, now the capital and court of Vajra. Declaimed the "foremost of the best of kings," (*nṛpavarya-mukhya*) or "lord among kings" (*rājendra*), and compared with Yudhiṣṭhira, Vajra is represented as a king of kings of realms all over India, if not the paramount overlord of India as a whole (*VDhP* I.1.2–8). The kings of India had assembled at the court of Vajra for the performance of his horse sacrifice, carried out ten years and one lunar fortnight after the current Age of Strife had begun (I.80.5–6).[13] The fourth and worst of a cycle of four ages, it was ushered in thirty-six years after the great battle of the Epic when Kṛṣṇa departed from the earth.[14] It was the age for which *bhakti*, which I render as "devoted participation" in Viṣṇu, as signified by *pūjā*, the honoring of images, was intended. In the earliest age, knowing the truth (*jñāna*) had alone enabled people to see the gods and had sufficed to lead them to the final goal of release. Ascetical feats (*tapas*) became necessary in the second age and sacrifice to the gods (*yajña*) in the third. Now, in the Age of Strife, the institution of images of gods (*surapratiṣṭhā*) was also required (I.73.20–34 and III.93.5–6). So, Mārkaṇḍeya's arrival with instructions on image-honoring was timely. The occasion chosen, a horse sacrifice, was suitable since it was apparently considered the proper setting for the recitation of the *MBh*, the *Rāmāyaṇa*, and the

---

the battle of Kurukṣetra, the Pāṇḍavas returned to Hāstinapura, the older capital of Kuru, performed the horse sacrifice (*aśvamedha*), and resumed their rule of the earth from that city.

[11]Alternatively, it could be the voice of Ugraśravas Sauti, son of Lomaharṣaṇa, who related the *MBh* to sages at a sacrifice.

[12]Vaiśampāyana, his pupil, related the Epic to Janamejaya, the son of Parikṣit, in response to a question from him, and imparted that text to Ugraśravas.

[13]Although the *VDhP* here names the kings of Madra, the Darads, Abhisāra and Darva, the Hūṇas, and Bāhlika, all near Kashmir, it names no king of that country, perhaps because, according to one account, its minor king did not participate in the great war. The king of Kashmir does make a cameo appearance in the war that Bharata wages against Gāndhāra.

[14]These ages were named after dice tosses: the first, the Kṛta or four spots, which I translate as the Age of Completeness; the second, Tretā or three spots, which I translate as the Age of the Trey; the third, Dvāpara or two spots, as the Age of the Deuce; and the Kali or one spot, as the Age of Strife.

Purāṇas to royal courts.[15] Yet this is also disquieting, for the very knowledge that Mārkaṇḍeya brings will have the effect of displacing the horse (and other Vedic) sacrifices from the center of concern in favor of a temple liturgy.

As illustrious as the court was, it was astonished when it saw Mārkaṇḍeya and his retinue of Brāhmaṇs appear before it:

> Those kings then saw sages the sight of whom was so scarce that those bearers of fame thought they must be in Brahmā's paradise. Out of attachment, they spoke these words to Vajra, the giver of many thousands [of cows to the Brāhmaṇs]: "It must be as a result of your favor (*prasāda*), O King, that Brāhmaṇs resembling Brahmā himself have appeared, as they used to do in the Ages of the Trey and Deuce, in this, the Age of Strife, that is now upon us. O King, you are of the same clan as Kṛṣṇa, that is why this court of yours is honored (*upās*) by these men, resembling Brahmā, whose lot is large and whose wealth consists of their austerities. By devotion to that Kṛṣṇa whose luminous will is infinite, even those kings of the past, unsurpassed in heroic valor but passed over/overcome by Kṛṣṇa may obtain release from Kṛṣṇa in the present. But this current Age of Strife is fierce and very violent, and since the opportunity of gazing on such men of high souls is hard to come by nowadays in a gathering of kings, be you pleased, O tiger among kings, to request of those best of the Brāhmaṇs the manifold orders of Viṣṇu (*vaiṣṇavān dharmān vividhān*) together with the esoteric teachings and abridgments (*sarahasyān sasaṃgrahān*)." (I.1.9–16)

As is clear from the marvelous appearance of Mārkaṇḍeya and the deferential treatment accorded him by Vajra, himself no ordinary king, this was no ordinary Brāhmaṇ. The reciter of the *VDhP* makes him resemble Brahmā, the god who is master of the Veda and of the Vedic sacrifice, the divine emanation of Viṣṇu who creates the world. Later in the narrative of the text, where Mārkaṇḍeya is himself the narrator, he reveals that he is indeed privileged, for he is the only man who survives from one grand cosmic formation (*mahākalpa*) to another. He does so by entering the mouth of a giant youth (*bāla*) who is none other than Aniruddha, one of the four major emanations of Viṣṇu (according to the Pāñcarātrins) and a homologue of Brahmā (I.78–79).[16] Mārkaṇḍeya is, thus, clearly an emanation of Viṣṇu himself.[17] Through its description of Mārkaṇḍeya, *VDhP* is clearly claiming

[15]R. C. Hazra, "The Aśvamedha, the Common Source of Origin of the Purāṇa, *pañca-lakṣaṇa* and the Mahābhārata," *Annals of the Bhandarkar Oriental Research Institute* 36 (1955), 190–203. The *VDhP* omits the frame, included in the *MBh* and some other Purāṇas, which has the sage narrator recite the text to a company of sages performing a Vedic sacrifice in the forest without royalty.

[16]After relating this cosmic event, Mārkaṇḍeya told Vajra: "That which happened in the past Cosmic Formation has been narrated by me, O King, to Yudhiṣṭhira, son of Dharma, in the Kāmyaka Forest" (I.81.26b–7a), a reference to his appearance in the *MBh* where he lectures the Pāṇḍavas on this event and related subjects; Mārkaṇḍeyasamasyā ("Session with Mārkaṇḍeya"), *MBh* III.179–221.

[17]We should not forget that many an Indian text states openly that its author was an ordinary man, not a sage, who completed his work on a date within one of the historic Indian eras. For example, Bhaṭṭotpala, a Kashmiri Brāhmaṇ, concluded his explication of the *Brihajjātaka* of Varāhamihira with: "This commentary is finished by me on Thursday, the fifth lunar day of the bright fortnight of the month of Caitra (March-April) in Śāka 888 (A.D. 966)"; see Avadhavihari Tripathi's introduction to Varāhamihira, *Bṛhatsaṃhitā* (Varanasi: Varanaseya-samskrta-visva vidyalaya, 1968), 1: ix.

divine presence: whenever his words, the contents of the *VDhP*, are recited, the words of Viṣṇu himself are to be heard.

Mārkaṇḍeya and his disciples came to the royal capital of India from a retreat in the forest. The *VDhP* nowhere gives the location of Mārkaṇḍeya's retreat, but it does suggest that it may have been situated at Badarikāśrama (Badrināth), the retreat of Nara-Nārāyaṇa situated near Lake Bindusaras and Mount Gandhamādana and Mount Kailāsa, the source of the Gaṅgā, the premier river of India in Purāṇic geography and the point from which India was recreated at the beginning of a cosmic cycle.[18] According to the *Nārāyaṇīya* of the *MBh*, Nārāyaṇa was the forest-dwelling aspect of Viṣṇu especially concerned with knowledge. Nara, the "man," was his permanent pupil. Another pair of divines, Vāsudeva Kṛṣṇa and Arjuna (whose dialogues figure so prominently in the *Bhagavadgītā*) were considered the princely emanations of Nārāyaṇa and Nara. The forest-dwelling Pāñcarātrins honored Nārāyaṇa as the supreme god, whereas the Bhāgavatas, householders of the plains, honored Kṛṣṇa as the highest form of Viṣṇu.

I should add here that the forest was assumed to be the place where relatively transcendent knowledge originated, whereas mundane or immanent knowledge was to be found on the plains. Against this background we can see that the pairing of Mārkaṇḍeya and Vajra duplicates these other couplings. The descent of Mārkaṇḍeya to the royal center of the Indian plains to impart the knowledge of the forest-dwelling Pāñcarātrins at the onset of the Age of Strife signals a rearticulation: both the Pāñcarātrins and the kings of India and their subjects are going to be refashioned in the discourse of the *VDhP*. The knowledge that the sage Mārkaṇḍeya has come to Indraprastha to reveal consisted not only of a world account but also of the rules or procedures required for transforming the activity of honoring images practiced by the forest-dwelling Pāñcarātrins into a fully elaborated temple liturgy of the plains-dwelling householders, one that would displace the Vedic sacrificial liturgy still practiced by the Bhāgavatas from its position of privilege in imperial polities. The knowledge that he delivers to his royal devotee, Vajra, is, thus, not, that transcendent text, the Purāṇa as first authored by Viṣṇu. It is itself a transformation of that text, one that is delivered out of grace for his devotees at the beginning of the current Age of Strife to meet the worsening conditions that would otherwise obtain in this age. Before we turn to a consideration of the text's representation of those conditions and the way it proposed to meet them, let us see what more we can squeeze from the text itself about the humans who participated in its authorship and use.

The evidence that the *VDhP* provides about its own past would have us believe that the text was composed by a forest-dwelling sage and delivered by him to a king of kings and his court. That Vajra would "reflect" (*cint*) daily on this

[18]When Vajra asks Mārkaṇḍeya about his future, the latter tells him that after he, Vajra, dies, the assembly hall (*sabhā*) that had been built at Indraprastha out of precious metals taken from lake Bindusaras, in the Himalayas, will be taken back there. Bindusaras, the source of the Bhāgīrathī Gaṅgā, was, of course, the site of the retreat of Nara and Nārāyaṇa. This cryptic reply to Vajra seems to imply that just as Mārkaṇḍeya has gone back to his place of origin, so, too, would the pillared hall revert to the lake at Badarikāśrama.

Purāṇa suggests that this text was to have a privileged position among the bodies of knowledge at the disposal of the king. This evidence is confirmed by the evidence of the text concerning those who were supposed to use the *VDhP* in the present, in the time following Mārkaṇḍeya's delivery of the text.

The daily routine prescribed in the *VDhP* for a king of kings called for him to listen to histories (*itihāsa*) in the morning and to reflect on instructions (*śāstras*) in the afternoon. There can be little doubt that the major texts intended here were, in the first instance, the *MBh* and, in the second, the *VDhP* itself; for, as we shall soon see, that text saw itself as a guide to the great Epic and instructions on a variety of topics. The text does not say so explicitly, but this should not surprise us, for the *VDhP* is quite tactful in the prescriptions it lays down for the king; it does not overemphasize the Pāñcarātra aspects of the royal routine. Its position is that all kings who adhere to the Vedas are de facto Vaiṣṇavas, even if they claim to be Śaivas. The best of kings, however, is a Pāñcarātrin.

We may infer, therefore, that the king of kings was not only supposed to listen to histories from the great Epic and the *VDhP*, he was also supposed to learn the instructions of the *VDhP* sufficiently well that he could reflect on them by himself. The expectation was that the king would be a generalized master of the contents of the text as a whole. He would, in addition, have a more detailed command of those parts of the text dealing specifically with the rules for royal order (*rājadharma*). Daily rehearsal of the text's contents would, of course, have reinforced his memory of them. One might point out here that the injunction to reflect daily on the instructions, was a command to engage daily in a practice of "*re*membering" (*smṛti*), of rethinking the knowledge of Viṣṇu in the continually changing circumstances of one's present, and not a rote process of retrieving knowledge from a static memory (as in a computer).

The king of kings was not the only one in the royal court who was assumed to know the contents of this text. The lists of qualifications for counsellors (*mantrin*), the senior and experienced men among the ministers of the king, seem also to presuppose their knowledge of relevant parts of the *VDhP*, those portions dealing with "resources" (*artha*), "guidance" (*nīti*), and the "science of weaponry" (*dhanurveda*). I think we can safely assume that many if not most of those in the royal court who were themselves Vaiṣṇavas, including the wives of ministers and politically high-ranking Śūdras, would have had at least some acquaintance with the text or with vernacular versions of portions of it. Moving out and down from this circle around the king of kings himself, it would also be reasonable to expect that the *VDhP* might have been known, again in part, to two other categories of persons. These were the wealthier merchants of the capital and of other towns, and the better-off farmers of the countryside, those who would have formed the councils of "subject-citizens" and been in frequent contact with the imperial court and other lesser lordly courts—and even, on occasion, conjoined with it. It is much less likely that the text was known, except perhaps by reputation, to "ordinary" villagers of the countryside. If scholars are referring to the beliefs and practices of this category of the population when they use the expression "popular Hinduism," then we must reject the view that the Purāṇas were and are, by definition, the texts of the "common man (and woman)." The *VDhP*, at least, was, during the century or so after its completion, primarily the text of an imperial king and his court.

Those who were most closely connected with the production and use of the *VDhP* were, apart from the king of kings himself, the Pāñcarātra adepts and priests connected to the court of a Vaiṣṇava king who had been persuaded to take that text as his guide to Viṣṇu's world account and the way of life that it supported. Just as Mārkaṇḍeya took the lead in the dialogues of the text, so Pāñcarātra adepts, we may assume, took the lead in the countless dialogues that contributed to the completion of the text. The *VDhP* urges its king of kings to appoint as his "palace priest" (*purohita*) a Brāhmaṇ skilled in two Vedas, the Yajur and the Atharva. He was also supposed to be learned in the "liturgical procedures" (*vidhāna*) of five Kalpas, a set of manuals associated with the Atharvaveda. The Yajurveda was the Veda most centrally connected with the performance of the grander Vedic sacrifices. It may be inferred from elsewhere in the text that a palace priest in Kashmir would have known the Black Yajurveda as redacted in the Kāṭhaka school. The Atharvaveda was, as is well known, the Veda most closely connected with the performance of a sequence of daily and annual "rites" by the king, apart from the multifire sacrifices. The palace priest that the *VDhP* calls for was thus of the sort one would have expected in a kingdom where Vedic liturgies were regularly performed.

The *VDhP*, however, complicates the situation, for it calls on the king of kings to appoint a "chronologer" (*sāṃvatsara*, "he who knows the entire year," often translated too narrowly and with the implication that his knowledge consisted of "superstition," as "astrologer"), under whose command the palace priest will be placed. This chronologer was supposed to have not only the qualifications normally expected in ancient India, but some additional and unusual qualifications, as well. Virtually every liturgical act the king of kings is commanded to perform comprises, from the standpoint of procedural knowledge, two sorts of material. One of these is Vedic, the other is Purāṇic. Generally speaking, the palace priest was to perform the Vedic portions and recite appropriate Vedic mantras. The Purāṇic portions of the rites, however, were to be performed not by the palace priest, learned in the Veda, but by the royal chronologer who, it is assumed, is learned in the rules and mantras of the *VDhP*.

Curiously, the *VDhP* makes no specific mention of another specialist one would not expect to find only at the court of a Hindu king but in command of his life-transforming practices. I speak here of the "royal preceptor" (*rājaguru*). I am tempted, therefore, to conclude that the capacities of royal preceptor, high priest, and chronologer were assumed, in the *VDhP*, to be exercised by one and the same man. If my reasoning here is correct, then we may go one step further in our search for the "author" of the *VDhP*: the person who played the largest part in "remembering" the text of Mārkaṇḍeya and compiling it was probably the very chronologer to whom so much responsibility is given in the text itself. But this author does not stand outside his text. The identity of the Pāñcarātra adept who takes on the roles of chronologer, high Vaiṣṇava priest, and royal preceptor is itself rearticulated by the same process of reworking and modifying existing traditions as is the identity of the text.

The central component of the disciplinary order that made itself into the author of the *VDhP* was a complement of sixteen liturgists (*ṛtvik*) required, according to the text, to perform the highest of all Pāñcarātra royal works—the installation of the image of a god in a monumental Vaiṣṇava temple (III.97). A chief liturgist, the Sātvata (Pāñcarātrin) adept who would be the supervisor of the temple and its liturgy, performed the actual installation of the fixed image, assisted by two priests (one a Sātvata who carried the images and another a priest of the Yajurveda who held the attendances to be offered), as well as a set of four priests (one from each Veda, who recited mantras from his Veda while holding waterjars). Three other Sātvatas were in charge of making attendances at an auxilliary altar before a portable image and three priests of the Yajurveda took charge of the oblations poured at another auxilliary altar into a fire. A dancer, flutist, and instrumentalist also did their part, as did the reciter of Purāṇa (*vācaka*). The chronologer (and royal preceptor) and builder, who made their interventions, completed this complement of liturgists. The complement of this complex liturgist was, of course, the imperial celebrant, in whose presence the installation was to be performed.[19]

To summarize: the "author" of the text was a complex agent, one consisting of Pāñcarātra adepts, palace priest, king of kings, and counsellor, as well as the chronologer himself, each of whom participated in the process of composition from a different perspective and brought to bear a different expertise or commitment. We can see these persons transforming themselves as disciplinary order and imperial court in the course of composing the *VDhP* itself. That is, the author takes on shape in the very process of authorship. What is more, the joint author at work here most likely spanned two or more generations. The text is a large one, organized in three parts. This could well be taken as an indication that the text was completed at three successive moments. We must, therefore, allow for the possibility that the process of composition may have continued for several decades, in which case not only the ideas and practices but the very composition of this joint author doubtless changed. All those who participated in this process probably thought they were inspired by Viṣṇu, but it was probably the Pāñcarātra chronologer and preceptor who "remembered" and then composed the text of the sage Mārkaṇḍeya in its completed form.

Naming Texts

The author of the *VDhP* was a complex agent, one that made and remade itself as it made and remade its text. The classic theory of the text considered the text either as an expression of an external state of affairs existing in the time and space of the author, or as the expression of an interior state of mind. The orientalist application of this notion to the Purāṇas argues that the expression in the first or empiricist instance is an inherently distorted expression of historical reality, and in the second instance is the mythological or symbolic expression of a monist, illusionist Hindu

[19] For a discussion of changes in the composition of priesthoods, see R. Inden, "Changes in the Vedic Priesthood," in *Ritual, State and History in South Asia: Essays in Honour of J. C. Heesterman*, edited by A. W. van den Hoek, D. H. A. Kolff, and M. S. Oort (Leiden: E. J. Brill, 1992), pp. 556–77.

philosophy. Neither of these positions has been easy to sustain, of course, because of the absence of a unitary author who could convey such expressions and, hence, provide the *VDhP* with the unitary essential content, the "textuality" that a proper text should have. Even a cursory glance at the diverse contents of the *VDhP* lets the scholar know that he or she will have to deal with what some of today's critics call the problem of "intertextuality," the problem of a text's heterogeneity and its connections with other texts, both within a genre, itself unstable, and with other genres.

The Indologists' solution to this problem has been to label the text as encyclopedic and to operate on the assumption that the text is only an accidental whole, a mere coagulation of past "influences." What I want to suggest here is that the text need not be seen either as the unitary product of a single author whose function is to express some outer or inner reality or as a mere hodge-podge whose only principle of unity is that of a casual sectarian convenience.

Instead, I argue, we can see the *VDhP* as a series of textual wholes, as a "scale of texts" that have been articulated by its complex author acting as a reader or user of other texts. It is possible to look at the complex author and text of the *VDhP* as articulative of a tradition embodying a way of life and not as the passive recipients of it. I begin to make my case for looking at this work as a series or scale of texts with the naming of the text and its supplements.

The title of the *VDhP* itself signals the importance of differences in the constitution of this text. It disturbs any effort we might make to reduce the text to a homogeneous unity. On the other hand, the very fact that the complex author of the *VDhP* has consciously given it such a name should make us hesitate before dismissing the text as a whole. Most secondary accounts call it the *Viṣṇudharmottarapurāṇa*.[20] Scholars have generally taken the title to mean a Purāṇa (or Mahāpurāṇa) consisting of "additions (*uttara*) to (the) Viṣṇudharma." This has led some of them to assume that the *VDhP* is appended to some other text, one containing the Dharma of Viṣṇu or entitled the Viṣṇudharma. There is textual support for this assumption, although it comes from outside the *VDhP* itself. A passage in the *Nāradīyapurāṇa* makes the *VDhP* into the Second Division of that *Viṣṇu Purāṇa*.[21] The editors of the printed text of the *VDhP* note this, citing the relevant passage from the *Nāradīya* in their foreword. The colophon that they print at the

[20]The printed version differs slightly, labeling the text a "Mahāpurāṇa." The use of this term is based on a distinction that has been made since at least the twelfth century between "greater" (*mahā*) and "lesser" (*upa*) Purāṇas (see n. 22 below).

[21]It describes a "great" (*mahat*) Vaiṣṇava Purāṇa as comprising two major divisions (*bhāga*). The first division is said to consist of six "books" (*aṃśa*). The second, we are told, contains texts called the Viṣṇudharmottaras, narrated with care by Sūta, Śaunaka (the sage to whom Sauti, son of Sūta, imparted the *MBh*), and others. It includes a variety of legends on Order; vows (*vrata*); major and minor observances (*yama, niyama*); instruction in the way of life leading to Order (*dharma*), and in the acquisition and distribution of resources (*artha*), on Vedānta (the end of the Veda or goal of Vedic liturgical action and learning), and on astronomy (*jyotiṣa*); tales of royal dynasties (*vaṃśākhyāna*); lauds or eulogies of the gods (*stotra*); descriptions of the epochs of Manu; and various other learnings (*vidyā*) "helpful to everyone"; *Nāradīyapurāṇa* (Bombay: Śrīveṅkateśvara Steam Press, 1905) I.94.1–20. From the detailed description of the contents of the first division, it is clear that the text published and translated as the *Viṣṇupurāṇa* is meant.

end of the last chapter of each of the three parts (*khaṇḍa*) of the texts states, in accord with the information given in the foreword, that the chapter stands in the appropriate part of the second division of the Viṣṇu Mahāpurāṇa. Hazra rejects this view in favor of his own, namely, that the *Viṣṇudharmottara* is the latter part of an unpublished Purāṇa called the *Viṣṇudharma*.[22] He also adds, without explanation, that both of these works were originally called Śāstras.[23]

The internal evidence of the *VDhP* itself, however, asks us to reject the view that the complex author of the *VDhP* attached its text as an appendix to either the *Viṣṇudharma* or *Viṣṇupurāṇa*. What is the nature of this evidence? Let us begin with the term "Purāṇa" and its variants. Although the text certainly presents itself by way of its contents and organization as a Purāṇa, it is not fond of naming itself as a Purāṇa. There is, however, one important exception to this general reticence. The very last verses of the text, cited above, relate that king Vajra "continued to reflect daily on the Purāṇa narrated by Mārkaṇḍeya" (III.355.5). This crucial passage leaves no doubt that the text saw itself as a Purāṇa, an originary account. We should also take this to embrace history (*itihāsa*), as the two are almost indistinguishable.[24] That is not, however, the only kind of text it claimed to be.

Mārkaṇḍeya, the "author" of the text, several times describes the text he relates as the *Viṣṇudharma*- ("together with additions") *sottara*. The text to which the first part of this name, *Viṣṇudharma*, "the Order [that is, ordered way of life] of Viṣṇu," refers was one of the instructional manuals on Order (Dharmaśāstra), in verse. This is possibly what Hazra has in mind when he somewhat misleadingly states that the text has been referred to as an instructional manual (*śāstra*).[25] If so, then *VDhP* appears to be claiming that it is the instructional manual on Order of the Vaiṣṇavas.

The suggestion of the *VDhP* that it is an instructional manual on Order would certainly seem to be justified, for it incorporates or paraphrases a large number of verses from the two texts of this class generally recognized as most important, the *Mānava* and *Yājñavālkya*.[26] But these two texts are peripheral to the Dharmaśāstra that the *VDhP* has appropriated under the name *Viṣṇudharma*. That text is

[22]Kane, in his criticism of Hazra's views, *HD* 5 (1962–74), 874, rightly rejects the idea that the *VDhP* is an appendix to a *Viṣṇudharmapurāṇa*, but he is prepared to see it as an addition to the *Viṣṇupurāṇa*.

[23]Hazra, furthermore, considers the *VDhP*, like the *Viṣṇudharma*, to be an Upapurāṇa. Many of the extant texts of the Purāṇas distinguish a set of eighteen named "greater" Purāṇas from a set, not fixed in name and number, of "lesser" Purāṇas. A passage in the *Dānasāgara*, a text composed by (or under) the king of Bengal, Vallālasena (c. 1158–1178), edited by Bhabatosh Bhattacharya (Calcutta: Asiatic Society of Bengal, 1956), p. 3, would seem to support the view that the *VDhP* was considered an Upapurāṇa. It clearly distinguishes between greater and lesser Purāṇas and classes a Purāṇa "called the *Viṣṇudharmottara* composed by Mārkaṇḍeya" as one of eight Upapurāṇas that it lists. Immediately after naming the *VDhP*, it lists a text called the *Viṣṇudharma*. It does not, however, refer to this text as an Upapurāṇa but as a Śāstra.

[24]The text seems also to have been unaware of any distinction between Mahāpurāṇas and Upapurāṇas. Either no such distinction existed at the time when the *VDhP* was closed or (less likely in my view) the text chose to ignore the distinction for fear that it would either have to accept its inferior standing as a "lesser" Purāṇa or lie in claiming to be a "greater" one.

[25]R. C. Hazra, "The Upapurāṇas," in *The Cultural Heritage of India* (Calcutta: Ramakrishna Mission Institute of Culture, 1958–1986), 2: 277.

[26]R. C. Hazra, *Studies in the Upapuranas* (Calcutta: Sanskrit College, 1958), 1: 198–99.

the *Viṣṇudharmaśāstra*, also known as the *Viṣṇusmṛti*. This is a peculiar text. Its opening (and closing) chapters consist of dialogues between Viṣṇu and his consort Śrī, exactly as one would expect in a Purāṇa. Indeed, the opening twelve verses of the *Viṣṇusmṛti* are to be found, with some variations, in the *VDhP* (I.3) and constitute the whole of that chapter, striking evidence of the closeness of the two texts. Moreover, when Śrī requests knowledge of Viṣṇu, she does so in language very much like that used by the major interlocutor of the *VDhP*, King Vajra. She desires to hear "the eternal rules for an ordered way of life (*dharma*) together with the esoteric teachings and abridgments (*sarahasyān sasaṃgrahān*)."[27]

The *Viṣṇusmṛti* is also peculiar in another respect. The learned designated this and other Dharmaśāstras as "the remembered" (*smṛti*) texts in relation to earlier texts on the same topic but in prose, the Dharmasūtras. The other Dharmaśāstras consist of fully versified elaborations and reworkings of the Dharmasūtras. Most of the text between the opening and closing chapters of the *Viṣṇusmṛti*, however, consists of a prose Dharmasūtra.

Now, the Dharmasūtras, aphoristic manuals (Sūtra, literally, "thread") on Order (*dharma*) for the estates and lifestages complement the Gṛhyasūtras, post-Buddhist guides that reposition the Vedic liturgy as a householder's practice (whence the term *gṛhya*, "pertaining to the household"). Together they formed the Smārtasūtras, that is, the Sūtras concerned with "remembered" practices—as distinct from the manuals on the "grand" or "multifire" sacrifices of the Vedic liturgy, those practices "deriving from the heard" (*śruti*), the utterances of the Veda itself, which make up the topic of the Śrautasūtras. Together with the Smārtasūtras, these texts made up the set of texts known as the Kalpasūtras, aphoristic manuals on "liturgical procedures." Tied directly to separate Vedic disciplinary orders (the so-called schools), these sets of texts were the ones most immediately concerned with the performance of the Vedic sacrifice.[28] It is quite clear that the Dharmasūtra contained in the *Viṣṇusmṛti* is none other than the "missing" Dharmasūtra of the Kāṭhaka order or school of the Black Yajurveda,[29] for which only the Gṛhya text of its Kalpasūtra is extant.[30] The Kāṭhaka or "northern" school of the Black Yajurveda has long been associated with Kashmir and environs, the "northern" country or quarter of India, just as others have been linked with western, eastern, and southern or peninsular

---

[27] *Viṣṇusmṛti*, edited with the commentary, *Keśavavaijayantī*, of Nandapaṇḍita, by Pandita V. Krishnamacharya (Madras: Adyar Library, 1964), I.62.

[28] Jan Gonda, "Ritual Sūtras," in *Vedas and Upanishads*, vol. 1.2 of *A History of Indian Literature* (Wiesbaden: O. Harassowitz, 1977), pp. 467–68. Although the learned considered the Dharmaśāstras as "remembered" in relation to the Dharmasūtras, they considered the Kalpasūtra s as "remembered" in relation to the Veda.

[29] Nandapaṇḍita, commentator on the text indicates this; see also Kane, *HD* 1 (1968–75), 112–27.

[30] Gonda, "Ritual Sūtras," *Vedas and Upanishads*, pp. 490, 527. The *Kāṭhaka Gṛhyasūtra*, also known as the *Gṛhyasūtra* of Laugākṣi, is still in use today in Kashmir (as reported to me in personal correspondence by the anthropologist, T. N. Madan). See Laugākṣi, *Kāṭhaka Gṛhyasūtra, with Extracts from Three Commentaries [Devapāla, Brāhmaṇabala, Ādityadarśana], Appendix, and Indexes*, edited by Wilhelm Caland (Lahore: Research Department, D. A. V. College, 1925) and *Laugākṣigṛhyasūtras, with Bhāṣyam of Devapāla*, edited with preface and introduction by Madhusudan Kaul Shastri, 2 vols., Kashmir Series, 49, 55 (Bombay: Nirnay-sagar Press, 1928–34).

India.[31] The *VDhP* itself is also implicitly affiliated with this disciplinary order, not just by virtue of its appropriation of the *Viṣṇusmṛti* but because it also appropriates parts of the Kāṭhaka Kalpasūtra (see below). Before Vaiṣṇava Brāhmaṇs succeeded in embedding the prose portion of the *Viṣṇusmṛti* in its Purāṇic frame, it had no doubt constituted a Kāṭhaka Dharmasūtra, a prose text on Order explicitly attached to the Kāṭhaka order. Hence, if the term *Viṣṇudharma* is taken to mean a text by that name to which the *VDhP* is attached or affiliated, it is most assuredly the *Viṣṇudharmaśāstra* and not the *Viṣṇupurāṇa* or the *Viṣṇudharmapurāṇa*, to which the *VDhP* has no such close links.[32]

Like its antecedent, the *Viṣṇudharmaśāstra*, the *VDhP*, thus, styles itself both a Purāṇa and a Dharmaśāstra, only much greater in scope and length than its ancestor. Let us now consider of what the "additions" indicated in the second part of its name consisted. The earlier Dharmaśāstras also claimed to be comprehensive. The *Smṛti* of Yājñavālkya (I.3), from which the *VDhP* takes much material, lists fourteen "sciences" (*vidyā*), ending with the Vedas themselves, which it considers the highest authority, and explicitly states that they are "receptacles" (*sthāna*) or "causes" (*hetu*) of *dharma*.[33]

The *VDhP* lists the very same sciences, with the difference that it ends with the two sciences which it considers the highest: "The four Vedas and [their six] ancillaries (*aṅga*), exegesis (*mīmāṃsā*) and logic (*nyāya*), Dharmaśāstra and the Purāṇa are the fourteen sciences" (I.74.32).[34] It then tells us what the ancillary sciences of the Veda were: phonetics (*śikṣā*), life-transforming practices (*kalpa*), grammar (*vyākaraṇa*), etymology (*nirukta*), astronomy (*jyotiṣa*), and meter (*chandas*) (I.74.33). These sciences, of course, implied still others, either by way of attachment or inclusion. The *VDhP* linked four minor (*upa*) Vedas to the four major ones—history (*itihāsa*), to the Ṛgveda, weaponry (*dhanurveda*), to the Yajurveda, music (*gāndharvaveda*), to the Sāmaveda, and last, health (*āyurveda*), to the Atharvaveda (II.22.129-30). The foremost of these was, of course, history, inseparable from the Purāṇas. The *VDhP* assumed that all of these knowledges had to do with the attainment of the goal of an "ordered way of life" (*dharma*) in the world as conceived by the Pāñcarātra Vaiṣṇavas, and it certainly does contain extracts or abridgments from virtually all of these sciences. These would have to be considered among the "additions" to the Viṣṇudharma in the *VDhP*. But these were not the only additions, or even the most important.

After naming the fourteen sciences, the *VDhP* then names another five sciences that it refers to as "bringing to an end" (*kṛtānta*), that is, as leading to the goal that is higher than and contrasted with ordered life in the world, namely, the goal of

---

[31] Louis Renou, "The Vedic Schools and the Epigraphy," in *Siddha Bharati*, edited by Vishva Bandhu (Hoshiarpur: Vishveshvaranand Vedic Research Institute, 1950), 2: 218–19. For evidence on the Vedic affiliation of the Brāhmaṇs of Kashmir, and on the general state of their learning in the nineteenth century, consult Bühler's "Detailed Report of a Tour in Search of Sanskrit MSS. Made in Kasmir, Rajputana, and Central India," *Journal of the Asiatic Society, Bombay Branch* 34, extra number (1877), 19–27.

[32] We may also conclude that the *Dānasāgara* classed both of these texts as Upapurāṇas.

[33] Kane, *HD* 1 (1968–75), 408–9.

[34] Atomism (*vaiśeṣika*), often paired with Logic, is apparently included here.

"release" or "liberation" (*mokṣa*) from life in the world. Four of these sciences are more or less distinct from the Veda: "Recognize Sāṃkhya, Yoga, Pāñcarātra, the Vedas, and Pāśupata as the five soteriologies (*kṛtāntapañcaka*) for the attainment of the Absolute (*brahman*), for calm living in the world of flux, and for assistance in mental well-being" (I.74.34–35a). This is a reiteration of the same set given in the *Nārāyaṇīya* text within the *MBh* (XII.337.59–63).[35] A section of the Mokṣadharma (rules for release) of the Śāntiparvan of the *MBh*, the *Nārāyaṇīya* is the oldest extant text on Pāñcarātra theology and its version of the science of liberation. It names the authors of these five sciences.

Sāṃkhya, founded by the sage Kapila, a manifestation of Viṣṇu, was concerned with the "enumeration of" or "discrimination among" (*saṃkhyā*) the twenty-five constituents (*tattva*) of the universe. Yoga, divulged by Hiraṇyagarbha (elsewhere, Patañjali), another form of Viṣṇu, was concerned with the "techniques" (*yoga*) by which one obtained release from the world. Many treated the two as complements, as did the Pāñcarātrins. They included their version of Sāṃkhya cosmogony in their own, and made the practice of yoga part of their daily liturgy. The Vedas, authored by Apāntaratamas, identified with Kṛṣṇa Dvaipāyana, here comprise not only the portion of the Vedas concerned with the sacrificial liturgy (*karmakāṇḍa*) and its exegesis, but the Upaniṣads, the portion of the Veda concerned with the attainment of release by knowing the truth (*jñānakāṇḍa*). The "definitive" supplement to these texts, often classed as exegesis of the latter part (*uttaramīmāṃsā*), was the *Vedāntasūtra* or *Brahmasūtra* of Bādarāyaṇa. This goal, together with the means for reaching it, was certainly approved of in Pāñcarātra, but it was displaced onto a former age by the goal of devoted participation (*bhakti*) in Viṣṇu, considered appropriate for the present Age of Strife and central to both the Pāñcarātrins and Pāśupatas.

Pāśupata and Pāñcarātra belong together in the sense that both were sciences advocating theism. The Pāśupata here consists broadly of the texts of the Theists who took Śiva, one of whose names is Paśupati ("lord of animals"), as the overlord of the cosmos, and performed a liturgy in his honor differing from that in the Veda. It designated not only those more narrowly calling themselves Pāśupata but also others such as the Śaiva Siddhāntins and the Kālamukhas (see Ali's chapter in this volume). They focused their liturgy on a five-faced representation of Śiva.[36] Śiva was the author of Pāśupata. The Pāñcarātrins of the *VDhP* considered Śiva to be a manifestation of Viṣṇu. They treated Śiva as Vāsudeva's instrument and, including his iconography within their own, condoned his path to liberation.

The Pāñcarātra itself consisted of the texts of the Theists who took Viṣṇu as overlord of the cosmos and who performed a liturgy that centered on an image of that god, called Vaikuṇṭha, consisting of the "four emanations" (*caturvyūha*) of Viṣṇu advocated by the Pāñcarātrins. Vāsudeva Kṛṣṇa or Viṣṇu, himself the author of Pāñcarātra and carved as a benevolent face, the eastern, was the highest. Saṃkarṣaṇa, elder brother of Kṛṣṇa, and represented as Narasiṃha, the Man-Lion,

[35] Kane, *HD* 5 (1962-74), 954.

[36] Sadyojāta Mahādeva (eastern), Vāmadeva (Bhairava) (southern), Aghora (Nandivaktra) (western), Tatpuruṣa (Umāvaktra) (northern), and Īśāna (Sadāśiva) (zenith) (*VDhP* III.48).

a descent of Viṣṇu who destroyed demons, was the next highest face, the southern, to be recognized as that of Śiva Paśupati. Pradyumna, son of Kṛṣṇa, was the third and western face, represented as fierce (*raudra*) and malevolent; he was also to be known as the sage Kapila, master of Sāṃkhya (and Yoga). The fourth face, to the north, was that of Aniruddha, son of Pradyumna, represented as Varāha, the cosmic Boar, the descent of Viṣṇu who rescued the Earth at the beginning of a cosmic formation, to be recognized as that of Brahmā, the embodiment of the Vedas.

The *Nārāyaṇīya* states that Nārāyaṇa is the goal (*niṣṭhā*) for all these sciences, whatever the tradition or the science.[37] Clearly it and the *VDhP* accord places to all five of the soteriologies listed. Yet there can be no doubt that it gives preeminence to the Pāñcarātra.

We are now in a position to name the "supplements" to the Vaiṣṇavadharmas in the *Viṣṇudharmottara*. The additions par excellence to which the term *uttara* referred were the chapters on Pāñcarātra theology and liturgy, the installation of images in Pāñcarātra temples, and the rules for performing vows with which the *VDhP* supplements the *Viṣṇudharma*. These constituted the very raison d'être for the text itself. It is none other than the Pāñcarātra to which it refers when, after naming the fourteen sciences dealing with life in the world and the five concerned with liberation from it, the *VDhP* turns, finally, to itself: "This, the Vaiṣṇava dharmas together with additions, is celebrated as the epitome (*sāra*) [of those sciences]. The whole of science/knowledge is thus declared to you; approved sciences by the hundreds and thousands [have originated] from them" (I.35b–36).

What were these texts that made up the Pāñcarātra? The Theists of early medieval India, the Pāñcarātra Vaiṣṇavas and those sometimes called Pāśupatas but calling themselves Śaivas, claimed to have texts generally called Āgamas ("that which has come [down to one]"), which they claimed to be another Veda or the essence of the Veda, authored by Viṣṇu or Śiva. Pāñcarātrins referred more specifically to their texts as Saṃhitās (the same term used to label the "collections" of Vedic hymns). Composed in metrical Sanskrit, there are supposed to be 108 texts in all. The Śaivas made similar claims about their Āgamas (or Tantras), 28 in number.[38] The Pāñcarātra chapters on theology and liturgy in the *VDhP* are very likely parallel to or even taken from the earliest Āgamas, possibly with some abridgment.[39]

---

[37] *MBh* XII.337.63b–4a.

[38] Texts generally list four orders of Pāśupatas: Pāśupatas proper; Kālāmukhas, an order that separates from the Pāśupatas; Śaivas or Śaiva Siddhāntins; and Kāpālikas; see David Lorenzen, *The Kāpālikas and Kālāmukhas: Two Lost Śaivite Sects* (Berkeley and Los Angeles: University of California Press, 1972), pp. 1–12.

[39] I have not seen any Saṃhitā that approximates that of the *VDhP*. The reason for this, most likely, is that the Pāñcarātrins periodically elaborated on and reworked these texts. Nearly all of the Saṃhitās and Āgamas that have come into scholarly hands seem to have been reworked in south India, but we should not infer from this that they were essentially and always south Indian texts. The Kashmiri commentator, Utpala, a Vaiṣṇava, names several of the Saṃhitās that the south Indian Pāñcarātrins name and possess; Gonda, *Medieval Religious Literature*, pp. 51–52. We must thus assume that the Pāñcarātrins and the Śaiva Siddhāntins were pan-Indian disciplinary orders in early medieval India whose adherents followed

Supplementation: Purāṇa as a Scale of Texts

There can be little doubt that the *VDhP* was the product of the process of "augmentation" or supplementation that V. S. Agrawala has indicated (see appendix at n. 128). Let me now do what he neglected to do—bring out the metaphysics that was at work here. The post-Buddhist ways of life (including "schools" of philosophy) that claimed the Vedas as authoritative generally classed the Vedas (including the Brāhmaṇas, Āraṇyakas, and Upaniṣads) as "the heard" (*śruti*). They classed other texts such as the Sūtras, "the remembered" (*smṛti*), as utterances that were not continually heard and (hence) remembered but were less reliably represented in the mind. Adherents of the Vedist way of life, those Brāhmaṇs whose voices are to be found in certain of the Smārtasūtras and their commentaries, called themselves Smārta. They emphasized this distinction and saw it as one between the more authoritative, self-existent words of the Veda, without author (*apauruṣeya*) either human or divine, and the less authoritative traditions of Smṛti, those "merely" remembered by sages and men. This was the position of the Mīmāṃsakas, exegetes among the Vedist disciplinary orders who made a fetish of the Veda and its sacrifice, denying the existence of any god and hence of the world as ordered by him in successive formations, epochs, and ages. A Purāṇa, as an account of the origin and ordered succession of the lives of the world, was clearly unnecessary here.

The Vedists also assumed that the Veda existed in higher and lower forms. The Veda in its higher form was "true knowledge" (*jñāna*) or "logos" (*vāc*, *śabda*). It was the unitary, transcendent, and unchanging knowledge on which the world was founded, but was knowable only by a person no longer subject to change, that is, one who had attained release. The Veda in its lower form was an ordered collection of actual utterances or statements. The Vedists claimed that the relationship between meanings and words in the Veda is fixed, and that the preservation of the particular word order in the text is both the sign of this permanence and its guarantee.[40]

The Theist perspective in the Purāṇas differed. It held that the Vedas did have an author, the supreme god, Viṣṇu (or some other form of the "divine personality," *puruṣa*). Although that god was eternal and unchanging, the cosmos—which, like the Veda, he also authored—was not. On the contrary, god caused the world and the people who inhabited it to undergo periodic changes described as the birth, growth (preservation), and decay of a living organism. The Veda in its higher form may have consisted of an eternal essence. The Veda in its lower form, however, was subject to the changes of everyday life. A single text at the beginning of a grand cosmic formation, the Veda's division into four "collections" (*saṃhitā*) of hymns was part of the life-process of the cosmos. The Purāṇas attributed it to Vedavyāsa, the "divider of the Veda." As one age gave way to another, sages divided the four Vedas further into "branches" (*śākhā*), disciplinary orders or schools, one of which

---

somewhat different procedures at different temples. After the establishment of the Delhi Sultanate, these orders underwent major disruption and or transformation, having a continuous history only in south India.

[40]M. Hiriyanna, *Outlines of Indian Philosophy* (London: Allen and Unwin, 1932), pp. 307–13.

was the Kāṭhaka order of Kashmir.[41] The idea here, nonetheless, was that the actual speech, the literal utterances of the Vedas as constituted in those branches, would continue to be transmitted without alteration by teachers and pupils (*guru-śiṣya*) and without interruption, "one after the other" (*paramparā*) down into the present. They were to be recited and transmitted "as heard" (*śruta*).

The Veda was, however, not the only text that Viṣṇu authored. That same Vyāsa, also known as Viṣṇu (or Kṛṣṇa) Dvaipāyana, is also said to have composed the Bhārata (the great Epic) and the Purāṇa, and transmitted these orally to their narrator, Sūta Lomaharṣaṇa (*VDhP* I.73.25–27; 74.24–31). As texts, the four Vedas and the Bhārata and Purāṇa, sometimes referring to themselves as the "fifth Veda," were, thus, coeval.[42] Texts classed as Remembered were not, as Indologists might think of them, subsequent in time to the Veda in the minds of the Pāñcarātra Vaiṣṇavas. The two were ultimately authored by Viṣṇu and both were, as texts, compiled at the same time by the same sage, Vyāsa. The difference was this: although the Veda as utterance remained fixed, eternally present in the world regardless of the capacity of people to know and understand it, Viṣṇu presented himself and the knowledge by which one could attain to union with him, in the form of Itihāsa, histories (of sages and princes) and Purāṇa, originary accounts (of the divine ordering of the world), which were tailored to the changing capacities of his devotees (compare Veda and Purāṇa with the narrower and wider notions of "instructions of the Buddha," *buddhavacana* in Walter's chapter in this volume). Pāñcarātrins and Pāśupatas apparently held the same view with respect to their Āgamas.

The written or fixed text that a man or men compiled on a given occasion was, of course, not the original unitary Purāṇa (or Āgama) that came into existence at the beginning of a cosmic formation and knowable only by a person who had attained liberation from the changing world, but one of the many Purāṇas made manifest on earth by Viṣṇu, through sages or adepts, on later occasions. Even here, however, we must not assume that the Pāñcarātrins thought that this version of a Purāṇa was remembered on their own, as was the case from the Vedist standpoint. The Theists would have held that the men who did this had the assistance of Viṣṇu and that their knowledge was, therefore, superior to that remembered by human agency alone. The Dharmaśāstras, the instructional manuals on Order, which they and the Vedists classed as the Remembered in relation to the Dharmasūtras, were, for this reason, to be read not as remembered by Vedist Brāhmaṇs alone but as remembered with the aid of Viṣṇu by the Pāñcarātra Brāhmaṇs.

The human authors of the *VDhP* and other Purāṇas thus more or less explicitly revalued the category of the Remembered. For them, it did not consist simply of what sages and men had recollected about the meaning of the Veda in words that remained outside of it. They permitted the Vedists to keep the Veda as

---

[41]When Vyāsa divided the Veda into four parts, he taught one of the resulting Vedas, the Yajurveda (along with the Bhārata), to Vaiśampāyana, who taught it in turn to his pupils, one of whom was Kaṭha, after whom this recension and its order of adepts were named.

[42]Some Purāṇas, for example the *Nāradīya*, go even further and claim that the Purāṇa is prior to the Veda. See Kane, *HD* 5 (1962–74), 915.

fixed signs retained in the minds and mouths of the Brāhmaṇs. At the same time, however, they made histories and originary accounts into the more immediate and accessible manifestations of a divine author. They supplemented the Veda by surrounding it in a shifting text revealed at critical moments by Viṣṇu himself in one of his manifestations to privileged sages and, through them, to kings and their subjects. Since Viṣṇu was omniscient and eternal, none of his knowledges could, of course, be said to be new. They could, however, be knowledges newly divulged. We thus find Mārkaṇḍeya explaining that some supplementary knowledges, to wit, the knowledges of the Pāñcarātra Saṃhitās, had been kept "secret" (*rahasya*, *guhya*) either by Viṣṇu or by his sage devotees until circumstances called for their divulgence. On other occasions, the sage tells us that a supplement in his text consists of knowledges that had once been revealed but had disappeared.

Roland Barthes, the French poststructuralist, provides one way of formulating the relationship that the Pāñcarātra Vaiṣṇavas create between the Purāṇa (or Āgama) and Veda. The Purāṇas were related to the Veda as, in Barthes's term, a second-order sign system. The Purāṇa as a whole was the framing signifier of the Vedic signified. It was a transforming, shifting signifier that denoted what the Veda was in differing circumstances. Each of the Purāṇic texts, in each of its redactions, was put forward by its advocates as a claim to be that knowledge.[43] The *VDhP* was one of those texts. This is a useful perspective, but Barthes still relies on binary opposition and in other respects finds himself unable to leave behind the structuralists' theory of language and culture as an abstracted, fixed system. As a result, his scheme does not address the dialogical process that goes on in the text as much as did Collingwood's idea of a scale of forms.[44]

I take a scale of forms to consist of overlapping classes. The notion of overlapping classes is important because it permits us to see the contents of texts, or more subtly, the discourses in them, as connected by relations not only of opposition but also of distinction, by differences not only of kind but of degree. It starts from the assumption, as far as texts are concerned, of a text's intertextuality, with the idea that a text is invariably related to other texts in a variety of ways. That is, a text is not created *ex nihilo* but from heterogeneous and overlapping portions of other texts. The author, as reader, may try to reduce this heterogeneity to a coherence. Any unity that might result, however, comes from a process of reworking his material and not from the unity of time, space, and author presupposed in the doctrine of expressive realism.

What, then, is the process by which such unities are produced? It is a dialectical process. This point needs some amplification. I do not want to say that texts are dialectically related in the senses usually attributed to a Marxian or Hegelian notion of dialectic, that is, as a series of oppositions that are negated. Collingwood's notion of dialectic is simpler and more permissive. He sees it as a process whereby two agents who are in a relation of nonagreement come to agreement through a process

[43] Roland Barthes, *Elements of Semiology*, translated by A. Lavers and Colin Smith (New York: Hill and Wang, 1968), pp. 89–94.

[44] R. G. Collingwood, *An Essay on Philosophical Method* (Oxford: Oxford University Press, 1933), pp. 54–91.

of discussion, argument, debate, and so on. To some extent, the relations between agents and the texts that they produce may also be thought of as eristical. This, according to Collingwood, is a situation in which two parties disagree and in which one tries to gain victory over the other through the use of lies, threats, deceptions, misstatements, and so on. More often than not, the relationship between agents is lopsided. One of the agents has or is accorded, or takes for himself, more authority than the other. I should also add, following Vološinov/Bakhtin, that dialogues take place among people speaking out of different discourses. Indeed, one of the main virtues of a scale of forms is that it recognizes explicitly what scholars of Bakhtin refer to as heteroglossia, the fact that people are commonly speaking from different positions and not communicating, getting or sending a message across—trying, in other words, to approximate the workings of a frictionless machine.[45]

If the activity of articulating unities and distinctions, additions and exclusions, in a scale of forms never starts from scratch, it also never finishes. As the circumstances in which agents find themselves repeatedly outstrips their capacity to know and act in the world, the work of constructing a scale of textual forms and traditions itself never ends. A text (or tradition) that an author (or disciplinary order) declares to be complete in one situation will have to be reworked in another. Texts at each level in the scale supplement and comment on the levels below. A text, whether in the form of a redaction or of a reading, is, hence, only momentarily and provisionally complete.

Using this idea, it is also possible to see the *VDhP* as occupying the apex of a scale of texts that its complex author has constructed and that includes the other texts that claim to belong to its tradition (Table 2.1). The texts are ordered vertically according to period or imperial formation and horizontally by the goal of the text—*dharma* or *mokṣa*—and then by genre of text. Texts in bold are explicitly related to or included in the *VDhP*, the other texts or genres of texts, only implicitly. At the bottom of the scale of texts are the Vedas themselves, not as they are or as Indologists read them, but as read by the composite Pāñcarātra agent who compiled the *VDhP*. If we pay attention to usage in the *VDhP*, we find that its agent privileges the mantras in the collection of hymns of the Kāṭhaka order over the other collections of the Yajurveda; and above all other hymns, it privileges the famous Puruṣasūkta, a hymn to and about Puruṣa as Nārāyaṇa, the forest-dwelling Pāñcarātrins' construct of god in his transcendent form. The effect of this particular dialogue is to turn the opposition of Vedists and Pāñcarātrins into a distinction: the impersonal absolute of the one is made into a distinct, anthropomorphic form of Viṣṇu. At the same time it also converts a difference of kind over the authorship of the Vedas into one simply of degree: Vedas and Purāṇas are both authoritative, one being only a lesser form of the other. Overall, the result of this dialectic process is to transform the Veda into a collection of hymns to the Pāñcarātra godhead. The *VDhP* also privileges the theist Upaniṣad of the Kāṭhaka order, the *Kaṭha*, in its view of the Upaniṣads and in its cosmology—for example, when it enumerates and names the constituents

[45]Michael J. Reddy, "The Conduit Metaphor—A Case of Frame Conflict in Our Language about Language," in his *Metaphor and Thought* (Cambridge: Cambridge University Press, 1979), pp. 284–324.

Table 2.1. The *VDhP* as the Apex in a Scale of Texts

DHARMA		MOKṢA	
Kārkoṭa Nāga Muktāpīḍa Lalitāditya (c. 724/5–760/1)			
Viṣṇudharmôttarāḥ:		**Pratiṣṭhākalpa** and **Śaṅkaragītā**	
Cālukya-Pallava (550–750)			
	Nīlamata	PĀÑCARĀTRA **Saṃhitās**	PĀŚUPATA Āgamas
Gupta-Vākāṭaka (320–550)			
DHARMAŚĀSTRA	PURĀṆA and ITIHĀSA		
Viṣṇusmṛti(-dharma)	**Rāmāyaṇa**		
		Nārāyaṇīya	
	Mahābhārata	**Bhagavadgītā**	
Post-Aśokan to Kuṣāṇa-Śātavāhana (2nd Century B.C. to 3rd A.D.)			
Manusmṛti and Yājñavalkyasmṛti		VEDĀNTA [Bādarāyaṇa]	
		SĀṂKHYA	YOGA
Post-Buddha to Aśoka (c. 268-39 B.C.)			
		MĪMĀṂSĀ	NYĀYA
VEDĀNGAS: Kalpasūtras **Kāṭhaka**: Dharma-, **Gṛhya-**, Śrautasūtras			
Buddha (480/430–400/350 B.C.) and Pre-Buddha			
VEDAS: Saṃhitās, Brāhmaṇas, Āraṇyakas, Upaniṣads			
		Kaṭhopaniṣad	
Kāṭhakasaṃhitā (Black Yajurveda)	**Puruṣasūkta** (Ṛgveda)		

of the universe.[46] Once again, this has the effect of making the Upaniṣads overlap with and anticipate the Pāñcarātra texts.

Next up the scale, we see the *VDhP*'s rendering of the Sūtras, manuals on the performance of the Vedic sacrifice and the attainment of release. So far as the former is concerned, it takes the position—enunciated in the *Bhagavadgītā* but quite at odds with that of the Vedists in the Kalpasūtras and their exegesis, the *Mīmāṃsā-sūtra* of Jaimini (read through its commentaries)—that the sacrifice is anact in

[46] *Kaṭhopaniṣat*, with Bhāṣya of Śaṅkarācārya and Prakāśikā of Rāmānuja, edited and introduced by Śrīdharaśāstrī Pāṭhaka (Poona: Oriental Book-Supplying Agency, 1919), I.3.9–11.

honor of Viṣṇu. With respect to the science of release, the Pāñcarātrins appear to have read the text that explains the Upaniṣads, the *Vedāntasūtra* of Bādarāyaṇa, as a text advocating the ontological position of the early Pāñcarātrins, *bhedābheda*, "identity-in-difference," and not *advaita*, "non-dualism," as constituting the relationship of god and man.

Still higher in the scale of texts is the *Viṣṇusmṛti*, itself a transformation of the earlier Kāṭhaka Dharmasūtra. That transformation, which enclosed the earlier prose text into a versified Śāstra, was not simply a formal change. Involved in it was a crucial move: making the honoring of an image of Vāsudeva with attendances (*pūjā*) the centerpiece of the daily liturgy to be carried out by a Vaiṣṇava who also adhered to the Veda. Here, too, we can see that a crucial overlap is created: image-honoring and fire sacrifice are made to seem continuous with one another by making the texts in which they appear into one text. Here, too, are the *Nārāyaṇīya* and the *Bhagavadgītā*, the texts in the *MBh* that provide the rationales for history, the narratives of gods, sages, and kings related in the Epics and Purāṇas. Of particular importance, of course, is the *Nārāyaṇīya*, the oldest Pāñcarātra text.

Finally, at the top of this Pāñcarātra scale of texts is situated the definitive or determining supplement, that of the *VDhP* itself. This consisted of its representation of the science of Pāñcarātra. Its proponents advocate the radical step of substituting its Pāñcarātra temple liturgy for the Vedic sacrifice, from which it appropriates dozens of Vedic mantras. So although the *VDhP* respectfully includes the earlier Smārta and Śrauta practices in its own world vision, it makes what they enjoined a weak option in it.

The Pāñcarātra of the *VDhP*, however, differs from the earlier Pāñcarātra of the *Nārāyaṇīya*. It closely resembles what I reconstruct as the project of the early versions of the Pāñcarātra Saṃhitās. The Āgamas in general are supposed to have four "legs" (*pāda*) or topics. The second and most important, that of liturgical undertaking (*kriyā*), has to do with the procedures for the construction of a temple and the installation in it of a permanently enlivened image. The Pratiṣṭhākalpa or procedure for installation (and the chapters leading up to it) in the *VDhP* corresponds to this topic; another part, the Śaṅkaragītā or song of Śiva, takes up the other three topics: the first "leg", on metaphysics, theology, and cosmology (*jñāna* or *vidyā*); the third on the procedures for initiation and the carrying out of the daily, monthly, and annual liturgy (*caryā*); and the fourth, on procedures for union with the godhead (*yoga*).

Even in their most reduced forms, the liturgies of these texts and their closest Saṃhitās presuppose a division of labor and a quantity of economic support that rules out the idea that these texts contained the liturgies performed either in the forest retreats or by adepts at small shrines without permanent images. These liturgies, furthermore, envisage a situation in which the older Vedic multifire sacrifices are no longer performed. Indeed, these texts position their temple liturgies (replete with procedures for their own fire oblations) as replacements for those Vedic sacrifices. The textualized procedures for temple construction and image installation replace those for the performance of multifire sacrifices, the *Śrautasūtra*, while those for periodic liturgical practices replace the *Smārtasūtra* (both *Gṛhya* and *Dharma*).

That is, just as the authors of these texts define themselves and their traditions as autonomous with respect to the Veda, so they also construe the liturgies they contain as autonomous with respect to the older Vedic multifire liturgy, just as the Pāñcarātra texts in the *VDhP* do. The earliest versions of these texts must, thus, be placed in the sixth to eighth centuries, and probably later rather than earlier, when brick and stone temples of the scale and complexity required by the Āgamic liturgy were first built.

So far I have talked about how the *VDhP* explicitly positions itself at the apex of a textual scale of forms. But the task of recovering the scale of textual forms that a text makes for itself cannot stop here. It is possible to show that there are exclusions or silences in almost any scale of texts—contexts not mentioned because the authors were unaware of them or because they wished for some reason to suppress them. I have already shown that the *VDhP* is attached to the Kaṭha order of the Black Yajurveda, but the *VDhP* makes no explicit mention of this. The reason for this is, of course, the imperial desire of the *VDhP*. It wishes to present its Pāñcarātra-oriented knowledge as universal and not as confined to one or another Vedic orders or schools. Besides, having displaced the Vedic liturgy with a universal one of its own making, Vedic affiliation did not matter as much as it otherwise might have.

There are two other examples of silences that are worth mentioning: Buddhism and locality. The relationship of the *VDhP* to Buddhism appears to have been more eristical than dialectical. The Buddhists were very powerful in the world of the *VDhP*, as we shall see. I would argue that the silence of its appropriation and rejection of Buddhist ideas and practices was a strategy, and neither unconscious nor a mere oversight. One example of this is the attempt to take command of the rainy season from the Buddhists by making it into a period of fasting and renewal that accompanied the season-long sleep of Viṣṇu. Unlike the Buddha, whose period of recline was the end of his life, Viṣṇu awakens after his period of "nirvāṇa" and resumes command of the world. Another is the appropriation of the form of the Buddhist monastery, a quadrangle with monk's cells along the sides facing onto a courtyard, for the Śaiva or Vaiṣṇava temple. Within these structures, worshipers saw the images of Hindu gods in occupation of cells reduced to the size of niches.[47]

The other example of silence concerns locality. The *VDhP* has a close relationship to the *Nīlamata* (*NP*), a Purāṇa that is about the Theist and royal wish to make Kashmir into an imperial kingdom. It proudly displays its regional markings and uses them to position itself in relation to India as a whole. It is likely that the earliest redaction of the text antedates the *VDhP*. Here again, I would suggest, the *VDhP* makes no allusion to this text because the author of the *VDhP* claims to articulate a world wish both for the order of Pāñcarātra Vaiṣṇavas and for their king of kings and his subjects, one that transcends the regional wish of the *NP*.[48]

[47] Ram Chandra Kak, *Ancient Monuments of Kashmir* (London: India Society, 1933), pp. 61–62.

[48] Ved Kumari Ghai, *The Nīlamata Purāṇa: Cultural and Literary Study; Text with English Translation* (Srinagar: Jammu and Kashmir Academy of Art, Culture and Languages, 1968–73; Ph. D Thesis, Banaras Hindu University, 1960), 2 vols. The first volume is based on the *Nīlamata or Teachings of Nīla*, edited by K. S. J. M. de Vreese (Leiden: E. J. Brill, 1936; Ph. D. dissertation, Leiden, 1936). Compilers

To sum up: the *VDhP* was supposed to be used (in varying ways) by a king and his associates—by his preceptor, chronologer, and chief priest, as well as his ministers and soldiers, and their wives. That text claimed not only to comprise the "epitome" of all knowledge, and especially of instructions on order and originary accounts (including History), but to do so from the perspective of Pāñcarātra Vaiṣṇavism. In its capacity as reader of these and other texts, the compound author of the *VDhP* has dialectically fashioned a scale of texts out of them. It has drawn into that scale the contents of those texts with whose discourses it was not in agreement so as to create agreement with its own position.[49] That is, all of the sciences to which it provided access, including the Veda, were not simply made available as separate, isolated bodies of knowledge that might somehow be useful. They were articulated in relation to one another and, either directly or indirectly, were made to appear as parts of the ontology and theology of the Pāñcarātrins. If the *VDhP* was an encyclopedia, it was one that placed a Pāñcarātra interpretation on every science, every tale, every practice that it included.

Purāṇa as Narrative

The *VDhP* was, I argue, both a narrative and discursive text. To a large extent, its narrative aspect was a function of the text as history (*itihāsa*), whereas its discursive aspect was a function of the text as instruction (*śāstra*). Yet these were very closely intertwined: narratives are used to prove discursive points by illustration, and discourses are made to serve as rationales of and guides to the narratives of the text. Since the narrative aspect predominates slightly over the discursive in the *VDhP*, I begin with that.

To a much greater degree than narratives about the change from the medieval (or traditional) to modern would allow, Purāṇic narratives were actively complicit in the shaping and transformation of polities and the disciplinary orders that sought their recognition and adherence. Because they were supposed to be the texts that told the history of the world, many of them were sites where the claimants of different ways of life, as practiced in disciplinary orders, translated their claims into the world accounts or imaginaries of local, regional, and imperial courts. As I have already indicated, I would not claim that people have used Purāṇas as a genre uniformly. I do think it plausible, however, that some people, namely, the Kashmir court of the eighth century, read the *VDhP* as a single narrative, a story which plots the activities leading to the hegemony of a four-faced image of Viṣṇu and its adherents, the adepts of the Pāñcarātra disciplinary or soteriological order, in an imperial formation embracing the "entire earth." The major device of this narrative is the descent or avatar of Viṣṇu prompted by events on earth, especially by acts

of one version of the *Brahmapurāna* directly appropriate this text: Ved Kumari Ghai, *Nīlamata*, 1: 11–14. The *Kṛtyakalpataru* of Lakṣmīdhara (1104–1154), in turn, uses large portions of that, especially in its *Niyatakālakāṇḍa*. See also, Yasuke Ikari, ed., *A Study of the Nīlamata: Aspects of Hinduism in Ancient Kashmir* (Kyoto: Institute for Research in Humanities, Kyoto University, 1994).

[49]One might argue that the complex author of the *VDhP* is itself a scale of authors with the chronologer/preceptor at its apex.

of humans—both men and women, high and low, rich and poor—signaling their devoted participation in that lord. (Compare this with the idea of the manifestation of post-Gautama forms of the Buddha, especially the Bodhisattva, in Walter's essay in this volume). These events are recursive and synergistic, bringing Viṣṇu's descent as divine favor inspiring still greater acts of devotion.[50]

The *VDhP* is divided into three parts (*khaṇḍas*), the first of which contains 269 Chapters (*adhyāyas*). The narrative of part 1 begins, as already noted, with the appearance of Mārkaṇḍeya and his acolytes at the court of Vajra, on the occasion of a horse sacrifice at the beginning of the Age of Strife. He took the lead in welcoming these extraordinary guests whose knowledge would be vital for the age. On behalf of his court, he asked them to impart this knowledge: "We kings, resorted to by your lordships, O Brāhmaṇs, have a request to make: be pleased, your lordships, as a favor (*anugraha*) to kings and out of a desire for the welfare for the world, to narrate the eternal orders (*sanātanān vaiṣṇavadharmān*); for after this there will be no further chance for kings to gaze on your lordships in this the Age of Strife" (I.1.19–20a). The sages agreed to do this not in the form of a monologue but through a process of dialogue in which Mārkaṇḍeya, we are told, "will allay all your uncertainties (*saṃśaya*), O Vajra" (I.1.21). The kings of the plains and the Brāhmaṇ forest-dwellers then sat down and began their discourse.

Holding to the Purāṇic form, Mārkaṇḍeya, the narrator, first relates how Viṣṇu caused the world to originate, beginning with the topic of cosmogony and ending with a description of Bhāratavarṣa or India (Chapters 2-11).[51] At every turn, the author reworks this material from a Pāñcarātra point of view. After several chapters on geography, Mārkaṇḍeya turns to the fourth Purāṇic topic, the genealogical succession of kings, giving an account of the Solar (*sūrya*) dynasty, in which the hero, Rāma Dāśarathi, one of the major manifestations of Viṣṇu, was born.

Mārkaṇḍeya tells Vajra, his royal pupil (chapters 23–71) of Bhārgava Rāma, the Brāhmaṇ who cleared the earth twenty-one times of Kṣatriyas. As Adalbert Gail correctly argues, the *VDhP* transforms Bhārgava Rāma, also called Paraśurāma, Rāma of the Axe, into a descent of Viṣṇu to lighten the earth of its burden.[52] As in so many of the histories in the Purāṇas, it is a retelling from a new point of view, that of the Pāñcarātra Vaiṣṇavas. Like other heroic manifestations of the cosmic overlord, Viṣṇu is supplied with a special weapon, a "jewel among bows" (*cāparatna*). The image of an archer is important not only in the saga of Bhārgava Rāma, but throughout this text, which is why I mention this detail here.

To return, this cycle of legends has an embedded section in which Viṣṇu reveals the most crucial knowledge of part 1, knowledge that he had kept a "secret"

---

[50]For the uses of narrative in forming "modern" polities, see *Nation and Narration*, edited by Homi K. Bhabha (London: Routledge, 1990)

[51]Cosmogony (chapter 2), regeneration (chapter 3), the first two defining topics of a Purāṇa. The wording of these chapters does not, by the way, correspond to that of the two text groups thatwhich Kirfel discovers in his critical edition (see appendix, n. 117).

[52]Adalbert J. Gail, *Paraśurāma: Brahmane und Krieger. Untersuchung über Ursprung und Entwicklung eines Avatāra Viṣṇus und Bhāktas Śivas in der Indischer Literatur* (Wiesbaden: O. Harrassowitz, 1977), pp. 54–101, for the *VDhP*. According to Gail, the first extended treatment of the legend is in the *VDhP*. Curiously, Gail makes no mention of the Paraśurāma episode as treated in *NP*, 1: 1165–1226.

(*rahasya*). This is a series of dialogues, called the Śaṅkaragītā, the "Song of Siva" (chapters 51–65). In them, Śiva, second only to Viṣṇu in the divine hierarchy of the text, is made to divulge to Bhārgava Rāma the rule or procedure for the five-part honoring (*pañcakālavidhāna*) of Vāsudeva. This was the highest life-transforming practice men were commanded to perform, according to the Pāñcarātrins, and comprised the daily liturgy in honor of Viṣṇu. The fifth part of it, the practice of yoga (*yogakāla*), was said to be the bow and arrow with which the Pāñcarātra adept reached the target of the transcendent Viṣṇu by piercing through the moon and the sun. This text is, of course, just what we would find in one of the Pāñcarātra Saṃhitās.

Now, as Gail points out, Rāma is not unproblematic as a descent of Viṣṇu. It would seem that the earliest Bhārgava Rāma preserved in the Epics was represented as a Vedist sage. Already in the *MBh*, though, he appears as a Śaiva ascetic and devotee of Śiva. This is probably the reason why the author of the *VDhP* makes Śiva the author of the Pāñcarātra liturgy and Śiva's prime devotee, Bhārgava Rāma, its first recipient on earth. Pāśupata Śaivism was probably predominant in Kashmir before the contents of the *VDhP* were disclosed to humanity.

Here we have the first major example in the *VDhP* of the deployment of historical narrative as an "illustrative proof" (*pramāṇa*). Viṣṇu was, in Pāñcarātra theology, the master of "deceptive appearances" (*māyā*). The authors of the *VDhP* wanted to show that Śiva was in reality Vāsudeva Kṛṣṇa, and that his preeminent devotee, Bhārgava Rāma, was actually the foremost Pāñcarātrin. Hence, when he cleverly asks the ascetic Śaṅkara—whom his followers continually depict, eyes closed and concentrated, as mentally representing someone—on just whom it is that the supposed overlord of the cosmos is meditating, he replies that it is none other than Vāsudeva, the one he considers the actual overlord.

Mārkaṇḍeya next conveys to Vajra the knowledge of the units of time made over to Bhārgava Rāma by Varuṇa, the lord of waters and regulator of the seasons (chapters 72–73). He follows this with an account of India's condition at the end of each cosmic period, including the end of an entire grand cosmic formation (*mahākalpa*) (chapters 74–81).

Still speaking to Vajra (chapters 82–105), Mārkaṇḍeya imparts to him the true knowledge of how the realm of the sky is distributed among a hierarchy of heavenly lords, foremost among whom are the planets (*graha*) and lunar mansions or asterisms (*nakṣatras*). He then proceeds to lay down the rules for honoring the images of these celestial lords. The procedure for this practice, one of the major "additions" to the *Viṣṇudharma*, includes as one part of itself the procedure for making oblations into a fire based on the short sacrifice (*pākayajña*) of the *Kāṭhaka Gṛhyasūtra*. Mārkaṇḍeya takes this procedure as the one to be followed on the occasion of every liturgical practice in the *VDhP* that calls for fire offerings.

The text returns (chapters 106–36) to another of the topics of a Purāṇa, *vaṃśa*: Brahmā's successive creation and population of the earth with various beings, the most important of which are kings and sages.

Mārkaṇḍeya next instructs his eager pupil on how the reverential offerings to the forefathers is to be carried out by a Pāñcarātra householder (chapters 137–47).

Here is but one instance in which the *VDhP* retains the practice of the Gṛhya-sūtras, but prescribes the addition of Pāñcarātra elements. For example, the ball of rice for the great-grandfather is identified with Vāsudeva, the highest manifestation of Viṣṇu; that for the grandfather, with Saṃkarṣaṇa; that for the father, with Pradyumna; and for oneself, with Aniruddha. Mārkaṇḍeya also states that the honoring of forefathers is not possible without the "luminous will" (*tejas*) of Viṣṇu (I.139.20–2).

The next section (chapters 148–200) is largely given over to stories of heroic devotees who, in accord with the Pāñcarātra prescriptions, performed certain vows (*vrata*) to Vāsudeva. Each of these histories is not only a retelling of preexisting stories, it is also a proof of the power of devoted participation in Viṣṇu to effect the outcome of events. Virtually all of these exemplary devotional events take place at sites in Kashmir and its hinterland that the *VDhP* singles out as especially propitious for the worship of Viṣṇu: the Vitastā (Jhelum), the major river of Kashmir, referred to here as Vaitasta, "the place where the Vitastā flows"; the confluence of the Candrabhagā (Chenab) and Tausi (Tawi) rivers, near Śākala (Sialkot), the capital of Madra (between the Ravi and Chenab rivers); Nṛsiṃhatīrtha on the banks of the Devikā (Degh); and a temple of Varāha (the giant-boar emanation of Viṣṇu) on the Sindhu (Indus).

The fourteen epochs of Manu, the remaining topic of a Purāṇa, form part of this section (chapters 175–91), each Manu being explained as a manifestation of Viṣṇu.

The last section of part 1 (chapters 201–69), is an extended retelling of a story from the *Rāmāyaṇa*.[53] Rāma sends his younger brother, Bharata, in response to the request of Yudhājita, the king of Kekaya and their mother's brother, to chastise the immoral Gandharvas of the neighboring country of Gandhāra. While Bharata marches, Nāḍāyana, the royal priest of the king of the Gandharvas, Sailuṣa, warns him in a series of hortatory tales (chapters 212–53) of the fates suffered by several villains. Bharata defeats the Gandharvas, and at the onset of the next rainy season institutes the performance of a Four-month Sleep (*cāturmāsya*), a liturgical practice celebrating the annual sleep of Viṣṇu, which lasts for the four months of the rainy season and begins and ends with five-day festivals. Once he completes the festival that marked the end of its performance, Bharata has the cities of Puṣkarāvati (Charsadda in western Gandhāra) and Takṣaśilā (Taxila in eastern Gandhāra) built for his two sons, Puṣkara and Takṣa, and himself returns to Ayodhyā.

Now, Kekaya is one of the regions of the Panjab (beyond the Jhelum), next to Madra, and its capital was Rājagṛha. Gandhāra (note the resemblance to Gandharva) is the country just northwest of Kekaya. It is bisected by the Sindhu River, with one capital in either moiety. All three of these countries are, of course, on the periphery of Kashmir. Bharata and his three brothers are, it is disclosed, none other than the four emanations of Vāsudeva Kṛṣṇa or Viṣṇu, the cosmic overlord of the Pāñcarātrins. The celebration of Viṣṇu's sleep that Bharata performs in Gandhāra

---

[53] *Rāmāyaṇa* VII.90–91. See the "critical" edition, edited by G. H. Bhatt et al. (Baroda: Oriental Institute, 1960–75) in 7 volumes.

is the major annual liturgical work that a Pāñcarātra king is ordered to perform in honor of Viṣṇu. With this "proof," we come to realize the true "subject" of this narrative: the overlord of the cosmos, as seen by the Pāñcarātrins, has manifested himself on earth as Rāma and his three brothers. One of them, Bharata, comes to save Kekaya, a Vaiṣṇava kingdom threatened by the offensive Gandharvas. After defeating them in a terrible battle, he transforms their country into a new Pāñcarātra kingdom by constructing two new capitals there and instituting Viṣṇu's four-month sleep which had been performed previously only by the forest-dwelling Pāñcarātra adepts and not by householders in the plains.

There are at least two ways of reading this story and part 1 as a whole. We may read it as a harbinger of events to come, a reading that is thrust on us by the contents of part 2. If, however, we think of part 1 as forming a complete text, we can read the text as content to institute Pāñcarātra Vaiṣṇavism among householder Brāhmaṇs in an imperial Pāñcarātra Vaiṣṇava kingdom with no wish to go beyond that.

Part 2 of the *VDhP*, comprising 183 chapters, has as its topic rules for royal Order (*rājadharma*), itself a topic of instructions on Order (*dharma*) more generally.[54] In this text, of course, rules for royal Order means the instructions to be followed by a Pāñcarātra Vaiṣṇava king. Puṣkara, the son of Varuṇa, who had learned these orders from Indra, king of the gods, relates them to Bhārgava Rāma, the Śaiva devotee earlier revealed to be a descent of Viṣṇu. The text thus continues with the dialogical form of a Purāṇa even though the emphasis in parts 2 and 3 will be much more on instruction than on history.

The first instructions Puṣkara gives Rāma (chapters 2–23) have to do with the procedure for the shower bath into kingship (*rājyābhiṣeka*) of a Vaiṣṇava king of kings whose intention it is to make the other kings of India submit to his rule. It is the replacement for the Vedic royal installation. Puṣkara next relates to Bhārgava Rāma the instructions a Vaiṣṇava king requires (chapters 24–131) so that he might govern, and all of the categories of people, animals, and things that make up the constituents of a Vaiṣṇava kingdom, successfully articulating their relationships. Included here are instructions on royal dependents and ministers, royal forts, the countryside, and revenue; householders, wives, and procreation; the care and feeding of cattle, horses, and elephants; rules for the estates and life-stages; a penal code; and rules on penances.

The next section (chapters 132–44) is concerned with the interpretation of omens and the pacification of their divine agents.[55]

Mārkaṇḍeya turns for the first time (chapters 145–50) to the relations a king should have with other kings. He then lays down the daily routine to be followed by a Vaiṣṇava king (chapter 151).

---

[54]Priyabala Shah has translated these chapters: *Pauranic Ritualism of the Fifth Century* (Calcutta: Punthi Pustak, 1993).

[55]These consist of extracts from the Saṃhitā of Garga the Elder. See R. Inden, "Kings and Omens," in *Purity and Auspiciousness in Indian Society*, edited by John Carman and Frédérique Apfel Marglin, issue of *Journal of Developing Societies* 2 (1986), 30–40.

Mārkaṇḍeya commends (chapter 152) a sequence of monthly and annual liturgical works that a Pāñcarātra king should perform, and details the procedures for these (chapters 153–62). The most encompassing of these works is Viṣṇu's four-month sleep. The same liturgical practice Bharata had instituted after his conquest of the Gandharvas, it is, as presented here, intended as a prelude to the beginning of a military expedition having as its purpose the triumph over the quarters by a Vaiṣṇava king of kings.

The last twenty chapters of part 2 of the *VDhP* are, accordingly, devoted to the topic of war:[56] the omens to watch for,[57] the times and circumstances for mounting a campaign, the procedures for beginning the march and for the day preceding the battle, the code of conduct to be followed in combat and afterward, and, finally, a condensed treatise on Dhanurveda, the science of weaponry and war vehicles.

Among the things a king successful in battle was supposed to do was to build temples. Once again, if we assume that the text ended with part 2, we could read the text as leaving the Pāñcarātra king who would be the paramount king of kings in India immersed in diplomatic and military activities and only thinking in vague terms of the temples he would build were he somehow to succeed. If, however, we read it with the instructions of part 3 in mind, we would be justified in reaching a stronger conclusion. Part 3 has the construction of large and elaborate temples and the institution of a complex Pāñcarātra temple liturgy as its unifying theme. Reading part 2 from this perspective, we would attribute to the Pāñcarātrins and their king, successful in his conquest of the quarters of India, the desire to replace the old horse sacrifice with the installation of images (*surapratiṣṭhā*) in a monumental Pāñcarātra temple, an act that would make Pāñcarātra Vaiṣṇavism preeminent, for the moment, among India's ways of life. This is, of course, the world wish that was central to the Pāñcarātra Saṃhitās. Those texts, however, because their readers were not in a position to neutralize the Vedic liturgy, were reluctant to specify the imperial coagent of this wish.

Part 3 of the *VDhP*, comprising 355 chapters, has just this complex of activities as its major concern. Mārkaṇḍeya tells Vajra (chapter 1) that the construction of temples is to be carried out by men who desire the highest welfare in this world and the next, and that this is especially so for the Age of Strife which, it will be remembered, had just begun before Mārkaṇḍeya appeared. The first 117 chapters, paralleling the contents of the main part of an Āgama—temple construction and image installation (*kriyāpāda*)—provide the procedures for this as if they were integral to the Vedic or Smārta tradition.

After preliminary chapters on the topics of semantics, meter, poetics, singing, and instrumental music, all to be parts of the temple liturgy, Mārkaṇḍeya delivers a

---

[56]Chapters 166–174 comprise a text, in prose, called the *Paitāmahasiddhānta*, of which chapters 168–74 have been translated by David Pingree, "The *Paitamahasiddhanta* of the *Vishnudharmottarapurana*," *Brahmavidya: The Adyar Library Bulletin* (Dr. V. Raghavan Felicitation Volume) 31–32 (1967–68), 472–510.

[57]Chapter 163 of the 1912 edition is lacking the text from the *Matsyapurāṇa*, edited by Hari Narayan Apte, Anandasrama Sanskrit Series, 3 (Poona: Anandasrama, 1907) CCXL.13–27 to CCXLIII.8, which thus adds three chapters to the text.

treatise on dancing, also an element of the temple celebrations (chapters 20–34). He next lays down to Vajra the rules for artistic representation in a text well known to art historians, the *Citrasūtra* (chapters 35–43). Mārkaṇḍeya then proceeds to describe the characteristics that sculpted images of the gods in the Pāñcarātra pantheon are to exhibit, in the *Pratimālakṣaṇa* (chapters 44–85). The most important of the icons to be fashioned is that of Vāsudeva Kṛṣṇa called Vaikuṇṭha, the image having four faces, and the major object of Pāñcarātra worship in the text.

Next comes an account (chapter 86) of the forms, in very general terms, of one hundred temples, replete with directions on which images are to be placed in which of them. Mārkaṇḍeya then describes (chapter 87) the characteristics that the temple referred to as Sarvatobhadra or "auspiciously open on four sides," the massive shrine housing the four-faced image of Viṣṇu, is supposed to be displayed. This is the summa of all temples, the temple that the Pāñcarātra king of kings is supposed to build after his conquest of the earth.

Our sage narrator details the elaborate rules for construction and installation that its builder, the paramount king of India, is to carry out. The treatises on this most important topic are grouped loosely (chapters 88 or 93–116) under the title Pratiṣṭhākalpa. Every day, the fivefold Pāñcarātra liturgy is to be performed in this temple. Every month, the procedure for the installation, without the elements peculiar to the installation itself, but including the daily liturgy, is to be undertaken by the Pāñcarātra king of kings. And at least once a year, on the day when Viṣṇu awakens from his slumber at the end of the rainy season, his image is to be given a grand shower bath (*bṛhatsnapana*) and taken through the streets of the capital in a procession of the god (*devayātrā*) (chapter 117). The leader of this triumphal procession carries a bow and arrow, a sign that the entire earth, ruled by a Pāñcarātra king of kings, has as its aim union with the overlord of the cosmos, Vāsudeva Kṛṣṇa.

The institution of this temple is the culmination of the narrative and of the career of its royal builder as a descent of Viṣṇu. With it, he completes both his kingdom and himself. But this is not the conclusion of the text.[58]

There follows a text called the Haṃsagītā or, the "Song of the Gander," in which Viṣṇu, taking the form of a gander, divulges instructions, that had become lost at the end of the Age of Completeness (first and best of the four ages), to a group of Brāhmaṇ sages for the benefit of the world.[59] In the last chapter of this colloquy, the gander shows himself to the sages as Viśvarūpa, the high god Viṣṇu, in "the visible form of everything," the ultimate proof Vaiṣṇavas offer of the cosmic overlordship of Viṣṇu (the first one of which appears in the *Bhagavadgītā*).

The *VDhP*, turning back to history from instruction, draws to an end with a cycle of dialogues extending the stories of the *Nārāyaṇīya*. Pāñcarātrins could

[58]Chapters 118–225 recommend Pāñcarātra vows (*vrata*) that devotees may undertake in order to obtain their desires.

[59]This is an omnibus condensation of Dharmaśāstra, including verses from both Manu and Yājñavālkya, as well as others. Although this *gītā* wanders over a wide range of topics, it focuses on three not treated extensively at an earlier point in the *VDhP*. One is the adjudication of disputes (*vyavahāra*) (chapters 324–38). The other two, closely related to each other, are the making of gifts of valuable things to qualified Brāhmaṇs (chapters 299–319), and the making of donations to Viṣṇu, the penultimate chapter (341) of the Haṃsagītā.

take the *Nārāyaṇīya* as their point of departure for understanding the Epic, just as Bhāgavatas could take the *Bhagavadgītā* as theirs. So it is hardly surprising that the *VDhP* goes over this ground. The dialogues of the reiterated *Nārāyaṇīya* concern the "highest favor" (*prasādam paramam*) shown by Viṣṇu to his devotees. Among these are Vasu Uparicara, a king rescued by Viṣṇu's mount, the eagle Garuḍa; and two Brāhmaṇs, Nārada and Viśvakṣena, treated as exemplary Pāñcarātra devotees. With the powers of divine sight (*divyacakṣus*) granted to them because of their devotion, they are able to see Viṣṇu as Viśvarūpa and as Narasiṃha, the Man-Lion. In the course of these dialogues, the narrator reveals protective mantras not given in the *Nārāyaṇīya*; by employing these, the devotees of Viṣṇu will, we are told, be able to attain to the highest goal, release from the world and union with Viṣṇu himself.

At last, we return to the court of Vajra, where the king of kings honors Mārkaṇḍeya after he has completed his delivery of the text and sees him off to his retreat in the Himalayas: "After the sage with the power of divine sight had finished speaking, the lord of kings did obeisance at the feet of the sage, as did his retainers and the other kings, circumambulated him, and entered his personal apartments (*svapura*). The sages themselves, dismissed by the wise Mārkaṇḍeya, did obeisance to the god Hari (Viṣṇu) and departed for their ashram"(III.355.3–4). Mārkaṇḍeya has brought Vajra into agreement with his position, so "the king Vajra, moreover, soul of Dharma whose highest goal was Nārāyaṇa, continued to reflect daily on the Purāṇa narrated by Mārkaṇḍeya and continued to enjoy his kingdom, protecting his subjects in accord with Dharma" (III.355.5). The Dharma that the text names of course is not Dharma in some general sense but life in the world as ordered by Viṣṇu and handed down through Mārkaṇḍeya.

I have argued that the *VDhP* embodies a self-conscious narrative. It begins with the arrival of the Pāñcarātra Vaiṣṇava preceptor, Mārkaṇḍeya, depicted as a manifestation of Viṣṇu, at the court of Vajra, a descendant of Vāsudeva Kṛṣṇa, and it ends with his departure for his retreat in the Himalayas. What is the "story" of the *VDhP* about? It is about the progressive manifestation of the Pāñcarātra godhead and concomitantly of those knowledges, previously withheld or misunderstood, that prove the validity of claims for divine truth. That narrative is totalizing (although not exclusivist) in its scope, involving a retelling of the origin and history of the world. It can, if one wishes, be seen as a "philosophy of history" or "universal history" in a quasi-Hegelian sense, that is, as a "master narrative" of humankind in which a divine plan is not only revealed but also realized in the course of the events narrated. It is the working out of a Vaiṣṇava world vision that is also a Kashmiri imperial wish (See Ali's chapter in this volume for the Śaiva world wish and Cōḻa imperial wish, and Walter's for the Buddhist vision and Okkāka imperial wish). The author and reader of the *VDhP* could even have taken this story on its first telling as a prediction: Viṣṇu will descend to earth in the Age of Strife and institute image-honoring. He will inspire a king of Kashmir with his "luminous will" (*tejas*), and that king, acting as Viṣṇu's willing instrument, his co-agent, will make India into a Vaiṣṇava kingdom. The reading of the completed text makes this sequence of events seem like the natural unfolding of some divine intention. That plan seems much more tentative, however, when we read the *VDhP* as complete at the end of parts I and 2. We shall see just how tentative the realization of these plans were when I turn to the historical situatedness of the *VDhP*.

The importance of this Purāṇa as master narrative also makes it possible for us to answer another question: why did Indian soteriological orders use the Purāṇas or dialogically related genres such as the Vaṃsa in the case of Sinhala Buddhists (see Walters) to make claims to hegemony? The reason is that such claims could not be sustained unless their authors could take command of history, of instructions in Order and of cosmogony, the three major topics of the Purāṇas apart from life-transforming practices themselves. Especially important was cosmogony. We have to remind ourselves that Indian ways of life were cosmological as well as existential and moral; they did not give up cosmology to a "secular" science, as most post-enlightenment European "religions" have done. Any disciplinary order that wished to claim preeminence in the world had to give an account of the world both in its cosmic and human respects. It also had to give an account of other accounts and demonstrate why its was the best.

The knowledges that intervene in the master narrative of the *VDhP* are not mere interpolations. They themselves often embrace as their "proofs" further narratives of events in which Pāñcarātra emanations, including devotees of the Pāñcarātra god, progressively remake the world into a Pāñcarātra Vaiṣṇava world. The knowledges that are so revealed and enacted are often explicitly didactic, instructing the devotee to perform certain acts in preference to others. Although these didactic chapters interrupt the flow of the narrative that some might wish the text to have, the knowledges they impart can be taken as integral to the narrative in the sense that without them, the listener would not always know why or how he or she should conduct himself or herself in the present and future as the persons of the narrated episodes did in the past.

It is important to emphasize the constitutive aspect of the narrative in the *VDhP*. The events presented are not to be taken as timeless exemplifications of universal norms that have always existed. The Pāñcarātra Vaiṣṇavas in the course of this narrative show themselves remaking their own knowledge of Vaiṣṇavism under the rubric of "remembering" it with Viṣṇu's inspiration. This rethinking itself has a close recursive relationship to acts that actually remake the world. When we start out, forest-dwelling Pāñcarātra Brāhmaṇs have come to the court of a Bhāgavata king, a Vaiṣṇava householder who performs the Vedic liturgy. Part 1 of the text has a Śaṅkaragītā as its guiding section. Unlike the earlier *Bhagavadgītā* which, offering no distinct liturgy for the honoring of images, leaves Vaiṣṇavas as performers of the Vedic liturgy, this Gītā constitutes Pāñcarātra Vaiṣṇava householder devotees so that they may institute the image-honoring of Viṣṇu on the plains of India in the Age of Strife. That part ends by revealing, in an extension of the *Rāmāyaṇa*, that one of the heroes of that epic had established an imperial kingdom in which Pāñcarātra Vaiṣṇavism was the hegemonic way of life.

Having done this, kings in part 2, are enabled, through the performance of liturgical and other practices revealed in that part, to constitute in full a Pāñcarātra Vaiṣṇava kingdom in India, and make it into the paramount polity within the Indian imperial formation by carrying out the practices related in the rules for royal Order with which part 2 is concerned. Finally, in part 3, organized around a Pratiṣṭhākalpa, a Pāñcarātra Vaiṣṇava imperial polity, having gained command of the world, rearticulates it as a Pāñcarātra scale of soteriological orders with a Pāñcarātra Vaiṣṇava temple liturgy at its apex; in it, the Pāñcarātra devotees of Viṣṇu attain an ultimate state. By the end of this narrative, then, major transformations have occurred. The way of life of the Pāñcarātra Vaiṣṇavas, confined at the beginning of the narrative to forest-dwelling Brāhmaṇs, becomes the hegemonic way of life for the "entire earth." The adherents of that disciplinary order do not do this, however, simply by causing a pregiven set of life-transforming practices to spread. They do it by transforming those practices in the process. Integral to this process was a discursive mode of knowledge embedded in this text, both in the formally narrative portions and in the didactic. Let me now attend to this argument.

Purāṇa as Discourse

People do not simply discover things and register them in texts. They discursively constitute them to some degree, that is, they make propositions about things that entail certain assumptions and presuppositions about the reality of the world. If a master narrative that pretends to remake the world is to convince, it must also, therefore, bring to bear existing discourses and deploy a discourse of its own. The text of the *VDhP* did not, thus, simply narrate the story of Pāñcarātra Vaiṣṇava triumph in the world. It claimed to offer a truer vision of the world, of how people should conduct themselves in it and of how they might attain to an ultimate state. It made arguments about the world as a Pāñcarātra Vaiṣṇava world, about cause and effect as well as about the significance of events in it. This discursive aspect was an integral aspect of the Purāṇic narrative. It was not a superficial and sectarian "interpretation" imposed by Brāhmaṇs on a more or less universal everyman's Hinduism. As I have already said, many of the narratives were themselves to be taken as "illustrative proofs" of Viṣṇu's presence, of his superiority to other divinities, of the efficacy of the Pāñcarātra devotional liturgy, and so on. Hence, if I wish to understand the narrative portions of the text as I think a medieval Indian listener would have, as well as within the frame of my own metaphysics, it is necessary for me to attend to a historical reconstruction of the discursive aspects of the text.

There are many examples of discursive practice that I could present here. Let me, however, discuss just one. It is the argument the *VDhP* makes for changing the relationship of the Pāñcarātra liturgy to the Vedic sacrifice. I have chosen this example not only because it is of great importance for the shifting objective that the complex author of the text wished to realize but because it has a great deal to do with the way in which that author has constituted the contents of its own text and related itself to other, earlier texts.

The disciplinary order of the Veda with which the *VDhP* was substantively connected was the Kaṭha "branch" (*śākhā*) of the Black Yajurveda. Yet the *VDhP* has refused, despite its profuse praise of the Veda and its acceptance of that text's validity, to attach itself to that branch or, for that matter, to any branch of the Veda. It has instead tried to attach the Veda and other bodies of knowledge to itself in a scale of texts by constituting itself as a guide to those sciences from the Pāñcarātra point of view. The reason for this is that the *VDhP* wished to bring about major changes in the relationship of image-honoring, in the form of the Pāñcarātra liturgy, to the fire sacrifice of the Veda. It desired to replace the Bhāgavata liturgy in Vaiṣṇavism with a Pāñcarātra liturgy that so far existed only in the autonomous Saṃhitās of the Pāñcarātrins, an order outside the Veda according to Smārtas. If the Pāñcarātrins succeeded, they would make the life-transforming practices of the Pāñcarātrins hegemonic among the ways of life of the imperial formation of eighth-century India.

The place of previous Smārta or Vedic discourse on the image or temple worship of Viṣṇu and Śiva was homologous with the place accorded to image-honoring in the Vedic liturgy itself. Just as the practice of image-honoring was classed with the lesser household sacrifices and made to be performed "outside the sacrificial terrain" (*bahirvedi*) of the Vedic multifire liturgy, so the texts on image-honoring were themselves classed with the Smārta- or Gṛhyasūtras, the texts advocating a householder liturgy, and added to them. Some of these texts, the precursors of the *VDhP*, actually presented themselves as "appendices."[60] Others more boldly represented these texts as parts of the larger Vedic textual ensembles, and presumed that the acts which they prescribed or recommended were to be added to the ongoing performance of the Vedic liturgy. The *Viṣṇusmṛti* to which the *VDhP* claimed to be an addition—just such an expansion of the textual material that had once formed the Dharmasūtra of the Kāṭhaka order of the Black Yajurveda—is an example of this.

The *VDhP*, highly conscious of its discursive antecedents, proposes to change all this. Before the appearance of Mārkaṇḍeya and his associates in the court of Vajra, a Pāñcarātra liturgy seems to have been performed only by Vaiṣṇavas who had left the householder (*gṛhastha*) stage and become forest-dwelling adepts (*vānaprastha*). They lived in small groups in retreats (*āśrama*) outside the plains of India, such as the famous Badarikāśrama near Mount Kailāsa and Mount Gandhamādana (now Badrināth) and Lake Bindusaras, source of the Gaṅgā in India. There, these Brāhmaṇs, who were "monotheists" (*ekāntabhāvin*), carried out their daily and annual liturgy centered on the honoring of an image (*pūjā*) of Viṣṇu with attendances of wild flowers and other relatively simple offerings. Vaiṣṇava householders—those designated by the more general term of Bhāgavata—continued to be the celebrants (*yajamāna*) of the Vedic sacrifices, supplemented by a relatively simple liturgy in honor of Viṣṇu's image. The idea was that Viṣṇu was the ultimate or true recipient of all those Vedic sacrifices. Earlier texts of the Bhāgavatas, the *Bhagavadgītā* of the *MBh* and the *Viṣṇupurāṇa*, consistently take this position.[61]

[60] Such, for example, were the *Pariśiṣṭa* of the *Atharvaveda* (or, more precisely, of the *Gṛhyasūtra* of Kauśika attached to that Veda) and the *Śeṣa* of the *Gṛhyasūtra* of Baudhāyana in the Taittirīya school of the Black Yajurveda. The *Pariśiṣṭa* has been edited by George Melville Bolling and Julius von Negelein (Leipzig: O. Harrassowitz, 1909–10); the *Śeṣa* is contained in R. Shama Sastri's edition of Baudhāyana's *Gṛhyasūtra* (Mysore: Government Branch Press, 1920), pp. 178–376.

[61] *Bhagavadgītā* 9.14–27; *Viṣṇupurāṇa* III.8.

Some Vaiṣṇava Brāhmaṇs and their wealthy household supporters had, however, begun to elaborate on these simpler liturgies, converting them into the lavish temple liturgies whose descendants continue to be performed at some temples today. They inscribed their procedures, which they claimed to have been directly divulged by Viṣṇu and to be independent of the Smārta and Śrauta rules, in their Saṃhitās. This move of some Pāñcarātrins, paralleled by Śaivas in their Āgamas, theatened to dislocate the relation between Pāñcarātrin and Bhāgavata, between Vedist and Theist.

Mārkaṇḍeya intervenes at this point. He would collapse the distinction between Pāñcarātra forest-dweller and Bhāgavata householder, and Theist and Vedist, with the knowlege he provides in the *VDhP*. This he would do in two ways. He would attach the capacity of celebrant for a Pāñcarātra liturgy to the king and his householder-subjects, while simultaneously expanding the scope of the Pāñcarātra liturgy itself as called for in the Pāñcarātra Saṃhitās. He accomplishes this suture by representing the Pāñcarātra liturgy he appropriates from the Saṃhitās as a newly disclosed practice appropriate to the Age of Strife for *both* Pāñcarātra adepts and householders living in the plains. This Pāñcarātra liturgy is largely to replace the older Vedic sacrifice. The centerpiece of this new royal and imperial "whole" is the image-honoring of Viṣṇu, conducted in a huge, elaborately adorned temple. The mantras of the Vedas are detached from the Vedic liturgy and made to reappear, in homologous places, as parts of the Pāñcarātra liturgy. Here, however, they must share the limelight with the newly revealed mantras of the Purāṇa. At this point, however, Mārkaṇḍeya departs from the program of the Saṃhitās. The householder liturgy of the Vedic ensemble, especially the so-called life-cycle rites, is retained intact—Vaiṣṇava householders are instructed to perform them in accord with the rules of the particular disciplinary order (*svakalpa*) of the Veda to which they are attached—but with certain Vaiṣṇava additions. The Śrauta, the grand or multifire liturgy from which the *VDhP* takes so many mantras, may be performed in the Age of Strife, but need not be. There is no choice, however, with respect to the honoring of Viṣṇu: it is obligatory in the Age of Strife for any person who would attain to the ultimate state.

One place where the *VDhP* presents the argument for this change is a chapter entitled "Account of the the Householder Way of Life" (*gṛhasthadharmuvarṇana*). The imparter of knowledge here is Puṣkara, son of Varuṇa, god of waters, and his listener is Bhārgava Rāma, that Brāhmaṇ emanation of Viṣṇu who had earlier received the procedure for the Pāñcarātra liturgy. The householder to whom the argument in this chapter is especially directed is the Brāhmaṇ. The chapter begins with Puṣkara urging the householder, assumed to be a Bhāgavata, to perform the traditional household and multifire sacrifices, reiterating the well-known idea that the householder has three debts to discharge (II.95.1–3a). According to the *VDhP*, "He becomes free of debt to the gods by sacrifices of animals, O bestower of honor, and if of little wealth, by honoring images (*pūjā*), fasts (*upavāsa*), and the keeping of vows (*vrata*); and by reverential offerings (*śrāddha*) and honorings (*pūjā*) he becomes free of debt to the forefathers. By abstinence as a student (*brahmacarya*), learning the Veda (*śruta*), and austerities (*tapas*), he becomes free of debt to the sages" (II.95.3b–5a). Here, into what is otherwise a standard passage from Dharmaśāstra, the *VDhP* has inserted the honoring of images and its attendant practices, but apparently only as an option for the householder of little wealth, one who cannot afford to make the expensive sacrifices of animals called for in the Śrauta liturgy. Without further elaboration at this point, the text rehearses the different daily sacrifices a householder should make (II.95.5b–11). Here the text says nothing to which either Smārta or Bhāgavata adherents would object.

Puṣkara next turns to the seasonal, annual, and occasional sacrifices, including the elixir of immortality (*soma*) sacrifice, horse sacrifice, and royal installation, all of which, it declares, are optional (12–18). By announcing that Viṣṇu is the recipient of these Śrauta works, the *VDhP* is setting forth the Bhāgavata doctrine of Viṣṇu's identification with the Vedic sacrifice, upon which it thus elaborates: "The sacrifice is Viṣṇu, whose luminous will is great, and he indeed is the sacrificer and the vessels of sacrifice and the materials of sacrifice, as well. One should sacrifice to that Hari, who consists of all the gods, every day, O Rāma; certainly, he should sacrifice to that god every year" (19–20).

Puṣkara then returns to the question of the householder's economic capacity to perform the multifire sacrifices. After entering into a number of complications in that regard and several legalisms regarding sacrificial fees—all of them, by the way, taken from earlier Dharmaśāstras—he leaves his listener in some confusion (21b–25a).

Puṣkara exploits this bewilderment by proceeding then to this declaration:

> Viṣṇu contains all of the gods; the daily (*pratyaha*) honoring (*pūjana*) of him in an image (*pratimā*) is obligatory (*kartavya*), O best of Bhṛgus, even though the Brāhmaṇs recognize Viṣṇu [as the recipient] in all sacrifices. Moreover, when he is "sacrificed" to with milk products and flowers as prescribed [i.e., in an image], the satisfaction of multitudes of various gods automatically (*svayam*) takes place [without the necessity of performing the Vedic sacrifices]. So the honoring of an image is to be performed with confidence (*śraddhā*), O scion of Bhṛgu, outside the sacrificial enclosure (*bahirvedi*). Since one must never sacrifice to Viṣṇu through the multitude of gods with reduced fees, O destroyer of enemies, the man of little wealth may/should, in accord with his faith, honor [Viṣṇu] every day with asceticism (*tapas*) [e.g., fasting]. When he fully honors (*saṃpūj*) the god with superior food (*paramānna*), perfumes (*gandha*), and incense (*dhūpa*), with sweet fragrances (*sugandha*) and excellent fruits, he obtains [the rewards of] all of the sacrifices. Therefore, is the noble-souled one to honor him every day. (II.95.25b-30)

At last, the author of the *VDhP* has revealed its Pāñcarātra position. What is that?

Earlier, the *VDhP* had made the argument that since Viṣṇu contains all the gods, sacrifices made to the gods other than Viṣṇu are really sacrifices made to him. This was the reason for continuing to perform Vedic sacrifices in a Bhāgavata environment. Now, however, Puṣkara turns that argument on its head. When Viṣṇu is honored in an image, all of the other gods are automatically honored. Worshiping the multitude of gods with the sacrifices in fire prescribed in the Vedas is, thus, rendered theologically obsolete. One may perform them if one wishes, but there is no theological reason for doing so. This is an "economic" argument in a double sense. The Pāñcarātrins are arguing that a person should be able to honor Viṣṇu, the god of devotion, in accord with his life-wishes, and should not be prohibited from doing so simply because he does not have enough wealth to pay the stipulated fee. Recourse to image-honoring permits a devotee of Viṣṇu to make his devotions when he does not have enough wealth to perform a Vedic sacrifice. As the *VDhP* text will point out in later chapters, every devotee of Viṣṇu, be he a Pāñcarātra adept, a king of kings at the top of the Vaiṣṇava chain of human beings or a poor Śūdra servant or his wife at the bottom, can participate in the temple liturgy in accord with his or her standing. The other sense in which Puṣkara makes an economic argument is from the standpoint of liturgical action. Why should a devotee of Viṣṇu dissipate his resources on the performance of a bewildering array of Vedic sacrifices aimed at the myriad gods when honoring the image of the overlord of all those gods is itself sufficient?

Implicit in this argument of economy is a deeper criticism of the Vedic sacrifice. The *VDhP* does not wish to do away with the Vedas, nor does it wish to dispense with fire sacrifices altogether. What it does desire to do as a discursive text is to replace an ensemble of liturgical practices in which the element of fire predominates with one in which the element of water is dominant. It wants to construct and institute a complex of practices in which the bathing of the sacrificer takes precedence over the offering of valued goods into a fire. The reason for wanting to make this shift is complex, and this is not the place for a full exposition of it. Let me just say that the centering of fire presupposed a cosmos in that the goods of men were transformed by that medium into the food which the gods needed, and that they returned in the form of rain, which men needed in order to grow food crops. The centering of water presupposed a cosmos in which an infinitely powerful and self-sufficient god could directly infuse his devotees with his will. This idea is central to the whole notion that Viṣṇu descends to earth at critical moments, for it is the "luminous will of Viṣṇu" (*vaiṣṇavatejas*) through which that god makes himself manifest in the world. It is by his will that he descends into his major avatars as well as into his devotees and the images they honor. Arguments about Viṣṇu's will are presented both explicitly and directly in certain parts of the text. They also appear, however, in implicit and oblique fashion, throughout much of the entire text. It is not accidental, for example, that the master and narrator of part 2, that on rules for royal Order, is the son of Varuṇa, the god of waters, and bears the name, Puṣkara, of the lake (in Rajasthan) conventionally placed first on the list of *tīrthas* or pilgrimage places, where the primary act to be done was a bath. Nor was it without purpose that the first twenty-three chapters of part 2 are given over to the disclosure of a rule for the shower bath into kingship of a Vaiṣṇava king of kings. But we need not go even this far afield to see the *VDhP* make this argument. All we need do is turn to the very next chapter of the text.

This begins the description of the procedure to be followed for a number of "optional" (*kāmya*) shower baths (*snāna*). Just as the purpose of the shower bath into kingship was to strengthen the will of a king to rule as a Vaiṣṇava by *infusing him*, through the medium of water containing fire, with the "luminous will" of Viṣṇu, so these more modest baths had as their purpose the infusion of the recipient of Viṣṇu's will for a variety of lesser purposes similar to those for which one might also have undertaken to perform the Śrauta sacrifices. Before one could perform any of the multifire Vedic sacrifices, one had to complete the setting up of the fires (*agnyādhāna*), a procedure to be carried out when the moon was in the lunar asterism called Kṛttikā (whose lord was Agni, god of fire). The first of the optional baths commended by the *VDhP* is called a Kṛttikāsnāna and is to include a fire sacrifice. It contains not a Vedic fire sacrifice but a more modest pouring of oblations into a fire (*homa*) as a preliminary part of itself. The claim made for this work leaves little doubt that the Pāñcarātrins saw this shower bath of water as supplanting the entire ensemble of sacrifices into fire: "He who periodically performs this work obtains the [result of having performed] the setting up of the fires. This work, as ordained, destroys enemies and bestows the prosperity of *every work of fire* (*sarvāgnikarman*). It bestows wealth as well as fame when performed optionally or regularly by those who know Dharma" (II.96.10; emphasis added).

Other arguments about the reasons for changing from a liturgy of sacrifice into fire to one calling for honoring images of gods with attendances are also to be adduced from the *VDhP*. I could, for example, point to the importance of the uses of the body. Making attendances in the procedure of honoring images purposely directed the senses and the desires and will of the worshiper onto the deity. They were supposed to have the effect of transforming the intellect, mind, and sensations into *bhakti*, that complicated mental condition I translate as "devoted participation."

What answer did the Bhāgavatas and the Vedists, especially the adherents of the Mīmāṃsaka interpretation of sacrificial action, give to the Pāñcarātrins? Whatever their response, it does not seem to have been persuasive. From the eighth century onward, the kings of India did, indeed, stop acting as celebrants of the multifire sacrifices. The fact that no manuscript of a Kāṭhaka Śrautasūtra has seen the light may be explained in part by the hierarchization of the Śrauta liturgy by the *VDhP*. Two of those sacrifices had been constitutive of Vedic kingship and, with supplements consisting of great gifts (*mahādāna*) to "qualified" Brāhmaṇs, of Bhāgavata kingship as well. These were the royal installation and the horse sacrifice. The one was supposed to empower an independent king to conquer his neighbors and become a king of kings, the other was supposed to enable a king of kings to rule successfully after he had so done.[62] The *VDhP* provides kings with replacements for these two life-transforming practices. One of these is the shower bath into kingship with which Puṣkara begins part 2 of the text. This practice incorporates elements from the older royal installation, including the major formula (*mantra*) of that rite. The replacement for the horse sacrifice is the installation of images, the placing and enlivening of an image of Viṣṇu in a spired, stone temple open on all four sides. Although this liturgical work, too, contained dozens of reapplied mantras from the Vedas, it is otherwise new, a rearticulation of Vedic speech and Pāñcarātra practice from the excluded Saṃhitās.

---

[62] R. Inden, "The Ceremony of the Great Gift (Mahadana): Structure and Historical Context in Indian Ritual and Society," in *Asie du Sud, traditions et changements*, edited by Marc Gaborieau and Alice Thorner. Colloques Internationaux du C.N.R.S. 582 (Paris, 1979), 131–36.

The *VDhP* has thus, in its completed form, boldly seized what Michel Foucault refers to as the "enunciative function" among the ways of life that people followed in "early medieval" India.[63] For the next few centuries, the Theist temple liturgy became hegemonic in India, displacing both the older Vedic fire sacrifices and the Buddhist monastery from their privileged positions in imperial polities. Yet it is well to keep in mind that the appearance of a master plan for establishing the hegemony of a Pāñcarātra liturgy that the completed *VDhP* gives needs to be seriously qualified. If, as I believe likely, the text was completed at three successive moments in time, the "divine plan" in the text can be read as more tentative than it appears on first sight. Part 1 is content to institute a Pāñcarātra liturgy of image-honoring—doubtless the appropriation of a Pāñcarātra liturgy from the Saṃhitās, itself a reworking of the liturgy once confined to forest-dwelling Pāñcarātrins—for the Brāhmaṇ householder. The elaboration of this liturgy performable by a king and a king of kings appears in part 2, but nothing is said there about the temple liturgy that part 3 of the *VDhP* constructs. There is, thus, no reason to assume that this totality existed before part 1 of the *VDhP*. We could just as easily see it as a whole that emerges in the course of the text's composition, as the flow of events in which that process was itself situated.

To sum up: whichever assumption we make, by the time part 3 is complete, the complex author of the *VDhP* has thoroughly reworked the scale of worshipers and the liturgical forms with which it had started. The soteriological order of Pāñcarātra Vaiṣṇavas had previously consisted of forest-dwellers who carried out a simple liturgy of image-honoring at retreats above the plains of India. The Bhāgavata order, by contrast, consisted of householders and kings of the plains who dedicated their performances of the older Vedic liturgy to Viṣṇu, remaining content to append a simple work of image-honoring to the older Smārta sequence. Procedures for an elaborate Pāñcarātra temple liturgy had come into existence, but its proponents had remained apart from the old Smārta liturgy. The effect of the dialectical reworking of the older and newer Pāñcarātra orders and the Bhāgavata was to articulate a single order out of them that could gain imperial support. Householders emerge as Pāñcarātrins, replete with a household liturgy centered on the worship of the four-faced image of Vāsudeva Kṛṣṇa; the king of kings, with a Pāñcarātra liturgy to perform for the welfare of his kingdom, which displaces the older Vedic liturgy, appears as a devotee of Vāsudeva; and finally, that king, as conqueror of the entire earth, is made into the builder of an elaborate temple and the celebrant of a complex liturgy in honor of the four-faced image of Vāsudeva Kṛṣṇa, styled the overlord of the cosmos.

Text and Historical Situatedness

I have argued that the *VDhP* can be seen as a narrative and discursive text, one that dialectically articulates itself and its intertexts as a scale of knowledges. Throughout

[63] Michel Foucault, *The Archaelogy of Knowledge*, translated by A. Sheridan (New York: Harper, 1976), pp. 88–105.

the discussion I have implied that a text is not merely a passive expression of the world in which it was situated; it was, I argue, agentive of that world. I have also implied that this was not a one-way process. Neither the author of the *VDhP* nor the text impressed itself on the world of shapeless matter from some transcendent perch outside it. The *VDhP* and its complex author were themselves part of their world. That world, seen as a complex tangle of agents and practices, also in part articulated the contents of the *VDhP* and its author. I now want to turn to this question in more detail.

I want to argue that a text's configuration cannot be separated from the historical circumstances in which the composite author of that text was situated. At the same time, I also want to show that a text may be seen as articulative of the historical situation in which it emerges. I would make this argument, of course, about any text, but here in the *VDhP*, as in many of the Purāṇas, we are talking about texts that claim to contain knowledge of cosmology and history and rules of conduct that are extraordinarily agentive, bristling as they do with eventful divine and human encounters and directions for action.

Time and Homology

For the purpose of prompting its readers and listeners to action, the text uses a device of *partial resemblance*. Through an active process of resemblance making, the user of the text comes to participate in the activities, and hence the agents, of the past and the future. Yet because the resemblances are partial, never total, neither the users nor those whom they resemble lose their several identities. The user of the text, its composite author/reader, may see itself as resembling agents of the past who provide the (previously unknown) rules for action which, if followed, will bring about a desired state of affairs that will resemble that of the past—only it will exist in the changed circumstances of the future. The chronologer/preceptor of the present who follows the orders of Viṣṇu delivered by Mārkaṇḍeya becomes like him, and becomes a Pāñcarātra devotee who spends his entire adult life honoring Nārāyaṇa and participating in him. The king who realizes the rules laid down for a Vaiṣṇava king likewise comes to resemble Vajra; he becomes a universal monarch. Both eventually attain to a permanent condition of participation in Viṣṇu in future lives.

In order to make my case credible, I must first deal with another assumption about the relationship of texts to historical events, one that is closely associated with—if not entailed—in both the idealist and structuralist approaches. Here I have in mind the assumption, brought to my attention elsewhere by the work of Foucault, that the text was concerned with transcendent knowledge as opposed to immanent power, and that it was consequently only marginally infected with the surface details of "sectarianism" and largely indifferent to the political constitution of India.

It is possible to read this dichotomous metaphysics into the *VDhP* (and other Purāṇas), but to do so does violence to the metaphysics of the text itself. The text certainly asserts that it constitutes a whole coming ultimately from the mind of a single Absolute, Viṣṇu. That mind in its highest, transcendent state was unchanging and unitary. The world it had created was, however, a world of change, of birth, growth, and death. As that world underwent its series of ontological changes, so too it underwent epistemological transformations. The way men came to know Viṣṇu in one age was not and could not be the way of knowing him in another. This metaphysics, which links epistemology to a changing ontology, does not therefore simply justify or rationalize the reframing of Smṛti texts; it requires it.

We could get around this "problem" by assuming, in the manner of the Advaita Vedānta ascribed to a classical or Purāṇic Hinduism, that the actual texts, like the visible world, are mere illusions or appearances distorting or imperfectly expressing the ideal original. To do this, however, we must dismiss the ontology of the Pāñcarātrins. As they present themselves here and in their Saṃhitās, the Pāñcarātrins do not occupy what they would consider the extremes of the Indian ontological spectrum. They adhere neither to the *advaita* or "non-dualist" position at one end nor to the *dvaita* or "dualist" position at the other. Rather the relationship they posit to exist between god and the world is one that resembles the *bhedābheda*, "identity-in-difference," stance of Bhāskara (eighth century) or the *viśiṣṭādvaita* "qualified non-dualist," position of the later Rāmānuja (1056–1137).[64] The Pāñcarātrins were, thus, not idealists but realists. Their purpose in the *VDhP* was not to avoid or ignore kings and their subjects. On the contrary, they wished to persuade them to transform the entire earth into a theophany, to rearticulate an imperial formation dominated by a Pāñcarātra temple and a Pāñcarātra king of kings.

This ontology of identity-in-difference makes the strategy of participation by resemblance possible. At work almost everywhere in the *MBh* and the Purāṇas is the idea that persons, situations, and events of the "present" are, and can be, homologous with those of the "past." I say "homologous" rather than "analogous" advisedly. For I am attributing to the Pāñcarātrins the belief that the persons of the present do, by correct thought, speech, and deed, come to participate in the beings of the past and the future. They do not simply become similar to them, they come to partake of their essence. The whole point of following the Pāñcarātra soteriology was, after all, to "make" *bhakti*, to participate in Viṣṇu, the Cosmic overlord who is at once both beyond time and time as process itself. Thus, far from assuming that the text and historical situation are opposed to one another, that the one expresses an ideal model of order "up there" and in the past whereas the other is an amorphous, empirical reality "down here" and in the present, they assume that the two are continuous with one another, overlapping realms that continually reconstitute one another.

---

[64]Eric J. Lott, *God and the Universe in the Vedantic Theology of Ramanuja* (Madras: Ramanuja Research Society, 1976), pp. 20, 36–37, and P. N. Srinivasachari, *The Philosophy of Bhedabheda* (Madras: Adyar Library and Research Centre, 1934), pp. 32–33. Surendranath Dasgupta, *A History of Indian Philosophy* ([1922] Delhi: Motilal Banarsidass, 1975) 3: 105, comments that, "The *bhedābheda* interpretation of the *Brahma-sūtras* is in all probability earlier than the monistic interpretation introduced by Śaṅkara. The *Bhagavadgītā*, which is regarded as the essence of the Upaniṣads, the older *Purāṇas*, and the *Pāñcarātra*...are more or less on the line of *bhedābheda*."

We have already seen that the *VDhP* acts as a "metatext," as a textual whole that transforms earlier texts into parts of itself. It construes the Pāñcarātra as a science situated in its present that tells its listeners how to know the sciences from the past. Here it exemplifies what Barthes refers to as the *denotative* aspect of a text that contains two levels of signs.[65] The text as a whole is a signifier in relations to its parts, which are taken as signifieds. A text can also have, argues Barthes, a *connotative* aspect. Here the text (or any part of the text) acts as a system of connotative signifiers for a second-order system of signs, which may lie outside the text itself. This is how, I submit, the users of the Epics and Purāṇas "read" these texts. They took the "histories" (*itihāsa*), the signs consisting of narratives of events in the distant past, as signifiers having events in the more or less immediate present as their signifieds. Or, to look at it from a dialogical standpoint, people conversed with the signs composing these texts; they treated them as living, as undergoing an active process of change in the present, as making things happen and not just as signifying them. One example of this in the *VDhP* that I have already mentioned is the war of Bharata against the Gandharvas of Gāndhāra. Given the long-standing rivalry of Gāndhāra and Kashmir, readers of the *VDhP* most likely took the Śāhis, the Turko-Iranians on the other side of the Indus (or the Kidāra Kuṣāṇas, before them), as homologues of those Gandharvas. They could also have seen the king of Kashmir (or one of the earlier Gupta monarchs) as resembling Bharata (denoted as the Pradyumna emanation of Viṣṇu). The fact that we are dealing here with signifiers that are, by definition, connotative rather than denotative makes it impossible to make an exact determination. But it is precisely this underdetermination of signifier by signified that has made it possible for the Epics and many of the Purāṇas to be used in so many different historical circumstances.

Having cleared the ontological ground, I will try in the remainder of this chapter to show how the complex author and reader of the *VDhP* and its text, whom Indologists have left floating above Kashmir (or the Panjab) between A.D. 600 and 1000, were historically situated, and sketch in how that situation was not only articulative of author and text but also how they articulated that situation.

Textual, Political Shifts

Kashmir of the sixth century was positioned at the intersection of three imperial formations. The Guptas (and their allies, the Vākāṭakas, in the Deccan), to the east and south of Kashmir, had represented themselves as the paramount kings of the world and as devotees of Viṣṇu from their Indic capitals in the Gangetic plains (though they also appear to have been indirectly supportive of Buddhism at the center of Nālāndā, in Bihar). The Kuṣāṇas, to the west and north of Kashmir, had claimed the title of Śāh or Śāhānśāh, taken from the Iranians, and most of them depicted themselves on their coins as devotees of Śiva from their capitals in Turkestan, Afghanistan, and Panjab (although some of them and many of their subject kings were devotees of Sarvāstivādin Buddhism, the "realist" position that

[65] Barthes, *Elements*, pp. 89–94

predominated among most orders in the northwest). Earlier kings of this dynasty (Kaniṣka, A.D. 78–102) had caused kings in India to submit.[66] The Guptas later caused their successors, the Kidāra Kuṣāṇas, to submit to them. The Sasanians, who also succeeded in contesting the rule of the Kuṣāṇas, and hence occasionally impinged on Kashmir, represented themselves as overlords of the world and as devotees of the Sun from their capital in Iran. A fourth imperial formation, to the north and east of the Himalayas, that of the Chinese, though only indirectly connected with Kashmir, would become closely involved before long.

During the sixth century, the Gupta-Vākāṭaka imperial formation met its demise. The Hūṇas, who had entered India from the northwest, had been among the more important agents of that decline, representing themselves as successors of the Iranian, Kuṣāṇa, and Indic overlords.[67] After the collapse of the Guptas, together with their Hūṇa Other, a new imperial formation appeared in India. The Sasanian polity regained its preeminence in eastern Iran, and Turks supplanted the Hūṇas not only in Turkestan (whence that name) but at Kapiśa (Kābul) and Jahuṇḍara or Zābul (Ghazni) in present-day Afghanistan, where they represented themselves as Śāhis. Kashmir, which had submitted to them as it had to the Hūṇas, became independent and a rival of the Śāhi imperial kingdom. The major claimants as successors of the Guptas to the east of Kashmir were the Puṣpabhūtis of Sthāṇvīṣvara (Thanesar), in the old Kuru country.

The king who emerged out of the struggle for paramountcy that ensued in north India was the Puṣpabhūti, Harṣavardhana (606–47).[68] He attempted to make his new capital, Kānyakubja (Kanauj) on the Gaṅgā in Pañcāla, the premier city of Āryāvarta (India north of the Vindhyas). Harṣa's main foes for the paramount overlordship of all India were the Cālukyas of the Deccan and the Pallavas of south India. Harṣa caused the kings of Jālandhara or Trigarta (Kangra), between the Śatadru (Satlej) and the Vipāśā (Beas), and (arguably) of Madra (Ṭakka), between the Vipāśā and the Vitastā, in the Panjab plains and hills, to become tributary kings. He could not, however, make the king of Kashmir submit.

The agent of Kashmir's political success was the first king, Durlabhavardhana (c. 626/7–662/3), of a new dynasty.[69] According to Kalhaṇa, poet-historian of

---

[66] B. N. Mukherjee argues provisionally for these dates in *The Rise and Fall of the Kushāṇa Empire* (Calcutta: Firma K. L. Mukhopadhyay, 1988), pp. 70–71.

[67] They had defeated the Sasanian emperor of Iran in 484 and established their predominance over a wide area, including Afghanistan, Kashmir, the Panjab, and Rajasthan. One of the Hūṇa lords, Mihirakula, may have headquartered for a while at Śākala (Sialkot) in Madra (Ṭakka). Their raids apparently caused severe dislocations throughout large parts of this region. The "heroic" efforts of Narasiṃha Gupta (c. 500–535), entitled Bālāditya ("rising sun"), to repel or disperse the Hūṇas, although successful, did not bring a reverse in the misfortune of the Guptas for long; R. C. Majumdar, "The Disintegration of the Empire" and "The Fall of the Gupta Empire," in *History and Culture of the Indian People* (*HCIP*) (Bombay: Bharatiya Vidya Bhavan, 1951–77) 3 (1954), 34–43; Upendra Thakur, *The Hūṇas in India* (Varanasi: Chaukhamba Sanskrit Series, 1967).

[68] Majumdar, "Northern India during A.D. 650–750," in *HCIP* 3 (1954), 131–32, and K. S. Saxena, *Political History of Kashmir (B.C. 300–A.D. 1200)* (Aminabad, Lucknow: Upper India Publishing House, 1974), pp. 38–45.

[69] If one adds twenty-five years to Kalhaṇa's dates for the Kārkoṭa Nāgas, in order to match the Chinese dates for Candrāpīḍa, the reign of the last king of the dynasty, Utpalāpīḍa, 853–855 (old reckoning)

Kashmir, this new dynasty, named Kārkoṭa Nāga after its serpentine founder, a Nāga, replaced the family that had ruled in Kashmir since the formation of that country and its permanent settlement by humans.[70] Kalhaṇa begins his narrative proper of Kashmir's past with a brief summary of the *Nīlamata* (*RT* I.25–27), showing that history was assumed to be an extension of a Purāṇa, an account of the divine origin and ordering of the world, and in this case, the country of Kashmir. For the bulk of his narrative of kings, however, Kalhaṇa draws on the inscribed eulogies and donative orders: "As a result of the donative orders of kings of the past [recording gifts of land for] installations [of images] and of movable goods and the plates of eulogies and the [colophons of] instructional manuals I have examined, the fatigue caused by endless errors has been stilled."[71]

Kalhaṇa reports that Durlabhavardhana received the shower bath into kingship, in aceord with the rule, with the waters of pilgrimage places poured out of golden jars, a statement to be read as a declaration that this king intended to establish an imperial kingdom (*RT* III.528). Durlabhavardhana seems to have made good his claim. Historians have inferred from the *Xiyouji*, the account of the Chinese Buddhist scholar and pilgrim Xuanzang (Hsüan Tsang), who visited Kashmir from 631 to 633, during Harṣa's reign, that Durlabhavardhana had forced the Śāhi monarch to cede the eastern province of Gāndhāra, Takṣaśilā (Taxila, Attock, and Rawalpindi districts), to him, as well as Kekaya (Siṃhapura) on the west bank of the Jhelum, south of Gāndhāra and southwest of Kashmir; Uraśā (the valleys of the Kishen Ganga and Kunhar rivers) to the west; Dārvābhisāra (Parṇotsa and Rajapurī) to the south; and possibly Brahmapura (Chamba) to the east.[72] He may have caused Madra to submit as Harṣa's polity collapsed. He is reported to have built a temple in the capital of Śrīnagara, presumably to mark his victory in establishing an imperial polity. The name of that temple, Durlabhasvāmin, "lord of Durlabha," indicates both that the temple was dedicated to Viṣṇu and that the king took Viṣṇu

---

ends in 880, overlapping the kings datable from other evidence of the next dynasty. We thus have to assume that some reigns are recorded as too long; Sunil Chandra Ray, *Early History and Culture of Kashmir* (Calcutta: U. N. Dhaur and Sons, 1957).

[70] Kalhaṇa, *Rājataraṅgiṇī*, ("River of Kings") (*RT*) III.528–30 and IV.1–38. See *Kalhaṇa's Rājataraṅgiṇī, a Chronicle of the Kings of Kaśmīr*, edited by Marc Aurel Stein (Bombay: Education Society's Press, 1892) and *Kalhaṇa's Rājataraṅgiṇī, a Chronicle of the Kings of Kaśmīr*, translated with introduction, commentary, and appendices by Marc Aurel Stein (Westminster: Archibald Constable, 1900; reprint, Delhi: M. Banarsidass, 1979). A more recent "critical" edition is *Rājataraṅgiṇī*, edited by Vishva Bandhu; Woolner Indological Series, 5,6 (Hoshiarpur: Visvesvraananda-Sansthanam, 1963–65) in 2 volumes. For empiricist textual criticism see Bernhard Kölver, *Textkritische und Philologische Untersuchungen zur Rājataraṅgiṇī des Kalhaṇa* (Wiesbaden: Franz Steiner Verlag, 1971). We should be careful not to treat this text as a "source," as a more or less realistic account of what happened; it is a poetical work whose author had a Śaiva outlook, and deserves further analysis from those points of view.

[71] *dṛṣṭaiśca pūrvabhūbhartṛpratiṣṭhāvastuśāsanaiḥ/ praśastipaṭṭaiḥ śāstraiśca śānto'śeṣabhramaklamaḥ//* (*RT* I.15); my translation; I rely in part on Kölver, *Textkritische*, reproducing a passage from Bühler, "Detailed Report," p. 7.

[72] D. Devahuti, *Harsha, a Political Study* (Oxford: Clarendon Press, 1983), pp. 72–73. Xuanzang, *Si-Yu-Ki [Xiyouji]: Buddhist Records of the Western World*, translated by Samuel Beal (London: Trübner, 1884), 1: 148–64; and Thomas Watters, *On Yuan Chwang's Travels in India, 629–645 A.D.*, edited by T. W. Rhys Davids and S. W. Bushell, 2 vols. (London: Royal Asiatic Society, 1904–5), 1: 258–85.

as overlord of the cosmos (*RT* IV.6). Noting his serpentine origin, the Kashmiri chronicler says that he supported the earth on his arm just as Śeṣa, the infinite cobra manifestation of Viṣṇu, supports the cosmos on his hooded head (*RT* III.529). The chief queen of Durlabhavardhana, Anaṅgalekhā—daughter, we are told, of the last (and sonless) king of the previous dynasty, whose kings were virtually all Śaivas, according to Kalhaṇa—had a Buddhist monastery, constructed and named after her, the Anaṅgabhavana (location unknown), reiterating the subhegemonic position of Buddhism in Kashmir (*RT* IV.3).

Harṣa, who took the Śiva of the Pāśupata order of Theists as the overlord of the cosmos (he also had leanings toward the Buddha) can hardly have provided the venue for the composition of the *VDhP*. Indeed, it is likely that his court was responsible for a Purāṇa of the Pāśupatas, the major Theist rivals of the Pāñcarātra Vaiṣṇavas.[73] Gāndhāra, which the *VDhP* represents as a country with a wicked way of life, could hardly have given rise to that text. It is also unlikely that Madra, which figures favorably in the *VDhP*, was the site of its composition, once it was conquered by Kashmir. I would not, however, want to rule out the possibility that part 1 of the *VDhP* could have been composed there and later been appropriated by a Kashmiri king.

Durlabhavardhana, the king of Kashmir, seems to have done some of the things one would expect the first royal recipient of the *VDhP* to have exhibited. He constructed an imperial polity in which Vaiṣṇavism displaced Śaivism as the preeminent form of Theism. Indeed, it is possible to see the Kārkoṭa Nāgas as reworking the Vaiṣṇava imperial kingship of the Guptas. Compelled around 635 to relinquish a tooth relic of the Buddha to Harṣa, however, Durlabha was far from being able to claim himself as paramount overlord of even north India.[74] He was in the position of an imperial king who was confined in his activities to the frontier of an imperial formation in which Harṣa and his overlord, Śiva or the Buddha, were supreme. Given the peripheral geographical position of Kashmir as well, it seems implausible that the wish of conquering the earth" would have seemed practicable to Durlabhavardhana.

Durlabhavardhana may not have seen the *VDhP* completed at his court, but it is quite likely that the Purāṇa of Kashmir to which the *VDhP* was closely related, the *Nīlamata Purāṇa*, was completed at his court. That text, the regional and royal antecedent of the universal and imperial *VDhP*, also claimed to have been delivered to a king by a Brāhmaṇ sage.[75] The author of the *NP* made Kashmir the center of an

[73]V. S. Agrawala makes this case for the *Vāmanapurāṇa* in *Vāmana Purāṇa, a Study* (Varanasi: Prithivi Prakashan, 1964), pp. i–iv.

[74]Devahuti, *Harsha*, pp. 111–13.

[75]He was named Bṛhadaśva. The name of his royal interlocutor was Gonanda, the king considered to have been the founder of the ruling dynasty of Kashmir that lasted until Durlabhavardhana established his dynasty, the Kārkoṭa Nāga. Bṛhadaśva tells Gonanda about the Brāhmaṇ Candradeva, who had received the liturgical procedures from Nīla, the king of Kashmir's serpents (whence the text's name), at the end of an earlier cycle of ages and related them to his king, Vīryodaya. The text as a whole presents itself as an extension of the *MBh*. King Janamejaya, great-grandson of Arjuna and son of Parikṣit (who was, remember, a contemporary of Vajra), asks Vaiśampāyana, the pupil of Vyāsa, composer of the Vedas, Epics, and Purāṇas, who had recited the *MBh*, why no king of Kashmir participated in the battle.

imperial Theist kingdom consisting of the countries of the northern quarter of India. That text enjoined the performance of a shower bath into kingship for the kings of Kashmir (*NP* 834–65), the rule for which the author of the *VDhP* transforms and adopts for its own. Even more interesting, the *NP* called for him to perform a four-monthly sleep in honor of Viṣṇu, in accord with the liturgical procedure of the Pāñcarātrins (*NP* 421–27, 729–33), to be found in full in their Saṃhitās. Here we have evidence that people in Kashmir were attempting to rearticulate an Indian polity as a Pāñcarātra theophany, but not one that incorporates the Vedic liturgy and the whole of India.

I think one can infer that this text reworks earlier discursive material (which may or may not have constituted a formal, written narrative). According to that, people took Kaśmīrā to be an incarnation of Umā, the spouse of Śiva, and held that her king and master was a portion of Hara, a move that itself seems to be a Śaiva response to the Vaiṣṇava notion that equates the kingdom with Bhū ("earth") and Lakṣmī ("mobile wealth"), or Śrī ("radiant prosperity"), and makes the king a portion of Viṣṇu (*NP* 245–46). The main river of Kashmir, the Vitastā, was also considered an incarnation of the spouse of Śiva in this earlier discourse about Kashmir (*NP* 247–74). The *NP* does not deny this, but frames this text in a narrative that makes the main feeder of the Vitastā, the Viśokā, an emanation of Lakṣmī, whose waters strengthen the otherwise hesitant Vitastā and purify them (*NP* 275–97). It also subordinates the king and his subjects to the Nāgas, a term used to denote the serpents who were the original inhabitants of Kashmir when it was a large lake, and also to name the many springs and smaller lakes and pools that punctuate the landscape of Kashmir after that lake is drained. Nīla is the king of these serpents of Kashmir and it is he who issues the orders that its human inhabitants, starting with its kings, are to follow if they wish to bring prosperity and avoid ruin. The *NP* represents this Nīla as virtually an emanation of Viṣṇu himself, and a great devotee of that god (*NP* 351–69). So by elevating the Nāgas over the early kings of Kashmir, the text also makes its Śaiva kings the instruments of Viṣṇu.[76] Even so, these kings do not come off well. Gonanda, founder of the

---

Gonanda was, Vaiśampāyana replies, too young, thus "explaining" the absence of a king of Kashmir in that text's account: Bühler, "Detailed Report," pp. 37–41. What the *NP* does not say is that the *MBh* considers the Kashmiris to be northern barbarians: VI.10.63–66. Arjuna defeats them in his conquest of the quarters: II.24.16. The Kashmiris, along with other "barbarians," attended Yudhiṣṭhira's royal installation and offered tribute: II.31.12; II.48.13.

[76]Xuanzang reports a Buddhist version of Kashmir's origin and history in which a Buddhist adept gets the Nāga lord of the lake to drain it and permit 500 Buddhist monks, served by poor people he purchased, to settle there. This is a retelling of a story in the *Mūlasarvāstivādavinaya*, second of the "three baskets" (*tripiṭaka*), the "canon" of Buddhism. This particular text is the Kashmiri reworking from about the third century of the first-century *Sarvāstivādavinaya* of Gandhāra: Jean Przyluski, "Le Nord-ouest de l'Inde dans le vinaya des Mūla-sarvāstivādin et les textes apparantés," *Journal Asiatique* 1914 (November-December), 493–568, esp. "La conversion du Cachemere," pp. 522–37. The story of the *Mūlasarvāstivādavinaya* appears to be a retelling of an "exploit" (*avadāna*) from the *Aśokāvadāna*, a Sanskrit Buddhist text of Mathurā: Jean Przyluski, "Avadana de Madhyāntika" in *La Légende de l'empereur Açoka (Açoka-avadāna)* (Paris: Paul Geuthner, 1923), pp. 340–42. It is extant only in the Chinese translation, *Ayuwangzhuan*, of the Parthian Faqin, around 300. Saṃghabhara, alias Saṃghavarman, a monk of Funan, translates a different recension of it in 512; Przyluski, *Légende*, pp. xi–xii. According to Xuanzang, Buddhism became predominant in Kashmir under Aśoka and

earlier dynasty, comes in for criticism. Vāsudeva had killed his father in a row, and Balabhadra of Mathurā (Saṃkarṣaṇa, equated with Ananta, the serpent on which Nārāyaṇa sleeps) slaughtered Gonanda himself after he only partially implemented the liturgical procedure laid down by Nīla (*NP* 7–9; 909–11). The successor of these Śaiva kings, the Vaiṣṇava Durlabhavardhana, by claiming to be of Nāga descent and, even in Kalhaṇa's account, a manifestation of Viṣṇu, implicitly claimed to inaugurate a new and better life in Kashmir, of which the *NP*, divulged by his serpentine counterpart Nīla, was articulative.

The effect of these discursive reworkings of the *NP* is, then, to transform Kashmir, previously a Śaiva kingdom subject to other kings—some of them Buddhist—into an imperial Vaiṣṇava kingdom. The *NP* did not, however, go so far as the *VDhP* in promoting Pāñcarātra Vaiṣṇavism. Although it placed Pāñcarātra Vaiṣṇavism in a position of primacy it also placed Viṣṇu and Śiva in a complementary relationship, and did so to the extent that it sometimes difficult to tell which is superior. For example, it included a rule for the main liturgical work of the Śaivas, the Śivarātri, but also told its listener to perform it in accord with the proedure declared for Viṣṇu's four-monthly sleep (*NP* 527–33). It also accorded open recognition to the Buddhists of Kashmir, which the *VDhP* did not (*NP* 709–15). The complex author of the *NP*, Durlabhavardhana and his court, had thus made Kashmir into the platform for a world vision (a social and political imaginary) from which the program of the *VDhP*, in which Pāñcarātra Vaiṣṇavism was unambiguously preeminent, could be launched.

Kashmir between Imperial Formations

The son and successor of Durlabhavardhana, Durlabhaka (662/3–712/3), entitled Pratāpāditya ("blazing sun"), was also independent. Like his father, he struck his own coins. Kalhaṇa reports that he constructed a new capital, named after himself, Pratāpapura.[77] It is, in my view, very likely that the composition of an early version of the *VDhP* was in process during the reign of this king.

The reason for this is that the political circumstances that had obtained during much of his father's reign had changed dramatically. Around 650, after the death of Harṣa, events were under way that were to bring about major changes in the

especially Kaniṣka, who held the third council of Buddhist monks there in order to fix the canon of the Sarvāstivādins. The servile Kashmiris and their kings, however, repeatedly abandoned Buddhism; Xuanzang, *Xiyouji*, 1: 149–58.

[77] In 1942, archeologists excavated a temple at Ṭāpar (identified with Pratāpapura). Its remains consist of a central sanctum and four ancillary shrines, all on a raised platform. Though not as large or complex as the Sarvatobhadra in the *VDhP*, it has the same basic design and was dedicated to Viṣṇu (fragments of two images of Viṣṇu Vaikuṇṭha were found). It is one of the largest temples in Kashmir, measuring 300 feet east to west and 250 feet north to south. Originally, scholars attributed this temple to Durlabhaka; G. M. D. Sufi, *Kashir* (Lahore: University of the Panjab, 1948), 1: 51 and facing plate. More recently, however, architectural historians have attributed it to Muktāpīḍa Lalitāditya, apparently on the grounds that Kalhaṇa does not say Durlabhaka built a temple in that town; *Encyclopaedia of Indian Temple Architecture; North India: Foundations of North Indian Style, c. 250 B.C.–A.D. 1100)*, edited by Michael W. Meister, M. A. Dhaky, and Krishna Deva (Delhi: Oxford University Press, 1988), part 1: 368; part 2, plate 739.

imperial formations of Asia—the Chinese, Turkish, and Iranian, as well as the Indian. The first two Tang emperors, Taizong (627–649) and Gaozong (649–683), had extended their command over the Buddhist oasis towns of Kashgaria or eastern Turkestan (Xinjiang/Sinkiang) during the reigns of Durlabhavardhana and Harṣa.[78] The annals of the Tang report that the Śāhis, the Turkish(?) kings of Kapiśa or Kābul, across the Indus from Kashmir, were their tributaries.[79] Harṣa himself is reported to have been enfeoffed by an ambassador of Taizong.

At the same time, around A.D. 650, the Arabs, claiming to be inspired by their new way of life, Islām, had completed their conquest of the Sasanian empire of Iran. The domains of that empire then included parts of western Afghanistan. It touched on the old kingdoms of Tokharistan (centered on Balkh) and of Kapiśa, ruled by the Śāhis, the western rivals of the kings of Kashmir. The scholars of medieval India, armed with the historian's hindsight, have paid great attention to the arrival of the Arabs on the Indic scene. To the rulers of this period, however, the rise of another nation was, if anything, more important than the replacement of the Sasanian empire with the Caliphate of the Arabs. I speak of the rise to imperial standing of the Tibetans, India's northern neighbors.[80]

During the second half of the seventh century, Tibetan armies greatly extended the area of Tibetan influence, making attacks along their southern borders.[81] The Chinese reported that in 678 the Tibetan armies had penetrated the Middle Region (Poluomen, equivalent to Brāhmaṇ in Chinese, *madhyadeśa* in the Purāṇas.), the upper and middle Gangetic plains of India. The major countries were Kuru (Haryana) and Pañcāla (western Uttar Pradesh); Kāśī and Kosala (western U.P.); and Magadha (Bihar). Tibetan sources state that they took command of Zhangzhung (also Guge), the area called Suvarṇagotra (land of gold) or Strīrājya (kingdom of women) in 653.[82] It is identified as the valley of the upper Satlej, the region

---

78 Edouard Chavannes, *Documents sur les Tou-kie (Turcs) occidentaux* (Paris: Libraire d'Amerique et d'Orient, 1900), pp. 259–79, and Howard J. Wechsler, "T'ai-tsung (reign 626–49) the Consolidator," in *The Cambridge History of China* (Cambridge: Cambridge University Press, 1978–91) 3 (1979), 219–30.

79 So, too, was the minor kingdom of Udyāna (Swat), just above and between Kapiśa and Kashmir. The kingdoms beyond them, Bāhlika or Tokharistan (Balkh or Bactria) below the Amu Darya (Oxus), and Sogdiana (capital of Samarkand) above it, both sent envoys and presents to the Chinese court.

80 The Tibetan monarch, Slon-brtsan-sgam-po (c. 608–650), constituted the larger part of the Tibetan region as an imperial kingdom. He obtained a Chinese princess (and, arguably, a Nepali princess, too) in recognition of his new standing, and is supposed to have introduced Buddhism and caused the Tibetan alphabet to be fashioned; R. A. Stein, *Tibetan Civilization* (Stanford: Stanford University Press, 1972), pp. 56–64; and Turrell V. Wylie, "Some Political Factors in the Early History of Tibetan Buddhism," in *Studies in History of Buddhism*, edited by A. K. Narain (Delhi: B. R. Publishing, 1980), pp. 365–72.

81 They posed a severe threat to the area on their northeast, near the Chinese capital of Zhangan. After 670 they took command of the "four garrisons," the Buddhist oasis principalities of Kashgar (Kashi), Yarkand (Shache), Kucha (Kuqa), and Khotan (Hotan), to the northwest, cutting the Chinese off from western Turkestan and Iran; Paul Pelliot, *Histoire ancienne du Tibet* (Paris: Libraire d'Amerique et d'Orient, 1961), p. 9.

82 Luciano Petech, *The Kingdom of Ladakh, c. 950–1842 A.D.* (Rome: Istituto per il Medio ed Estremo Oriente, 1977), pp. 8–9.

around the Tibetan Mount Kailāsa.[83] I think we may infer from this that Tibetan armies had descended onto the Gangetic plains along routes that came through the Kathmandu Valley of Nepal, tributary to Tibet, and, from the newly acquired territory of Zhang-zhung, through Kumaon and Garhwal, along the Alaknandā and the Gaṅgā. It is likely that the Tibetans (who would at this time been seen simply as cruel barbarians and not as Buddhists) despoiled Badarikāśrama, the most important retreat in India of the forest-dwelling order of Pāñcarātra Vaiṣṇavas. They would also have been in a position to threaten Kanauj and to demand tribute from the lords of India's Middle Region. Vaiṣṇavas considered the area around Badrināth to be the source of the Gaṅgā and the ontological center of India, and many thought of Kanauj, in the plains below, as the political center of northern India or Āryāvarta. Hence the Tibetan presence must have had serious consequences. At the very least their raids and exactions can be seen as enough of an intervention in the political affairs of northern India to keep any of the contenders for supremacy there from reconstituting an empire before the first quarter of the eighth century.

The Tibetan armies seem to have devoted relatively little attention to the countries southwest of Kashgaria and Zhang-zhung, that is, to the north of Kashmir along the trans-Himalayan valleys of the Indus.[84] Although the Tibetans attempted conquests in this area, they do not seem to have constituted a serious threat to it or to Kashmir.

The circumstances that arose as a result of the political and military maneuvering I have described in brief can be summed up as follows from the standpoint of Durlabhaka, the king of Kashmir. The rulers of the Turkish kingdoms immediately to the west of Kashmir were in disarray as a result of Chinese aggression from the north and Arab assaults from their west. They were, therefore, hardly in a position to threaten Kashmir. Neither, for the moment, were the Arabs, caught up in internal quarrels, nor the Chinese, cut off by the Tibetans.[85] These latter had, to be sure, caused great mischief in the Gangetic plains. Partly as a result of their dominance, the political center of India as a whole had shifted to the south. The donative orders of the Cālukyas of Vātāpī (Badami) claimed they had become the paramount kings not only of the Deccan but of the entire subcontinent after king Pulakeśin defeated Harṣa. The Tibetans had not, however, been very successful in establishing their presence in the area north and east of Kashmir. So the damage they had done in the Middle Region of India actually worked to the relative advantage of the Kashmiri

[83]This is not to be confused with Suvarṇabhūmi, identified in Theravādin Buddhist discourse with Burma.

[84]The countries at issue here were, from west to east, Gilgit (Little Polü/Bolor), Baltistan (Great Polü/Bolor), and Ladakh (Mar-yul). The latter two regions are today inhabited by Tibetan speakers. Kalhaṇa calls them Sūkṣmabhuṭṭa and Bṛhadbhuṭṭa, Little Tibet and Great Tibet. There is, however, evidence that in the seventh and eighth centuries the peoples of this region (or at least their rulers), like those of Kashgaria, were Indo-Iranian speakers and that they (or, once again, their rulers) were Buddhists or, possibly, Śaivas: Luciano Petech, *A Study on the Chronicles of Ladakh* (Calcutta: n.p., 1939), pp. 97–105.

[85]H. A. R. Gibb, *The Arab Conquests in Central Asia* ([1923] New York: AMS Press, 1970), pp. 15–28; M. A. Shaban, *Islamic History: A New Interpretation* (Cambridge: Cambridge University Press, 1971), 1 (A.D. 600–750 [A.H. 132]), 173–75.

monarch. He was also able—and this is the major point—not only to strengthen his regional kingdom; he was able to see the situation as one in which Viṣṇu was urging him to think of making Kashmir the center of a pan-Indian imperial formation.

Toward the end of Durlabhaka's reign, the political circumstances again changed, giving further impetus to the world and imperial wish I am imputing to the Kashmiri court. The eldest son and designated successor of Durlabhaka was Candrāpīḍa. The Chinese had regained their command over the oasis towns of Kashgaria in 692, and had begun to jockey for position with the Arabs and Turks against the Tibetans.[86] The Arabs under Qutaybah bin Muslim (705–715), once again pressed eastward, executing the Śāhi, Nezak Śāh, in 709.[87] The same year that Candrāpīḍa took the throne, 712/13, Arab armies conquered Sind, taking the city of Mūlasthāna (Multan), south of the Madra country.[88] The Tang Annals record for that year a mission sent by Candrāpīḍa, followed seven years later by an imperial decree granting him the title of king of Kashmir.[89] Changes had also taken place in the Middle Region of India. The kings of Nepal (the Bagmati Valley) and of the Gangetic plains to the south had, in 703/4, successfully revolted against their Tibetan overlords.[90] It is possible that the king of the Middle Region reported to have overthrown Tibetan rule was Yaśovarman of Kanauj.[91] This king later attempted to conquer the quarters and rearticulate the Middle Region as an imperial kingdom. He then allied himself with the king of Kashmir and the Tang emperor, to counter a renewed Tibetan and Arab threat.

As for Candrāpīḍa himself, he apparently wished an alliance with the Chinese emperor. This would help him against the Tibetans and the Arabs, who were again threatening the Indo-Iranian world with which Kashmir was conterminous. Candrāpīḍa appears thus to have been laying the groundwork for a military campaign against his more immediate rivals, the first step one would take in a conquest of the quarters. One of the rivals Candrāpīḍa had in mind was almost certainly the Śāhi king of Kapiśa and western Gāndhāra. He was, I would contend, the homologue of the wicked Gandharva king against whom that past emanation of Viṣṇu, Bharata, had fought. The other potential rival of whom Candrāpīḍa might have been thinking was the king of Kanauj.

If the political circumstances of Candrāpīḍa's reign favored the disclosure of a Pāñcarātra text placing the king of Kashmir at the center of a kingdom embracing the entire subcontinent, so did the immediate circumstances with regard to ways of life. Candrāpīḍa was a Vaiṣṇava, as his dynastic predecessors had been. He seems,

---

[86] Pelliot, *Histoire ancienne*, pp. 10–11; Chavannes, *Documents*, pp. 287–92; and Denis Twitchett and H. J. Wechsler, "Kao-tsung (reign 649–83) and the Empress Wu: the Inheritor and the Usurper," in *The Cambridge History of China* 3 (1979), 286.

[87] Gibb, *Arab Conquests*, pp. 29–58.

[88] H. C. Ray, *The Dynastic History of Northern India (Early Mediaeval Period)* ([1931–36] New Delhi: Munshiram Manoharlal, 1973), 1: 6–11.

[89] Narayan Chandra Sen, *Accounts of India and Kashmir in the Dynastic Histories of the Tang Period* (Santiniketan: Visva-bharati, 1968), pp. 17, 31; and Chavannes, *Documents*, pp. 209, 293.

[90] Don Y. Lee, *The History of Early Relations between China and Tibet, from Chiu t'ang-shu, a Documentary Survey* (Bloomington: Eastern Press, 1981), p. 28.

[91] Majumdar, "Northern India during A.D. 650–750," in *HCIP* 3 (1954), 128–31.

however, to have had a Vaiṣṇava guru of special importance. This man, Mihiradatta, is the only preceptor of a Kārkoṭa Nāga king mentioned by Kalhaṇa (*RT* IV.80). Further evidence of the high esteem in which Mihiradatta was held is the fact that he himself was able to build a temple to Viṣṇu (*RT* IV.80). Finally, there is the evidence of royal names. The king who first hears the *VDhP* is named Vajra, the "Adamantine One." The kings of Kashmir, like many of the kings of India, took titles ending with the word *āditya* or "sun." Now it just so happens that the royal title taken by Candrāpīḍa was Vajrāditya, the "Adamantine Sun" or "Diamond Sun." It is thus quite likely that Vajrāditya, homologous with the Vajra whom the author of the *VDhP* made the recipient of that text at the beginning of the Age of Strife, was intended as the historic recipient of the very same text. Nor is it implausible to think that Mihiradatta, his soteriological preceptor and the homologue of Mārkaṇḍeya, was the historic Pāñcarātra adept who completed the last redaction of the *VDhP* and revealed it at the Kashmiri court. Such a textual event had probably occurred before in Kashmir's history when (as I earlier suggested) Durlabhavardhana, the grandfather of Candrāpīḍa, received the *NP*, a text rearticulating the Theist and predominantly Śaiva kingdom of Kashmir as one predominantly Vaiṣṇava. Part 2 of the *VDhP* ends with chapters on warfare. I am tempted to think that the complex author of the *VDhP* had completed part 2 of the text before Candrāpīḍa's death, at that moment when the Kashmiri court was itself preparing for a protracted military campaign.

It is highly probable that Candrāpīḍa, entitled Vajrāditya, was the king of Kashmir who became the historic recipient of the *VDhP*, a text remembered by his preceptor, with the aid of Viṣṇu, which was supposed to inspire him to world conquest. There is a problem here, however. Candrāpīḍa may have been the first king of Kashmir to hear the *VDhP*, but since he ruled for only eight years and eight months (c. 712/13–720/1), he could not have completed the sequence of tasks called for by that text. Nor could his younger brother, Tārāpīḍa (c. 720/1–724/5), his elder brother's murderer and successor, whose reign was an even shorter four years and twenty-four days (*RT* IV.39-125). His younger brother, Muktāpīḍa Lalitāditya (c. 724/5–760/1), who succeeded him, is reported to have ruled for thirty-six years, seven months, and eleven days, and it was he who completed what his eldest brother had only begun. After a successful campaign against the Tibetans in conjunction with Yaśovarman of Kanauj, he renewed his dynasty's relationship (in 733) with the Tang emperor.[92] He then broke his alliance with Yaśovarman, defeated him, and took command of Kanauj. Thence he proceeded on a conquest of the quarters, of which Kalhaṇa gives an ornate account (*RT* IV.126–80). Probably accompanied by the defeated Yaśovarman, Lalitāditya campaigned in eastern India in 735–736 and then in the Deccan and south India in 736–737.[93] What made possible Lalitāditya's successful conquest of the quarters beyond north India was the

[92]Chavannes, *Documents*, notes, p. 53.

[93]The most engaging reconstruction of this conquest of the quarters is that of Hermann Goetz, "The Conquest of Northern and Western India by Lalitāditya-Muktāpīḍa of Kashmir," in his *Studies in the Art and History of Kashmir and the Indian Himalaya* ([1952] Wiesbaden: Otto Harrassowitz, 1969), pp. 8–22.

failure of the Cālukyas' will as the paramount overlords of the Indian imperial formation. Weakened by a war of position with their rivals in south India, the Pallavas, the Cālukya court had apparently not been able to prevent first Yaśovarman and then Lalitāditya from undertaking the conquest of the quarters. Furthermore, preoccupation with the Pallavas left the Cālukya polity unattended in the north Deccan, which was under the command of underlords who called themselves Rāṣṭrakūṭa. The eulogies in their donative orders report that a Rāṣṭrakūṭa underlord of the Cālukya, Vijayāditya (696–733), Indra I, abducted the princess, Bhavagaṇā, possibly the daughter of Maṅgalarāja Satyāśraya or his younger brother, Pulakeśin Avanijanāśraya, who had recently become underlords of Lāṭa (Gujarat), after 722. The son of this marriage was Dantidurga (c. 733–757), who successfully supplanted the Cālukya, Kīrtivarman II (744/5–757), as paramount overlord (c. 750–752).[94] Interestingly, Kalhaṇa represents Muktāpīḍa as receiving homage from a Raṭṭā of Karṇāṭa who was acting as king of the Deccan. Most likely this was Bhavagaṇā, acting for her son who would have been a minor in 736–737.[95] Lalitāditya returned to Kashmir for the last time, to deal with a Tibetan threat in 747, about the same time that the grown Dantidurga began his active career, at which point the reach of the will of Lalitāditya's polity greatly diminished. His interventions in the Deccan and south India were nonetheless consequential. Quite possibly Muktāpīḍa's maneuvering strengthened the position of the Rāṣṭrakūṭas at a critical point in their career, and helped them support the claim of their protegé, Nandivarman II Pallavamalla (c. 731/2–796), a Vaiṣṇava, to the Pallava throne, on which he had been placed (at the age of twelve), apparently against the wishes of the Cālukyas.[96] Pāñcarātrins may have begun to displace the older Bhāgavatas in south India with his support. To conclude, if this admittedly speculative account of the *VDhP*'s historic debut is correct, if Vajrāditya was the first historic king to receive the text but his youngest brother, Lalitāditya, was in fact the first to fulfill its world vision, it explains why the text of the *VDhP* bears the homological signature of the one, Vajrāditya, while the earth herself came to be marked by the other, Lalitāditya.

Whether the first historic recipient of the *VDhP* was Candrāpīḍa or not, Kalhaṇa's account of the victories he achieved and of the temples he built, combined with the archeological evidence of these, leaves no doubt that Lalitāditya, and not Vajrāditya, was the first king of Kashmir who was able to carry out the orders of Viṣṇu issued in the *VDhP*. No subsequent ruler of Kashmir was as renowned as Muktāpīḍa Lalitāditya, for no other king of that country could claim to have conquered all of India, and no other monarch undertook there the construction of

---

[94]A. S. Altekar, "The Rāshṭrakūṭa Empire," in *HCIP* (1955) 4, 1–3.

[95]Goetz, "Conquest," pp. 16–17.

[96]Under their crown prince, Vikramāditya (733/4–744/5), they invaded the Pallava capital, Kāñcīpuram, and installed their own candidate, Skandaśiṣya Citramāya (c. 731/2–744/5), whereupon Nandivarman took refuge with Dantidurga, aiding him in his exploits. Dantidurga reinstated him in 744/5, the year of Vikramāditya's death: T. V. Mahalingam, *Kāñchīpuram in Early South Indian History* (Bombay: Asia Publishing House, 1969), pp. 137–85. If the Kayya mentioned in Kalhaṇa as the king of Lāṭa is to be identified with Karka II, the Rāṣṭrakūṭa whom, Altekar infers, Dantidurga placed in command of Lāṭa, then this would tend to confirm the guess that Lalitāditya and Dantidurga were allied, for Kayya is named as one of the Kashmiri king's court; *RT* IV.209–10.

as many permanent structures for the housing of different disciplinary orders as he did.[97] Here again I am tempted to think that the complex author of the *VDhP* completed part 3 of the *VDhP*, the largest of the three, and the one so elaborately concerned with enumerating temple types and the construction of a Sarvatobhadra temple for the image of Vāsudeva Kṛṣṇa, in conjunction with the "conquest of the quarters" by which Lalitāditya made India into his imperial formation.

Text Composition and Empire Building as Mutually Articulative

Lalitāditya did not simply claim to be the ruler of the earth. He and his court set out to prove it. This proof consisted of a concerted effort to make Kashmir the center of the Indic earth, and the centerpiece of that project was the construction of a Sarvatobhadra temple that displayed Pāñcarātra Vaiṣṇavism as the preeminent way of life in the Indian imperial formation. The *VDhP* was, I shall argue, as much involved in this project as the imperial project was involved in the composition of the *VDhP* itself.

The rulers of India had had a strong inclination in the past to consider the region called the Middle Region the center of India, an Āryāvarta. Any imperial kingdom that wished to establish paramountcy within the entire Indian imperial formation had to take this into account if it wished its claims to be taken seriously. Chinese and Tibetan incursions had already damaged the credibility of Āryāvarta's claims, and the Cālukyas of the Deccan had challenged its presumption of centrality—(as would their successors, the Rāṣṭrakūṭas, who were to rearticulate themselves as imperial rulers, with their Middle Region in Karṇāṭaka, after Lalitāditya's sun in Kashmir had set).[98] Clearly if Lalitāditya wished to establish his supremacy over India, he would have also to meet the challenge of making Kashmir the Middle Region of India. I have already shown that the *NP* and its royal readers had represented Kashmir as an imperial kingdom by telling stories about the origin and landscape of Kashmir and the countries around it, and by instituting a complex liturgy that turned Kashmir into a regionally triumphant theophany. My reading of Kalhaṇa, the *VDhP*, and the archeological evidence shows that Lalitāditya, supplementing these discursive and liturgical practices with the more radical program of the Pāñcarātra Saṃhitās, went one step further.

Indian kings made or remade their kingdoms by building new capitals, in the course of which they necessarily displayed the nature and extent of their claims to hegemony. Here is how Muktāpīḍa Lalitāditya deployed a strategy of city building

[97] Jayāpīḍa (c. 770–801), the grandson of Muktāpīḍa and a Pāñcarātrin, was said to have emulated his grandfather; he twice attempted to conquer the quarters, but did not enjoy great success: D. C. Ganguly, "Central and Western India," *HCIP* IV (1955), 114–15. The only other kings before 1000 who could even be compared in power with Muktāpīḍa are Avantivarman (c. 855–83) and Śaṅkaravarman (c. 883–902); but both of these kings were, at least publicly, Śaivas: Ray, *Dynastic History* 1: 115, 117, 121. The more expansionist of the two, Śaṅkaravarman, had himself to contend with a king named Bhoja, the most powerful of the Pratīhāras. He was the first king since the rise of imperial Tibet to succeed in reestablishing Kanauj as the capital of northern India and claimed, in that regard, the title of "Overlord of Aryavarta"; Majumdar, "Rise and fall of the Pratihara Empire," in *HCIP* 4 (1955), 28–32.

[98] R. Inden, *Imagining India* (Oxford: Blackwell, 1990), chapter 6.

so as to instantiate his claims. The Purāṇas generally defined the Middle Region as that region drained by the Gaṅgā, premier river of the whole of India, and its tributary, the Yamunā. From a cosmogonic standpoint, the center of this region was Prayāga. Located at the confluence of these two streams, it was the pilgrimage place where Viṣṇu reclined on his serpent-couch, the only place that escaped inundation when the deluge came. It was the plains homologue of the other major Vaiṣṇava place of pilgrimage, Badarikāśrama. The political center of this Middle Region was Kānyakubja. Kalhaṇa depicts Lalitāditya as taking command of that center (which, with the historian's hindsight, he probably made more important than it was).[99] He says of Lalitāditya that "The land of Kānyakubja from the bank of the Yamunā to that of the Kālikā was as much in his power as the courtyard of his palace" (*RT* IV.145, tr. Stein) and that "swelled with pride, the king granted the land of Kānyakubja with its villages to the [shrine of] Āditya [which he erected] at that [town of] Lalitapura" (built by his architect while Lalitāditya was away) (*RT* IV.187, tr. Stein); but that was not all that Lalitāditya did. He located the new capital of Parihāsapura that he built in Kashmir near the confluence of the Vitastā (Jhelum) and Sindhu (Sind) rivers.[100] The reason for this choice of location was that Lalitāditya and other Kashmiris, having listened to the discourse of the *NP*, had come to consider the Vitastā and Sindhu to be homologous with the Yamunā and the Gaṅgā, respectively, and that the confluence of the two was a Prayāga.[101] Lalitāditya and his court filled out this homology by making Parihāsapura a new Kanauj.

The archeological evidence indicates that this was not just an idle thought. Stein and later scholars have described the remains of six major structures on the plateaus at this site, corresponding to six that Kalhaṇa describes in his chronicle.[102] The three (A–C) on the lower of the two plateaus were Buddhist: a stupa or pagoda built not by the king but by a minister, Cankuna; a "royal monastery" (*rājavihāra*); and a meeting hall with a giant (*bṛhat*) image of the Buddha, facing east.[103] The three (D–F) on the higher of the two plateaus were probably Vaiṣṇava. One housed the (presumably four-faced) image of Viṣṇu that Kalhaṇa calls Parihāsakeśava, after the new capital Muktāpīḍa built. Another had installed in it the image named after himself, Muktākeśava. The third apparently contained an image of Viṣṇu as the "giant boar." Standing high above this ensemble was a pillar mounted by Viṣṇu's vehicle, the eagle.[104] At least two of these temples appear to have been larger than

[99] Its position, tentative after the death of Harṣa, was not secured until the rule of the Pratihāras in the ninth century: D. C. Sircar, *The Kānyakubja-Gauḍa Struggle from the Sixth to the Twelfth Century A.D.* (Calcutta: Asiatic Society, 1985), pp. 20–21.

[100] Not to be confused with the Indus River.

[101] Ved Kumari Ghai, *Nīlamata Purāṇa, Cultural Study*, pp. 29-30, 45.

[102] M. A. Stein in note F on *RT* IV.194–204 in 2: 300–3; Ram Chandra Kak, *Ancient Monuments of Kashmir* (London: India Society, 1933), pp. 146–49.

[103] A [Cankuna's stupa] on a platform 127'6" square surrounded by a wall 400' x 300'; B [Rājavihāra], with 26 cells, about 170' square; C [Caitya], 27' square on a double platform about 160' square]

[104] D [Muktākeśava], Peristyle = 258' x 209' (Sahni); E [Parihāsakeśava], 295' x 247' (Sahni); F [Mahāvarāha]; and Govardhanadhara = Garuḍadhvaja, 54 cubits high.

the other large temple of Lalitāditya that remains standing in Kashmir, the temple of the Sun at Martand.[105]

The *VDhP*, we recall, describes a Sarvatobhadra temple.[106] The text clearly places this temple, to be used for the installation of the main liturgical image of the Pāñcarātra Vaiṣṇavas, the Vaikuṇṭha, peculiar to the Kārkoṭa Nāgas, at the apex of this scale of temple forms.[107] It was to be the site for an elaborate liturgy that demonstrated the superiority of Pāñcarātra Vaiṣṇavism. Unfortunately the ruinous condition of the remains at Parihāsapura does not permit us to ascertain whether the two large temples of Viṣṇu that Lalitāditya erected there were built along lines recommended for a Sarvatobhadra temple, as was his other temple at Pratāpapura and that of the later Avantivarman[108] The evidence leaves little doubt, however, that Lalitāditya built monumental temples in the course of demonstrating his and the Pāñcarātrins' claim to universal precedence. The author of the *VDhP* faced a difficulty in doing this, however, one that was closely coordinated with the problem of making Kashmir itself into a Middle Region. We may suppose that Lalitāditya attempted to build temples in accord with the Sarvatobdhadra plans of the *VDhP*, for that text addresses this problem. In the course of doing so, he provides us with an excellent example of how the *VDhP* and its historical circumstances were articulative of one another.

The Kashmiri style of temple building, which used a hipped or pyramidal roof (*kūṭa*) and trefoil arched doorways (*candraśālā*) instead of porticos, was not only distinct from other styles, it was apparently one that even the *VDhP* recognized as regional rather than universal or imperial—good enough to be followed in Kashmir's imperial kingdom, but hardly sufficient for a Kashmiri court and a Pāñcarātra disciplinary order that wished to make claims to hegemony over all of India, the "entire earth," for its way of life. The style that the *VDhP* recognized as emblematic of a claim to universal rule was the style associated with the Gangetic plains, and especially the Middle Region of India in the sixth and seventh centuries. This style included a curvilinear spire (topped with an *āmalasāraka*, myrobalan), commonly called a *śikhara*, as its roof.[109] Examples of temples built in this style can be found near Kashmir in Kangra (Masrur) and Rajasthan (Osian), and in the Panjab (Kafirkot) from the eighth century.[110]

Here is what the complex author of the *VDhP* did to solve this problem. It began the chapter on temple types, named after mountains, with a description of

[105]The enclosure wall of Martand measures 220' x 142'; the shrine has three distinct chambers: the outer (*ardhamaṇḍapa*) is 18'10" sq.; the middle (*antarāla*) is 18' x 4'6"; and the innermost (*garbhagṛha*) is 18'5" x 13'10." The height was about 70'; Kak, *Ancient Monuments*, pp. 131–33, Plates 53, 73.

[106]R. Inden, "The Temple and the Hindu Chain of Being," in *L'Espace du temple: Espaces, itinéraires, médiations*, edited by Jean-Claude Galey, Collection Purusartha, 8 (Paris: EEHESS, 1985), pp. 53–73.

[107]T. S. Maxwell gives a brief but critical review of the literature on this image, of which numerous examples have come to light; in *Viśvarūpa* (Delhi: Oxford University Press, 1988), pp. 125–30.

[108]For the Avantisvāmin temple at Avantīpur, see Percy Brown, *Indian Architecture (Buddhist and Hindu Periods)* (Bombay: D. B. Taraporevala Sons, 1971), plates 137 and 138.

[109]Later texts refer to this temple style as Nāgara: M. A. Dhaky, *The Indian Temple Forms in Karṇāṭa Inscriptions and Architecture* (New Delhi: Abhinav, 1977), pp. 7–8.

[110]The superstructures of the latter are of particular importance; Maurizio Taddei, *India* (Geneva: Nagel, 1970), p. 99, plates 144, 147–49; see also Brown, *Indian Architecture*, plate 82.

the temple called Himavān, which I read as an elaboration of the stone temples extant in Kashmir. The *VDhP* actually describes these under the name of the Śveta temple. Nowhere, however, does the text say that the Himavān and its variants are particular to Kashmir. As the text proceeds, permuting and varying temple features, types that are quite different from this first group appear. All of this prepares the way for the description of the Sarvatobhadra in the next chapter. The main shrine of that temple, the one that was to house the four-faced image of Vāsudeva and his eight consorts, was to have porticos (*maṇḍapa*) and to be built with curvilinear towers (*śikhara*) surmounted by cogged ringstones (*āmalasāraka*) provided with tracery work (*jāla*) and dormer windows (*gavākṣa*). At the same time, however, the text calls for smaller ancillary shrines to be be built around this one in the Himavān style.

Some might consider this mixing yet another product of Hinduism's inherently wandering, dreamy mind. I prefer to see it as an example of how historical circumstances acted to articulate the text. The author of the *VDhP* constructed a new composite temple type because it envisioned the prospect of transforming the Kashmiri imperial kingship into the paramount kingship of India. In order to accomplish this, the complex author of the text thought it desirable to appropriate the temple style that princes recognized as emblematic of universal rule, that of the Gangetic plains, and combine it with an elaboration of the local Kashmiri style—the latter clearly in a peripheral position yet also clearly acting to distinguish the Sarvatobhadra from temples built in this general style elsewhere in India. The distinctive style that emerged from this rearticulation would have the effect of marking Kashmir as the universal center. It is a great pity that the archeological evidence is not good enough to show whether or not Lalitāditya's Pāñcarātra temples were full realizations of the Sarvatobhadra plan.[111]

Squaring the Kashmiri style with the universal style of northern India was not the only problem Lalitāditya and his Pāñcarātra preceptor had to confront in their drive to constitute a Pāñcarātra Vaiṣṇava kingship as the paramount kingship of India. Just as important was the problem of how to relate Theism (whether Pāñcarātra or Pāśupata) as the hegemonic way of life in India to Buddhism. As already noted, Vaiṣṇavas appropriated various Buddhist forms and combined them with their own to fashion new Vaiṣṇava forms. Although Buddhism was subhegemonic in seventh and eighth century Kashmir, it had exercised hegemony there, especially when Kashmir was a part of the Kuṣāṇa-Śātavāhana imperial formation of the first and second centuries A.D.. Next door, however, in the rival kingdom of the Śāhis and among the Turkish and Indo-Iranian rulers to the north and west of Kashmir, Buddhism continued to prevail over Theism.[112] Lalitāditya apparently

[111]Although Martand had a semi-portico (*ardhamaṇḍapa*) rather than four full porticos, it appears to have had a hipped roof, but the claim being made on its behalf was not the same as for the Pāñcarātra temples.

[112]Of Kapiśa, center of the Śāhi imperial kingdom before Turks took it, Xuanzang says: "The king is a Kṣatriya by caste. He is of a shrewd character (nature), and being brave and determined, he has brought into subjection the neighbouring countires, some ten of which he rules. He cherishes his people with affection, and reverences much the three precious objects of worship. Every year [periodically] he

met this challenge by making a Buddhist and a Turk, Cankuna, one of his major ministers and giving him permission to build a large stupa on a site at Parihāsapura, the new capital. Moreover, Kalhaṇa records the king himself as having built a royal monastery and stūpa at the same place. These structures were even larger than the Vaiṣṇava temples Lalitāditya built.

On first sight this would seem to contradict the notion of Theism as the hegemonic way of life of the imperial formation that Muktāpīḍa articulated; and, indeed, Buddhists could claim that their way of life was or remained hegemonic in that formation. A closer look, however, at Kalhaṇa and the *VDhP* tells us otherwise. In the first place, by the seventh and eighth centuries many of the Buddhist structures and images that kings had erected were gigantic.[113] It would hardly have done for Lalitāditya, as overlord of the earth, to support the erection of Buddhist structures that were smaller than those of his predecessors if he was to outshine them. Contemporary Vaiṣṇava and Śaiva temples were, however, smaller affairs. So Lalitāditya could outbuild his Vaiṣṇava and Śaiva rivals without resorting to gigantism. But then how would he manage to persuade people that Theism and not Buddhism was the hegemonic way of life of the world?

Kalhaṇa's text lets me argue that Lalitāditya adopted a two-pronged strategy. First, he used a distinction between quality and quantity to get around the problem of Buddhist gigantism. Lalitāditya, we are told, spent the same amount of money on each of the five structures that he himself built at Parihāsapura. He also spent equivalent amounts for the images erected in four of them, 84,000 measures of metal. The catch was that he did not use the same metal for those images. He caused the image of the Buddha to be made of copper, and had the three Vaiṣṇava images made of (or decked with) the more precious metals: Parihāsakeśava and Garuḍa of silver, Muktākeśava and Mahāvarāha of gold. As a result, the images in the lower shrines would have been larger than in the higher shrines, but consist of an inferior form of metal.[114]

We can detect a second strategy in the *VDhP*. The way in which that text represented the Buddhist "reliquary" monuments (*stūpa*) made it possible for Pāñcarātra Vaiṣṇavas of the time to see these monuments as Vaiṣṇava structures. The text devotes a chapter (III.84.1–15) to the design for erecting what it refers to as an *aiḍūka*. This is none other than a tall pagoda (or dagoba) corresponding in most details with at least one miniature stūpa represented in a Kashmiri bronze of the period.[115] After saying how the structure is to be constructed, it then tells what each of the elements signifies within a Theist cosmology. The round pole that sticks up through the top is Brahmā, the rounded part of the structure, which it calls a phallic sign (*liṅga*), is Śiva, and the base is Viṣṇu. Nowhere does the *VDhP* directly label the structure as

makes a silver figure of Buddha eighteen feet high and at the same time he convokes an assembly called the Mokṣa Mahāpariṣad where he gives alms to the poor and wretched, and relieves the bereaved." *Xiyouji* 1: 54–55.

[113]For example, the temple at Nālāndā and the image of the Buddha at Bāmiyān.

[114]We would also expect the larger Buddhist buildings to be less ornate and the smaller Vaiṣṇava ones more ornately and delicately carved.

[115]The so-called Rockefeller bronze sits beween two of these stūpas; Pratapaditya Pal, *Bronzes of Kashmir* (Graz: Akademische Druck und Verlagsanstalt, 1975) pp. 106–7, plates 30a, 30b.

Buddhist, but it clearly indicates this in two ways. First, it gives Buddhist names for the four guardians of the directions it places in the sides of the rounded structure, where people would expect to see images of the Buddha. Moreover, all of them are to be garbed like the Sun, that is, in the dress of Indo-Iranians and Turks, the major devotees (in Pāñcarātra Kashmiri eyes) of the Buddha, rather than of Kashmiris and other Āryas. This iconographic placement has the effect of making the Buddhas into guardian deities of Viṣṇu's world (returning a favor which Buddhists had long ago extended to Indra, Brahmā, and other Vedic deities). Second, the name it gives to the structure is a term that the *MBh* used to denote buildings that Śūdra kings would build at the end of the Age of Strife when the world was turned upside down.[116] People used the term *aiḍūka* (or *eḍūka*) itself to designate a wall or other structure that contained bones and other rubble. To call a stūpa a refined rubbish heap was hardly flattering, but also accurate if we remember that it was supposed to contain "relics" of the Buddha, and that a Theist temple would not incorporate any human remains.[117] So the *VDhP* accommodates the large and distinctively Buddhist stupas that any imperial ruler of its time would have had to build or to allow to be constructed.[118] The text provides it with a denigrating name while describing it in honorific terms as a building that should be built; it indicates that it is somehow foreign, yet shows how it can be homologized with and placed in a Theist cosmological framework.

To sum up: true knowing for people living in the world was, in the epistemology of the *VDhP*, a question of being able to recognize homologies, of being able to see the resemblances of one's present situation with those of the past. To do this, however, was not simply a matter of "imitating" the fixed knowledge of a remote, dead past. People lived in a world that was seen to be changing. True knowledge in an ultimate sense was permanent and eternal, but only Viṣṇu and those who had become permanently like him had this perfect knowledge. People, situated in a changing world could not have such knowledge. They had to "remember" (*smṛ*) knowledge of Viṣṇu, with his help in one of his sagely manifestations, in their own present circumstances. This was a gradual, ongoing process, one that a person could come even close to completing only after a long period of time encompassing several lives. It was also a changing process. Different persons in changed circumstances had to use differing modes of knowledge and perform different acts in order to attain to full participation in Vāsudeva Kṛṣṇa.

My own attempt to "determine" the human, historic composer and listener of the *VDhP* by showing homologies is "speculative," but then there is no way, given the process by which such a text came to be composed, that we could ever establish its authorship and provenance in such a way as to satisfy conventional

---

[116] III.188.64–66.

[117] The term pagoda, from the Portuguese *pagode* is apparently a "corruption" of the Sinhala term *dāgäba* (whence dagoba in English). This term is derived from the Pāli term *dhātugabbha* (Skt., *dhātugarbha*), "container of constituent ingredients (of the Buddha)."

[118] Pratapaditya Pal, "The *Aiḍūka* of the *Viṣṇudharmottarapurāṇa* and Certain Aspects of Stūpa Symbolism," *Journal of the Indian Society of Oriental Art.* New Series 4 (1971–72), 49–62, takes the most sensible approach to this interesting structure, and I largely follow his lead.

empiricist criteria. Nonetheless, this approach does allow us to reconstruct the actual practices of the Vaiṣṇavas of the period, something that the older authorist and contextualist approaches to the Purāṇas do not permit. We do not, however, simply see the practices of eighth-century Indians through the *VDhP*. Instead of treating the *VDhP* as a document, as a more or less accurate "sourçe," we look upon the practices of text making and text use as an integral part of this new cultural history.

Conclusion

The first person to have the *VDhP* recited by a bard in his king's court was undoubtedly a Pāñcarātra Brāhmaṇ who saw himself as a homologue of the great sage Mārkaṇḍeya; and his royal listener, the man who was supposed to carry out the orders of Viṣṇu revealed in the text, surely thought of himself as a homologue of Vajra, if not of Vāsudeva Kṛṣṇa himself. I have looked at the *VDhP* as a text both articulative of and articulated by a complex author. I have shown how that author, through a dialogical process, articulated not only itself but the intertexts of Indian traditions as a scale of texts from a Pāñcarātra perspective. Finally, I have shown how the text was both articulative of and articulated by its historical circumstances. Both the discursive focus and the narrative ordering of the contents of the text can be made sense of in detail by seeing them as a dialogical response to the political and soteriological situation that obtained in the seventh and eighth centuries, in Kashmir and, more widely, in India. The text was not, however, just a passive response to events. It was also an intervention. It called on an imperial court to articulate the kingdoms of India in an imperial formation that would appear as a manifestation of the Pāñcarātra representation of Viṣṇu. At the same time, it also called for the Bhāgavata Vaiṣṇavas (albeit without naming them as such), an order of householders that performed the Vedic liturgy but dedicated it to Viṣṇu, to accept the leadership of the Pāñcarātrins. Once an order of forest-dwellers who dedicated themselves exclusively to honoring images of Viṣṇu, some had descended to the plains to establish their liturgy in houses and temples, albeit without Vedic mantras and fires. The result of this double articulation was to be an imperial formation centered on Kashmir, one in which the Theism of the Pāñcarātrins and Pāśupatas, with its liturgy of images and temples displacing the older Vedic orders' sacrificialism, would be instituted as hegemonic. The textualized knowledge that had advocated the repositioning of these orders through the deployment of temple liturgies had been a new genre of texts, the Āgamas (in the wider sense). By suturing these texts to the older Vedic and Bhāgavata textual traditions in texts such as the *VDhP* and transforming themselves into temple liturgists, Theists in the eighth to tenth centuries made it possible for themselves and the imperial courts who followed this Theism to secure their hegemony over both the Vedic and Buddhist ways of life.

Kashmir's day in the sun lasted for perhaps twenty-five years. Kashmir continued to be an imperial kingdom, but under a new dynasty it opted for a Śaiva order as the preeminent form of Theism. As the Middle Region of India, however, it gave way to the Rāṣṭrakūṭas of the Deccan, who retained their paramountcy for some two centuries. Many later orders of Vaiṣṇavas claimed descent, directly or indirectly, from these Pācarātrins of Kashmir. At each turn, however, these orders reworked themselves in dialogue with other orders and with the polities of the imperial formation in which they were situated. The texts in which they inscribed their practices and represented their tradition also changed. It would seem, for example, that the imperial formation to which that of the Rāṣṭrakūṭas finally yielded, the Cōḻa, had relatively little use for Purāṇas such as the *VDhP*. Under the Cōḻas and their major rivals and allies, the Āgamas came into their own as the definitive supplements to the Veda over much of imperial India.

As a result of my treatment of the *VDhP* as a text, I have been able to create new historiographic possibilities. By using the *VDhP*, the *NP*, and Kalhaṇa's *River of Kings* to read each other, we are better able to reconstruct the practices the two Purāṇas recount and the historical poem presupposes. I have thus shown, through a detailed analysis of the *VDhP*, that, if we alter our notion of a text as monological (and the authorist and contextualist assumptions that notion carries with it), a very different view of the Purāṇas is possible. We can then see them as dialogical, as both articulative of and articulated by the realities in which they are situated. We can see a Purāṇa as the claims of a complex and shifting author and reader to rework Indian textual traditions, supplementing them and transforming them into a scale of texts from the point of view of one or the other of India's soteriological or disciplinary orders, the so-called sects.

Appendix: Authorism and Contextualism, Empiricism and Idealism in the Study of Purāṇas

Trained to believe that the essences of different genres can become blurred and overlaid in the course of time, philologists have attempted, since the time of H. H. Wilson, to cure these "perversions" through the comparison and editing of manuscripts. This enterprise has been dominated by an incoherent mixture of contextualism and authorism inflected by empiricist (or positivist) and idealist assumptions. Assuming that there was indeed an original Purāṇa, embodied in an ur-text that conformed to the norms of the genre, philologists have beavered away.[119] They have inventoried the Purāṇas, scoured other texts for references to them,

[119]H. H. Wilson, whose annotated translation of the *Viṣṇupurāṇa*, published in 1840, continues to be read today, criticized the earlier investigations into the "mythology and traditions" of the Hindus from the empiricist standpoint of a nineteenth-century philologist. His predecessors were erroneous because they had not adhered to the methods of "inductive philosophy" which, said Wilson, "draws its conclusions from the careful observation and accumulation of facts"; *The Viṣṇu Purāṇa: A System of Hindu Mythology and Tradition, Translated from the Original Sanskrit and Illustrated by Notes Derived Chiefly from Other Purāṇas*, translated by H. H. Wilson, introduced by R. C. Hazra (Calcutta: Punthi Pustak, 1972), pp. lxx, lxxi. Wilson hoped that his translation of the *Viṣṇupurāṇa*, which he thought conformed most fully to the generic definition of a Purāṇa, would help to inaugurate a "sound and comprehensive survey of the Hindu system."

and prepared "critical" editions and translations of them.[120] The most recent of the attempts to survey Purāṇic texts and the scholarship on them is the excellent monograph of Ludo Rocher.[121]

Contextualist and empiricist Indologists' treatment of the *VDhP* does not differ from these more general treatments of the Purāṇās. One has attempted a critical edition of the chapters assumed to contain one essence of the text, the rules of kingship;[122] another has attempted a more extensive edition of that other essence of the *VDhP*, information on iconography and architecture.[123] Still others

---

[120]Maurice Winternitz, *A History of Indian Literature*, translated by S. Ketkar (Calcutta: University of Calcutta) 1 (1927), 517–86; Hazra, "The Purāṇas," 240–70 and Hazra, "The Upapurāṇas,"in *The Cultural Heritage of India* ([1937] Calcutta: The Ramakrishna Mission Institute of Culture, 1958–86) 2 (1962), 271–86. Wilson based his own translation of the *Viṣṇupurāṇa* on his critical reading of seven manuscripts of that text: *Viṣṇupurāṇa*, p. lxxi. A German philologist, Willibald Kirfel, extended this project when he published his critical edition of the chapters from the printed texts of some dozen Purāṇas in 1927. His object was to discover the extent to which there was an original text corresponding to the generic essence of a Purāṇa. He concluded that there most probably was no ur-text, at least not one that is presently recoverable: *Das Purāṇa Pañcalakṣaṇa, Versuch einer Textgeschichte* (Bonn: Kurt Schroeder/Verlag, 1927), p. xlviii. Haraprasad Shastri raised serious doubts about this generic essentialism, but to little avail; "The Maha-Puranas," *Journal of the Bihar and Orissa Research Society* 14 (1928), 323–40.

The same year that Kirfel published his study also saw the publication of the first fascicle of the critical edition of the *Mahābhārata* (*MBh*), edited by Vishnu S. Sukthankar et al. (Poona: Bhandarkar Oriental Research Institute, 1927–59) in 19 volumes. Philological scholarship on the Purāṇas has, since Independence, taken its cue from that effort. A Purāṇa Committee was established by the All India Kashiraj Trust at Varanasi in 1959; Suniti Kumar Chatterji, "The Purāṇas: Projected Critical Editions by the Kasiraja Trust of Varanasi," *Purāṇa* 1.1 (July 1959), 12–15; Anand Swarup Gupta, "A Brief Account of the Works of the Purāṇa-Department of the All India Kasiraja Trust," *Purāṇa* 1.1 (July 1959), 16–20. The Trust began the publication in that same year of a journal, *Purāṇa*, and to date has published, under Gupta, critical editions along with English translations of three *Purāṇas—Vāmana* (1967 and 1968), *Kūrma* (1971 and 1972), and *Varāha* (1981), with the *Matsya* to follow soon. It purports to follow roughly the principles laid down by Sukthankar in his "Prolegomena" for the *MBh* 1: i–civ. He took a manuscript in the Śāradā script from Kashmir as the "norm" because "it contains relatively little matter that is not found, at the same time, *in all other versions of both recensions*" (p. xlvii, emphasis his). The oldest dated manuscript (A.D. 1511) was in Nepali (p. lix). The Devanāgarī manuscripts are based on the southern, eastern, or northern traditions (p. lxii). That is, there is no text preserved from the so-called Aryan heartland (Haryana, Uttar Pradesh, and Bihar).

[121]Ludo Rocher, "The Purāṇas," in *Epics and Sanskrit Religious Literature*, vol. 2.3 of *A History of Indian Literature*, edited by Jan Gonda (Wiesbaden: O. Harrassowitz, 1986), 3. Also worthy of mention is the detailed and helpful *Epic and Purāṇic Bibliography (up to 1985) annotated and with indexes*, compiled under the direction of Heinrich von Stietencron (Wiesbaden: O. Harrassowitz, 1992), part 1 (A–R); part 2 (S–Z, Indexes).

[122]A pupil of Kirfel, Hans Losch, in *Rajadharma: Einsetzung und Aufgabenkreis des Königs im Lichte des Purāṇa's* (Bonn: Universität Bonn, 1959), has edited 21 chapters of part 2, collating them with similar or identical passages in the *Matsya* and *Agni* Purāṇas and using those passages that appear in later digests to provide alternate readings. Although a useful compilation, this effort does not yield a common, prior text. The *Matsya* includes many of the chapters on statecraft contained in the *VDhP*, but does not contain those on the royal liturgy that the latter text includes. The compilers of the *Agni* employ a different principle: they include abridged versions of both kinds of chapters. My own view is that the text of the *VDhP*, longer than both the others (instead of shorter, as a proper ur-text ought to be), is the earliest of the three.

[123]Priyabala Shah has produced a critical edition of these chapters, III.1–118, in *Viṣṇudharmottara: Third Khaṇḍa* (Baroda: Oriental Institute, 1958). There is a separate edition of the *Citrāsūtra*, III.35–43, edited by Asoke Chatterjee (Varanasi: Varanaseya Sanskrit Vishvavidyalaya, 1971), and the earlier

have analyzed the contents of the text in order to place it in time and space. The more modest efforts from this empiricist angle have reached the following conclusion. Most of the manuscripts collected are from Kashmir and in the Śāradā script of that region, or are based on a Kashmir manuscript.[124] The text itself, moreover, exhibits a greater familiarity with the rivers and pilgrimage places (*tīrthas*) of Kashmir and of the adjacent Panjab region.[125] The *VDhP* incorporates verses from the *Bṛhatsaṃhitā* of Varāhamihira, who wrote in Malwa in the sixth century.[126] Abu Riḥān Alberūnī, the Arab savant who stayed in India (A.D. 1017–30) appears to have had a manuscript of the text in his possession and includes numerous excerpts from it in his *Kitāb-u'l-Hind*.[127] The *VDhP* is, thus a text composed in Kashmir or the adjacent Panjab sometime between A.D. 600 and 1000.

Although no ur-text true to the Purāṇic genre has emerged from these labors, some of the scholarship that has resulted is certainly useful. Rocher is, therefore, correct in the rather skeptical position that he takes with respect to the methods of text criticism.[128] We can infer from his doubts that authorism and empiricism might prepare a scholar to make sense of his own textual tradition, where to a certain extent this metaphysics has been made to come true, but it has not served him well in the Indian case, especially when dealing with the Purāṇas and Epics. Insofar as one remains committed, whether implicitly or explicitly, to this notion of

---

translation by Stella Kramrisch, *The Viṣṇudharmottara (part 3): A Treatise on Indian Painting and Image-Making* (Calcutta: University of Calcutta, 1928).

[124]Hazra, *Studies in the Upapuranas*, 1: 155–57, and Shah's introduction to her edition, *Viṣṇudharmottara: Third Khaṇḍa*, 1: xv–xviii. The only "complete" printed version of the text is the one edited by Madhusūdana and Mādhavaprasāda Śarmā and printed at the Śrīveṅkaṭeśvara Steam Press at Bombay in 1912. Like other Sanskrit works printed there, it takes the form of an ancient manuscript with elongated pages. Reprinted with a preface (*bhūmikā*) consisting of a summary of the contents in Sanskrit, by Cārudeva Śāstrī, and a second volume, an alphabetical index of verses by Nag Sharan Singh (Delhi: Nag Publishers, 1985).

[125]Hazra, *Studies*, 1: 214–16. Although Hazra is correct about the prominence given to places in the Panjab, he is on less firm ground regarding Kashmir. There is only one story about a site in Kashmir itself. But at I.139.9–16, in connection with reverential offerings to the forefathers (*śrāddha*), the *VDhP* states that Nṛvarāha, after rescuing the Earth at the beginning of a cosmic formation, becomes a stone image at Vārāhaparvata (Baramula in Kashmir), and gives the rule for offering balls of rice (*piṇḍas*) there.

[126]Kane, *HD*, 5 (1962–74), 876–78, 910, who thus disposes of attempts to place the text in the "classical" Gupta period. Hazra had placed the text between A.D. 400 and 500, claiming that it did not refer to or utilize the works of Varāhamihira: *Studies*, 1: 205–12. P. Shah placed it between 450 and 650, *Viṣṇudharmottara: Third Khaṇḍa*, 1: xxvi. Much earlier, Georg Bühler, in his review of *Alberuni's India*, had opted for A.D. 500 as the latest date for the composition of the *VDhP* on the grounds that Brahmagupta, who completed his astronomical work, *Brahmasphuṭasiddhānta*, at Bhinmal, Rajasthan, in A.D. 628, is said by later commentators to have based it on the Paitāmahasiddhānta, a text that he found in the *VDhP*; *Indian Antiquary* 19 (1890), 408. But the only inference that can safely be drawn from this statement is that by the time of these commentators, an independent text of the *Paitāmahasiddhānta* no longer existed. For the date of Varāhamihira, see R. C. Majumdar, "Astronomy," in *HCIP*, 3 (1954), 323.

[127]Bühler's review of Edward C. Sachau's English translation of *Alberuni's India: An Account of the Religion, Philosophy, Literature, Geography, Chronology, Astronomy, Customs, Laws and Astrology of India, about A.D. 1030* (London: Trübner, 1888) in 2 volumes; *Indian Antiquary* 19 (1890), 381–410.

[128]Note also the controversy that Madeleine Biardeau started regarding the value of "critical editions": "Some More Considerations about Textual Criticism," *Purāṇa* 10.2 (July 1968), 115–23; A. S. Gupta, "A Problem of Puranic Text-Reconstruction," *Purāṇa* 12.2 (July 1970), 304–21, replies.

author and text, one will continue to confront insurmountable obstacles in coming to grips with texts that have been rewritten several times over.

Some Indologists, confronted with the persistent failure to come up with discretely authored texts, have lapsed into philological formalism, content to display their methods for the dissection of dead texts. Others, however, were tempted by other forms of contextualism. Many, for example, believed that the Epics and Purāṇas were originally the expressions of a warrior class, the Kṣatriyas, when India was, presumably, in a "heroic" or "barbaric" stage of development that ended with the great war of the *MBh.* Later, a class of priests appropriated these texts, vastly distorting and overlaying the historic, bardic kernel of the text with religious and mythological material. The whole point of textual criticism here has been to recover this heroic order in its pristine historic representation.[129]

Efforts to reconstruct the political chronology of an "ancient" India after the great war, using the Epics and Purāṇās as "sources" are similar. And social historians have attempted to discern what was going on in Indian society.[130] The Protestant or secularist outlook regarding the generic authors of the Purāṇas, the Brāhmaṇs, is a psychological reductionism of the utilitarian variety: they made additions to the Purāṇas with an eye on their own household budgets, foisting innumerable superstitious practices, virtually all of which brought economic benefit to themselves, onto a credulous populace. Not surprisingly, the empiricists have tended to see the Hinduism of the Purāṇas as symptomatic of India's decline from a more heroic or secular condition to one of increasing religion and superstition, especially after the "classical age" of the Guptas and the onset of the "middle ages." Needless to say, few empiricists have been prepared to take these texts seriously as expounding different ways of life.

The result of strict adherence to the authorist and empiricist approach to the Purāṇas has, of course, almost invariably entailed the atomization of the texts as transmitted in manuscript form. Subjected to the withering gaze of the philologist, the Purāṇic corpus disintegrates. Some scholars have objected to this approach from the perspective of a philosophical idealism that can be traced to the romantic, mostly German, response to the rise of a cosmology of science. Responding to the scholars who want to disintegrate a Purāṇa and date its separate parts, Vasudeva Sharana Agrawala says:

> But the problem of the Purāṇa literature is not in the hands of chronology, for it should be clearly understood that in almost all the Purāṇas the process

[129] F. E. Pargiter, *Ancient Indian Historical Tradition* ([1922] Delhi: Motilal Banarsidass, 1972). U. N. Ghoshal summarizes the attempts to reconstruct political history before the Bharata battle out of the Purāṇic genealogies in *Studies in Indian History and Culture* (Bombay: Orient Longmans, 1965), pp. 37–48.

[130] The most important work done under this heading is probably that of Rajendra Chandra Hazra. His doctoral dissertation, completed in 1936 and published in 1940, remains the most ambitious and detailed attempt to write a history of Hinduism out of the Purāṇas. Like those before and after him, Hazra held that the critical analysis of the Purāṇas was necessary if scholars were to be able to use them as sources for religious and social history; see "The Purāṇas," in *The Cultural Heritage of India* 2 (1962), 266; and his *Studies in the Puranic Records on Hindu Rites and Customs* (Dacca: University of Dacca, Bulletin no. 20, 1940).

> of *Upabriṃhaṇa* [or augmenting] was operative from the very beginning and upto later times. It is pejorative to speak of it as interpolation. It is legitimate to understand *Upabriṃhaṇa* as a sacred obligation of authorship to keep the text up to date by revising its contents as often as necessary—an approved method applicable to our Encyclopaedias in modern times. The hand of editing or redacting is visible in all the Purāṇas. It should therefore be accepted that the existing Puranic texts have gained in size and scope by the deliberate technique of *Upabriṃhaṇa.*[131]

This view, which appears to be grounded in an Indian cultural distinction, seems on first sight to be a definite improvement on the empiricist idea of authorship. Rocher, himself an empiricist, emphasizes the importance of the Purāṇas as "oral" texts, pointing to the role of the bard (*sūta*, the later *bhāṭ*) and, like Agrawala, questions the validity of attempts to treat them as closed texts attributable to historically locatable authors. Yet Agrawala's view is not without difficulties, for he and those who concur do not provide an explanation from within any Indian metaphysics of the "sacred obligation" to augment the Purāṇas. On the contrary, his comparison with modern encyclopedias suggests that ancient Indians had a theory of knowledge that was progressing, like modern science, toward the truth. Elsewhere, Agrawala implies just the opposite, that the varying Purāṇas express the unchanging metaphysical truths of the Vedas.[132] Rocher's invocation of an oral tradition does not really solve anything, either; it simply defers the difficulties encountered in coming to terms with texts that existed in *both* oral and written forms to the problem of understanding the formation and use of oral texts. He also seems momentarily to have forgotten that some of the most important texts in ancient India were transmitted orally.[133]

As we might expect, idealists have been prepared to see the Purāṇas as religious texts, and many studies interpreting their religious contents have appeared. At last, perhaps, we are on the right track.[134] Unfortunately, however, the idealists are just as essentialist and antihistorical as the empiricists. The difference is that the essence that the idealists presuppose, religious rather than linguistic, is a classical Brahmanism or Hinduism expressed by the religious leader or philosopher. That religion consists of the sacrificial "cult" of the Brāhmaṇas and "pantheist mysticism" of the Upaniṣads. Its highest, most authentic flowering was that of

[131] Agrawala, *Matsya Purāṇa—A Study* (Ramnagar, Varanasi: All India Kashiraj Trust, 1963), pp. iii–iv.

[132] Agrawala, "Editorial," *Purāṇa* 1.2 (1960), 118–19.

[133] This deferral runs into problems when, for example, Stuart H. Blackburn reports that for the bow tradition of singers among the low-caste Nadars, "palm-leaf manuscripts are considered the most authentic form of a story"; *Singing of Birth and Death: Texts in Performance* (Philadelphia: University of Pennsylvania Press, 1988), p. 28. Frits Staal would seem to oppose Rocher's link of orality with instability in a tradition in his argument about the precise oral transmission of the Veda: *The Fidelity of Oral Tradition and the Origins of Science* Mededelingen der Koninklijke Nederlandse Akademie von Wetenschappen, Afd. Letterkunde, 49.8 (Amsterdam: North Holland Publishing Company, 1986), pp. 23–29; Staal goes too far, though, in implying that orality was the essence of Indian high tradition. David Pingree criticizes him in a review for downgrading the importance of writing and manuscripts in Indian traditions, reminding us that more manuscipts have been recovered from India than from any other comparable area; *Journal of the American Oriental Society* 108.4 (1988), 637–78.

[134] Most notable here are the monographs of V. S. Agrawala, *Matsya Purāṇa—A Study* and *Vāmana Purāṇa, a Study* (Varanasi: Prithivi Prakashan, 1964).

Smārta or "traditional" Brahmanism, as interpreted in Mīmāṃsā ("exegesis" of the sacrificial texts), and especially in the Advaita ("non-dualist") Vedānta of the philosopher Śaṃkara, the creative genius held up here. Consistent with this assumption, the idealist strain of scholarship considers the "religious" rather than the "historical" portions of the Purāṇas as their essence, and the scholars who have taken this approach have tended to be historians of religion first and philologists second.

The idealist stance, like the estheticist tendency of authorism, sees the Purāṇas as texts that are expressive of mind—not of the individual geniuses of their authors but of the spiritual genius of the Hindu mind. Idealists consider the Hinduism of the Purāṇas as the historical outcome of the progressive (or, perhaps, degenerative) "influence" of an elite, Aryan, pantheist, and spiritualist religion on a folk, popular, or mass religion that is non-Aryan, polytheistic, and materialist. They suture the "sectarian" religions of Vaiṣṇavism and Śaivism to the elite Brāhmaṇic subject of classical Hinduism by treating their devotionalism as lower, popularized forms of the ideal, unitary religious essence of India. The Purāṇas are texts that are both indexical of that influence and, at the same time, the instruments of it. Or, couched in more relational terms, the Purāṇas are expressions of a great religious tradition that has clothed its abstract, elite philosophy in mythological and symbolic language so that everyone, even Śūdras and women, can understand it. As for the authors, the idealists tend to see the Brāhmaṇs who composed and transmitted the Purāṇas and the bards who recited them not as self-seeking, but as the imperfect instruments of their transcendent religion. That religion itself is the true, unchanging and unitary Author of these texts. The result of this approach is to elide over differences because, it is assumed, they are inherently divisive. They are to be tolerated only if some underlying (and inevitably banal) unity can be teased out of them. Since, in my estimate, the problematic of most of the Purāṇas is that of differences among disciplinary orders, study of the contents of these texts remains perennially postponed.[135]

Roland Barthes, the French structuralist, distinguishes "works" from "texts." A "work," briefly, is the closed expression of a particular "author." A "text," by contrast, is open and "authorless." The reader is the one who determines its meaning, and since there are many readers there are many significations.[136] It would seem that the Purāṇas are nearly perfect exemplifications of the Barthean text. That being the case, the direction scholarship on such texts would want to take is to look at the way in which different Indian users of the Purāṇas, situated in different circumstances, have understood these texts. Alas, this has not been the direction of more recent scholarship. Rocher's criticisms of previous and ongoing efforts to edit and analyze the Purāṇas are, in my view, largely correct. One cannot, however, agree with the major reason for his criticisms and with the "consequences" he thinks

[135] Studies attempting uncritically to combine both empiricist and idealist approaches in a formulaic way abound; see for example Siddheswar Jena, *The Narasiṃha Purāṇam: A Study*, "Foreword," by H. V. Stietencron (Delhi: Nag Publishers, 1987), the first in a Purāṇa Vidyā Series.

[136] Barthes, "From Work to Text," in *Textual Strategies: Perspectives in Post-structuralist Criticism*, edited by J. V. Harari (Ithaca: Cornell University Press, 1979), pp. 73–81.

should follow for future research. His argument that the Purāṇas are essentially oral texts and that the manuscript versions of these texts are "accidental" compilations leads him to conclude that we should abandon dealing with the written Purāṇas as whole works, for no such things exist or ever have existed. What we should do instead is to take up the study of what Rocher refers to as mini-Purāṇas, the stories, legends, and other parts of the written Purāṇas, because these are more "basic" than the "conglomerations" in which they have been transmitted.[137] He argues that the comparison of these smaller texts will not lead us back to their originals, but will give us "at least some idea of the vast richness with which certain themes have been treated." He shows that some scholars have already, in effect, done this. The difficulty that I have with this is that it brings us full circle; was it not the very richness of these texts that we were trying to account for and reduce in the first place?

Certainly Rocher's point about mini-Purāṇas is not without basis. Many present-day Hindus probably do know the Purāṇas in the form of extracts rather than as integrated wholes. Indian religious practices have not escaped the process of commodification and the atomization of knowledge accompanying it that has occurred in India over the last two centuries. There are also good reasons to believe that people in India have always made use of extracts and condensations in a range of circumstances. There is no reason, however, why we should assume that oral texts must necessarily be fragmentary. More importantly, it does not follow that using extracts from the Purāṇas precludes the use of the written Purāṇas as wholes.[138] Finally, the impression that this approach leaves—that popular, orally transmitted knowledge is presumed to be an almost pointless flux of stories and that Purāṇic texts, in Sanskrit, virtually nobody's mother tongue, are arbitrary, unconscious accumulations—brings us back to the orientalist notion of an Indian mind unable to escape from its dreamlike imagination.[139] We are also close to the postmodernist's infinite play of signifiers or the "magical realism" that supposedly characterizes (Third) World literature.

The predominant use that Western scholars have made of the Epics and Purāṇas in recent decades rests squarely on the orientalist idea of a prerational Indian mind. Sidestepping the problems both of philology and of looking at Purāṇas

[137]Rocher, "Purāṇas," p. 98.

[138]Paul Hacker has tried to combine, in a thoughtful way, both empiricist and "history of ideas" approaches in "Zur Methode der geschichtlichen Erforschung der anonymen Sanskritliteratur des Hinduismus" [1961] in his *Kleine Schriften*, edited by Lambert Schmithausen (Wiesbaden: Steiner, 1978), pp. 8–17, and "Purāṇen und Geschichte des Hinduismus: methodologische, programmatische und geistesgeschichtliche Bemerkungen" [1957] in his *Kleine Schriften*, pp. 1–7. Carrying on Kirfel's project in "The Sānkhyization of the Emanation Doctrine Shown in a Critical Analysis of Texts," in *Kleine Schriften*, pp. 167–204, he argues that the core of the *Mārkaṇḍeya* is the oldest of the Purāṇa texts (c. A.D. 300), followed by the *Vāyu* and *Brahmāṇḍa* nucleus (c. A.D. 335), that of the *Padma*, then the *Viṣṇu* (c. A.D. 500), and, finally, the *Kūrma* (7–8th century). In at least one respect, his willingness to take seriously the later parts of these texts as intellectual projects, Hacker anticipates what I urge in this essay—looking at a text as a scale of forms.

[139]R. Inden, *Imagining India*, chapters 1 and 2.

as textual wholes, Indianists have produced numerous studies of selected parts of them—for example, of cycles of "myths" about a god or goddess or some other topic—that are psychoanalytic, cultural, or structuralist in approach.[140]

[140]The book by the Jungian scholar Heinrich Zimmer, *Myths and Symbols in Indian Art and Civilization*, edited by his student Joseph Campbell (New York: Pantheon, 1946), whose own *The Masks of God: Oriental Mythology* ([1962] London: Penguin, 1976) carries on this tradition, can be taken as one of the founders of this selective approach. Alf Hiltebeitel, *The Cult of Draupadī* (Chicago: University of Chicago Press, 1988–91) and Madeleine Biardeau, "Études de mythologie hindoue," *Bulletin de l'École Française d'Extrême-Orient* 54 (1968), 19–45, 55 (1969), 97–105, 58 (1971), 17–83 published under the same title (Paris: Maisonneuve, 1982); 63 (1976), 111–263, 65 (1978), 87–237, partly follow Georges Dumézil. Wendy Doniger, *Asceticism and Eroticism in the Mythology of Śiva* (London: Oxford University Press, 1973), partly follows Claude Lévi-Strauss. For criticisms, see R. Inden, *Imagining India*, pp. 122–27.

3

Buddhist History

The Sri Lankan Pāli Vaṃsas and Their Commentary

Jonathan S. Walters

> In the time of King Dāṭhopatissa the Younger there was a monk named Dāṭhāvedhaka living in the Kurundacullaka cloister (*pariveṇa*) in the Jetavana monastery, and another monk named Dāṭhāvedhaka living in the Kolambahālaka cloister in that very place. These two were rogues, with the thoughts of rogues; exalting themselves and hating others, having wrong beliefs that differ from those of the exalted disciplinary order, they had given up looking on the next world with fear.... Defecting from the grammar and the text of the facts, they wrote down and stored these words which illustrate false meaning: "The residents of the Mahāvihāra came into being on their own"—these and other words different from the [true] teaching. Therefore all of that should be taken as falsehood. (*Vaṃsatthapakāsinī* I.176)

Revising Histories

For more than a century scholars have relied upon the Pāli Vaṃsas—*Dīpavaṃsa* (*Dpv*), the "Chronicle of the Island" (early fourth century), *Mahāvaṃsa* (*Mhv*), the "Great Chronicle" (a fifth-century revision of *Dīpavaṃsa*), and *Vaṃsatthappakāsinī* (*VAP*), the "early medieval" commentary on *Mahāvaṃsa*—as "primary sources." From them they have gleaned countless "historical facts" now to be found in the histories of ancient India and Sri Lanka. I wish to challenge this "common-sense" understanding of history in the Pāli Vaṃsas. The idea that the facts of the past recorded in the Vaṃsas constitute "history" is a relatively recent idea, forged by George Turnour during the late 1830s. Revised and expanded by philologists such as Wilhelm Geiger, but never dismissed, this idea continues to frame scholarly study of the Vaṃsas. I present the history of this idea, the situation in which it was produced, the thoughts of the human agents who produced it, and its subsequent appropriation and development, in the appendix to this chapter. Here I suggest that "history"—thought about the past in the then-present—proceeded in precolonial Sri Lanka within an episteme (to borrow M. Foucault's useful term) consisting of a temporal scheme and anthropology quite foreign to modern sensibilities, one that leads me to consider the Vaṃsas as "successions" of the Buddha's presence rather than as mere "chronicles" of events.

The notion of an episteme is itself problematic, however; ideas change over time. If we want to think of the Vaṃsa authors as historians, then it is not enough to discuss abstractly the rules, presuppositions, and canons for authenticity; for these historians themselves were simultaneously articulating those rules in new and creative ways. This is particularly the case with respect to the "commentary" on the histories themselves. Rather than a simple clarification of the earlier texts, it is a supplement that makes major revisions of them. As my main contribution, therefore, I examine the circumstances articulative of each Vaṃsa, and the world that users of each Vaṃsa attempted to realize in accord with the text's life-wish. Intertextual evidence—descriptions of the composition of each Vaṃsa in the earliest part of the later *Cūlavaṃsa*, the "Little Chronicle" (narrating history from the beginning of the fourth to the end of the twelfth centuries), plus contemporary epigraphic, archeological, and textual evidence—will allow us better to see the ways in which these Vaṃsas reflected and reacted to the circumstances that produced them, as well as the ways in which they participated in and changed those very circumstances.

Buddhist monks and nuns of two disciplinary orders residing at two institutions outside the walls of the old capital, Anurādhapura, the Mahāvihāra, (the "great monastery") and Abhayagirivihāra (the "monastery [built on the hermitage of the Jain monk] Giri [by king] Abhaya") had differing world wishes. Those who succeeded in convincing royal courts of the rightness of their view were able to gain hegemony for their representation of Sri Lanka's past. It is their histories that appear in the Vaṃsas. Scholars have, I argue, accepted these partisan rearticulations of a past, "corrected" for its minor chronological deficiencies and shorn of its "supernatural" elements, as an account accurately reflecting events that happened. If we attend to the debates embedded in this history, if we see the text as dialogical, it is possible to tell a more interesting history, one that sees people in Sri Lanka as making their polity and way of life rather than as the passive guardians of a pure, early Buddhism.

I conclude with two points. First, I elaborate upon my critique of recent trends in the historical study of Vaṃsa "ideology" produced by readings of the Vaṃsas as a monological text. Second, I discuss some more general implications for the reconstruction of Buddhist history made possible by reading pan-Buddhist texts as dialogical.

Buddha's Presence in the Calculable and Incalculable Past

Historians in Western-style universities throughout the world share assumptions about the nature of time (it is linear, progressive, divided into "historic" and "prehistoric," and so on.) and connectedness (which is limited to empirical causality). It takes a bit of effort for us to conceive of "history" as being anything different. But we need only think of traditional Christian historians—for whom time was constituted by an omnipresent eternity, and who predicated connectedness in history upon God as cosmic agent—in order to see that the modern view is one among many. Most modern historians claim to have rejected the old Christian framework and proceeded with their studies according to their own theoretical principles. Historians of history cannot, however, limit their understanding of historical thought to the study of pagan and Christian prefigurings of the modern European and reject out of hand as "theocratic" or "mythic" all other histories.[1]

Scholars who have treated the Vaṃsas as history have ignored the indications that they were written within (and should be understood within) a temporal and causal framework different from that which we know in the modern West. If we are to understand the Vaṃsas as history (that is, if we are to reconstruct the manner in which their Sri Lankan authors thought about their own past) we must understand the temporal and causal framework upon which they are based.

The earliest Pāli Vaṃsa extant is not one of the famous Sri Lankan Vaṃsas. It is the *Buddhavaṃsa* (*BV*, "Successive Lives of the Buddhas"), written in India during the second or first century B.C.[2] It is not only the oldest Pāli "history," it also constitutes the actual beginning of the *Mhv*, *Dpv*, and *VAP* (the latter, in fact, quotes extensively from the *BV* and its commentaries). The Vaṃsas under discussion present themselves as continuations of or successors to the *BV*; they took *BV* as their epistemological and ontological foundation, thus paralleling the process by which royal eulogies present themselves as continuations of the Theist Purāṇas, providing Buddhist versions of the "successive lives" of the gods. So the inquiry must begin where the Vaṃsas themselves begin: with an explication of their philosophical foundation.

The *BV* is in one sense a biography of Gotama Buddha. It details the process of his self-perfection, during which he became Buddha and set forth the monastic "disciplinary rules" (*vinaya*) and "teachings" (*dhamma*) for the enlightenment of his followers. But the *BV* is also a "biography" of other Buddhas (*bodhisatta/bodhisattva*).[3] Twenty-four of these preceded Gotama Buddha in time, six of whom lived in the present world age (*kappa/kalpa*), a notion dialectically related to the Theist idea of cosmic formations. The remainder lived before this world—before time—began. The biographies of these previous Buddhas all parallel the "this-life" biography of Gotama precisely; they differ only in detail. Accordingly, each of the prince Buddhas was enlightened under a different kind of tree, which in turn was venerated by his adherents. In like manner, for each Buddha the text provides the name of the prince, his parents, his wife, his only son, the length of his ascetic withdrawal, the names of his chief disciples, the name of his chief attendant, and so forth. Gotama, the Buddha (480/430–400/350 B.C.), prince Siddhattha, son of Suddhodana and Māyā, married to Yasodharā, with whom he fathered Rāhula before withdrawing into asceticism for six years after which enlightenment (*bodhi*) was attained beneath a fig tree (*assatha/aśvattha*), and so on, is merely the most recent example of a type.

---

[1]This is unfortunately what R. G. Collingwood does in *The Idea of History* ([1946] Oxford: Clarendon, 1956, p. 14.

[2]Jonathan Walters, "Stupa, Story, and Empire: Constructions of the Buddha Biography in Early Post-Aśokan India," *Sacred Biography in the Buddhist Traditions of South and South-east Asia*, edited by Juliane Schober (Honolulu: University of Hawaii Press, 1997), 160–92.

[3]The second term given here and below is the Sanskrit.

Table 3.1. Vaṃsas and Theravāda "Canon" of Mahāvihāra as a Scale of Texts

Post-Cōḷa (12th Century)		
	Cūlavaṃsa	
Mahinda IV (956–72)		
	Vaṃsatthapakāsinī	
Dhātusena (455–73)		
	Mahāvaṃsa	
Mahānāma (406–28)		
Buddhaghosa's Commentaries: Samantapāsādikā, etc.		
Siri Meghavaṇṇa (301–28)		
	Dīpavamsa	
Vaṭṭagāmaṇi (89–77 B.C.)—Writing of the Mahāvihāra Canon		
TIPIṬAKA (Three Baskets):		
I.VINAYA	II.SUTTA/DHAMMA	III.ABHIDHAMMA
(Disciplinary Rules)	(Teachings)	(Metaphysics)
3.Parivārapāṭha	Khuddakapāṭha	
	Sīhalaṭṭhakathā-	
	Mahāvaṃsa	
Aśoka (c. 268–39 B.C.) and Post-Aśokan—Vibhajja- and Sarvāstivādin Split		
	Buddhavaṃsa	7. Paṭṭhāna
	Apadāna	6. Yamaka
	Jātaka	5. **Kathāvatthu**
	Petavatthu	4. Puggalapaññatti
	Vimāṇavatthu	3. Dhātukathā
		2. Vibhaṅga
	5. Khuddakanikāya (15)	1. **Dhammasaṅgaṇi**
Buddha (480/430–400/350 B.C.) and Post-Buddha—Fixing/s of Canon in Memory and Speech		
	4. Aṅguttaranikāya	
	3. Saṃyuttanikāya	
	2. Majjhimanikāya	
2. Khandhakā	1. Dīghanikāya	
1. Suttavibhaṅga		

The *BV* rests upon a two-dimensional conception of time. According to the one, a notion of "calculable" (*sankheyya*) time and causation that resembles modern notions, Buddhas lived, founded Disciplines, and died during certain time and in certain places; their succession connects the past to the present. But the *BV* also charts out another unfathomable (*acintiya*) dimension of time-place that cannot be conceived in terms of calculable time and causal connection alone. Accounts of previous world ages involve discussions of kings who lived before the first king was crowned, and places that existed before the world was created: a time-place that no map can chart. The incorporation of these pre-primordial periods into history depends upon a conception of "incalculable" (*asaṅkheyya*) time that overlaps with the calculable. Gotama Buddha as Bodhisatta meets (in the *BV*) all the previous Buddhas. He works at his self-perfection in their presence, then moves on to the next life. Though conceived on a greater scale than post-Enlightenment thinkers can countenance, this still constitutes a diachronic biography of the Buddha. But as a Buddha he also participates in a reiteration of infinitely existing practices. Buddhahood existed long before Gotama the Buddha; the duration of his life is calculable within this world age and even in the time-before-time, but the duration of Buddhahood itself is incalculable (the *BV*'s narrative of it begins "100,000 world ages and four incalculables" ago). History, for authors in the tradition that began with *BV*, includes both the calculable and incalculable dimensions of time. This is why "succession" of the Buddha's presence translates Vaṃsa better than "chronicle" of events; unlike chronicles, Vaṃsas assume that the incalculable overlaps with and informs the calculable.

The connectedness of the present to this incalculable past cannot be explained so simply as genealogy or chronology allow in the calculable dimension of history. One can trace neither a dynasty back to a king who reigned before the first king in the world nor a monastic lineage back to Buddhist monks who lived before the Buddha first preached his teachings. The connectedness is, instead, meritorious (or deleterious) action and its consequences (*kamma*/*karman*). Although the present king's lineage cannot predate the first king, the effects of deeds that he did (*kamma*) even during times-before-time are still ripening in him at the present moment. Similarly, someone born during a Buddha era (like the present era), especially someone who joins the monastic community, is surely experiencing the good consequence of having glanced at a Buddha in some forgotten previous Buddha era.

The *BV* is one of several related texts, probably the latest in the Pāli canon as defined by Sinhala Buddhists today, which explore the ramifications of this *kamma*-based (incalculable) connectedness in history. These texts are gathered together in the Collection of Miscellaneous Texts or Khuddakanikāya of the Suttapiṭaka, the "basket" of discourses (*sutta*) or Teachings (*dhamma*); this is the second of the "three baskets," the Tipiṭaka, into which these Buddhists order their texts (the first being the Vinaya, on monastic disciplinary rules, and the third, the Abhidhamma, on metaphysics); see (Table 3.1).[4] All share the same style and grammar (which in turn are continued by the *Dpv* and the *Mhv*).[5] The *Jātaka* details the good

[4]The two texts of the Vinaya are the *Suttavibhaṅga*, including the text for "release" (*pātimokkha*) from offenses, divided into rules for monks (*Bhikkhu-*) and nuns (*Bhikkhuṇīvibhaṅga*), and *Khandakā*, divided into a *Mahā-* and a *Cullavagga*. There are four major collections Nikāyas in the *Suttapittaka*, Dīgha-, Majjhima-, Saṃyutta-, and Aṅguttara-, the Khuddaka- being the fifth.

[5]Étienne Lamotte discusses the difficulties involved in determining the history of this material:

kamma Gotama cultivated in previous lives, which led him to Buddhahood in the present, and shows that his disciples were already connected to him by having participated in meritorious actions (*puññakamma*) with him during previous Buddha eras. The *Apadāna* ("Glorious Deeds") elaborates the previous good *kamma* of famous monks (*bhikkhu*) and nuns (*bhikkhunī*), who met the same previous Buddhas (and each other) in previous lives, whereas the *Vimānavatthu* and *Petavatthu* describe the effects of good and bad *kamma*, respectively, on the lives of ordinary people.

A vision of the world as a vast tapestry of interconnected *kamma* emerges in these Khuddaka texts: across the expanse of cosmic time, a large number of people transmigrate, meeting up as subject-citizens in the same kingdoms and even as members of the same families; because they have also participated together in Buddhist gift-giving, devotional, and meditative practices during the eras of previous Buddhas, they are able as a complex, dispersed agent to achieve, during the time of Gotama Buddha, the ultimate goal, "cessation" (*nibbāna/nirvāṇa*) of *kamma* and rebirth. These cosmic biographies provide illustrations of transmigrations in "cosmic flux" (*saṃsāra*) that successfully directed themselves toward escape from it.

The story, moreover, does not end with the Buddha's death; the interconnections of *kamma* that resulted in the final liberation of the Buddha and his disciples are ongoing to the extent that there are people in polities who continue to perform the life-transforming practices taught by the Buddha. The *BV* assures us that another Bodhisatta, a future Buddha, Metteyya/Maitreya, is nearing the achievement of Buddhahood; those Buddhists whose *kamma* was not developed enough to achieve cessation during the present Buddha era will be able to achieve it during Metteyya's. Knowledge of the events of incalculable history thus has immense soteriological relevance.

The beginning of each of the Sri Lankan Vaṃsas, by paraphrasing the biography of the Buddha in the *BV*, locates the history of the island within this two-dimensional time-place. That history continues through all the world ages up to the present, until Gotama becomes Buddha and lives out his most famous life which, according to the Sri Lankan Vaṃsas (but not the earlier canonical sources), included three visits to that island.

Most of the material in the Vaṃsas, it is true, belongs to calculable history, consisting of the genealogy of kings in this age and Buddhist history in this Buddha era. The kings of Sri Lanka are portrayed as genealogical descendants of the first king in this world age, Mahāsammata, and the monks of Sri Lanka's Mahāvihāra monastery (to the south of the capital, Anurādhapura) are portrayed as "descendants" of the Buddha in this Buddha era in a line of succession (*paramparā*) from his original disciples, by virtue of their higher ordination (*upasampadā*) into the

---

"Khuddakanikāya and Kṣudrakapiṭaka," *East and West* 7.4 (January 1957), 341–48. The suggestion that these texts need to be considered together is supported by the fact that in Buddhist Sanskrit tradition the parallel Kṣudraka texts and historical materials are similarly grouped together as Avadāna ("Glorious Deeds") of the Buddha and adherents of his teachings.

monastic order. But incalculable history intervenes in this royal genealogy, in the form of an event central to the Vaṃsa tradition.

That event is the "pleasing" (*pasanna*) of the first Sri Lankan king said to have become a Buddhist, Devānaṃpiyatissa (c. 250–10 B.C.) in the year believed to correspond to 247 B.C.[6] Mahāmahinda Thera, son of the great Aśoka Maurya (c. 268–39 B.C.) himself, is said to have led a party of five Buddhist monks and one layman to the Island in order to effect the institution (*patiṭṭhāna/pratiṣṭhāna*) of the Buddha's Discipline (*sāsana*, "instructions," "dispensation," "religion") there. As the first step, Devānampiyatissa dedicates his pleasure garden, the Mahāmeghavana (later site of the Mahāvihāra), to Mahinda and the community of monks. At the moment that this pious offering is made, the earth quakes. Astonished, Devānaṃpiyatissa asks Mahinda the reason, and he replies that the practices of the Buddha have just been instituted in the island for the fourth time. Although only slightly more than two centuries of the present Buddha era had elapsed, this offering had an unfathomably ancient (incalculable) history. Seven more earthquakes occur as Mahinda drops flowers on seven sites within the pleasure garden, which he explains were the sites of seven liturgical edifices that existed there during three previous Buddha eras: an enclosure (*mālaka*), a bathing tank, a *bodhi*-shrine, a confessional meeting (*uposatha*) hall, an alms hall, a refectory, and a stūpa. Devānaṃpiyatissa proceeds to (re)build these edifices on those sites. In telling about the sites, Mahinda relates details about the previous Buddha eras during which the Buddha's practices existed on the island.[7] These details are presented systematically as "the thirteen subjects and the four names" (*Dpv* XVII.3–25). For each of the four Buddha eras in question, the text provides the name of the island, the name of the capital, the name of the king, details of the affliction (that the Buddha visited the island to eradicate), the relics he left, the name of the stūpa the king built, the name of the lake (in the capital), the name of the sacred mountain, the name of the royal pleasure garden, the type of sacred tree, the name of the monk (who like Mahinda brought Buddhist

[6]The term *pasanna/prasanna* is generally translated "conversion," but its semantic range distinguishes it from the Christian notion of how religions acquire followers. In the Pāli sources, people (who are often already what we would term "Buddhists" to some degree) participate in certain life-transforming practices, including the "honoring" (*pūjā*) of images and stūpas and Bodhi trees, hearing sermons (*dhammasavana*), adopting moral precepts, and gift giving (*dāna*), which generates in them a certain mental pleasure (*cittapasāda, pasanna*); this mental pleasure—an affirmation of the value of participation in Buddhist life-transforming practices—in turn becomes the foundation for the generation of further good *kamma* and eventually *nibbāna*. For further thoughts on this subject see my "Stupa, Story and Empire" and "'Rethinking Buddhist Missions" (Ph.D. dissertation, University of Chicago (1992), 1: 208–10. I take dates for the Sinhala kings from K. M. De Silva, *A History of Sri Lanka* (Berkeley and Los Angeles: University of California Press, 1981), pp. 565–70, who summarizes the findings of the authors of the University of Ceylon's *History of Ceylon*, edited by S. Paranavitana and K. M. De Silva (Colombo: Ceylon University Press, 1959–95) in 3 volumes, about the proper Western equivalents for the Buddha era dates provided in the Vaṃsas. He warns (p. 565) that the dates up to Sena I (A.D. 833–853) are only approximate. Although he does not mention it, the reason for this is that the dynasty of Sena's successors was the first to leave enough epigraphic documents to "verify" the Vaṃsa chronologies.

[7]It is significant that Mahinda, an adept (*arahant*), is identified in these histories as the source of details from incalculable history. Only an adept (or Buddha) has direct knowledge of the incalculable past, and so placing the details in Mahinda's mouth lends credence to their claim to reliability.

texts and practices to the island), the name of the nun (who like Mahinda's sister Saṃghamitta brought a branch of the Bodhi tree to the island), and the name of the Buddha. The names of the three previous Buddhas and their sacred trees are, of course, also to be found in the *BV*; the remainder of the account appears nowhere else except in the Vaṃsas.

The institution of the Buddha's Discipline on the island by Mahinda and Devānampiyatissa is an event in calculable history, and these characters constitute essential links in that history (Devānampiyatissa himself is a descendant of Mahāsammata, the primordial king in this world age; Mahinda, the monastic ancestor of the Sinhala monks, is the pupil of a pupil...of the Buddha who founded this Buddha era). But their actions—the dedication and reception of royal funds and support for the Buddha's Discipline—reiterate life-transforming practices from that unfathomably ancient past before the world had even been created. Long before the time of Mahāsammata, during the Kakusandha Buddha era when Sri Lanka was called Ojadīpa and the capital was called Abhayapura, King Abhaya built those liturgical edifices on those same sites in what was then his own pleasure garden. And on Ojadīpa there was also a community of monks tracing its line of succession back to a Buddha, even though Gotama—the Buddha of the present age—was still experiencing rebirths as monkeys and birds.

By implication, later Sri Lankan kings who make offerings to the society of monks living in Devānampiyatissa's pleasure garden (the Mahāvihāra) participate in a rectitude that is twofold, paralleling the two-dimensional time at work in these histories. Those kings do what their ancestors did, remaking their own worlds with Devānampiyatissa as paradigm; those same kings also do what good kings did before the world even began. The same may be said of the monks who live within that pleasure garden, carrying on the tradition of their predecessors in this Buddha era and of their counterparts in previous Buddha eras.

Scholarly studies have focused on the calculable history contained in these texts to the exclusion of what I have dubbed the *kamma*-based or incalculable, but I believe that the latter constitutes the more important history within Vaṃsa literature. The texts give early monastic lineages, but do not trace them up to the then-present. Similarly, they document the fact that after the reign of Yasalaka Tissa (A.D. c. 52–59), the kings of Sri Lanka were not genealogical descendants of Devānampiyatissa. I am not suggesting that calculable historical rectitude ceased to be important at all—monks to this day do not question the fact that their lines of succession, if they could be traced back, would lead to one of the Buddha's own disciples. And even into the British period, Sri Lankan kings continued to claim Śākyan descent. But these links are left vague (and even dubious) in the Vaṃsa literature; the history that is driven home in these texts is that of the incalculable, the history of meritorious (and deleterious) action. Kings are judged, one after another, on the basis of their cooperation with and offerings to the Mahāvihāran monks living within Devānampiyatissa's old pleasure garden. And the monks deemed purest are those in Mahinda's Mahāvihāra fraternity, when compared to those in the two main rival disciplinary orders of the Anurādhapura period, the residents of the Abhayagirivihāra and the Dakkhiṇavihāra. History in the Vaṃsas is thus a succession of kings and monks judged more or less pious on the basis of their participation in incalculable history, in the infinitely reiterated Discipline that merged with the calculable history of this age when Devānaṃpiyatissa instituted Mahinda—and the Buddha's Discipline—at the Mahāvihāra.

Precolonial Sri Lankan historians conceived of the world as a place in which even complete knowledge of calculable history back to Adam himself cannot explain what really happens across time—what the present really is. More important than who a king's mother was, in the eyes of the authors of the Pāli Vaṃsas, is the question of his *kamma*: what merit, and what demerit, did he accrue as king? How will this affect where he is going? Did he assist, or injure, the instituted Discipline on the island? These questions, which conclude the account of each king's reign, are not idle. The king shapes the soteriological future of his subjects (and his enemies): he makes the teachings more or less accessible, he provides a meritorious or deleterious example, he forges connections for the future cessation of his subjects' cosmic wanderings, or he does not. Everything is connected. His subjects are subjects because they have previously been connected to him in one way or another; if he is on his way out of rebirth (the soteriological goal) some subjects will be led there, too. Thus everything depends on his participation (or lack thereof) in the incalculable dimension of history, the point in calculable time(s) at which a door out of suffering was opened on the island: the great gift of the Mahāvihāra to Mahinda.

There is no evidence that the Vaṃsa authors considered themselves personally capable of obtaining knowledge about the incalculable past. This capability depends, according to Buddhist anthropology, upon a highly advanced state of self-perfection. It is a power that belongs to adepts and especially to the Buddha himself. As privileged knower, he was able to teach the *BV*, the truth about these unfathomably ancient times and, as a result, his disciples were able to cultivate knowledge of their own previous lives in that same unfathomable past. There is every reason to believe that the Vaṃsa accounts rely on older texts preserved by the "ancients" (*porāṇā*: great elders of the past), beginning with the *BV* but no doubt including the *Sīhalaṭṭhakathā-Mahāvaṃsa*, which recorded such knowledge as obtained by people who did, the Vaṃsa authors believed, have these magnificent powers.[8] The Vaṃsa authors studied the calculable past with an assumption that it proceeds from and overlaps with the incalculable past. The Vaṃsa authors did not necessarily have the power to know the incalculable past as an adept does, but they surely had the very human ability to think about how these ancient records of the incalculable past might relate to, and give direction for the improvement of, the calculated present.

That the Vaṃsa authors understood the then-present in terms of the incalculable past is evident in the chronological system they employ. The *Dpv* was apparently a first attempt to order the ancient records of political history on the basis of a Buddha era, although different chronological systems often continue to

[8]For the *Sīhalaṭṭhakathā*, which is no longer extant but has been partially reconstructed by scholars, see the appendix to this chapter.

appear side by side in it. The later *Mhv* goes one step farther; it gives precedence to the chronology of the Buddha era (calculated according to the number of years since the death of the Buddha) over that of the political (calculated according to the number of dynastic or regnal years). All subsequent Vaṃsas use this method. This was a remarkable innovation. It was not just a question of converting an unconnected jumble of reigns and dynasties in the older *Sīhalaṭṭhakathā-Mahāvaṃsa*, each with its own new numbering, into a single coherent chronology and thereby anticipating "scientific" history. Calculating time according to the Buddha era (like dating according to the Christian era) provided a special kind of coherence: its imposition transformed political history into soteriological history.

History that is calculated according to the date of the Buddha's final Cessation (*parinibbāna*) is charged with the knowledge that there is an incalculable past at work in the present. The Buddha's life transformed time-place by introducing the possibility of escape from the tedium of transmigration. Across the vast expanse of time that the Buddha revealed in the *BV*, no fewer than twenty-five Buddhas have opened this "door to deathlessness" (*amatadvaraṃ*) and instituted Buddha eras and Disciplines of differing durations. Humanity today, as during the time of the *BV*, still enjoys the presence of Gotama Buddha, in which this door remains open. Calculation of time according to the Buddha era presumes this significance.

Thus, when the authors of the Vaṃsas placed political history in the Buddha era, they transformed it. The fact that a particular king lived and acted during a Buddha era, at a date that could be calculated only so long as the memory of the Buddha's date and his teachings remains, subjected that king and his actions to the critique that knowledge of incalculable history makes possible. The Vaṃsas consistently end their descriptions of each king with an evaluation of his reign according to the precedents of incalculable history. Did he progress on the Path or regress? Was he driven by good motives or bad ones? Did he extend the Buddha's Discipline by example and by charity or not? And what morals were to be drawn for contemporary royal practice? These evaluations, of course, were of no interest to the scientific historians. But they constituted the primary purpose of the precolonial Sri Lankan Buddhist histories. Their authors wished to show how the presence of the Buddha, reiterated in ever-changing circumstances and hence continually in need of rethinking, provided the basis for future reiterations of the Buddha's Discipline in daily life. The Buddhist historians were, in other words, engaged in the process of continually articulating Buddhist practices with those of the polity in which those practices took place.

The Buddhist emperors among the Śuṅgas and early Śātavāhanas (second and first centuries B.C.) constituted their empires on the basis of a homology between the cosmic polity represented—in the *BV* and *Khuddaka* texts that it supplements—as transmigrating through successive Buddha eras until it reaches Cessation in the present Buddha era, on the one hand, and the disciplinary practices of Buddhists living in India at that time, on the other.[9]

---

[9]Walters, "Stupa, Story and Empire."

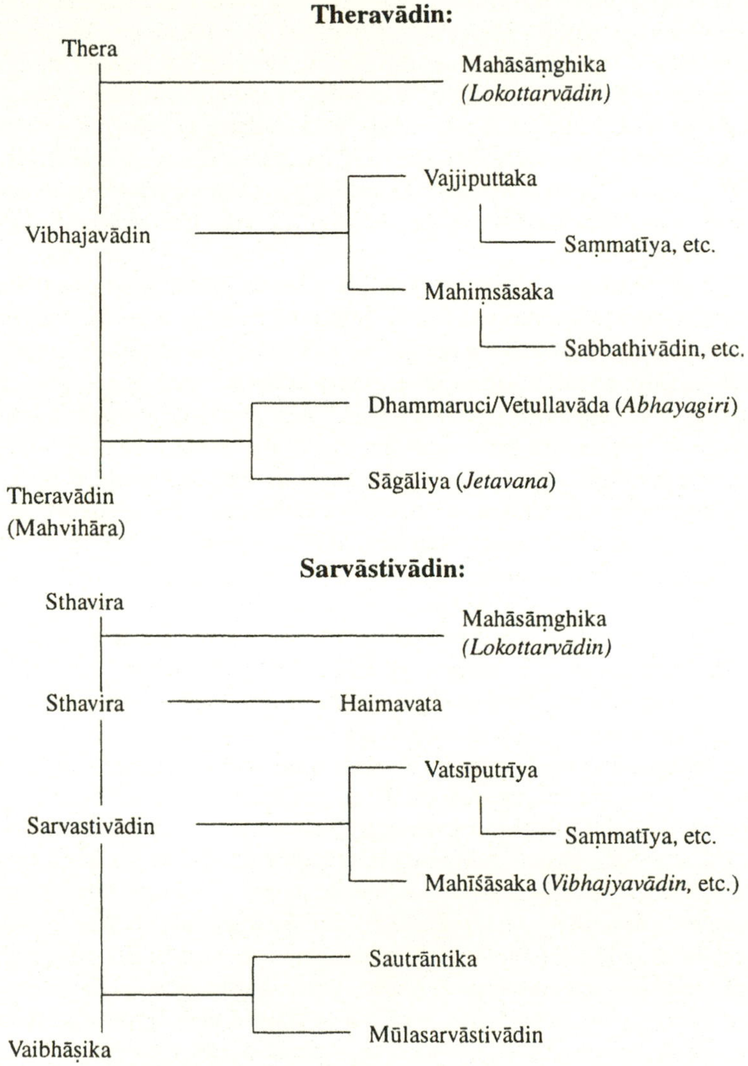

Figure 3.1. Histories of Buddhist Disciplinary Orders

Crucial to this history were representations of successive "councils" (*saṃgīti*) held under imperial aegis in order to resolve disciplinary and philosophical disputes among the differing disciplinary orders (*nikāya*, often referred to as "sects" or "schools"). After the Kuṣāṇa kings of northwest India (first century A.D.) displaced the early Śātavāhanas as paramount overlords of India, the order that emerged as preeminent under the Kuṣāṇas was the Sarvāstivādin, adherents of the "doctrine that 'everything exists'" who claimed to be the true heirs of the "elders" (*sthavira*), the earliest monks (Figure 3.1). Those monks produced a new interpretation of the cosmic Buddha biography, the *Divyāvadāna*. That text, a supplement to the *Kṣudraka* in their Sanskrit "canon," continued the cosmic story of *BV* beyond the lifetime of the historical Buddha, in order to "chronicle" subsequent Buddhist history, including Buddhist expansion into Gandhāra and Kashmir and the reigns of Aśoka Maurya and the Kuṣāṇa emperor Kaṇiṣka. This appropriation and reinterpretation of the *BV*'s cosmic Buddha considered time the locus of reality, and simultaneously constituted Gandhāra-Kashmir as the center of an Indo-Iranian world extending far into Central Asia.

The major rivals of the Sarvāstivādins were the Mahāsāṃghikas ("those of the Great Society [of Monks and Nuns]" implying that they were the true heirs of the Buddha), resident in eastern India. One disciplinary order that emerged from it under the Guptas (successors of the Kuṣāṇas in north India), the Lokottaravādin (whose "doctrine emphasizes the other world"), authored the *Mahāvastvavadāna*, a response to the Sarvāstivādin view that the whole world is real with the view that the real is to be found only in the other world. They excised from the cosmic Buddha biography in it all reference to Aśoka and the time that had elapsed since the Buddha was alive. Their thought thus shifted from the "reality" of human history to the "reality" of timelessness.

The Lokottaravādins were only one among many Buddhist disciplinary orders in the second, third, and fourth centuries who began to effect radical shifts in the locus of Buddhist epistemology and ontology, both among those of the so-called Lesser Vehicle, Hīnayāna, and those of the Great Vehicle, Mahāyāna (a distinction of the latter which, by employing the adjective "great," implies they are the true successors of the Buddha). This shift dialogically participated in the political reality of the age. It appears from the epigraphic record that after the Kuṣāṇa paramountcy, Buddhists were increasingly displaced in Indian imperial formations. The later Śātavāhanas, beginning with Gautamīputra Śrī Sātakarni (first and second centuries A.D.) sponsored Buddhist activities at Nasik (Maharashtra) and Dhanakaṭaka (Amarāvatī, Andhra Pradesh), and the imperial Ikṣvākus (second and third centuries) allowed their queens and daughters to sponsor Buddhist activities at Nāgārjunikoṇḍa and other sites in Andhra Pradesh. But the emperors themselves and the world visions according to which they shaped their empires were mostly Theist, and the emergent Śaiva and Vaiṣṇava cosmic stories, the Purāṇas and Epics, supplanted the Buddhist claims to the command of historical time. The simultaneous Buddhist epistemological shift away from the command of historical time in their discourse thus responded to the actual displacement of Buddhist claims to the command of space in Jambudīpa, the Indian world.[10] Buddhists who made no further claim to imperial status were welcome participants in a Theist empire. And Buddhists of this sort did indeed thrive within Indian kingdoms during the Gupta-Vākāṭaka and Pallava-Cālukya imperial formations. Buddhists (both Mahāyāna and "proto-Mahāyāna") instead claimed primacy in the evaluation of precisely

[10]Comparable to Bhāratavarṣa rather than Jambudvīpa in Vaiṣṇava and Śaiva cosmography. Sometimes I use the term "mainland" to translate the term, where it differs from the "island" (*dīpa*) of Sri Lanka.

those things that early Buddhists eschewed and so left to "heretics": essences, eternal entities, soteriological shortcuts, the nature of the ultimate.

Dīpavaṃsa: A Plea for Survival

These shifts were having profound repercussions in Sri Lanka. The Vaṃsas claim that the true Buddhist disciplinary order of Sri Lanka is Theravāda/Sthaviravāda (the "doctrine of the Elders"), that of the earliest monks. Yet a disciplinary order of that name first appears in inscriptions at Nāgārjunikoṇḍa in Andhra Pradesh (second or third century A.D.). There, donors endowed nuns from Sri Lanka with a monastery in which, the inscriptions state, they "pleased" Buddhists from all over Asia.[11] Histories of disciplinary orders by Buddhists of this period other than those of the Mahāvihāra are also at odds with their account.

The Sarvāstivādin Vāsumitra (c. 4th century), says in his history that the Mahāsāṃghikas split off from the Sthaviras a century after the Buddha's death. These latter divided, a century later, into Sarvāstivādin and a residual, unchanging Sthavira calling itself Haimavata ("of the Himalayas," implying that it lost out and fled to the mountains).[12] From this point on, Vāsumitra says no more about Sthaviras as a separate, unmodified order. We are thus allowed to infer that the Sarvāstivādins are the Sthaviras and, hence, the foremost successors of the Buddha. Other Sarvāstivādin stories affirm their claim of supremacy over the Mahāsāṃghikas, while at the same time seeming to accept that the Sarvāstivādins lost out in their dispute with the Mahāsāṃghikas, just as the Haimavata did in their encounter with the Sarvāstivādins. One relates that Aśoka, paramount king of India, held a council one hundred years ("a long time") after the final Cessation. As a result of the bad judgment that he exercised on this occasion, five hundred Sthavira adepts fled to Gandhāra and Kashmir, which that king, after he repented, gave to them.[13] The monks favored at the council were the founders of the Mahāsāṃghika order. The Sthaviras were the ancestors of the Sarvāstivādins (Figure 3.1).

Where are the Theravādins of Sri Lanka in this history? From the Sarvāsti-

---

[11] D. C. Sircar and A. N. Lahiri, "Footprint Slab Inscription from Nagarjunikonda," *Epigraphia Indica EI* 33 (1959–60), 247–50; J. Ph. Vogel, "Prakrit Inscriptions from a Buddhist Site at Nagarjunikonda," *EI* 20 (1929–30), 7–8, 22–23; Nalinaksha Dutt, "Notes on the Nāgārjunikoṇḍa Inscriptions," *Indian Historical Quarterly* 7.3 (September 1931), 651–53; Walters, "Rethinking Buddhist Missions," 302–6; Jonathan Walters, "Mahāyāna Theravāda and the Origins of the Mahāvihāra," *Sri Lanka Journal of the Humanities* 23.1–2 (1997), 100–19; Walters, "Mahāsena at the Mahāvihāra: the Interpretation and Politics of History in Medieval Sri Lanka," in *Invoking the Past: The Uses of History in South Asia*, edited by Daud Ali (New Delhi: Oxford University Press, 1999), pp. 322-66.

[12] André Bareau, "Trois traités sur les Sectes bouddhiques attribués à Vasumitra, Bhavya et Vinītadeva; [1] Le cycle de la formation des schismes (*Samayabhedoparacanacakra*) de Vasumitra," *Journal Asiatique* 242 (1954), 235–66; Jiryo Masuda, "Origin and Doctrines of Early Indian Buddhist Schools" in *Asia Major* 2 (1925), 1–78. André Bareau records a story to this effect of the commentator Paramārtha: *Les Sectes Bouddhiques du Petit Véhicule* (Saigon: École Française d'Extrême-Orient, 1955), p. 111.

[13] The seventh-century Chinese pilgrim Xuanzang (Hsüan-tsang), *Xiyouji*, translated by Samuel Beal as *Si-Yu-Ki: Buddhist Records of the Western World* ([1884] Delhi: Motilal Banarsidass, 1981), 1: 150–51, relates this. Some consider this king to have been Aśoka Maurya. Others see here an earlier Kālāśoka.

vādins, according to Vāsumitra, other orders emerge after another century elapses. These are the Vātsīputrīya, characterized as Pudgalavādin ("those who hold that the personality' [exists]), the foremost order of which is the Saṃmatīya; and the Mahīśāsaka, the first of those elsewhere called Vibhajyavādin ("those who distinguish" some things as existing and others as not), which terms suggest that these orders were defined by their opposition to one another. As will be seen below, the monks of the Mahāvihāra used the term Vibhajyavādin as a synonym for Theravāda. We are thus led to conclude that in this and other contemporary histories apart from their own, the Theravādins of Sri Lanka are to be derived from the Vibhajyavādin, possibly the Mahīśāsaka, more than three hundred years after the death of the Buddha.[14]

If those claiming to be Theravādin were not as old as they claimed, they were also not as doctrinally pure. Disciplinary orders that arose after the practices of the Great Vehicle became prominent appear to have been mostly Mahāyāna in their orientation. The Theravādins, despite the standard scholarly view, were among them. Although the Theravādins at the Mahāvihāra in Sri Lanka apparently did not participate in the Mahāyāna tendency, those at the rival Abhayagiri monastery did. According to the Vaṃsas themselves, monks at Abhayagiri took up the Vetullavāda/Vaitulyavāda, identified as a Mahāyāna canon that overlapped with the Madhyamaka literature.[15] They did so during the reign of Vohārika Tissa (A.D. 209–231) who, along with a successor named Goṭhābhaya (249–262), is said to have suppressed this teaching, but only temporarily.[16]

Inscriptional evidence from Sri Lanka, though scarce, also backs the view that in the second and third centuries a cosmopolitan Buddhist establishment flourished at Abhayagirivihāra.[17] Support for the ecumencial Abhayagiri monks had reached a fever pitch at the end of the third century, under Mahāsena (274–301). *Mhv* states that during Goṭhābhaya's suppression of the Vetullavāda, he deported

---

[14]Bareau, author of the most comprehensive study to date of "Hīnayāna" disciplinary orders, concludes that the Theravāda of Sri Lanka emerged as a branch of the Vibhajyavāda as late as the fourth century A.D.!; *Sectes bouddhiques*, pp. 169, 183.

[15]For citations see G. P. Malalasekera, *Dictionary of Pāli Proper Names* ([1937] London: Pali Text Society, 1974), 2: 918.

[16]*Dpv* XXII.43–45; *Mhv* XXXVI.41, 111–12.

[17]Unambiguous donations to the Abhayagirivihāra were made by Amaṇḍagāmaṇī (c. 19–29): Senarat Paranavitana, *Inscriptions of Ceylon* (Colombo: Department of Archaeology, 1970) (*IC*) 2.1: 46; and Gajabāhu I (c. 114–36): *IC* II.1, 88; as well as by ministers or generals of Mahallaka Nāga (c. 136–43): *IC* 2.1: 109; and Bhātika Tissa II (c. 143–67): *IC* 2.1: 113. Gajabāhu I also made a donation to the Dakhhiṇavihāra: *IC* 2.1: 87; so did several officials of an unidentified king at the beginning of the third century: *Epigraphia Zeylanica* (*EZ*) 7 (1984), 99–106. No unambiguous evidence for royal donations to the Mahāvihāra exists from this period. However, a donation to the Mahāvihāra dated to the reign of Bhātika Tissa II was made by one of his ministers; *IC* 2.1: 116–17. It must be noted, however, that this sole Mahāvihāra donation proved by lithic inscription includes references to the residents of the rival Abhayagirivihāra and Dakkhiṇavihāra as well, but the stone is too effaced to determine why they were mentioned. R. A. L. H. Gunawardana discusses the evidence available for determining which regional monasteries were affiliated with which disciplinary orders, and reaches similar conclusions about the importance of the Abhayagiri; *Robe and Plough: Monasticism and Economic Interest in Early Medieval Sri Lanka* (Tuscon: University of Arizona Press for the Association of Asian Studies, 1979), esp. pp. 8–21; 36.

sixty Abhayagiri monks to India (Nagārjunikoṇḍa?). The disciple of one of them, a Cōḻa (south Indian) monk named Saṃghamitta, came to Sri Lanka "embittered against the Mahāvihāra," no doubt because it had supported Goṭhābhaya's suppression of the Vetullavāda. During the reign of his successor, Jeṭṭhatissa I (263–273), this "disgruntled" monk gained the king's favor and was placed in charge of young Mahāsena, whom he inculcated with hatred for the Mahāvihāra. After he had ascended the throne, the villainous Mahāsena, under this monk's guidance, destroyed the buildings of the Mahāvihāra, forced the monks into exile for nine years, and carried off its riches to the rival Abhayagiri.[18] The very survival of the less cosmopolitan Mahāvihāra, clinging to a now-archaic Buddhology, was uncertain.

The *Dpv* intervenes in this situation. It ends with the reign of Mahāsena, dead by the time of its composition. There are good reasons to think that the reign of Mahāsena was roughly "the present" for the author of the *Dpv*. The text's language suggests that his deeds were still recent history:

> When Jeṭṭhatissa died his younger brother King Mahāsena reigned for twenty-seven years. Once that king thought, "Of the two sorts of monks in the Discipline, which speak the true teachings (*dhamma*) and which speak untrue teachings (*adhamma*)? Which feel shame and which are shameless?" Contemplating this matter and searching for people who feel shame, he saw [instead] evil monks disguised [as renunciates] who were not genuine renunciates; he saw agitated men, like putrid corpses covered in black flies, disguised [as renunciates but] not genuine renunciates: Nasty Mitta and Evil Soṇa, and other shameless people. Approaching the evil monks, he asked them about the meaningful teachings. Nasty Mitta and Evil Soṇa and other shameless people connived in secret in order to corrupt the virtuous [king]. Dressed in delusion, those immoral men depicted as unlawful the [calculation] from conception of the twenty years [required for] the higher ordination, which has been permitted [by the Buddha] in the [story] about Kumārakassapa [in the *Mahāvagga* of the Vinaya].[19] Those shameless ivory-whores depicted as permitting the practice of [using] ivory [fans], which is prohibited in the story [in the *Cullavagga* of the Vinaya amid the stories about the transgressions] of the "Gang of Six."[20] As regards these matters and others, many additional shameless monks, craving material gain, unjustifiably depicted [the true] as untrue teachings. Precisely because of his association with rogues, that king Mahāsena did bad things as well as good things as long as he lived; [now] he has gone [to an evil state] according to his *kamma*. Therefore, shunning from

[18]*Mhv* XXXVI.11–25; XXXVII.

[19]The first foot of this verse is clearly corrupt; I read *upasampadaṃ gabbhavīsaṃ* for *ubhosamaggabhāvissaṃ*, following Oldenberg (who follows the *VAP*); Hermann Oldenberg, edited and translated by *The Dīpavaṃsa: An Ancient Buddhist Historical Record* ([1879] New Delhi: Asian Educational Services, 1982); G. P. Malalasekera, ed., *Vaṃsatthappakāsinī* (London: Pali Text Society, 1935), 2: 676–77.

[20]This verse contains a play on the term *danta*, "ivory": *dantavattakaṃ* ("practice of ivory") and *dantagaṇikā* ("whores who work for ivory"). The latter term may also pun on a second meaning of *danta*, "tamed," meaning "they by whom whores are tamed" (or even "they whose whores work for ivory"). The term is, at any rate insulting in a fashion particularly apt for portraying corrupt monks. My interpretation of the reference to the *Cullavagga* here follows Oldenberg, who follows the *VAP*.

afar all association with rogues as though it were a snake or a viper, one ought to do things in life that benefit its purpose. (*Dpv* XXII.66–76; my translation)

The virulence with which *Dpv* slings insults at the historical characters (for example, substitution of the nickname Dummitta, literally "bad friend" for Saṃghamitta, "friend of the community") suggests that they were still remembered. Similarly, the author of this text lambastes monks on the "other side" of some unstated disagreement. The *Dpv* author, I infer, assumed that the audience would be familiar with the details of the events being debated. I thus conclude that this text was written as a polemical work within the context of contemporary debate centered upon the events of Mahāsena's reign.

This inference is confirmed by the continuation of the *Mhv*, the twelfth-century *Cūlavaṃsa* (*Cv*). The son and successor of Mahāsena was Siri Meghavaṇṇa (301–328). He approached the Mahāvihārans and asked them to tell him what damage his father had wrought at their monastery and after hearing this he undertook the restoration of the Mahāvihāra.[21] This account which, we are told, Siri Meghavaṇṇa heard "from the beginning" at the Mahāvihāra, that is, starting with the journey of Mahinda, "pleaser of the island," to bring the Discipline of the Buddha, was probably the *Dpv* itself. If *Dīpavaṃsa* was the account provided to Siri Meghavaṇṇa of the history of Mahāsena's destruction "from the beginning," then the fact that it ends with Mahāsena was hardly accidental, as scholars have argued.[22]. *Dpv* evaluates Mahāsena's action, implicitly suggesting that it violates the truths of both calculable and incalculable history, and concludes its narrative with him because that is what the entire presentation was leading up to: a demonstration that the Mahāvihāra is worth continuing because it embodies these truths.

Many scholars have suggested that the *Dpv* may have been composed by a Mahāvihāran nun or nuns. This hypothesis seems reasonable, given the unusual amount of detail *Dpv* provides about famous nuns and convents, and its list of revered nuns "living now" (no comparable list of monks exists in *Dpv*). The suggestion that a nun wrote *Dpv* becomes especially interesting in light of the prominence that Sri Lankan Theravādin nuns (*theriyā*), presumably of the Abhayagiri persuasion, seem to have enjoyed at Nāgārjunikoṇḍa, as discussed above. If nothing more, this evidence suggests that nuns were considerably more important than scholars generally allow.[23] Additionally, if we read the *Mhv* account of Mahāsena's reign as saying that only the Mahāvihāran monks were expelled from the monastery—if the monks had indeed been destitute (and denied access to their libraries) for nine

[21] Wilhelm Geiger, *Cūlavaṃsa* (London: Pali Text Society, 1925–27) XXXVII.53–90.

[22] Wilhelm Geiger, *The Dīpavaṃsa and Mahāvaṃsa and Their Historical Development in Ceylon* (German ed., Leipzig: A. Deichert, 1905), translated into English by Ethel M. Coomaraswamy (Colombo: H. C. Cottle, Government Printer, 1908), p. 64; Regina T. Clifford, "The *Dhammadīpa* Tradition of Sri Lanka: Three Models Within the Sinhalese Chronicles," in Bardwell Smith, ed., *Religion and Legitimation of Power in Sri Lanka* (Chambersburg, Pa.: Anima, 1978), pp. 40–41.

[23] The best account to date is R. A. L. H. Gunawardana, "Subtile Silks of Ferreous Firmness: Buddhist Nuns in Ancient and Early Medieval Sri Lanka and their Role in the Propagation of Buddhism," *Sri Lanka Journal of the Humanities* 14 (1988, published 1990), 1–59.

years—then we could explain why the task of pleading for mercy should have fallen upon the remaining nuns.

Because Siri Meghavaṇṇa was "pleased" by this history, he honored an image of its originary hero, Mahinda, at Mihintale (where the latter first began to please the rulers of Sri Lanka and their subject-citizens), and led it in lavish procession to the Mahāvihāra. He did not, however, close down or dishonor the monastic establishment at Abhayagiri. On the contrary, Siri Meghavaṇṇa instituted elaborate attendances (*pūjā*) to the famous relic of Buddha's tooth at Abhayagiri, brought to Sri Lanka from Kaliṅga country (eastern India) during his reign. Teeth of the Buddha were common palladia in Indian Buddhist kingdoms of the time, so the public celebration of the same things in Sri Lanka would have marked Sri Lankan participation in interregnal Buddhist networks.[24] Siri Meghavaṇṇa, an underlord of Samudragupta, arranged with him to have rest houses built for Sinhala pilgrims and scholars at Bodh Gayā, another mark of his interregnal interests.[25] My reading of the *Cv* account, then, is that Siri Meghavaṇṇa effected a "division of labor" between the two monasteries. He recognized the Mahāvihāra because of its local significance as the site where the Buddhist disciplinary order brought by Mahinda supposedly continued to be preserved, while at the same time he recognized the Abhayagirivihāra because of its pan-Buddhist importance. The Abhayagiri was, thus, to continue unhindered as a center of cosmpolitan Buddhist learning, while the Mahāvihāra, bastion of an archaicizing and interregnally unpopular Buddhist order, Hīnayāna Theravāda, would also be continued.

The continuation of the Mahāvihāra was an achievement won by the *Dpv* author, who presented its version of the past in order to make its case convincing. The account convinced many Buddhists in Sri Lanka as well as India, beginning with Siri Meghavaṇṇa, that it should survive. It even convinced an entire tradition of Western scholars that its originary claims were true. The *Dpv* succeeded as a text because it made four major moves.

First, the author composed the text in Pāli, thus reviving that language as the medium for Buddhist textual production among the beleaguered Theravādins of the Lesser Vehicle. Of course the most ancient canonical texts already existed, composed in Pāli (or perhaps some cruder, but comparable, Prākrit, a "precultivated" language). But these texts were at least five hundred years old when *Dpv* was composed. For centuries Sri Lankan Buddhists had been composing their own literature in Elu (proto-Sinhala), rather than in Pāli.[26] Meanwhile, in India (and perhaps also

[24]Xuanzang, *Xiyouji*, tr. Beal, 1: xxviii, xxxiii, xxxv, 45, 67, 92 (teeth), lxxviii (the travelling bowl), xxxi, lvii (footprints), and Index, "Buddha's hair and nails," sometimes thought exclusively the domain of Sri Lankan traditions. I discuss this in "Rethinking Buddhist Missions," pp. 403–10. As late as the twelfth century Kaliṅga claims to the Abhayagiri tooth were credible: Don Martino De Zilva Wickremesinghe, "Polonnaruva: Slab-Inscription of the Vāḷāikkāras," *EZ* 2 (1912–27), 242–55; S. Paranavitana, "Polonnaruva Inscription of Vijayabahu I," *EI* 18 (1925-26), 330–38.

[25]Sylvain Lévi, "Les Missions de Wang Hiuen-Ts'e dans l'inde," *Journal Asiatique* (1900), 316–17, 401–11.

[26]The definitive Mahāvihāran supplement to the Vinaya texts, in Pāli, was the *Parivārapāṭha*, which *Dpv* represents as having been rejected by the monks of Abhayagiri; this probably took place under the Sinhala king Vaṭṭhagāmaṇi (c. 89–77 B.C.).

at the Abhayagiri) Buddhists had been composing their literature in Sanskrit, the cultivated language (including a "hybrid," Sanskrit mixed with Prākrit), and/or regional languages. It was a startling innovation to compose the *Dpv* in the archaic "language of the texts," Pāli, which the commentators named "Magadha" (after the Indian kingdom where it supposedly originated). This accounts for the roughness of the Pāli in *Dpv*, which led Wilhelm Geiger to characterize it as "a first, although clumsy, effort."[27]

Now, if the *Dpv* was written merely to address a Sri Lankan audience, why was an archaic language employed? The most obvious answer is that composition in Pāli, in śloka meter, consciously like that of the Khuddaka texts, set the *Dpv* squarely within the Buddhist canon. It appeared to be a direct supplementation of the Buddhist revelations contained in those texts, and thus substantiated the claim of Mahāvihāran learning and practice to its great antiquity, thereby justifying its rejection of the cosmopolitan teachings of the day. The revival of Pāli can also be seen as having a wider purpose, an appeal to an interregnal audience. Pāli provided a vehicle for the mobilization of Theravāda Buddhists (wherever they might be) in order to fend off the then-prevalent Sarvāstivādins and Lokottaravādins.

The second move of the *Dpv* was to give a history of the disciplinary orders entitled Ācariyavāda (the "doctrines of the teachers," especially of those departing from its own: V.39–54) that seems to respond to that of Vāsumitra. Far from representing the original Sthaviras as having either lost out to changing rivals and taken refuge in the Himalayas, or transmuted into the Sarvāstivādins, it claims that the disciplinary order of the Mahāvihāra in Sri Lanka is that of the original Theras: "There are seventeen doctrines that have split off [from the Buddha's original teaching as codified at the First Council]; one doctrine has not split off. All of them, together with the doctrine that has not split off, number eighteen. The best [doctrine, namely, that] of the Theravādins is like a great banyan tree; nothing added, nothing lacking, it is the complete dispensation of the Jina. The other doctrines are like thorns on the tree" (V.51–52, my translation). The first of the Vibhajjavādin orders, the Mahiṃsāsaka (Mahīśāsaka), was not, claimed the *Dpv*, derived from the Sabatthivādins (Sarvāstivādin), but the other way round.

The monks and nuns of Mahāvihāra could not, however, sustain these bold claims without some skilled suturing (Figure 3.1). In its main narrative, *Dpv* uncontroversially relates that Ajātaśatru, king of Magadha, the most powerful kingdom in the Buddha's time and afterward, called a First Council in the sixteenth year after

[27] *Dīpavaṃsa and Mahāvaṃsa*, p. 68. Geiger understood the history of the Vaṃsas to be a triumphal history of poetical refinement. Like most scholars before and after him who have studied these texts, he believed that the Vaṃsa authors merely expressed ideas and facts that already existed; they represented objectively, through translation, the old eyewitness accounts of history. Their creativity, for Geiger, lies in their ability to repeat it all nicely. There are numerous difficulties, however, with his perspective: it does not explain why or for whom there should be a desire to make this material fine literature in the first place; it cannot account for the heavy commentarial style of a text like *VAP*; it does not account for the selective choice all the Vaṃsa authors made about which material to beautify through translation; and it makes no sense that for a thousand years people would strive simply to translate beautifully what already exists in their own language into some other language, only to discard the original once the process has climaxed.

the Buddha's death (c. 385/35 B.C.) at his capital, Rājagṛha (Rajgir in Bihar), to determine the teachings and disciplinary rules of the Buddha. Then the Vaṃsas tell of two more councils, both occurring under Aśokas. The Second Council, which took place under a Kālāśoka at Vaiśālī (Basarh in Bihar) "one hundred years" after the final Cessation, saw the Mahāsāṃghikas and Theravādins separate. The Third, which Aśoka Maurya called on the advice of his preceptor, Moggaliputta Tissa, supposedly 236 years after the final Cessation, dismissed from the Saṃgha all monks who did not avow themselves Vibhajjavādins on the basis of a text composed by that monk, the *Kathāvatthu* ("A Matter of Dispute"). It denounces the "wrong views" of the orders that have divided off from the original.

The disciplinary orders differentiated themselves in these histories mostly by the ontological "propositions" (*vāda*) they held. They classed the texts in which they argued these propositions as belonging to the third of the "three baskets," the Tipiṭaka, to which they assigned "canonical" texts, the Abhidhamma, concerned with metaphysics. The *Kathāvatthu* was the Theravāda supplement to Abhidhamma that differentiated the Theravādins from their opponents (Figure 3.1).[28] The major opponents among these orders, as we can infer from the very term Vibhajjavādin, were those entitled Pudgalavādin (those who hold that the "personality" exists) and Sarvāstivādin (those who hold that "everything exists"). The Sarvāstivādins in particular took pride in their elaboration of Abhidharma.[29] With this text as a guide to the corrected canon for would-be Theravādins, dispatching rivals and their incorrect texts, the residents of Mahāvihāra could, they thought, boast that "the Theravāda is well grounded, free of doctrines other [than those which the Buddha preached], the protector of the glorious teachings, full of meaning; it will last as long as the Discipline, so long as there are noble disciples of the Buddha in the Discipline" (*Dpv* IV.24–25, my translation).[30] This reworking of the history of Buddhist orders and their textual canons, which dismisses the claims of the Mahāsāṃghikas and Sarvāstivādins by appropriating Aśoka for the Theravādin cause, hoped to secure a place for the Theravāda at the Mahāvihāra, a Buddhist disciplinary order that was probably a newcomer on the global Buddhist scene.

The third move of the *Dpv* was to identify the lineage of the Sri Lankan kings (*rājavaṃsa*) as of Okkāka/Ikṣvāku descent. It represents Ikṣvāku, founder of that line, as the first king of the Śākya branch at Kapilavatthu of the Solar dynasty of Kosala (eastern Uttar Pradesh) at Ayodhyā, through Amitodana, younger brother

---

[28]It was one of the seven texts that came to make up this Piṭaka. The others are *Dhammasaṅgaṇi*, *Vibhaṅga*, *Dhātukathā*, *Puggalapaññatti*, *Yamaka*, and *Paṭṭhāna*.

[29]Their key text, one of seven, was the *Jñānaprasthāna*, supposedly authored by Kātyāyanīputra. Two explications of this text were crucial, the *Vibhāṣā* of Aśvaghoṣa and the *Mahāvibhāṣā* of Vasumitra. Some monks of this order rejected the Vibhāṣās ("commentaries") in favor of the Sūtras alone and founded an order known as Sautrāntika; the earlier then became known as Vaibhāṣika. Others, claiming to adhere to an "original" (*mūla*) Vinaya, also formed a separate order, the Mūlasarvāstivādin.

[30]The *Kathāvatthu* is so highly dialogical that it is almost impossible to disentangle it from its opponent texts, for example the Maudgalāyanaskandhaka, the first chapter of the *Vijñānakāya*, one of the Abhidharma texts of the Sarvāstivādins, which purports to refute the views of the author of the *Kathāvatthu*, Maudgalāyana, i.e., Moggaliputta; Vasubandhu, *Abhidharmakośa*, translated and annotated by Louis de la Vallée Poussin (Paris: Paul Geuthner, 1923–31), xxxiii–iv.

of the Buddha's own father (*Dpv* X.1–9.) The text thus portrayed the Sri Lankan kings as the true heirs to the Ikṣvāku legacy, a claim that the Ikṣvākus of Andhra had earlier staked out for their imperial kingdom in which, at Nāgārjunikoṇḍa, Sri Lankan Buddhists had received their first recorded recognition. The text also portrayed the kings of Sri Lanka as Śākyas, kinsmen of the Buddha himself. It thus resurrected an earlier Buddhist claim to the command of time, subordinating human action (calculable time) to the endless reiteration of the Buddha's presence (incalculable time). Like *Divyāvadāna*, it soteriologically charged later Buddhist history, retelling the Aśoka legend as the story of Mahinda's activities in Sri Lanka (rather than as the story of another disciple, Madhyāntika, who "pleased" Kashmir, home of the Sarvāstivādins). The *Dpv* goes further, permeating *all* history since the final Cessation with the incalculable. *Dpv* describes the here-and-now of Sri Lankan kingship, monasticism, architecture, literature, geography, and economics explicitly as a continuation of the cosmic story that constituted earlier Buddhist empires in India.

The fourth move of the *Dpv* was to associate Mahinda, the "pleaser" of Sri Lanka's first Buddhist king, Devānaṃpiyatissa, with the Mahāvihāra. It thus accorded that monastery the privilege of being the first to receive Buddhist teachings in Sri Lanka, a privilege that had no doubt also been claimed by their rivals at the Abhayagiri (in their Vaṃsas, which unfortunately have not survived). When Siri Meghavaṇṇa brought Mahinda's image from Mihintale to the Mahāvihāra, he validated this claim.

Far from being a defective or biased memory of the past, the *Dpv*, through these moves, attempted to rearticulate the events of the past in order to check the disarticulation of the place of the Mahāvihāra among Buddhist monastic institutions and within the polities of the present. Together they repositioned its author, the Theravādins of the Mahāvihāra, and the kingship of Sri Lanka both interregnally and internally. Interregnally, the text represents the Theravāda monks and nuns of the Mahāvihāra as the authentic heirs of the Buddha, and represents the kings of Sri Lanka as descendants of the legendary Okkāka, displacing the earlier Ikṣvākus of Andhra as the kings with an imperial wish and upholders of the Buddha's Discipline. Internally, *Dpv* repositions the Mahāvihāra in relation to the Abhayagirivihāra, securing a place of honor for it and its Bodhi tree and great stūpa within the royal liturgy.

It is important to caution, however, that *Dpv* goes no further than to position the Mahāvihāra and the Anurādhapura kings as worthy of recognition by other Buddhist orders and kings. It does not contain any anti-Abhayagiri statements, nor does it suggest that the Sri Lankan kings are the only descendants of Okkāka. Composed at a time when the Mahāvihāra was fighting for its life and the Sri Lankan kings were in no position to challenge more powerful Indian dynasties, one can hardly expect otherwise.

Mahāvaṃsa: Glimpses of Empire

About a century after the composition of *Dpv*, during the reign of King Mahānāma (406–428), the Chinese pilgrim Faxian (Fa-hien or Fa Hsien) spent three years in Sri Lanka studying with the Buddhists at the Abhayagiri. There he received copies of the Mahīśāsaka *Vinaya* and a large number of Mahāyāna texts in Buddhist Sanskrit (*Fan*). He describes the Abhayagiri monks as "Mahāyānists" and details the splendor with which Mahānāma celebrated the tooth relic festival there. The Mahāvihāra, on the other hand, he describes as a smaller and less-populated monastery. His description thus suggests that Siri Meghavaṇṇa's "division of labor" actually obtained.[31]

During the reign of King Mahānāma, Buddhaghosa, the man who was to become the great commentator on Sri Lanka's Theravāda version of the Buddha's teachings, arrived there from India. *Mhv* represents him as a Brāhmaṇ from near Bodh Gayā, prompted to go to Sri Lanka to look for true Buddhist texts by the monk who initiated him (XXXVII). More likely, he came from Andhra Pradesh.[32] Many of the important "medieval" works in Pāli, in fact, were written by south Indians.[33] Buddhaghosa was only the first. Buddhaghosa found the *Dpv* account especially convincing. Throughout his work, he cites *Dpv*, by name and as "the Purāṇa," implicitly comparing it with the Theist Purāṇas, originary accounts which also had accounts of royal lineages as one of their topics.[34] Buddhaghosa frames his commentary on the disciplinary rules (*vinaya*), the *Samantapāsādikā*, with the *Dpv* account of disciplinary orders and relies on it in his commentary on that Abhidhamma text crucial for these Theravādins, the *Kathāvatthu*, identifying the "wrong views" denounced in that text with the various orders deemed "heretical" in the *Dpv* account (Table 3.1).[35] With the compilation of his commentaries (*aṭṭhakathā*), Buddhaghosa had appropriated the early Buddhist canon for the resurgent Theravādins of the Mahāvihāra.[36] As a result of his work of supplementation, the old Pāli canon as a scale of texts became again a living thing, accessible to contemporary monks and nuns, and the Theravāda Buddhist disciplinary order became a plausible rival of the other Indian orders whose scales of texts were newer and had been periodically refreshed. The view that Mahāvihāran Theravāda Buddhists built themselves up in a conscious rivalry with other Theravāda adherents is strengthened by recent scholarship showing *Visuddhimagga*, a concise restatement

---

[31] Beal cites Faxian in his introduction to Xuanzang, *Xiyouji*, 1: lxx–lxxvi.

[32] A. P. Buddhadatta, "Who Was Buddhaghosa?" in his *Corrections of Geiger's Mahāvaṃsa, etc: A Collection of Monographs* (Ambalangoda, Ceylon: The Ananda Book Company, 1957), pp.142–57.

[33] Gunawardana, *Robe and Plough*, pp. 264–5.

[34] Buddhaghosa, *Samanta-Pāsādikā*, edited by J. Takakusu (London: Pali Text Society, 1924), I.62, 70, 71 (*tenāhu porāṇā*); 74, 75 (*vuttaṃ pi c'etaṃ Dīpavaṃse*). It is possible that when Buddhaghosa cites "the ancients" (*porāṇā*) he means not *Dpv* itself but the source of *Dpv*, that is, the *Sīhalaṭṭhakathā-Mahāvaṃsa* (and/or the men who wrote it), in which case these *Dpv* verses are also quotations from that ancient source.

[35] One should also mention here the more or less contemporaneous commentary on the Sarvāstivādin *Mahāvibhāṣā*, the *Abhidharmakośa* and its *Bhāṣya* of Vasubandhu.

[36] Sri Lankan tradition has ascribed virtually all the commentaries on the canonical texts to Buddhaghosa, including those that later scholarship has shown to be otherwise.

of the Theravādin world vision that constitutes Buddhaghosa's most important work, to be the Mahāvihāran reworking of an earlier Abhayagiri attempt called *Vimuttimagga*.[37]

After the reign of Mahānāma, Sri Lanka was conquered by "Tamils" (probably Pāṇḍyas), and ruled by six "Tamil" kings in succession.[38] The interest of south Indians in Sri Lanka during this period was thus more than doctrinal: it was also political. The two interests may have been intimately connected. Buddhaghosa took his full-fledged Theravāda option back to the mainland. The interregnal implications of this discursive activity—the renewal of Buddhist claims to the command of time—were no doubt grasped by the south Indian kings whose subjects were engaged in them. Theravāda Discipline in the medium of Pāli provided one possible foundation for a south Indian political formation that could remake the Indian world to be potentially if not actively hostile to the configuration of Theists and Buddhists that prevailed in the Gupta-Vākāṭaka imperial formation.

Dhātusena (455–473) formed alliances with various Sri Lankan factions and succeeded in defeating these south Indian overlords. It is possible that Dhātusena also formed alliances with some south Indian rulers, such as the Kaḷabhras, during this moment of Pallava dispersion. He became a great benefactor of the Mahāvihāra, ornamenting all its buildings, effecting repairs, and donating to it eighteen large monasteries with reservoir tanks, and eighteen smaller monasteries. Then, in order to celebrate his victory, he instituted a huge festival—the venue, I argue, for the performance of the texts of the Khuddaka in the period when they were also imperial discourses.[39] Like Siri Meghavaṇṇa, he honored an image of Arhant Mahinda at Mihintale, under the command of the Abhayagirivihārans, then had it taken in a lavish procession to the Mahāvihāra.[40] As part of the ceremony, Dhātusena ordered a redaction of the Buddhist canon and a "revision of the *Dpv*," that is, the composition of *Mhv*.[41] Dhātusena undoubtedly understood, as had his "Tamil" overlords earlier, that there were important implications in the Mahāvihāran perspective on history. As a bastion of Sri Lanka's own Buddhist order, which nevertheless was beginning to attract the attention of south Indian Buddhists (through the works of Buddhaghosa and his Indian successors), support for the Mahāvihāran account of history was tantamount to the declaration that "true" Buddhists, those of Sri Lanka,

---

[37]Gunawardana, *Robe and Plough*, pp. 22–23.

[38]The word "Tamil"—which in English denotes a language and an ethnic identity—does not properly translate the Pāli term *damiḷa*, which specifically means "enemies"; Damiḷas may or may not be Tamil, and Tamils may or may not be Damiḷas, but all Damiḷas are (political and military) enemies of the Sri Lankan kings. When the Vaṃsa authors want to specify the identity of a certain group of Damiḷas, they use the name of the country in which they live (Pāṇḍya, Kaliṅga, etc.). The inadequacy of translating the term *damiḷa* as "Tamil" becomes especially manifest in the seventeenth-century Sinhala Vaṃsa text *Rājāvaliya*, where the equivalent Sinhala term *demaḷa* is applied to enemies as far-flung as the Chinese and the Portuguese.

[39]Walters, "Stupa, Story and Empire."

[40]In this reign, we have a definite indication that non-Mahāvihārans controlled Mihintale: *Cv* XXXVIII.75–76 and cf. Gunawardana, *Robe and Plough*, p. 19 n. 72.

[41]*Cv* XXXVIII.43–60. I argue this, *contra* Wilhelm Geiger in "Rethinking Buddhist Missions," pp. 329–30 n. 152.

ought to command time for themselves, at least locally, and potentially on a global scale.

The *Mhv* does not extend the history of the *Dpv*, and ends, as did the earlier text, with the reign of Mahāsena. The most significant difference between the *Dpv* and the *Mhv* is in its retelling of that history and especially its "epic" treatment of King Duṭṭhagāmaṇī (c. 161–137 B.C.). The first king to unify the island and throw off foreign rule, Duṭṭhagāmaṇī receives little mention in the *Dpv*, but occupies nearly half the *Mhv*. As Regina Clifford has argued, an exemplary Duṭṭhagāmaṇī was propounded at this time because Dhātusena was a king who succeeded in doing just what Duṭṭhagāmaṇī did.[42] The *Mhv*, written to celebrate the victory of Dhātusena, portrays Duṭṭhagāmaṇī as a king devoted exclusively to the Mahāvihāra. The project that the authors of the *Mhv* attribute to him is not just gaining autonomy for the revivalist Theravāda of the Mahāvihāra within the Sinhala polity. Their focus on the meritorious deeds of Duṭṭhagāmaṇī implies that for the sake of the true (Theravāda) teachings and discipline, the Sri Lankan kings have to be prepared to rebel against Indian imperial overlordship and, if possible, institute their own overlordship.[43]

Consistent with its projection of empire, the *Mhv* also urges recognition of the superiority of the Mahāvihāra over the dissident monks and nuns of the Theravāda in Sri Lanka, appending to the *Dpv* account of disciplinary orders a single strophe which indicates that new orders also emerged from the Theravāda of the Mahāvihāra in Sri Lanka (V.13): Dhammaruci and Sāgāliya (Figure 3.1), and we know from later sources that these (pejorative?) terms come to refer to the residents of the Mahāvihāra's two rival monasteries outside of Anurādhapura, Abhayagiri (sometimes called Uttaravihāra, the Northern Monastery) and Dakkhiṇavihāra (the Southern Monastery, which breaks away from Abhayagiri) or Jetavana (east of the city, later displacing it), respectively.[44] From the perspective of *Mhv*, the Mahāvihāra should no longer be accorded a position secondary to the adherents at the other Theravādin monasteries on the island; it should gain their recognition of its supremacy because it alone preserves the tradition that has come down unbroken from the Buddha himself.

The monks and nuns of the Mahāvihāra produced the *Dpv*, the first Pāli text of Sri Lanka, as a challenge to the privileged position enjoyed by the residents of the Abhayagirivihāra in the fourth century. More than that, by claiming to be the descendants of an originary Buddhist order uncorrupted with later Great Vehicle practices, it also posed a challenge to the "idealist" Buddhists who were coming into prominence in the Gupta-Vākāṭaka imperial formation in response to the "realist" Buddhists who had prevailed when imperial rulers recognized theirs as superior to

---

[42]Clifford, "The *Dhammadīpa* Tradition of Sri Lanka," p. 39.

[43]For a new reading of Duṭṭhagāmaṇī's unification of the island, see R. A. L. H. Gunawardana, "Prelude to the State: An Early Phase in the Evolution of Political Institutions in Ancient Sri Lanka," in Seminar for Asian Studies (The University of Peradeniya, Sri Lanka), Discussion Paper No. 11, July 13, 1983 (unpublished).

[44]Gunawardana, *Robe and Plough*, pp. 14–16, 33–34; Walpola Rahula, *History of Buddhism in Ceylon* (Colombo: Gunasena, 1956), pp. 84, 92; A. M. Hocart, "The Dhammaruci Sect," in *Memoirs of the Archaeological Survey of Ceylon* New Series 1 (1922–24), 15–17.

other ways of life. The complex author of the *Dpv* composed that text as part of its fight for survival (in the wake of Mahāsena's disastrous reign). The complex author of the *Mhv*, in rewriting the earlier text, transformed its strategy. Rather than merely claiming a place for Sri Lankan kings and Mahāvihāran monks within a larger imperial formation, *Mhv* claimed pride of place for them within the world it began to imagine. For nearly four centuries after Dhātusena, however, no king was in a position to do anything more than dream about a world in which a Sri Lankan king and the Theravāda order he supported would exercise such power.

Around the middle of the sixth century, the Gupta-Vākāṭaka imperial formation gave way to the Pallava-Cālukya, with important consequences for Sri Lanka. The *Cūlavaṃsa*, the Little Chronicle that continues the history of the Great Chronicle from the point of view of the Theravādins of the Mahāvihāra, portrays the sixth to eighth centuries, especially after the Pāṇḍya Kaḍuṅgōṇ (c. 590–620), and his contemporary, the Pallava Siṃhaviṣṇu (c. 586–610) regained dynastic command over their kingdoms,[45] as hard times. Mahāvihāran lands were taken; the Abhayagiri and Jetavana monks were far wealthier, more privileged and powerful; kings fought incessant civil wars, seldom secure on their thrones; famine, plague, and foreign invasions kept the people in misery.

Xuanzang, who was interested in the newer Buddhist orders, recorded reports he heard of Sri Lanka during his visit to South Asia in the early part of the seventh century. His account echoes that of Faxian: the Abhayagiri (where monks studied the texts of all Buddhist disciplinary orders) was ascendant, while the Mahāvihārans were "opposed to the Great Vehicle and adhered to the teaching of the Little Vehicle"[46] out of royal favor. But Xuanzang found something that Faxian did not: the presence of Sthaviras of the Mahāyāna tendency at Bodh Gayā, in Kaliṅga, in several other north Indian kingdoms and, of course, at the Abhayagiri in Sri Lanka.[47] In central and south India, and of course at the Mahāvihāra in Sri Lanka, he found Sthaviras adhering to the Hīnayāna.

Contemporary accounts of disciplinary orders confirm Xuanzang. Bhavya's account of the seventh century says that some Sarvāstivadins are called Vibhajyavādin, the name the *Mhv* gives the original Sthaviras.[48] The Mūlasarvāstivādin account of Vinītadeva (eighth century), which the Chinese and Tibetans take up, lists four main Buddhist orders, with subdivisions—Sarvāstivādin, Mahāsāṃghika, Saṃmatīya, and Sthaviravādin. It also includes Vibhajyavādins among the Sarvāstivādins. It differs, however, in clearly according a separate place to Sthaviravādins, although it does not award them the global pride of place they claimed for them-

[45] T. V. Mahalingam, *Kāñcīpuram in Early South Indian History* (Bombay: Asia Publishing House, 1969), pp. 56–62.

[46] Xuanzang, *Xiyouji*, tr. Beal, 1: 247.

[47] The connection of the Sthaviras of Bodh Gayā with those of Sri Lanka is amply documented: Sylvain Lévi in "Les Missions"; J. Fleet, "Bodh-Gaya Inscription of Mahanaman: The Year 269," *Corpus Inscriptionum Indicarum* 3 (1888), 274–79; D. K. Barua, *Buddha Gaya Temple: Its History* (Buddha Gaya, India: Buddha Gaya Temple Management Committee, 1981), pp. 42–45, 52–53; Gunawardana, *Robe and Plough*, pp. 244–47.

[48] André Bareau, "Trois traités 2: L'explication des divisions entre les sectes (*Nikāyabhedavibhaṅga-vyākhyāna*) de Bhavya," *Journal Asiatique* 244 (1956), 166–91.

selves, reserving that for the Sarvāstivādins. Quite the contrary, by listing its subdivisions as Mahāvihāravāsi, Abhayagirivāsi, and Jetavanīya—the residents of the three main monasteries around Anurādhapura—it implies that the Sthaviravāda was confined to Sri Lanka (Figure 3.1).[49]

The Sri Lankan kings seem to have been largely dependent upon the Pallavas after the seventh century, when the Pallavas reconstructed Sinhala kingship.[50] The published Sri Lankan inscriptions up to the ninth century were articulated by and articulative of this situation. Only a few crude epigraphs in Sinhala record benefactions, all of them to the Abhayagirivihāra or Dakkhiṇavihāra.[51] Elaborate epigraphs in Sanskrit (in Gupta and Pallava Grantha scripts) by Sri Lankans, however, record Sri Lankan benefactions on the mainland. There are also elaborate Sanskrit inscriptions preserved in Sri Lanka itself, again in the Pallava Grantha script, evidence of the dependence of the Theravāda in Sri Lanka upon the Buddhist idealism favored by the Pallavas (and of the Sri Lankan king upon his Pallava overlords): for example, the huge Sanskrit *Trikāyastava*, a Mahāyāna devotional text based on the doctrine that Buddhas have several bodies, incised on a boulder at Mihintale.[52] A stūpa at Mihintale contained, along with the traditional Buddha relics, fragments of an eighth-century Pallava copper-plate manuscript of two central Mahāyāna texts, the *Prajñāpāramitā in Fifty Thousand Ślokas* and the *Kāśyapa-parivarta*.[53] Like their Mahāyāna compatriots in kingdoms on the mainland, the monks at the Abhayagiri thrived in the Pallava empire (even though they conceded the overlordship of the cosmos to Śiva). Other kings in southern India also supported both Mahāyāna and Hīnayāna Buddhist orders. The imperial Viṣṇukuṇḍin king, Govindavarman Vikramāśraya, indicated that he was an adherent of Mahāyāna, but was also supportive of all "vehicles" (*yāna*).[54] One local king, Harivarman, obtained permission from his father, Pṛthivīmūla, to dedicate a "great monastery" to monks from Sri Lanka (Tāmbraparṇīya).[55]

The Abhayagiri Theravāda also enjoyed a place in the larger South and Southeast Asian world. Its Mahāyāna construction of Theravāda in its Vaṃsa, and its version of the canon (which the Abhayagiri monks caused to be "widely diffused")

---

[49]André Bareau, "Trois traités 3: Le compendium descriptif des divisions des sectes dans le cycle dela formation des schismes (*Samayabhedoparacanacakrenikāyabhedopadarçanasamgraha*) de Vinītadeva," *Journal Asiatique* 244 (1956), 192–200. The Mūlasarvāstivādins were, apparently, Sarvāstivādins who claimed to adhere to an "original" (*mūla*) Vinaya.

[50]Compare *Cv* XLVII with E. Hultzsch, "Kasakudi," *South Indian Inscriptions* (*SII*) 2.4 (1913), 353–61.

[51]S. Paranavitana, "Inscriptions on the Steps near 'Burrows' Pavillion' at Anurādhapura," *EZ* 4 (1934–41), 136–41; Paranavitana, "Rock-Inscription of Dāṭhopatissa near Dakkhiṇa-Thūpa, Anurādhapura," *EZ* 5 (1965–66), 65–72.

[52]S. Paranavitana, "The Trikāyastava in an Inscription at Mihintale," *EZ* 4 (1934–41), 242–46.

[53]S. Paranavitana, "Indikaṭusāya Copper Plaques," *EZ* 3 (1928–33), 199–212. The *Prajñāpāramitā* literature, as is well known, contains lengthy arguments about why texts of the Buddha's teachings (*dharmadhātu*) are more important than his bodily relics (*rūpadhātu*), which are usually interred in Sri Lankan stūpas.

[54]S. Sankaranarayanan, *The Vishṇukuṇḍins and Their Times (An Epigraphical Study)* (Delhi: Agam Prakashan, 1977), pp. 142–43, 153–56.

[55]Sankaranarayanan, *Vishṇukuṇḍins*, pp. 143, 187.

were apparently attractive to monks and laity beyond Sri Lanka and the Pallava polity (unfortunately, only small fragments of Abhayagiri literature survive today, mostly embedded within Mahāvihāran texts).[56] Scholar-monks from all over South Asia, even Tibet, visited the Abhayagiri in the seventh to ninth centuries, and their monks stayed at such important northern centers as Nālāndā and Bodh Gayā, and even established a branch in Java.[57]

The Pāli Buddhist canon of the Hīnayāna Theravādins at the Mahāvihāra, framed by the writings of Buddhaghosa, was disseminated among Indian Buddhists in the Pallava and Pāṇḍya kingdoms and gained footing among some of them.[58] It does seem, however, that the monks affiliated with the Mahāvihāharan Theravāda were opposed to the cosmopolitan Buddhist world of the Abhayagiri monks and the Sri Lankan kings, which would account for the fact that no royal dedicatory inscriptions to the Mahāvihāra have been published from this period. The Mahāvihārans were unwilling participants in a polity supporting Mahāyāna Buddhists—ultimately Śaivas—and they adopted a primarily eristical relationship to both. The few Hīnayāna Theravādins who reached Nālāndā were expelled for being so belligerent in their scorn of the latest Tantric teachings.[59] The Mahāvihārans in south India (or their Theravādin counterparts and offshoots there) during this period were engaging in different kinds of dialogue as well, attempting to establish their own supremacy in the south of the mainland over the persistent Jains and, especially, the growing dominance of Śaivism in Andhra Pradesh and Tamil Nadu.[60]

During the Pallava-Cālukya imperial formation of the sixth to eighth centuries, Theravādin monks and nuns had thus constituted the Theravāda order, in both its Mahāyāna and Hīnayāna forms, as an important presence in an interregnal Buddhist world that did not yet, despite Buddhological claims to the contrary, know a sharp distinction between "northern" and "southern" forms. Though often portrayed by scholars as a division that dates back to the Kuṣāṇa kings (before the quintessentially "southern" disciplinary order, the Theravāda, had been invented), nine hundred years later the interregnal Buddhist world was considerably more complex in its ordering than this distinction allows: Hīnayāna as well as Mahāyāna Buddhists and their texts from "northern" disciplinary orders as far flung as Tibet and China were continuous with those of the "southern" orders of Sri Lanka. By the middle of the eighth century, the Pallavas and their opponents in the Deccan, the Cālukyas, were in decline, largely as a result of their battles with each other. This enabled the Rāṣṭrakūṭas, formerly underlords of the Cālukyas, to displace both them and their Pallava foes as the paramount kings of India.[61] The Rāṣṭrakūṭas were apparently determined not to have their paramountcy qualified as had been

[56] Xuanzang, *Xiyouji*, tr. Beal, 1: 247.

[57] Gunawardana, *Robe and Plough*, pp. 242–81.

[58] T. N. Vasudeva Rao, *Buddhism in the Tamil Country* (Annamalainagar: Annamalai University, 1979).

[59] Gunawardana, *Robe and Plough*, pp. 244–45.

[60] For Buddhist-Jain debates in south India during this period, see B. L. Rice, *Inscriptions at Śravaṇa Belgola* (Bangalore: Mysore Government Central Press, 1889), pp. 45–46, 136.

[61] R. Inden, *Imagining India* (Oxford: Blackwell, 1990), pp. 244–62.

that of the Cālukyas, by an imperial power to their south. Their interventions in that region helped to destabilize political order there. The Pāṇḍyas and the Cōḻas, the most powerful kings in the region, battled each other when they were not fighting together against the Rāṣṭrakūṭas, while the other regional kings—such as Ceras, Keralas, Kaliṅgas, lingering Pallavas, and the Sinhalas—were embroiled in constantly shifting alliances with one or the other of these powers, or with the Rāṣṭrakūṭas against both. This very flux made it possible for a newly consolidated kingship in Sri Lanka to engage in the construction of an imperial kingdom that realized the vision of the *Mhv*.

Vaṃsatthappakāsinī: Sinhala Conquest of the Mainland

The Okkāka dynasty of Sri Lanka, first in the ninth to early eleventh centuries, and then again in the last part of the twelfth, attempted to institute the Mahāvihāran world vision by gaining supremacy over its long-time rivals and by attempting, through alliances with these several south Indian kingdoms, to achieve political supremacy in southern South Asia. By the end of the tenth century they were convinced that the world would become one of Mahāvihāran Theravāda Buddhists. Their imperial vision was not, however, a timeless ideology simply waiting to be realized. It was a detailed project that took textual form. The court of the Okkākas, in collaboration with the Mahāvihāran monks was, I am convinced, responsible for the composition of an imperial Purāṇa in the form of a commentary on the *Mhv*: the very commentary that has allowed George Turnour and later scholars to read the history in the Pāli Vaṃsas.

This commentary, entitled "Illumination of the Purpose (or Meaning) of History" (*Vaṃsatthappakāsinī*) gives little direct internal evidence for dating. It is certainly later than the reign of Dāṭhopatissa II (659–667), since the *VAP* refutes charges made against the Mahāvihārans by Jetavana rivals during his reign (*VAP*, 1: 176).[62] The *VAP* is no later than the thirteenth century, because it was used by the author of a text from that period.[63] But when we look for evidence external to the textual tradition, it is possible to date it much more precisely. The inscriptions erected by kings of the Okkāka dynasty, with claims that came evercloser to mirroring precisely the *VAP* world vision, preserve a record of the process by which the Mahāvihāra became the site for a formulation of Sri Lankan imperial hopes, a process that culminated in the final composition of the *VAP* and the Sri Lankan assumption of overlordship on the mainland. Without the *VAP* we cannot imagine the Sri Lankan kings taking seriously the claims they made in their inscriptions during the Okkāka ascendancy; without the global political ascendancy of the Okkāka kings, we cannot imagine the *VAP* having been written. I contend that the *VAP* both

---

[62] He is one of several "medieval" kings said to have repeated Mahāsena's action by seizing Mahāvihāra lands despite entreaties not to (*Cv* XLV.29–31). The only published inscription from the reign of this king records a donation to the rival Dakkhiṇavihāra (i.e., the Jetavana): Paranivatana, "Dakkhiṇa-Thūpa."

[63] Malalasekera, *VAP*, 1: cvi. Geiger dated *VAP* to 1000–1250, although Malalasekera demonstrates here that *VAP* may be somewhat earlier. Note that Malalasekera abbreviates "*VAP*" as "*MṬ*" (for *Mahāvaṃsa-ṭīkā*, a later epithet applied to the text; the *VAP* calls itself *Vaṃsatthappakāsinī*).

articulated and was articulated by the imperial hopes of Sri Lankan kings in the Okkāka dynasty, a dialogical process that I shall explicate in the following pages.

The *VAP* opens with a complex Pāli poem whose language suggests that this commentary is an example of something like the classical Western text, composed at a particular moment by a discrete author:

> Having honored the lord of the world who ought to receive honors (*pūjā*),
> who became the unsurpassed sun for tractable people-lotuses,
> who illuminated the sky of the excellent solar clan with radiant energy rayed by the glorious teachings (*dhamma*),
> who had vast majestic power in the dispersion of the darkness of delusion,
> and [having honored] his teaching and his disciplinary order, the mine of virtues,
> I shall give an explanation of the uncertain purpose (or meaning) of the verses of the *Mahāvaṃsa*:
> Pay close attention to it, excellent men! (*VAP*, 1:1.)

But the gloss on the meaning of this verse complicates the situation. In a lengthy discussion of how one should listen to "the injunctions of the enlightened one" (*Buddhavacana*, a term here predicated on "explanation of the uncertain meaning of the verses of the *Mhv*," 1:4), the text blurs the distinction between the author and his audience. Apparently quoting other texts, the *VAP* addresses its analysis of listening to "you (*tumhe*), who have come to listen to the teachings." "Listening to the teachings" (*dhammasavaṇaṃ*) is an action performed by "listeners" (*sotūhi*, *VAP*, 1: 4) a category that includes both teachers and students (*ācāriyasissehi*, 1: 3). The teachers (called "blossoming people-lotuses") and students (called "tractable people-lotuses" who "blossom" through an understanding of the meaning of the *Mhv*) thus overlap in a single group of "listeners," who are united in "the sphere of good men" (*sappurisabhūmi*). Listeners are enjoined to "fall into this sphere of good men forcibly, as though thirsty when water's received, or destitute when the recipient of great wealth," a metaphor explained at length (1:4–6). The text further explains that "listening carefully" is a practice that includes both teaching with care and studying with care as two sides of the same coin (1:10–11).

The *VAP*'s introduction (1:12) proceeds to outline a fivefold requirement for the introduction to any book of teachings (*gantha*): after homage has been paid to the Buddha, the book should be described according to its name, according to the number of recitation portions (*bhaṇavāra*), according to the number of chapters (*pariccheda*), and according to its usefulness or purpose (*payojanaṃ*). The homage required of the *VAP* as of any book has already been paid in the first verse and gloss thereon. But the *VAP* does not proceed to explain its own name (given only in the colophon). Instead, the *VAP* explains the meaning of the name of the book upon which it comments, *Mhv*. Thus it proceeds to define itself according to the divisions not of itself, but of the *Mhv*. So the *VAP* is not a book of teachings at all: it is a preaching of and listening to the meaning of a book (the *Mhv*) by teachers and students assembled together in the sphere of good men. As the hearers of the *VAP* are taught how to listen carefully (*sakkaccaṃ*), a distinction—evident also in its chosen title—is introduced between the letter (*byañjana*) and the purpose or meaning (*attha*) of this "Teaching of the Buddha" (1: 6). That is, the authors of this text position it as a supplement to the letter of the *Mhv*, the "meaning" (*attha*) of which, as intended by the Buddha himself, is now to be made manifest.

The *VAP*, then, records the proceedings of a "committee of inquiry" charged with interpreting the Mahāvihāran Vaṃsa (then five hundred years old). It represents itself as a textual practice whose purpose is unambiguously defined as setting forth a disciplinary procedure for attaining cessation; and studying the *Mhv* is integral to this. The committee's membership is easily reconstructed. Surely the "teachers" were Mahāvihāran Buddhist monks, who possessed privileged access to the Mahāvihāran archives and the necessary facility in Pāli language and textual exegesis. The "students" must have come from the educated nobility and members of the royal court.

According to *VAP* schematics, the purpose of *this* Teaching should, first, be listened to through the "door" of the ear and identified with the Teachings themselves; second, it should be defined according to its "meaning" (*attha*) in Magadha (i.e., Pāli) common usage, which opens up the "door" of the mind to the Teachings; third, it should be grasped and existentialized, forcibly, which is "realization" through the mind-door (1:6). Since *this* Teaching is none other than the Mahāvihāran articulation of an imperial imaginary, the implication is that this world vision should be identified as the word of the Buddha, understood literally, then truly listened to, that is, put into effect. The *VAP*'s reading of the *Mhv* is the blueprint for a Mahāvihāran imperial project, promising important results (1: 3–4). The complex author of the *VAP* thus authorizes itself. Its contents, skilfully articulated, comprise the "definitive" account of the world that its listeners are to hear again and again and think through for themselves and for the world they live in.

The Mahāvihāran imperial project called for the king and other "listeners" to the Teaching of the Buddha inscribed in the *Mhv* as "explained" by the *VAP*, to recognize Mahāvihāran supremacy over their major rivals, the Abhayagiri and Jetavana monks and their Mahāyāna practices. Like the texts on which it comments, the *VAP* makes a number of moves designed to gain preeminence for its account of the world. The most obvious move it makes is to attack the Abhayagiri and Jetavana monks as non-Theravādin, heretical offshoots of the Mahāvihāra. I have pointed out that the *Mhv* adds to the *Dpv* list of disciplinary orders the statement that two groups named Dhammaruci and Sāgāliya (Figure 3.1), seceded from the Theravāda in Sri Lanka, but it does not say where they were or when this happened, because monks with different views all claiming to follow a Theravāda rule probably lived in the same monasteries. The *VAP* eliminates this ambiguity, identifying these heretical orders with the Abhayagiri and Jetavana monks, and explains that their secession involved the adoption of false disciplinary rules (*vinaya*), and refutes anti-Mahāvihāran statements it alleges them to have made (1: 175–76), which the epigraph to this chaper specifies.

The specific charges that the Mahāyānists made against the Hīnayānists of the Mahāvihāra during the reign of King Dāṭhopatissa were, according to the *VAP*, written down and stored in a library (or, carved on stone and erected; Pāli: *likkhitvā ṭhāpesuṃ*). These charges are not spelled out in the *VAP*, but they are characterized with the statement that "the residents of the Mahāvihāra came into being on their own" (*Mahāvihāravāsino pāṭiyekkā jātā ti*: 1: 176), which the *VAP* vehemently denies. It would seem that these charges represented a counterattack on the Mahāvihāran claim to be the unadulterated Theravādins; it points out rather bluntly the probable fact that the Mahāvihārans articulated this position for themselves only a few centuries before the reign of Dāṭhopatissa. The Hīnayānists state in their Vaṃsas that the Mahāvihāra was the first monastery in Sri Lanka, founded by Devānampiyatissa himself. Abhayagiri is said to have seceded from Mahāvihāra during the reign of Vaṭṭagāmaṇi (89–77 B.C.) and the Dakkhiṇavihāra, later displaced by Jetavana, from the Abhayagiri.[64] If, having convinced its listeners that this was the right chronology, the text could also claim that the monks at Mahāvihara were unsullied Theravādins and that those at the other monasteries were the seceding Mahāyanists called Dhammaruci and Sāgāliya, they would secure their recognition as supreme.

More subtly, *VAP* retells the Mahāsena episode to include direct rebuttals of rival perspectives on the events of Mahāsena's reign, in which even Mahāsena is portrayed as a king who was convinced by the Mahāvihāran monks that the Mahāvihāra does after all deserve pride of place in Sri Lanka (2: 681–82).[65] Most interesting, it includes a curse, from a now-lost commentary on *Dpv*, upon any monks who disagree with the *VAP* interpretation of Mahāsena's reign (2: 683).

More subtle still, the *VAP* moves to appropriate and thereby undermine the Abhayagiri Vaṃsa literature. The compilation of the *VAP* was no simple matter. It involved the study and interpretation of a vast amount of canonical and post-canonical literature, which is copiously quoted or cited. That is, its listeners were actively engaged in determining "authentic" doctrine on the basis of their study of all existing literature (most of which, unfortunately, no longer exists). Among the texts most commonly cited by the *VAP* is a Mahāvaṃsa of the Abhayagirivihārans. This citation of the rival chronicle has naively been taken as "evidence of a wide tolerance and keenness for truth and precision."[66] Indeed, the *VAP* incorporates passages from the rival Vaṃsa in a convincing way, appearing to have left a record of all important differences it contained. But the *VAP* only cites this rival history for information about Mahinda and his predecessors, usually after introducing the quotation as "not at odds with the [orthodox] tradition." The implication is that everything else in the Abhayagiri Vaṃsa about the later history of Buddhism in Sri Lanka *is* at odds with the tradition.

The *VAP* makes another move to gain Mahāvihāran supremacy in its formulation of a Theravādin liturgy that could supplant the Dhāraṇī, the Mahāyāna practice of chanting protective spells in Sanskrit. Inscribed Dhāraṇī stones discov-

---

[64]Because this king favored Abhayagiri, the monks at Mahāvihāra, it is claimed, wrote down their texts (*Dpv* XX.20–21) (Table 3.1).

[65]One of the most important historical issues surrounding this reign seems to have focused upon the integrity of the Mahāvihāra's *sīmā* or liturgical boundary. The *Dpv*, *Mhv*, and *VAP* all attack the "other side" in the debate over this issue, in strikingly different ways; Walters, "Mahāsena at the Mahāvihāra."

[66]Malalasekera, *VAP*, 1: cxi; compare his dismissal of the rival chronicle: 1: lxv–lxvii.

ered in the precincts of Abhayagiri and Jetavana indicates its prevalence there in the eighth and ninth centuries.[67] Scholars have long noted that the Theravādin Buddhist practice of Paritta (Sinhala, Pirit), reciting protective spells in Pāli, represents a non-Mahāyāna (or "Mahāyāna-influenced") alternative to Dhāraṇī recitation. But there has been little attempt to trace the history of the Paritta liturgy. People recited Parittas even before the time of Aśoka, as evidenced by references to it in the Suttas used in the present-day liturgy.[68] But this in no way indicates that Paritta was a fixed part of Theravāda liturgy. The commentaries of Buddhaghosa (fifth century) give no evidence of a systematized Paritta liturgy. The first reference to such a codified liturgy appears, not surprisingly, in the *VAP*, which glosses the *Mhv* statement that Buddha thrice circumambulated the island with an explanation that, as he did so, he chanted "the Paritta which is called Mahāparitta" (*VAP*, 1: 81, 95). So *VAP* establishes the primacy of Paritta for protecting the island/the polity, with reference to a particular Paritta liturgy.

Among the lengthiest supplements to the *Mhv* made by the *VAP* is an elaboration of the Okkāka genealogy. Through a rather complex argument, the *VAP* clarifies the *Mhv*'s representation of the Okkāka/Ikṣvāku dynasty, sprung from the primordial king in this world age, Mahāsammata, as "the pure lineage" (*suddhavaṃsa*) into the premier line of which (the Śākya), the Buddha himself was born. Because the Buddha was a Śākya and Okkāka, the *VAP* argues, he was at the head of all Kṣatriya families (*sabbakhattiyakulamuddhani*: 1: 40, 136). It then demonstrates that every branch of the Śākya line of the Okkāka dynasty had been exterminated with one exception: the lineage of the Sri Lankan kings through Amitodana, the Buddha's paternal uncle, and Amitodana's grandson, Paṇḍukābhaya, king of Sri Lanka, whose Kaliṅga wife was another grandchild of Amitodana. As a result, only the Sri Lankan kings were entitled to claim overlordship among the Okkākas and Kṣatriyas of Jambudīpa (a list of whose kingdoms, including important ones on the mainland, the *VAP* conveniently supplies: 1: 130).

What the *VAP* does for the interregnal positioning of the Okkākas of Anurādhapura through its discourse on genealogy it also does for their internal positioning. In the *Mhv* genealogies, certain royal lines appear to be independent of the Anurādhapura ruling house, most notably that of Kälaṇiya (southwestern Sri Lanka) (2: 431).[69] But according to the *VAP*, these royal houses, too, were branches of the Anurādhapura dynasty. Thus the "independent" kingdoms of the south—those an Anurādhapuran ruler had to defeat in order to unify the island, a necessary first step toward world conquest—are shown to be dependent on Anurādhapura; a unified Sri Lankan polity is justified genealogically.

---

[67]Gunawardana suggests that Tibetan *Tantras* were actually far better known in ninth century Sri Lanka than scholars have generally thought: *Robe and Plough*, pp. 255–56. This was still the case in the fourteenth century; C. M. Fernando, tr., *The Nikāya Sangrahawa* (Colombo: H. C. Cottle, 1908), pp. 9–10.

[68]For example, the Aṭānāṭiya-sutta of the *Dīghanikāya*; Lily De Silva, "Paritta: The Buddhist Ceremony for Peace and Prosperity in Sri Lanka," *Spolia Zeylanica* 36.1 (1981), 3–22.

[69]See my *The History of Kelaniya* (Colombo: Social Scientists' Association, 1996), chapter 2.

The *VAP* completed this glorification of the Anurādhapuran monarchy as an imperial lineage with the only procedure for the shower bath into kingship (*abhiseka*, "coronation") of an Anurādhapuran king in the entire history of the literature. It appears in the *VAP* retelling of Aśoka's own interactions with Devānampiyatissa, and is advocated as correct for an Okkāka, Śākya king (1: 305–7). As underlords of the Pallavas, it is likely that earlier kings in Sri Lanka had received the shower bath from them. If the Sri Lankan kings were to be overlords they needed their own distinct procedure for the shower bath into kingship, and the *VAP* provides it. Moreover, in detailing the construction of the vessels from which the shower bath is to be given, the *VAP* stipulates that the clay must be obtained from seven specific sites within the Mahāvihāra where, according to the *Dpv* and *Mhv*, the adept Mahinda declared buildings to have existed in the times of previous Buddhas (*VAP*, 1: 307). The *VAP* leaves no doubt that undergoing its shower bath into kingship entails enactment of the Mahāvihāran world vision: the clay required for the Okkāka emperor's coronation is to be found where the endlessly reiterated presence of the Buddha was truly to be found, at the feet of the Mahāvihāran monks.

Last, the *VAP* moves to counter the Mahāyāna idea of the Bodhisattva-king. The *Mhv* not only declares the Buddha to be "born in the pure lineage"; it also calls him "born in the lineage of Mahāsammata, the primordial king." In its explanation of this apparent redundancy, the *VAP* makes a startling revelation about the relationship of the Buddha to the paramount kingship of Jambudīpa. To have been born of Mahāsammata means not only that the Buddha was a descendant of Mahāsammata, which is already established by the epithet "born in the pure lineage;" it also means that during previous lives he himself intervened in that lineage, being repeatedly reborn as his own ancestors. The Buddha *was* many of the great world-emperors of the pure lineage and not just the first, Mahāsammata (1: 120–24). According to the *VAP*, which follows the *BV*, after the Buddha had gained enlightenment in the time of a previous Buddha, 100,000 world ages ago, he decided to remain in cosmic flux (*saṃsāra*) as a Bodhisatta, a future Buddha, deferring his own cessation for the good of others. The *VAP* account here innovates: after his death at that time (when his name was Sumedha), he ascended into the Brāhma heaven, where he decided that, for the good of the world, he would be reborn as Mahāsammata and institute kingship on earth. The *VAP* divulges this before discussing the Mahāsammata lineage, stating that it must be understood "first of all" that the great paramount kings in the lineage of Mahāsammata were actually incarnations of the Buddha himself, as Bodhisatta/Bodhisattva.

This idea of a Bodhisatta would have startled Buddhists and Theists throughout post-Pallava South Asia. The claim that the king is a Bodhisattva was certainly a familiar one during Pallava times, when Mahāyāna-leaning kings' liturgical practices, even in Sri Lanka, often centered upon honoring images of Bodhisattvas, especially Avalokiteśvara.[70] The kings' claims to be a Bodhisattva were rooted in a Mahāyāna revelation that all good Buddhists are or should become Bodhisattvas, a

[70] John Clifford Holt, *Buddha in the Crown: Avalokiteśvara in the Buddhist Traditions of Sri Lanka* (New York: Oxford University Press, 1991).

revelation flatly denied by Mahāvihāran Theravādins, who insisted that at present there is precisely one Bodhisatta, Gotama Buddha's next successor, Metteyya. The Mahāyāna imaginary dominated the Buddhist disciplinary orders and kingdoms of the Pallava-Cālukya imperial formation, participating in dialogues and debates with the predominant imperial Śaiva knowledges and practices; the royal liturgical practice of enthusiastic participation with and honoring of images of Avalokiteśvara nicely paralleled contemporary Theist practices relating to Śiva, just as Buddhist thought about Avalokiteśvara as the very body of history, even of the entire universe, approximated Śaiva theology. The iconographic similarity between Śiva and Avalokiteśvara (and other Bodhisattvas) in Pallava art is so striking that images of them easily could be mistaken for each other; sculpture thus became a site for discourse on the relationship between Śiva and Avalokiteśvara, which ranged from assimilation to outright antagonism.

The complex author of the *VAP* did not, however, simply "borrow" the predominant Mahāyāna imaginary of the king as Bodhisattva. Instead, it developed a Pāli alternative to that world vision by reworking the Khuddaka texts of the Pāli canon. There, as in *Divyāvadāna* of the Sanskrit Sarvāstivādin canon, the web of connection to Gotama himself bears fruit in eventual, polity-wide cessations; the king who organizes and sponsors Buddhist practices helps to foster the corporate conditions that make possible the continuing development of this interconnected web of *kamma*. But even in the *Dpv* and *Mhv*, we find no indication that the king's prominence in this polity-wide soteriology was based upon anything more than his ability to create the occasions for Buddhist practice; no matter how pious the king, he was not to be considered the only Bodhisatta, the future Buddha, Metteyya. The notion of the king as Bodhisatta, which pervades post-*VAP* Sri Lankan historical literature and so has been considered by scholars to be a timeless Theravādin ideal, was a remarkable innovation effected by the complex author of the *VAP*).[71] *VAP*'s disclosure that the Buddha's birth lineage (genealogy) overlapped with his *kamma* lineage (lives as Bodhisatta)—the disclosure that calculable and incalculable dimensions of history proceed as one when a Bodhisatta condescends to be born as a

[71]The Sri Lankan king Siri Sanga Bodhi (247–249), in whose reign the Vetullavāda seems to have flourished unimpeded, is called *mahāsatta* ("great being") in the *Mhv*. This term (Skt., *mahāsattva*) is a well-known epithet of—almost synonym for—*bodhisattva* in Buddhist Sanskrit literature. The use of this term would appear at first glance to suggest that the Mahāvihāra Theravādins of Sri Lanka already had their own idea of the king as Bodhisatta. But the term *mahāsatta* is *not* a well-known epithet for the Bodhisatta in Pāli; this instance apart, according to Rhys Davids and Stede's *Pali Text Society Pali-English Dictionary*, the term is used to mean Bodhisatta only once in all the Pāli canonical and commentarial literature, and that in a very late commentary. I would suggest that the use of this term fits quite well with my argument: the imagining of the king as Bodhisatta did not enter Mahāvihāran world accounts until the composition of the *VAP*, since choosing the Buddhist Sanskrit word rather than the Pāli one immediately positions Siri Sanga Bodhi's imaginary as a response to "Mahāyāna" ontology. By implication, Sri Lankan kings who adopted "Siri Sanga Bo" as their throne name before the composition of the *VAP* were probably inserting themselves into the hegemonic Mahāyāna milieu, in which every good Buddhist aspires to become a Buddha in the future (that is, to live as a Bodhisattva in this life), rather than the Theravādin milieu, in which only a single Bodhisatta exists for soteriological succor.

Buddhist paramount king—made it possible for a powerful Mahāvihāran Buddhist king to be, not only *a* Bodhisattva, but truly *the* Bodhisatta.

Although this position moved the Mahāvihārans even further from the terms of the debates about Śiva and Avalokiteśvara that had dominated the positioning of Buddhists vis-à-vis Theists in the Pallava-Cālukya imperial formation, the *VAP*'s imaginary of the king as Bodhisatta bears striking similarity to the Vaiṣṇava imperial imaginary that had been developed by the Guptas and reworked by the Kārkoṭa Nāgas of Kashmir (see chapter 2). There, Viṣṇu himself takes birth as a series of avatars in the remote past, implying that he has also taken birth as the great kings of the immediate past and present, just as the Bodhisatta is born as various paramount kings and may therefore be born again as a paramount king, in the same genealogical line, in the present.

The implications of the *VAP*'s revelation were startling: the paramount kings have been endowed with the presence of the Buddha. They appear on earth in order to deepen their own interconnections with their subjects, who will be their followers during their future Buddhahood. Now if the coming Buddha is to be found, like his predecessor Gotama Buddha, incarnate in the Śākya branch of the Okkāka dynasty, and if the only extant descendants of Okkāka rule Sri Lanka, then a Sri Lankan king who attains imperial status must also be the coming Buddha. Participation in his Buddhist polity effects *kamma* that links subject-citizens to the becoming-Buddha, the king; the soteriological efficacy of such links is attested to in the cosmicized biographies of Gotama Buddha and his followers.

That Buddha's presence should manifest itself in the great king makes perfect sense in light of the *Dpv* and *Mhv* understanding of what Buddhas do in Sri Lanka. According to both these texts (and elaborated by the *VAP*), four previous Buddhas (Gotama included) associated themselves with the island in order to institute their Discipline (*sāsanaṃ patiṭhāpetuṃ*), namely, the teachings and disciplinary rules of the Mahāvihārans. The king who truly listens to the *VAP*—not only hearing its sound and ascertaining its meaning but also wilfully bringing that meaning into existence—does precisely the same thing: he gains recognition for the Mahāvihāran rendering of the Buddhist way of life as supreme in Sri Lanka by displacing rivals in Anurādhapura, and then he moves abroad to gain recognition for it in South Asia at large.

Realizing the Okkāka World Vision: Sena I to Mahinda IV

The defeat of the Sri Lankan king Sena I (833–853) seems to have focused the attention of Sinhalas on this imperial project. He made a donation to the Jetavana, recorded in Sri Lanka's last Sanskrit inscription.[72] Sena I apparently built a hall at the Abhayagiri monastic complex devoted to reconciliation among equal numbers of representatives from the four major divisions of the interregnal Buddhist world

[72] Sena I may have been the author of this inscription in Nāgarī characters on a stone slab; Don Martino De Zilva Wickremasinghe, "Jetavanārāma Sanskrit Inscription," *EZ* 1 (1904–12), 1–9. Gunawardana gives the (somewhat circumstantial) evidence associating it with Sena I in *Robe and Plough*, pp. 250–55.

as construed by Sarvāstivādins of the period: the Sarvāstivādins, Mahāsāṃghikas, Saṃmatīyas, and Sthaviravādins (those of Abhayagiri, I assume).[73] Sena I was still operating under the assumptions of the old Pallava ascendancy. During Sena's reign, the Pāṇḍyas conquered Sri Lanka and forced Sena I to flee south following the retreat of the Sri Lankan army from its last stand at the Abhayagirivihāra. The Pāṇḍyas under Śrīmāra Śrīvallabha (815–862), after sacking the kingdom and stealing a gold Buddha statue with gem-set eyes from the Ratanapāsāda at the Abhayagiri Śrī Mahābodhi tree (the centerpiece of royal donations to the Abhayagiri in the Pallava-Cālukya imperial formation), sued for peace (*Cv* L.12–42).[74] Sena I submitted and "agreed to everything, bestowed favors on the ambassadors to their hearts' content, presented them with a couple of elephants as well as with all his jewels and sent messengers to the Paṇḍu king, thinking of his own advantage."[75] Sena, regarded as a traitor in later Sinhala texts for "adopting false faiths,"[76] was apparently forced to bow down to the Pāṇḍya imperial way of life: Śaivism.

The Śaiva canon (codified by the Cōḻas but extant under the earlier Pāṇḍyas) makes it very clear that the Śaivas were ordering themselves in opposition to the Jains and Hīnayāna Theravādins. The latter are referred to as Therars and Sakkiyas (or Śākyas—perhaps a reference to the imperial designs that the Mahāvihāran view implied). The diatribes against these Jains and Buddhists by the Śaiva adepts make sense only if both groups actually posed a threat to Śaiva supremacy in the region.[77] Some of these accounts detail assemblies in which Buddhists and Śaivas debate about the truth of the universe, while Sri Lankan and south Indian kings adjudicate.

The most important of these accounts is a story surrounding the Śaiva adept Mānikkavāsagār, the second part of which claims that during the ninth century a king from Sri Lanka came to Madurai, the Pāṇḍya capital, with Buddhist monks, in order to win the favor of the Pāṇḍya king.[78] The Buddhist position was, however, soundly defeated by the Tamil adept, and the king of Sri Lanka recognized the superiority of Śaivism and received initiation into it. (His daughter is credited with reciting an entire portion of the Śaiva canon).[79] Sena I is the only king of the ninth century to whom these records might refer. From the Śaiva perspective, Buddhist

---

[73]Gunawardana, *Robe and Plough*, pp. 247–55.

[74]Wilhelm Geiger, tr., *Cūlavaṃsa*, translated from German by Mrs. C. Mabel Rickmers (Colombo: Ceylon Government Information Department, 1953), 1: 140 n. 4.

[75]Cv L.39–40; Geiger's translation.

[76]Gunawardana, *Robe and Plough*, p. 248.

[77]See T. N. Vasudeva Rao, *Buddhism in the Tamil Country*, pp. 207–49 and K. A. Nilakanta Sastri, "An Episode in the History of Buddhism in South India," in D. R. Bhandarkar et al., eds., *B. C. Law Volume* (Calcutta: Indian Research Institute, 1945), 1:35–49 for texts and translations from the Śaiva canon containing anti-Jain and anti-Buddhist tirades.

[78]Vasudeva Rao provides a synopsis in *Buddhism in the Tamil Country*, pp. 228–31, as does Rev. G. U. Pope, *The Tiruvācagam* (Oxford: Clarendon, 1900), pp. xxx–xxxii, lxvii–lxxii. A translation in German verse is available in H. W. Schomerus, tr., *Śivaitische Heiligenlegenden (Periyapurāṇa und Tiruvātavūrar-Purāṇa)*, Religiöse Stimmen Der Völker, Texte Zur Gottesmystik Des Hinduismus, 2(Jena: Eugen Diederichs, 1925), pp. 264–80.

[79]The initiation of a Sri Lankan king into Śaivism during the ninth century is also recorded in the *Rājataraṅginī*; Vasudeva Rao, *Buddhism in the Tamil Country*, pp. 230–31.

imperial designs had been defeated in India; the Pāṇḍyan way of life had won over the Sri Lankan king and his Therars.

But the final act of this drama had actually just begun with the submission of Sena I to the Pāṇḍyas. In the reign of his son and successor Sena II (853–887), who ascended the throne as an underlord of the Pāṇḍyas, a Pāṇḍyan prince came to Sri Lanka and requested his assistance in a rebellion. Sena II agreed, launched a huge force, and succeeded in sending the Pāṇḍyan king in flight to the Cōḻas. Sena II conquered Madurai, crowned his ally king of the Pāṇḍyas, and returned to Sri Lanka victorious, carrying with him the previously pillaged booty. His victory festival included the reinstatement of the prized gem-set Buddha image on its rightful throne (*Cv* LI.27–49).

The first part of the Mānikkavāsagār story claims that a Sri Lankan king, offended by Śaivas living in his capital, launched an attack on Madurai in order to "rip the god Śiva off his golden throne." The story ends abruptly here, and continues with the Sri Lankan king's submission to the Pāṇḍyas. But I think that the order of the stories has been reversed: Sena II did not submit, he succeeded. The Cōḻas, who later conquered Sri Lanka, rewrote the story to make it look as if the attempt at stealing Śiva had failed.

Sena II extended the practice, begun by his father, of erecting inscriptions on stone pillars placed all over Sri Lanka. These epigraphs have a common script, style, and language, and always grant certain immunities to Buddhist monasteries or villages attached to them.[80] To mark his new imperial standing, he began the practice, continued until the thirteenth century, but only sporadically thereafter, of erecting these pillars with an interregnal "bodyguard" of Pāṇḍyas, Cōḻas, Keralas, Javanese, and/or Kaliṅgas, who supported the Sri Lankan king's sovereignty.[81]

The Mahāvihāran historian reports that Sena II inscribed the Abhidhamma section of the Theravāda canon and the Paritta texts on plates and celebrated his shower bath into kingship in association with them (*Cv* LI.79). The disciplinary orders seem to have distinguished themselves most decisively with their ontologies which, more often than not, named the orders. Within the scales of Buddhist texts that each order maintained, these ontologies were inscribed in the Abhidhamma. A text of the Abhidhamma, the *Kathāvatthu*, was, it will be remembered, the text the Theravādins of the Mahāvihāra had used to position themselves against the Sarvāstivādins and Lokottaravādins. The Abhidhamma now distinguished the Theravāda from the Mahāyāna, which had attacked it mercilessly in texts beginning with the Prajñāpāramitā literature. It is known that the Abhayagiri and Jetavana possessed plates inscribed with such Mahāyāna texts called Dharmadhātu, which were treated like Buddha relics in their liturgy. The plates Sena II had inscribed with the Theravāda Abhidhamma were an alternative to these. The inscription of the Paritta is particularly interesting because its recitation was to become an important Theravāda practice in the *VAP* world vision. I read the Vaṃsa as attributing

[80]Gunawardana, *Robe and Plough*, passim.

[81]C. E. Godakumbura, "Pillar-Inscription from Mihintale," *EZ* 5 (1956–66), 320–24; and Godakumbura, "Tāmaravāva Pillar Inscription," 281–86.; S. Paranavitana, "Mannar Kacceri Pillar Inscription," *EZ* 3 (1928–33), 100–13.

to the triumphant Sena II a change of royal policy, a tentative effort to displace the authority of the Abhayagiri and Jetavana monasteries onto the Mahāvihāra. The use of the plates so inscribed in the shower bath into kingship clearly implies that the conquering king has committed his kingship to the Mahavihāra, and that the Buddhists of the Mahavihāra now endow the king with their will.

Sena II's brother and successor, Udaya II (887–898), introduced the practice of heading his grants with a royal eulogy (*praśasti*), apparently modeled after contemporary imperial inscriptions on the mainland. Intertextual reading of Okkāka inscriptional rhetoric and the *VAP*'s interpretation of the history of Sri Lanka enable us to trace the emergence of the Okkāka imperial imaginary during the ninth and tenth centuries. Udaya II claimed for the first time in an inscription that a king of Sri Lanka, his elder brother, was "descended from the lineage of Okā [Okkāka], the victorious hero, comparable to a forehead ornament unto the island of Sirilak [Sri Lanka], he of abundant splendour, a mass of splendour, who by its fulness illuminated the whole expanse of Jambudīpa and conquered Madhurā (Madurai)."[82] To the interregnal supporters in his brother's inscriptions, Udaya adds the chief of the army, whose name appears to be south Indian. He also made a donation for the preservation of the Bodhisattva image at the Abhayagirivihāra, which, as I noted above, was central to Sena's attack on Madurai and his victory celebration thereafter.

Udaya refers to his brother and heir Kassapa IV (898–914) as "his highness...who has worn the precious stones of the Pāṇḍya," and refers to Kassapa's chief consort as born in the royal lineage in Kaliṅga country, announcing an imperial marriage alliance.[83] When he ascended the throne, Kassapa IV added to his inscriptional list of cohorts officials from the court of a Pāṇḍyan king named Dappula and "Kiling Agbo (Kaliṅga Agrabodhi)," presumably a king of his wife's royal lineage.[84] He is the first Okkāka king who claimed to have brought all of Sri Lanka under a single royal canopy and thus to have established the internal power that allowed Sri Lankan kings to look across the sea with imperial eyes.[85] Kassapa IV recorded in stone his donations to the Mahāvihāra as well as the Abhayagiri, but there is no evidence that Kassapa IV furthered his brother Sena's displacement of the Mahāvihāra's rivals. Sena II and his brothers were thus the founders

[82]Paranavitana, "Paṅḍuvasnuvara Pillar-Inscription of the Reign of Udaya II," *EZ* VI (1973), 12–20, ll. A1-A15; Paranavitana, "Giritale Pillar Inscription," III (1928–33), 138–48. Gunawardana seems not to be aware of these inscriptions when he states, twice, that Udaya II's successor, Kassapa V, was the first king to claim Okkāka descent; *Robe and Plough*, pp. 173–74; Gunawardana, "The Kinsmen of the Buddha: Myth as Political Charter in the Ancient and Early Medieval Kingdoms of Sri Lanka," in Bardwell Smith, ed., *Religion and Legitimation of Power in Sri Lanka* (Chambersburg, Pa.: Anima Books, 1978), p. 102.

[83]S. Paranavitana, "Paṅḍuvasnuvara," *EZ* 6 (1973), 12–20, ll. A16–B12. I disagree with Paranavitana's view that Kaliṅga here means Sumatra. Called a place where an altar for the tree of Enlightenment (*bodhimaṇḍa*) has been established, this is the country of the *Kaliṅgabodhijātaka*, that is, the Kaliṅga in eastern India.

[84]C. E. Godakumbura, "Pillar-Inscription from Mahakalattava," *EZ* 5 (1956–66), 340; Don Martino De Zilva Wickremasinghe, "Kiribat-vehera Pillar-Inscription," *EZ* 1 (1904–12), 161.

[85]Don Martino De Zilva Wickremasinghe, "Moragoḍa Pillar-Inscription of Kassapa IV," *EZ* 1 (1904–12), 205; Paranavitana, "Two Fragmentary Inscriptions from Kälaṇi," *EZ* 6.1 (1973), 1–7.

of a dynasty that lasted, through twists and turns, for the rest of the history of Sri Lankan kingship, but in the absence of any specific indication that either of them was familiar with the range of topics in the *VAP*, it is most probable that the *VAP* was composed after their reigns.

Kassapa IV's successor Kassapa V (914–923) claimed to be the "son of the great king [Sena II] who won the fame of victory by conquering the Pāṇḍya country," and to be "descended from the Okkāka dynasty, the pinnacle of the illustrious Kṣatriya race, and lord, by lineal succession of kings, of the island of Lankā."[86] These claims, whose language resembles that of the *VAP*, were made in the ninth year of Kassapa's reign, after the dedication of a monastery at the Mahāvihāra to which he granted full immunities from taxes, impingement by royal officers, and so on. A far more elaborate slab-inscription discovered in Anurādhapura records Kassapa's construction of a different monastery for the Abhayagiri three years earlier.[87] It does not, however, just grant immunities; it attempts to regulate the Abhayagirivihāra and its sister monastery at Mihintale, as the Vaṃsa states (*Cv* LII.44), ordering the monks there to keep detailed financial accounts (LII.55) and prohibiting them in various ways from taking full possession of the donated monastery—including a prohibition on readmitting monks who have been deported to India, indicative of the defensive stance the Mahāvihāra's rivals were forced to take by the emergence of Okkāka world-making activities (LII.54). Finally, he recognized as monks only those who knew *Catubhāṇavarapāli* or *Mahā Pirit Pota*, the Mahāvihāran Paritta liturgy (mentioned here by name for the first time) (LII.55), a requirement the *VAP* made of its adherents. Although Kassapa V represented himself as a supporter of both the Mahāvihāra and the Abhayagiri, in reality his "honoring" of the Abhayagiri was more an attack than encouragement. The Mahāvihāra simply received gifts; the donations to the Abhayagiri came with strings attached. Kassapa V was trying to position the Abhayagiri within a polity that recognized the Mahāvihāra as supreme, a move no doubt offensive to the Abhayagiri and Jetavana monks.

Kassapa V, like his father Sena II, had text of the Abhidhamma inscribed on golden plates, and in a public festival recited it himself (*Cv* LII.47–50).[88] He had one book of the Abhidhamma, the *Dhammasaṅgaṇi*, encrusted with jewels and installed it in a specially built temple, in which he celebrated a yearly festival (LII.50–57). This Theravādin answer to the popular Abhayagiri *Dharmadhātu* is even called a "relic" (*dhātu*) in a contemporary inscription.[89] Kassapa V built several other monasteries in the Mahāvihāra, such as a victory temple called Maricavaṭṭi, and turned them over to the "Theravaṃsa"—a curious designation of the Theravāda that

[86]Don Martino De Zilva Wickremasinghe, "Bilibäva Pillar-Inscription," *EZ* 2 (1912–27), 38–43. The term translated "pinnacle" (*kot*) = Pāli *ketu*, flag or banner, a common metaphor for "head" or "top," and obviously reminiscent of the *VAP* position that the Sri Lankan king is "at the head" of all Kṣatriya clans.

[87]Don Martino De Zilva Wickremasinghe, "Anurādhapura Slab-Inscription of Kassapa V," *EZ* 1 (1904–12), 41–57.

[88]Wickremasinghe, "Anurādhapura Slab," p. 52.

[89]Paranavitana, "Inscriptions of the Stone Canoe within the Citadel, Anurādhapura," *EZ* 3 (1928–33), 133 n. 3.

may indicate the special importance of Vaṃsa discourse among the Mahāvihārans during this period (LII.61). Then, in a eulogy Kassapa V bragged (to the Abhayagiri monks) about these donations to the Mahāvihāra—stating that he had thereby "raised the standard of the Discipline"—an action that no doubt smarted![90]

The most blatant demonstration of the newly articulated order was Kassapa V's renewal of an old practice, recorded even by Faxian, in which the kitchen of the royal palace would feed thousands of monks daily, at a refectory called "Mahāpāli Hall."[91] In Kassapa's reign, stone troughs called "gruel boats" were installed for this purpose in the precincts of the Abhayagiri and the Jetavana monasteries (none have been discovered in the Mahāvihāra).[92] The inscription on one records its installation by the guard in the (Mahāvihāran) temple containing the *Dhammasaṅgaṇi* relic (*Cv* LII.133). It is thus possible that these boats were used in a humiliating alms giving to the rival monks, who were forced, as it were, to eat from troughs. That is, it was an act that disarticulated the relationship of these "oppositional" monks to the Discipline. It is significant that two other inscriptions on the Mahāpāli gruel boat record the fact that the Jetavana monks forfeited their shares of gruel to raise money for repairs—indicating the dire situation in which this rival monastery found itself—and called for a 6.25 percent tax on paddy to fund the same project (LII.133–6). In this light I should point out that even as he placed severe restrictions on the rights of Abhayagiri and Mihintale monks to dissent, Kassapa V also prohibited them to refuse the gruel.[93] If I am right about what these stone troughs represented—the reiteration of "honoring" that offended—it is no surprise that the rivals were refusing alms-food at the palace, and trying to get their hands on cash instead.

The eulogy of the inscription at the Abhayagiri gives further indication still that Kassapa V was operating within and helping to foster a Mahāvihāran world vision. Kassapa calls himself a king "who accomplished [the purpose] of the Discipline (*sasun ariyū*)...who in various ways interconnected diverse peoples with the Buddha...yearning in his heart, 'I shall institute the Discipline' (*sasun sitvāmi* = Pāli *sāsanassa patiṭṭhāpayissāmi*) he explained that teaching [the Pāli Abhidhamma philosophy embodied in *Dhammasaṅgaṇi*] in the presence of his own respected teacher and praised the virtues of the Buddha in his own language" (*Cv* LII.46–67, my translation). Since he did not go so far as to identify himself as a Bodhisatta, he probably knew the *VAP* only in the initial stages of its composition. It is significant in this regard that Kassapa V was presented with an opportunity to help the Pāṇḍyas, as allies, and defeat the Cōḻas, but called his army back because of plague (LII.78). His reign also witnessed severe famine (LII.81).[94] These factors seem to have hindered the imperial designs of Kassapa V, although this scholar-king may well have initiated the conference that ultimately codified the imperial world vision as the *VAP*. The mother of Kassapa's commander-in-chief provided a

---

[90] Wickremasinghe, "Anurādhapura Slab,"p. 51.

[91] Beal cites Faxian in his introduction to Xuanzang, *Xiyouji*, 1: lxxiv–lxxv.

[92] Paranavitana, "Stone Canoe," *EZ* 3 (1928–33), 131 n. 1.

[93] Wickremasinghe, "Anurādhapura Slab," p. 55.

[94] Wickremasinghe, "Anurādhapura Slab," p. 51.

monastery for forest-dwelling (*araññakavāsīnaṃ*) Mahāvihāra monks, described generally as "lamps among the elders" or, more specifically, as the "illuminators of the Vaṃsa of the Theravādins" (LII.64), in which case we have a reference to the listeners of the Illumination of the Meaning of the Vaṃsa, *VAP*.

Kassapa V was succeeded by Dappula III (923–924), whose successor Dappula IV (924–935) is our next possible candidate for listener to the *VAP*. He was another son of Sena II, and consequently a half-brother of Kassapa V. His claims are not much more elaborate than Kassapa's, except that he adds the first specific mention of the shower bath into kingship to the eulogies of this period, which may indicate that he had already instituted this facet of the Okkāka world vision.[95] He is also the first to claim that Sena II's conquest of Madurai "made the other Kṣatriya families of Jambudīpa his underlords" (*Cv* LII.139, my translation). An inscription of Dappula IV also contains the first explicit curse upon those who act against the intention of the inscribed royal edict, pointing to the curse on those who disagree with the *VAP* reading of Mahāsena's reign, in that text, the first literary evidence of such a curse.[96] Mahāvihāran reflection on the purpose of the *Mhv* was not yet a claim that the Sri Lankan king is the Bodhisatta and universal overlord. But the participants in the sphere of good men clearly were continuing with the composition of the *VAP* during Dappula IV's reign.

Dappula IV was succeeded by a series of weak kings, though I should note that in the reign of Udaya III (935–938) the Cōḻas scored a decisive victory against the Pāṇḍyas. The Pāṇḍyan king fled to his ally in Sri Lanka, left the Pāṇḍyan regalia in Udaya's hands, and then returned to Kerala in order to secure military support for the reconquest of his kingdom (*Cv* LIII.7–10). A strong alliance was thus forming, with Udaya already king of the Sinhalas and Pāṇḍyas, preparing for a confrontation with the Cōḻas. During the reign of Udaya IV (946–954), the Cōḻas attacked Sri Lanka in the interest of recovering the Pāṇḍyan regalia and quashing the growing anti-Cōḻa federation (LIII.40–46). The king fled to the mountains, and foiled the Cōḻas' quest.

During this period the last of the great Rāṣṭrakūṭa emperors, Kṛṣṇa III (939–967), mounted a strong offensive against the Cōḻas, who had been emerging since their conquest of the Pāṇḍyas as the most powerful kings in the south. Kṛṣṇa claims to have gained the subservience of the Sri Lankan king, who is not named.[97] But this relationship with the Rāṣṭrakūṭas seems to have served the Okkāka kings in Sri Lanka well. As the Cōḻas attempted to defend themselves against the Rāṣṭrakūṭas they left a temporary power vacuum to their south. Into this turbulent situation entered Mahinda IV (956–92), most likely the first to listen to the fully elaborated text of the *VAP*.

Mahinda IV was the son of Kassapa V. He thus might have been listening to the *VAP* while his father and/or uncles were ruling, which would explain why they appear to have articulated certain aspects of the Mahāvihāran world vision without

---

[95] Paranavitana, "Koṇḍavaṭṭavan Pillar-Inscription of Dappula V [sic]," *EZ* 5 (1956–66), 139.

[96] C. E. Godakumbura, "Ellevewa Pillar-Inscription of Dappula IV," *EZ* 5 (1956–66), 378.

[97] D. C. Sircar, "Rashtrakuta Charters from Chinchani, Grant of the Time of Kṛishṇa III," *EI* 32 (1957–58), 55–60; R. G. Bhandarkar, "Karhad Plates of Krishna III," *EI* 4 (1896–97), 289.

being listeners themselves. Even as heir-apparent, and ruler of the southeastern part of the island, Mahinda IV was the first to claim descent from the Buddha's father through the latter's nephew, Paṇḍukābhaya.[98] Thus even before he ascended the throne, Mahinda IV was evaluating his own political position on the basis of his knowledge of the Vaṃsas. In the first year of his reign, after conquering rebels in the southeast, Mahinda IV erected a pillar on which he claims to be the son of "the Kṣatriya lord, descended from the royal line of the Okkāka dynasty, which, abounding in an assemblage of benign, boundless, and transcendental virtues, has caused other Kṣatriya dynasties of the whole of Jambudīpa to render it homage."[99] The document also makes reference to his exalted shower bath into kingship.

Mahinda IV was a supporter not only of the Mahāvihara but also of the Abhayagiri and Jetavana monasteries. Like his father Kassapa V, he erected elaborate slab inscriptions in the precincts of the latter monasteries and at Abhayagiri's branch, Mihintale. They state that the king convened conferences, arrived at determinations about what constitutes valid monastic disciplinary rules, and then effected them. These regulations were stricter even than Kassapa's: the monks were required to submit to the disciplinary rules of the Mahāvihāra, to chant Paritta, to accept limited rights as landholders, and apparently to submit to the adjudication of royal officers or even the Mahāvihāra monks.[100] Mahinda IV spent a lot of money at the rival monasteries and even praised them in flowery language in his inscriptions, but it is clear that this honoring was also repositioning them, bringing them under Mahāvihāran rule.[101] Like his father, he bragged in his inscriptions at the rival monasteries about his improvements in the Mahāvihāra (228). Again imitating Kassapa V, Mahinda IV thus regulated and insulted only the rivals; his Mahāvihāran inscriptions are less ornate, but they come with no strings attached.[102]

Mahinda IV boasted about his work on two of the very buildings Kassapa V had bragged about: the Maricavaṭṭi and the *Dhammasaṅgaṇi* relic house. These temples were Kassapa's displays of victory and repositioning of the Abhayagiri, respectively. Knowing perfectly well what the "honoring" of Mahāyāna Buddhism by the Sri Lankan kings implied, the Cōḻas under Parāntaka (907–954) had destroyed these very buildings, along with the Mahāpāli Hall (site of the gruel boat) and the temple of the Tooth-relic (which at an undetermined moment during this period became the domain of the Mahāvihārans), when they invaded the island during the reign of Udaya IV (*Cv* LIV.44–46). Mahinda's reconstruction of these buildings was hardly nostalgic: it answered the Cōḻa challenge. Mahinda IV also attacked the Cōḻas, and under the commander of his forces, Sena, he achieved

---

98 Godakumbura, "Kirinda Pillar Inscription of Apā Mihindu," *EZ* 5 (1956–66), 271–79.

99 Don Martino De Zilva Wickremasinghe, "Rambäva Slab-Inscription," *EZ* 2 (1912–27), 64–70.

100 Don Martino De Zilva Wickremasinghe, "The Two Tablets of Mahinda IV at Mihintale," *EZ* 1 (1904–12), 75–113; Wickremasinghe, "Jetavanārāma Slab-Inscription (No. 2) of Mahinda IV," *EZ* 1 (1904–12), 230–41; Wickremasinghe, "Rambäva," *EZ* 2 (1912–27), 70.

101 Wickremasinghe, "Jetavanārāma Slab-Inscription (No. 1) of Mahinda IV, *EZ* 1 (1904–12), 213–29; S. Paranavitana, "A Fragmentary Slab-Inscription found at the Buddhist Railing near the Eastern Dāgäba, Anurādhapura," *EZ* 3 (1928–33), 226–29.

102 Don Martino De Zilva Wickremasinghe, "Vessagiri Inscriptions," *EZ* 1 (1904–12), 29–39.

astounding victories in the south of the mainland (LIV.12–16).[103] He added these victories to his eulogies. In one of them he stated, "With his glory he illumined the island of Laṅkā; with the prowess of victorious lords, displayed in the precincts of the Palace, constantly filled with wonderful presents offered by various kings of Jambudīpa, he brought glory upon prosperous Laṅkā. With [the rise of] his majestic power he drove away from Laṅkā the Drāviḍa foe [*damila*], just as the rising sun dispels darkness from the sky, and sheds lustre upon the world" and claimed to be one "who brought to his feet all the riches of the whole of Jambudīpa by means of the valour of his ...Commander-in-Chief, Sena."[104] Even earlier, Mahinda IV had effected edicts in league with Kaliṅgas, Pāṇḍyas and Tamils and forged marriage alliances with the Kaliṅgas and the rulers of Śrī Vijaya, in Java (*Cv* LIV.9).[105] After his military victories against the Cōḻas, the dominant power in south India, and the death of the Rāṣṭrakūṭa Kṛṣṇa III, paramount king of India, Mahinda IV, with a powerful confederation behind him, was genuinely in a position to claim paramount overlordship.

Accordingly, he states that his shower bath was a shower bath into world supremacy (*lov uturā bisevnen bisesvä*)[106] and that he had attained for himself transcendental virtues and "the way to cessation."[107] The rhetoric of his inscriptions after the victory over the Cōḻas closely resembles that of the *VAP*; he shines light upon the world through the effulgence of his majestic energy, like the Buddha in the *VAP*, a sun for the Solar dynasty. Most important, he concludes an inscription with this statement:

> The regulations thus enacted should always be maintained with due regard to the descendants of our dynasty, the Kṣatriya lords devoted to the Buddha, who have received the assurance [made by] the omniscient Lord of Sages, the pinnacle of the Śākya race, that none but the Bodhisattas would become kings of prosperous Laṅkā; who are wont to wear the white scarf to serve and attend on the great community of monks on the very day they celebrate the coronation festival after attaining to the dignity of kingship, bestowed by the great community of monks for the purpose of defending "the bowl and the robe" of the Buddha.[108]

Thus Mahinda IV included in the Okkāka eulogy the final and most important element of the *VAP* imperial imaginary: the representation of the king as the Bod-

---

[103]Don Martino De Zilva Wickremasinghe, "Vessagiri," *EZ* 1 (1904–12), 34–5.

[104]Don Martino De Zilva Wickremasinghe, "Jetavanārāma (2)," *EZ* 1 (1904–12), 225; Wickremasinghe, "Vessagiri," pp. 34–35.

[105]S. Paranavitana, "Inscription on 'Vessagiri' Slab No. 2B," *EZ* 6.1 (1973), 28.

[106]Wickremasinghe, "Jetavanārāma (2)," pp. 234 l. 5; 221, ll. 3–4.

[107]Wickremasinghe, "Vessagiri," I, 34.

[108]Wickremasinghe, "Jetavanārāma (2)," p. 240. This "assurance" was revealed as Buddha's word (*Buddhavacana*), for the first time in history, by the *VAP*. Although scholars generally think of the "Bodhisatta-king" imaginary as ubiquitous in Theravāda history and timeless in the sense that it has always existed, it is important that we recognize the historicity of the perspective. This idea emerged only when the Sri Lankan kings had reached an unprecedented level of global power and prestige—only when the homology between the Sri Lankan king and the great world conquerors of the Okkāka lineage was credible.

hisatta. Victorious over the Cōḻas, allied with important South and Southeast Asian kings, the Śākya pinnacle of all Kṣatriya clans, the world-conquering Bodhisatta who shines light on the Solar dynasty—Mahinda IV represents himself as the Okkāka king who truly listened to the *VAP*, who truly fashioned his own kingship on the basis of the Mahāvihāran world vision.[109] Between about 963/4 and his death in 972, Mahinda IV was one of the most powerful kings in the Indian world. His polity realized the world wish in the *VAP*, a work that his Theravādin polity completed.

History after *Vaṃsatthappakāsinī*

The only scholars who have written about the Okkāka dynasty and its representation in epigraphic records as a separate topic for historical study, R. A. L. H. Gunawardana and Lakshman Perera, have dismissed the claims made in Okkāka royal eulogies as "myths" of legitimation or meaningless hyperbole.[110] My critical reading of the *VAP*, which elucidates the ontology upon which these eulogies are based, undermines the long-lived scholarly belief that Sri Lanka has always been a religious or cultural island whose only interaction with the mainland has been the result of periodic Indian aggression against it. This view reflects the representation of Sri Lanka first as a territorial division in the British empire and then as an independent nation, as well as the monological approach to texts and history, more than it reflects the actual position of Sri Lanka as a polity vis-à-vis other South Asian kingdoms during the ancient and medieval periods. It was, as much as those centered in Tamil Nadu or Bengal, an active participant in Indian political formations until the fall of Kandy (1815). Contemporary mainland inscriptions leave no doubt that the island's Okkākas, during two centuries after the time of Mahinda IV posed a serious threat to other contenders for the overlordship of south India, especially the Cōḻas, the eventual victors in the battle for sovereignty. Taking seriously the claims made by the Sri Lankan Okkāka kings is justified by the fact that their contemporaries did so.

By the end of the tenth century, the Cōḻas had emerged victorious in their struggle with the Rāṣṭrakūṭas, and were ready to consolidate their position further south. The first great Cōḻa world conqueror, Rājarāja I (985–1014) launched an attack against the Sri Lankan King Mahinda V (982–1029) between 1001 and

---

[109] An inscription dated to the tenth or early eleventh century on paleographic grounds (the name of the king no longer survives, but I assume that it must have been Mahinda IV) states that anyone failing to comply with the regulations it enacts will "not be born in the kingdom of the Great Maitreya the Buddha." This curse would be weighty only when the Bodhisatta happens to be the reigning king, and participation in the polity is thereby soteriologically efficacious; S. Paranavitana, "Two Inscriptions from Eppāvala," *EZ* 3 (1928–33), 188–92.

[110] Gunawardana, "Kinsmen of the Buddha"; Lakshman S. Perera, "The Royal Lineage in the Prasastis of the 8th-10th Century Inscriptions," *Ceylon Historical Journal* 2.3 (January 1953), 230–36. Paranavitana simply dismisses the Okkāka claim that Sena II caused all other Kṣatriya clans to render him homage, declaiming "the inappropriateness of referring to a king of Ceylon as having subdued all the kings of India…"] as though it were obviously an impossible fantasy; "Koṇḍavaṭṭavan Pillar Inscriptions," p. 139 n. 7.

1004. Although he failed to capture the Pāṇḍya and Sri Lankan regalia, he did defeat the king, who was forced to flee (*Cv* LV.14–22).[111] His successor, Rājendra Cōḻa I (1012/14–1044) launched another attack in 1017/18 and this time the Cōḻas were successful.[112] Rājendra subsequently added to his inscriptional eulogy the statement that he conquered, "the crown of the king of Iram [Eelam, Sri Lanka], (*who was as impetuous as*) the sea in fighting; the exceedingly beautiful crown of the queen of the king of that (*country*); the crown of Sundara and the pearl-necklace of Indra, which the [Pāṇḍya] king of the South had previously given up to that (*king of* Iram); the whole Ira-maṇḍalam [island of Sri Lanka] on the transparent sea."[113] Mahinda V was captured along with the regalia, and he and his family were carried off to India to die in exile (LV.22–33).[114] These were real victories against a formidable foe. Rājarāja I "was pleased to destroy...Ila-maṇḍalam, (*which was the country*) of the warlike Singalas."[115] He states that the conquest of Sri Lanka "made (*him*) famous (*in*) the eight directions."[116] Rājendra I boasts more about his conquest of Sri Lanka than any other single victory in his conquest of the quarters. And he appropriates for his family descent from Ikṣvāku, progenitor of the Solar dynasty.[117]

The Cōḻa victory over Sri Lanka included an attempt at appropriating its Buddhist imperial significance. Rājarāja erected Buddhist monasteries in his own name at the major western and eastern seaports of Sri Lanka, and Rājendra I erected inscribed slabs (subsequently smashed and surviving only in fragments), including one containing his elaborate eulogy boasting of his conquest of Sri Lanka, in order to demonstrate that the Cōḻa was now the Bodhisatta.[118] He moreover sponsored the construction (under the direct supervision of Mahinda IV's old Buddhist ally, the king of Śrī Vijaya in Java) of an elaborate Buddhist temple at Nāgapaṭṭaṇam, the seaport on the mouth of the Kāverī River in Cōḻamaṇḍalam (Thanjavur Dt.), central domain of the Cōḻa empire.[119] This site continued to be of great importance to the survivals of pan-Asian Buddhism even into the seventeenth century.[120] The Javanese king named this temple "Cūḍāmaṇivarman" after his father, a name that punned on the stūpa which Indra, king of the gods, built in his heaven when the

[111] K. V. Subrahmanya Aiyer, "The Larger Leiden Plates of Rajaraja I," *EI* 22 (1933–34), 257; E. Hultzsch, "Inscriptions in the Vishnu Temple at Ukkal: [Rajaraja I]," *SII* 3.1 (1899), 7–8.

[112] K. A. Nilakanta Sastri explains the overlapping reigns in *The Cōḻas* (Madras: University of Madras, 1935–37), 1: 231, 293.

[113] Hultzsch, "Tamil Inscriptions in the Rajarajesvaram Temple at Tanjavur [Rajendra-Chola I]," *SII* 2.1 (1891), 108; Hultzsch, "Tirumulai Rock Inscription of Rajendra-Chola I," *EI* 9 (1907–8), 233.

[114] S. Paranavitana, "Fort Hammenhiel Tamil Inscription," *EZ* 6.1 (1973), 28–30.

[115] Hultzsch, "Inscriptions at Ukkal," p. 7.

[116] Hultzsch, "Inscriptions at Ukkal," p. 15.

[117] H. Krishna Sastri, "The Tiruvalangadu Copper Plates of the Sixth Year of Rajendra-Chola I," *SII* 3 (1929), 413.

[118] S. Paranavitana, "Fort Hammenhiel"; A. Veluppillai, "Two Short Inscriptions of Velgam Vihāra," *EZ* 6.1 (1973), 65–67; Veluppillai, "Four More Inscriptions from Nātanār Kovil or Velgam Vihāra," *EZ* 6.1 (1973), 88–92.

[119] Subrahmanya Aiyer, "Larger Leiden Plates," p. 257. This temple should be looked to as the paradigm for the "seven-storeyed vihāra" in Polonnaruwa and the similar architecture at Angkor Wat.

[120] Gunawardana, *Robe and Plough*, pp. 262–63, 265.

Buddha came to visit, according to the Mahāvihāran recension of the *Jātaka*. And so it was in the Cōḻa empire where the king among kings erected a temple for visiting Buddhists. As in the days of Nāgārjunikoṇḍa, Sri Lankan Theravāda was again one Buddhist disciplinary order among many in the Śaiva king's world.

For nearly forty years the Cōḻas actually ruled Sri Lanka, pillaging the northern part of it from their eastern base at Polonnaruwa.[121] What the Cōḻas did in Sri Lanka was reprehensible, but the Okkākas themselves were partially to blame: the virulence of their challenge to Cōḻa hegemony between the tenth and twelfth centuries, which included raids and pillaging expeditions in Cōḻa country, provoked them to respond. Both had positioned themselves as close rivals for imperium.[122] Six kings claiming to be carriers of the Okkāka torch "ruled" in the southeastern part of Sri Lanka between 1029, when Mahinda V died in exile, and 1055, when a new contender emerged among the Sri Lankans: Vijayabāhu I (1055–1110). Forming alliances with various political and military factions in Sri Lanka and in India, Vijayabāhu succeeded in raising the royal canopy and forcing the Cōḻas out of Sri Lanka. He posed enough of a threat that Rājendra II (1052–1064) felt he had to counterattack (and boasted of his victories, including the capture of the Kaliṅga king in Sri Lanka).[123]

During the reigns of Vijayabāhu's successors, Jayabāhu I (1110–1111), Vikramabāhu I (1111–1132) and Gajabāhu II (1132–1153), the Cōḻas and/or strong-arm mercenary forces from south India like the Vēḷāikkāras dominated the scene in Sri Lanka.[124] Sri Lankan kings ruled at the old Cōḻa capital, Polonnaruwa, but only by virtue of marriage alliances with Cōḻa princesses; and their Buddhist city was dotted with Śaiva shrines.

Parākramabāhu I (1153–86) made the final attempt to realize the world vision of the *VAP*. He united the island, expelled the Cōḻas, and even harassed them in India, attacking Madurai, sending Kulaśekhara (the Pāṇḍya king) fleeing to his Cōḻa overlords, and installing Vīra (the Sinhala candidate) on the Pāṇḍya throne. Rājādhirāja (1163–1181), the ruling Cōḻa emperor, ordered the Sri Lankan generals to be killed and their heads hung on the gates of Madurai, and reinstated Kulaśekara on the Pāṇḍyan throne, claiming in subsequent inscriptions to have saved his kingdom from falling into the hands of the Sinhalas.[125] The Okkāka empire was not merely the product of Sri Lankan imagination; it was an imperial threat to which

---

[121] George W. Spencer reproduces the polemics and hyperbole of the *Cv* (and modern Sri Lanka), which hold that the Cōḻa destruction in Sri Lanka somehow lay outside any world vision: "The Politics of Plunder: The Cholas in Eleventh-Century Ceylon," *Journal of Asian Studies* 35.3 (1976), 405–19.

[122] Richard Davis, *Lives of Indian Images* (Princeton: Princeton University Press, 1997), provides a much more sophisticated analysis of plunder in South Asian polities.

[123] E. Hultzsch, "Inscriptions at Manimangalam [Rajadhiraja]," *SII* 3.1 (1899), 57–58; S. Paranavitana, "Panākaḍuva Copper Plate of Vijayabāhu I," *EZ* 5 (1956–66), 23–27; Don Martino De Zilva Wickremasinghe, "Ambagamuva Rock-inscription of Vijayabāhu I," *EZ* 2 (1912–27), 202–18.

[124] Paranavitana, "Polonnaruva Inscription of Vijayabāhu I," *EI* 18 (1925–6), 330–38; Paranavitana, "Slab-Inscription of the Vēḷāikkāras," *EZ* 2 (1912–27), 242–55; Paranavitana, "A Tamil Pillar-Inscription from Māṅkanai," *EZ* 6.1 (1973), 7–11; A. Veluppillai, "A Tamil Pillar Inscription from Rankot Vihāra, Polonnaruwa," *EZ* 6.1 (1973), 67–79.

[125] V. Venkatasubba Ayyar, "The Pallavarayanpettai Inscription of Rajadhiraja II," *EI* 21 (1931–32), 184–93; Venkatasubba Ayyar, "Tiruvalangadu Inscription of Rajadhiraja II," *EI* 22 (1933–34), 91–92.

the Cōḻas responded accordingly. Subsequently, Kulaśekara changed sides, conspired with the Sri Lankans, and revolted against the Cōḻas, tearing the decapitated Sri Lankan generals' heads from the gates of Madurai. The Cōḻa king retaliated, reinstating Vīra Pāṇḍya on the Madurai throne.[126] Parākramabāhu I allied himself with former Okkāka allies, especially the Kaliṅgas and the Javanese, launched a successful invasion of Burma and, consequently, declared himself pinnacle of the Kṣatriya Okkākas and paramount king, reponsible for the salvation of his subjects.[127] The last of Sena II's direct descendants to occupy the Sri Lankan throne, he was perhaps more deserving of the Okkāka title than any of them.

An inscription of Parākramabāhu I implies that Kassapa V and Mahinda IV had tried "strenuously" to bring rival disciplinary orders under the Mahāvihāra.[128] Certainly Parākramabāhu—hero-king of the *Cv*—attempted to do so. He had colossal Buddha images (now called Gal Vihāra) carved into the side of a rock formation in the city of Polonnaruwa; in their midst he had inscribed a huge royal proclamation called a Katikāvata (reminiscent of the slabs erected by Kassapa V and Mahinda IV at the Abhayagiri and Jetavana). It consisted of regulations of the monastaries on the island, a demonstration of the king's power to adjudicate contesting viewpoints about history, monastic discipline, and interpretation of the Buddha's teachings.

Parākramabāhu's inscription leaves no doubt that he fully accepted the Mahāvihāran perspective on Sri Lankan Buddhist history. The inscription begins, like the Vaṃsas, with a reference to the cosmic Buddha biography of *BV*, commencing "four incalculable and one hundred thousand eons ago." The narrative continues up to the foundation of the Abhayagirivihāra, which is portrayed, like subsequent splinterings of the Saṃgha in this "course of decadence," as a decided break with Buddhist tradition. A descendant of Mahāsammata, Parākramabāhu is responsible for the provision of the true Discipline to his subject-citizens, in order to save them from rebirth in hell, and so finds the divisions of the Saṃgha intolerable. He orders all monks in rival monasteries to give up their robes and undergo again their higher ordination (*upasampadā*) under the guidance of a monk from the Mahāvihāra: only Mahāvihāran monks would be recognized as monks, and all monasteries would hence become branches of the Mahāvihāra.[129] This "unification" of the island's disciplinary orders under the aegis of the Mahāvihāra, which was overseen by the forest-dwelling (*araññakas*) Mahāvihārans, differs little from what Mahāsena tried to do for the Abhayagiri order centuries earlier, except that it is far subtler, based upon the *VAP*'s complex historical argument. We may never know what outcry it raised from the rivals, because their defeat was (eventually) permanent. The fact that only Mahāvihāran Vaṃsas have survived is evidence of this: the texts of the rivals disappeared after Parākramabāhu's unification of the Saṃgha.

[126]C. W. Nicholas, "The Reign of Parakramabahu I," *History of Ceylon* 1.2 (1960), 475–76; Nilakanta Sastri, *Cōḻas*, 2: 98–107.

[127]Paranavitana, "Devanagala Rock-Inscription of Parākramabāhu I," *EZ* 3 (1928–33), 312–25 and note 127 below.

[128]Nandasena Ratnapala, ed. and tr., *The Katikāvatas* (Munich: R. Kitzinger, 1971), pp. 127–35.

[129]Gunawardana's analysis suggests that in fact Parākramabāhu's obliteration of the rivals was not as complete as is usually assumed: *Robe and Plough*, passim.

That the Mahāvihāran Theravāda disciplinary order became the very definition of "southern Buddhism" should not be seen as the inevitable resurgence of the true Discipline of the Pāli canon. It was, rather, in many ways, an accident of geography. Beginning in the eighth, ninth, and tenth centuries, Arab and then Turkish Muslim armies destroyed many of the major northern centers of the interregnal Buddhist world (in modern north India, Pakistan, Afghanistan, and Central Asia.) The remaining "northern" disciplinary orders (in Tibetan and Chinese domains) were cut off from their "southern" counterparts. Little surprise that by the tenth century, "Mahāyāna" disciplinary orders in the south like those that formerly had thrived in Anurādhapura as purveyors of cosmopolitan Buddhist knowledge, finding the former Buddhist world in shambles, increasingly lost ground to the "Hīnayāna" Theravāda that had always been concentrated in south India and Sri Lanka.

Although the dominance of the Mahāvihāra in Sri Lanka—the articulation of an exclusively "Hīnayāna" Theravāda tradition with Sri Lanka as its home—was permanent, its political significance in the larger imperial formations of South Asia proved only transitory. Parākramabāhu's Kaliṅga allies helped keep Sri Lanka from the Cōḻas for another forty years, with the backing of Parākramabāhu I's own commander-in-chief. Niśśaṅka Malla (1187–1196), who calls himself "Kaliṅga Cakravartin" ("Kaliṅga Wheel-turning Monarch," never before used in Sri Lankan eulogies) in his inscriptions, even made two expeditions to the Pāṇḍya country and "tarried" at Rāmeśvaram—where Sri Lanka still commanded a military outpost—erecting a victory pillar there. He also performed the "weight in the balance" (*tulābhāra*) ceremony there, the same place Parāntaka Cōḻa had performed it in order to display his appropriation of paramount kingship from the Rāṣṭrakūṭas.[130] Perhaps the Cōḻas knew that this dynasty was on its last leg, and simply allowed Niśśanka Malla to taunt them in this way; or perhaps he really did have sufficient military force to sustain his claims to have no rival in all of Jambudīpa. Within ten years, however, the Cōḻas captured the military outpost at Rāmeśvaram.[131] They sent a "ruthless" Kaliṅga prince to Sri Lanka, named Māgha (1215–1236), who seized the "Kaliṅga" throne of Sri Lanka at Polonnaruwa for the Cōḻas and wreaked havoc on the countryside, focusing on liturgical edifices.[132] Sri Lankan kingship emerged from this final confrontation weakened, and reduced to hiding out in the fortress-palaces from which it tried to survive in the wake of new, and even more powerful, Indian and Western colonial empires. *Cv* can be seen as a product of imperial defeat. It constituted a new kind of identity for Sri Lankans, one that is not undermined by submission to more powerful emperors. *Cv* is thus ripe for a dialogical interpretation. Rather like the *Dpv*, it exhibits an historical consciousness stressing continuity and survival rather than innovation and expansion, the

[130] Don Martino De Zilva Wickremasinghe, "Dambulla Rock Inscription of Kīrti Niśśaṅka Malla," *EZ* 1 (1904–12), 121–35; "Polonnaruva: 'Galpota' Slab-inscription," *EZ* 2 (1912–27), 98–123; "Polonnaruva: A Slab-Inscription of Niśśaṅka-Malla," *EZ* 2 (1912–27), 153–6; "Kantalāi Gal-āsana Inscription of Kitti Niśśaṅka-Malla," *EZ* 2 (1912–27), 283–90.

[131] Sirima Wickremasinghe, "Successors of Parakramabahu I," *History of Ceylon* 1.2 (1960), 521–25.

[132] Wickremasingha, pp. 525–28.

local rather than the global, peace at the cost of submission to the Cōḻas as more desirable than ceaseless military conflict with them. To the extent that the present interpretation does not examine the situation in which *Cv* was produced, it thus remains incomplete.

The Sri Lankan kings never again attempted to realize the world wish of the *VAP*. Instead, subsequent Sri Lankan history is the story of subtle and complex attempts at a dual strategy. On the one hand, its ruling society of kings and monks tried to find a place for some sort of less ambitious Sri Lankan kingship first within the Śaiva and Vaiṣṇava empires of India, and then in the Christian empires of the West.[133] On the other hand, Sri Lanka did attempt to position itself as the center of a Theravāda Buddhist world in Southeast Asia. Probably under Parākramabāhu I, if not under Mahinda IV himself, the *VAP* was disseminated along with most of Sri Lanka's Pāli canon throughout Southeast Asia, and rearticulated by the monks and kings of Burma, Thailand, Cambodia, and Laos within their polities from the eleventh century onward. Possibly people once used it in Java, as well. Monks in Southeast Asia versified the *VAP* as an extension of the *Mhv*, and it continued for centuries as the textualized world wish for the "further Indian" Theravāda Buddhist empires of the late precolonial period.

Conclusion: Vaṃsas as Dialogical

Like the Purāṇas of Theist disciplinary orders, the Vaṃsas of the Theravādin Buddhist orders can be seen as dialogical moments in a scale of texts, each of which supplements the earlier ones with its own interpretation. The lowest text in this scale is the *Buddhavaṃsa*, the first Theravādin revelation of incalculable time and its soteriological implications for present-day polities (Table 3.1). The *Sīhalaṭṭhakathā-Mahāvaṃsa*, itself a collection of documents compiled at the Mahāvihāra before the fourth century, supplemented *Buddhavaṃsa* with the details of Indian and Sri Lankan history, thereby envisioning the Anurādhapura kingdom as a continuation of the cosmic polity depicted in the *BV* and related texts. Though no longer extant, we can affirm with Geiger and others that the authors of the major Vaṃsas that do survive today—the *Dpv*, *Mhv* and *VAP*—preserved much of the *Sīhalaṭṭhakathā-Mahāvaṃsa* by embedding portions of it within their own more grandiose narratives. The *Dpv* took up the basic format and actual passages from the earlier Sinhala Vaṃsa and versified them, somewhat crudely, in Pāli. This textualization permitted later monks to refer to the *Dpv* as "the Purāṇa."

Composed at the very beginning of the fourth century A.D., perhaps by Mahāvihāran nuns who were the only residents left in the Mahāvihāra after Mahāsena's destructive reign, the *Dpv* defers to the rival monastery and limits its petition to the survival of the Mahāvihāra in whatever position of inferiority to the Abhayagiri. The complex author of the *Mhv*, at a moment of relative strength for both

---

[133] I show, for example, that the Sri Lankans submitted to the emperors of Vijayanagar in "Vibhīṣaṇa and Vijayanagar: An Essay on Religion and Geopolitics in Medieval Sri Lanka," in *Sri Lanka Journal of the Humanities (Special Jubilee Edition)*, 17-18.1–2 (1991–92), 129–42.

Mahāvihāran monks and Sri Lankan kings in the fifth century, reworked this Purāṇa into something more than a refined poetic version of the *Dpv*, advancing the (still cautious) claim that the Mahāvihāra should be considered superior to its rivals, and its bolder statement that Sri Lankan kings need not submit to mainland overlords if their power be great and their motives sincere. The *VAP* supplemented the *Mhv*, not merely with the minor details extracted from the *Sīhalaṭṭhakathā-Mahāvaṃsa* that so delight positivist historians but more important, with its own innovative interpretation: a full-fledged Mahāvihāran world vision, which transformed the *Mhv* into a blueprint for imperial formation. All these texts narrate the same history, but they do so in strikingly different literary forms, and according to strikingly different political agendas, as was appropriate to the historical circumstances in which they were composed.

By way of conclusion I examine two areas on which the revised history resulting from my changed approach sheds important light: the contemporary scholarly portrayal of a generic Vaṃsa "ideology" or "ideal," and scholarly approaches to the study of Buddhist history more generally.

One of the most important features of recent scholarship is its focus on the Mahāvihāran idea of Dhammadīpa. This sees Sri Lanka as an island and light of the Buddhist way of life in and for the rest of the world, and is said to appear in the Vaṃsas.[134] Scholars take this "ideology" to be inherently Sinhala, an essence that preexisted the composition of the actual texts in which it is first expressed. The "ideal social order" embodied in the king as lay person par excellence (i.e., Bodhisatta) "legitimizing" his sovereignty by providing material support to the Buddhist monks par excellence (the Mahāvihārans), then "influences" history, or is influenced by it, but it always remains outside of history. In fact, scholars have doubtless identified many of the aspects of the full-fledged Mahāvihāran world vision. But their monological approach to texts leads them to consider these imperial imaginaries to be the very essence of Sri Lankan Buddhism. The authors of the Vaṃsas "document" or "express" it; they do not create it and rework it as complex authors engaged in debate with others.

The dialogical approach employed in this study of the available evidence leads me to a very different conclusion about the idea of the Dhammadīpa. The complex author of the *VAP* was able to locate its imperial world vision in the *Mhv*, but there is no evidence that the Mahāvihārans who composed the *Dpv* and *Mhv* even contemplated one. Those texts are significant—and have continued into the present, unlike the Abhayagiri historical texts—precisely because later monks made them a foundation upon which they could develop a world vision in the seventh to ninth centuries until, near the end of the tenth century, they "listened" to it for the first time. This vision, later ideologized as the Dhammadīpa, remained, rather like a

[134]As Steven Collins has pointed out to me, this idea appears nowhere in the Vaṃsas themselves. As far as I have been able to discern, the earliest published use of the term in its timeless sense occurred only in 1942, and the author quotes statements made by Lord Passfield in the House of Commons: Ven. Bhikkhu Metteyye, "Lord Buddha—The First Liberator of Slaves," *Maha Bodhi Journal* 50 (April-June 1942), 178–79. I can only conclude that the Dhammadīpa was invented in the middle of the twentieth century as an ideologization of the *VAP*/Okkāka world vision.

myth, a hypothetical description of reality until Mahinda IV actually constituted the world around it. He and his successors as Metteya (Maitreya) the Bodhisatta and Okkāka the paramount king would institute the Discipline of the Buddha, as understood by the Mahāvihāran monks of Sri Lanka, in order to transform South and Southeast Asia into a predominantly Buddhist world.

I single out the idea of Dhammadīpa simply because it has been so prevalent in the scholarship. My analysis, though, has implications for all the facets of "the Theravādin social order" that scholars have hypostasized. For example, it is clear that "patronizing" Theravādin orthodoxy at the Mahāvihāra in order to "legitimize" kingship was a late phenomenon (arguably a tenth-century innovation) that could have "legitimized" nothing in earlier periods, and that ultimately "legitimized" Okkāka kings quite differently—more realistically, more directly, more actively—than scholars have so far imagined. Indeed, this study suggests that scholars have been wasting time searching for transcendent Theravāda Buddhist essences since Theravāda Buddhism itself, as an independent disciplinary order, only began to exist in the third or fourth century A.D., and "orthodox" Theravādin thought did not gain ascendancy over "Mahāyāna" Theravādin thought, even in Sri Lanka, until the ninth or tenth century!

The enterprise of studying Vaṃsas as "authentic history" first emerged among colonial British civil servants seeking to appropriate Ceylon by appropriating its past. In the last quarter of the nineteenth century and the first half of the twentieth century Sinhala Buddhist "nationalists" turned the *Mhv* against those who had spawned it in the first place. They ideologized the British (mis)reading of the Vaṃsas as containing a positivist history in which the Sri Lankan polity is essentially and timelessly Mahāvihāran Theravāda Buddhist, then took up this ideology in order to justify the very expulsion of the non-Buddhist British imperium. The stamp of scholarly authority is then lent to this ideologization of the misreading by neopositivist writings on the "ideal social order" supposedly expressed in the *Mhv*. Within the first decade of Independence, and especially during the 1980s and 1990s, this ideologized misreading, in the form of "Sinhala chauvinism," has become the rallying cry of a civil war wreaking truly tragic consequences for the nation generally and its Tamil (Theist) members, in particular.

Tenth-century imperial rhetoric—which was played out politically, which failed, and which the Sri Lankans had themselves abandoned by the thirteenth century—has been made into the essence of Sri Lankan consciousness both before and after the historical period in which it was actually current. This is more than an epistemological problem; it is a political problem. For this imperial rhetoric—insidiously, though largely unconsciously, transformed in the minds of "scientific" historians into the language of ceaseless ethnic struggle on the part of a Sri Lankan state that "uses" religion to "legitimate" homicidal frenzies—has been reworked into a program for modern Sri Lanka by the very scholars who now shake their heads wondering how such terrible things can be happening there. I believe that if scholars begin to examine the manner in which historical thought is produced, both in medieval Sri Lankan monasteries and in the modern academy, it will be a crucial step toward recovering the options of a more differentiated, contingent history that has been lost in Sri Lanka.[135]

Reading the Vaṃsas as dialogical rather than monological texts reveals dimensions of their history that empiricist and positivist historians, as discussed in the appendix to this chapter, never even considered. The recovery of these histories in turn causes us to rethink certain aspects of received tradition about Buddhist history more generally (itself in large part constructed on the basis of monological readings of the Sri Lankan Vaṃsas).

Because the Vaṃsa authors were active participants in the interregnal Buddhist world, rather than the isolated conservatives Buddhological scholarship usually portrays them to have been, their texts made claims about a larger Buddhist history. These claims have been evaluated as though they had been intended as contributions to Colonial European archives rather than to the discourses of the time-places in which their authors lived; some scholars reproduce these claims as "authentic history" while others denounce them according to the same standard. A dialogical reading allows us, instead, to treat those claims as part of the Buddhist history we are trying to understand. Scholars have too often blindly reproduced the polemics rather than asking what the polemics were for. What was at stake in these claims? Who made them? What was happening around them at that time-place? Why and where did they dispute? How did different sides in various disputes constitute the authenticity of their own positions? How did they combat the positions of rivals?

When we begin to ask and answer these questions, the monological essence "Buddhism" begins to recede; there is no single "Buddhist history," but a history of multiple Buddhist representations of the Teachings and Discipline. Giving up the essentialized Buddhism of these interpretations in order to recover actual Buddhists engaged in making their own histories, we are forced simultaneously to reconsider some important mainstays in Buddhological scholarship. My work on the Vaṃsas has suggested that the quintessential "Hīnayāna" Buddhist disciplinary order already encodes responses to the supposedly later "Mahāyāna" orders; that the Mahāvihāran Theravāda became hegemonic in Sri Lanka some thirteen centuries later than scholars have admitted; that the division of the Buddhist world into "Northern" and "Southern" schools occurred later still; that "medieval" develop-

[135]Obviously, scholarship alone cannot solve the problems in Sri Lanka. But just as the mass media have been employed in order to reinforce the communalist program that has torn Sri Lanka asunder, so they can be employed in order to undermine that program. There are hopeful signs at the time of this writing that steps in this direction are now being taken, as the Sri Lankan press begins to focus upon the needs and goals common to all ethnic groups in the country, and as Lāṅkika ("Sri Lankan") begins to displace "Sinhala" and "Tamil" as terms of national identity. But undoing the damage done by scholarly constructs requires redressing the construct of Sri Lankan history as well as the construct of modern social divisions. It is incumbent upon the Sinhala press, broadcasting corporations, textbook designers, and especially politicians to make use of scholarly reexaminations of the complex manner in which the traditional Sri Lankan polities, both before and after the Okkāka dynasty, worked to forge union rather than disunion among different linguistic and religious social groups, on the basis of subtle grammatical and theological epistemologies which, hierarchical though they surely were, constituted all Sri Lankans as parts of a larger whole, and moreover understood Sri Lanka itself to be part of a still larger whole. It is especially incumbent upon scholars to start making those reexaminations.

ments in South Asian Buddhist thought and practice were active engagements with prevalent Theist philosophies and practices rather than passive absorptions of their "influence"; that far from gradually and inevitably "disappearing" in post-Gupta South Asia, Buddhist forms of thought and practice remained real contenders for imperial prestige as late as the twelfth century, and finally did not so much "disappear" as get obliterated. But my work has wider implications still for the study of Buddhist history.

Clearly, historians can no longer rest content treating "medieval" Buddhist monks and nuns as though they had been operating according to an empiricist philosophy of history that had yet to be invented, thousands of miles and years away. Taking seriously the statements about the nature of time and connection made by the Vaṃsa authors makes possible my reconstruction of a particularly Mahāvihāran Theravāda Buddhist historiography rooted in the philosophical and literary traditions of the historians who worked according to it; this in turn has made possible a new reading of their texts, and consequently serious revisions of modern scholarly constructs based upon those texts. But the Theravāda of the Mahāvihāra was only one among many "medieval" Indian Buddhist disciplinary orders, and the same reconstructive work needs to be done on the historiographies of rival historians. This will allow us to see more clearly how Sarvāstivādins or Mahāsāṃghikas countered the claims of their Theravādin rivals—for "dialogue" is a two-way street—and in turn will clarify that historiography itself was an important arena for dispute among the "medieval" South Asian disciplinary orders.

Virtually all Indian Buddhists maintained versions of the Buddhist "canon," the Tipiṭaka/Tripiṭaka. Parts of these canons—certain texts of the Vinaya and Sutta/Sūtra Piṭakas—were "closed," and disciplinary orders, especially the "Hīnayāna," maintained roughly similar versions of these texts, even though minor differences in the various monastic disciplinary rules (*vinaya*) often functioned as hooks upon which doctrinal disputes were hung, and the interpretation of these shared texts by philosophers and commentators varied widely. However, other portions of these canons, especially the texts of the Khuddaka/Kṣudraka or "miscellaneous" division of the Sutta/Sūtra, and the texts of the "metaphysical" Abhidhamma/Abhidharma Piṭakas, were "open" (Table 3.1).

My work on the Pāli Vaṃsas makes it clear that these "open" divisions of the canon became key sites for the disputes of "medieval" Indian Buddhists. The "miscellaneous" literature included all the elements that in their various ways constituted the "philosophies of history" of the various orders, that is, their own versions of the *Jātakas*, narratives about the successions of the Buddha's lives and Apadāna/Avadāna, stories about the nature of the cosmic polity he instituted. Each disciplinary order continually supplemented these "open" texts with new revelations dialogically related to the supplements being composed in rival orders. Extant examples suggest that these historical supplements were used to frame the monastic Vinaya or disciplinary rules contained in the canons of the different orders, being after all claims about why such-and-such a disciplinary order is superior to all others, made on the basis of (highly contested) claims about the history of the "councils" through which its canon was supposedly transmitted into the present. Thus the Sarvāstivādin *Divyāvadāna* was apparently appended to the *Mūlasarvāstivādavinaya*;[136] the Lokottaravādin *Mahāvastvavadāna* was intended as an introduction to the Mahāsāṃghika version of the Vinaya; and Buddhaghosa introduces his commentary on the Pāli Vinaya with an abbreviated *Mhv* after the fashion of the old Sinhala commentary. As a result, the practice of any particular monastic discipline embodied an entire set of historical claims (often focused upon King Aśoka) and practices (rooted in philosophical doctrines) peculiar to its own disciplinary order. Likewise, the epistemologies and ontologies that underlay these historical traditions, embodied in the various Abhidhamma/Abhidharma literatures, battled each other in a tradition of dialogical supplementation throughout most of the Indian Buddhist history; historical claims about the "councils," produced on the basis of these philosophical musings, in turn bolstered the claims of different philosophical traditions to be supreme.[137]

Monological readings of these texts may discern changes over time within a particular disciplinary order, but they have not adequately addressed the nature of the changes across disciplinary orders; in Buddhological scholarship Sarvāstivādins or Theravādins talk to themselves, and talk to the scholars who study them, without talking to each other. But if anything about these disputes is clear, it is that these groups were seldom talking only to themselves, and were never talking to the practitioners of a foreign epistemology which had not even been invented; they were talking to each other. Interregnal sites of pilgrimage such as Sārnāth and Bodh Gayā, interregnal universities such as Nālanda and Kāñci, interregnal exchanges of scholars and monks, interregnal diplomatic, commercial, and military encounters, and interregnal literary transmissions enabled Buddhists thoughout "medieval" South Asia to remain aware of the thoughts and practices of rivals and to address them in the ongoing constitution of their own traditions.

It is time to stop arguing about whether the Sarvāstivāda compendium *Abhidharmakośa* or the Theravāda commentarial tradition surrounding *Kathāvatthu* represents the "authentic" metaphysics of the Buddha; whether Aśoka "really" privileged Kashmir or Khotan or Sri Lanka. Those polemics belong to the "medieval" South Asia we are trying to understand. It is time instead to start exploring the implications of the fact that the compilers of these inconsistent or even contradictory traditions were contemporaries, aware of one another, and acting as agents in a "real world" where philosophical-historical disputes were simultaneously political challenges. When Kassapa V recited aloud his jewel-encrusted *Dhammasaṅgaṇi*, he was not simply displaying his erudition for the edification of his Mahāvihāran subject-citizens; he was launching an imperial program. Prior to the advent of colonialism, Buddhists did not argue about "historical truth" in

---

[136]The Mūlasarvāstivādins, who rejected the Abhidharma, seem to have made its Kṣudra texts into the third Piṭaka.

[137]One might point to instructional concerns, as well. The *Parivārapāṭha* and the *Khuddakpāṭha* both appear to have been supplements that acted as condensations or catechisms of the canon or its parts: K. R. Norman, *Pāli Literature Including the Canonical Literature in Prakrit and Sanskrit of All the Hīnayāna Schools of Buddhism* in vol. 7.2, *A History of Indian Literature* (Wiesbaden: Otto Harrassowitz, 1983), 26–29, 40, 57–58.

quite the way that empiricists and later positivists have wanted to claim; instead, their arguments were about hierarchies of polities and disciplinary orders within the then-present. Rather than take sides with Buddhist polemicists of the ancient past, it is time for scholars to start recovering the dialogical moments that make up the history under scrutiny.

Nor is it the case that texts represented the only sites for these dialogical encounters with practitioners of rival Buddhist disciplines. Rather, Buddhists developed an entire range of such sites, including architecture, iconography, public debates and disputations, diplomacy and liturgy; these, like their texts, provided forums for inter-Buddhist, as well as Buddhist-Theist, dialogue. Yet in the heavily textualized climate of "medieval" South Asia, it was in their texts that Buddhists most explicitly and most carefully carried on their mutual contests for supremacy and the truth, both incorporating and reworking, affirming and attacking, portions of their rivals' texts; it was in their texts that Buddhists argued about proper architectural style, about iconographic standards, about the doctrinal interpretations that were debated publicly, about the rules of interregnal diplomacy, about correct liturgical form. It is thus in their texts that we must look first, and that we must look for the dialogical, if we are to see Buddhists as engaged and powerful agents of the South Asian polities in which they lived.

Appendix: Colonial and National Readings of the Pāli Vaṃsas

Pāli "chronicles" come prepackaged for modern academic consumers. The *Dīpavaṃsa* and *Mahāvaṃsa* have long been available in English and German translations. These translations largely predetermine how each Vaṃsa will be read. Carefully indexed, complete with lists of kings and scholarly introductions, these translations transform Pāli poems of the fourth and fifth centuries into nineteenth-century Western European historical reference books, prose works with numbered paragraphs and footnotes. Although Roman-script editions of the original poems and of the commentary on the *Mhv* also exist, scored for easy comparison with the translation and each other, scholarship, in the West at least, has focused almost entirely upon the translations.

My concern is not with the "accuracy" of the translations by conventional philological standards; I have found them to be fairly good for my purposes.[138] Instead, my concern is with the interpretive framing of the Pāli Vaṃsas. That framing carries with it assumptions that are not transparent; they are the product of historical thought by the people responsible for the translations and editions, along with their colleagues. These assumptions are also not unproblematic. But they appear both transparent and unproblematic, within the frame in which they come. The purpose of the present section is to examine this framing: how has it come to

[138]There are, of course, problems: A. P. Buddhadatta, *Corrections of Geiger's Mahāvaṃsa, etc.: A Collection of Monographs*, reprinted from *University of Ceylon Review* (Ambalangoda, Ceylon: Ananda Book Company, 1957). Beyond purely linguistic errors, translations of necessity encode certain perspectives and presuppositions that belong to the translator rather than the author of the text being translated. As a result, new historical knowledge necessitates (and is produced by) new translation.

pass that certain assumptions about the Vaṃsas seem transparent and unproblematic to us today? Who made these assumptions, and in what circumstances? To what theories of knowledge do these assumptions commit us, and how do they delimit the questions that scholars can ask about the Vaṃsas?

George Turnour's Mahāvaṃsa

On August 5, 1835, James Prinsep, secretary of the Bengal Asiatic Society, read a letter to the assembled members that was to become a turning point in the study of Indian history. The author of this letter, George Turnour, was an important civil servant in Ceylon.[139] Writing from Kandy, July 10, 1835, Turnour thanked the society for his recent election to honorary membership. He considered himself "peculiarly fortunate" to receive election at that time, for he was then "engaged in the translation of a valuable historical work in the Pāli language...[which] contains, besides detached historical fragments, a *chronologically connected* Buddhistical History of India.[140] Turnour was referring to the *Mhv*, and in the course of his interactions with Prinsep and other members of the society, over the next three years, he was to lay foundations for the study of Indian and Sri Lankan history that remain solid to this day.

Turnour did not "discover" the *Mhv*, although his contribution is often described in that way. Rather, the *Mhv* existed in numerous manuscripts throughout Sri Lanka and Southeast Asia, and Westerners before Turnour had seen it. But these early orientalists did not have access to the commentary on the *Mhv* called the *Vaṃsatthappakāsinī* (*VAP*) (sometimes called the *Mahāvaṃsaṭīkā*), and they were consequently unable to understand the poetic expressions of the *Mhv* it-

---

[139]He was born there in 1799, where his father, third son of the earl of Winterton, was a civil servant. After receiving his education in England under the guardianship of Sir Thomas Maitland, governor of Ceylon (1805–1811), Turnour returned to Sri Lanka in 1818, entered the civil service, and quickly rose in rank; Sir James Emerson Tennent, *Ceylon: An Account of the island Physical, Historical, and Topographical, with Notices of Its Natural History, Antiquities and Productions*, 3d rev. ed. (London: Longman, Green, Longman and Roberts, 1859), 1: 312. He began to study Pāli in 1826 with the help of Buddhist monks in the vicinity of Ratnapura, where he was stationed as agent of the government; Kitsiri Malalgoda, *Buddhism in Sinhalese Society, 1750–1900: A Study of Religious Revival and Change* (Berkeley and Los Angeles: University of California Press, 1976), p. 179 n. 24. It may be that his interest in the history of Buddhism was first sparked by the directive of the Kandy Board of Commissioners (December 16, 1825) that he investigate a dispute between Kandyan (Malvatta) and Low-Country monks over the ownership of Adam's Peak (Sinh. Siri Pāda = Skt. Śrī Pāda), in the island's central highlands; Malalgoda, *Buddhism*, p. 86. After he was transferred to Kandy, in 1828, for five years Turnour was too busy to return to his Pāli studies; Turnour's own account in Major [Jonathan] Forbes, *Eleven Years in Ceylon: Comprising Sketches of the Field Sports and Natural History of That Colony, and an Account of Its History and Antiquities* (London: Richard Bentley, 1840), 2: 324–25. The same account is to be found in the 1836 and 1837 editions of the *Mhv* (citations below). Around 1833 he renewed his aquaintance with the Pāli texts under the guidance of monks at the famous Malvatta Vihāra, and on the basis of their library; Malalgoda, *Buddhism*, p. 179 n. 24. He remained there until he was transferred to Colombo in 1838 and appointed to the Supreme Council. He left Sri Lanka in 1841 due to ill health, and after a brief stay in England he went to Italy for its healthful climate. He died at Naples on April 10, 1843.

[140]James Prinsep, "Proceedings of the Asiatic Society," *Journal of the Asiatic Society of Bengal* (*JASB*) 4.2 (July 1835), 407.

self.[141] Then in 1827 Turnour's Pāli teacher secured for him a number of palm-leaf manuscripts from the Mulgirigalla Vihāra near Tangalle, which included a copy of this commentary, and with its assistance Turnour became the first Westerner to decipher accurately the root text.[142]

In 1833 Turnour published his initial findings about the *Mhv* and other "Buddhistical Annals."[143] Advance notice of another "edition" that same year discouraged Turnour from the work in which he was already actively engaged, namely, a translation and edition of the *Mhv* on the basis of his precious commentary.[144] But once Turnour had seen its flawed work—which he criticized as both incomplete and inaccurate—he set out to complete his task.[145]

It was precisely this goal that led Turnour to open correspondence with his orientalist colleagues in Calcutta during the summer of 1835; Turnour realized that the *Mhv* provides a dated chronological history of India that links up with the records of ancient Western historians, a link that made possible for the first time a "scientific" (empiricist) history of ancient India. The *Mhv* gives "Candagutta" (= Candragupta) Maurya (c. 317–293 B.C.) as the name of the grandfather of Aśoka (c. 268–239 B.C.), whereas the fragmentary records of Megasthenes's well-known embassy to India mention "Sandracottus" (= Candragupta) as the ruler whose court he visited.[146] Once a specific date from "reliable" Western authorities had been synchronized with the date of an event (the coronation of Aśoka) in an Indian chronology (the Buddha era of the Vaṃsas), an absolute chronology and, hence, a scientific history of India became possible. The *Mhv* thus played a role in the history of Indology analogous to the Rosetta Stone in the history of Egyptology. This analogy is especially apt because the (Pāli) language of the *Mhv* became

---

[141]Tennent, *Ceylon*, 1: 311–15; cf. Turnour's own account in Forbes, *Eleven Years*, 2: 269–70. Note that the poetic style of the *Mhv* is cast here as a bother to the orientalist, but is not discussed in its own right. It did not occur to Turnour to ask *why* the *Mhv* is in verse; he recognized that it *is* in verse and set out to find a commentary that would help him to render it into prose.

[142]Tennent, *Ceylon*, 1: 314–15; Turnour, in Forbes, *Eleven Years*, 2: 324–25.

[143]George Turnour, *An Epitome of the History of Ceylon, Compiled from Native Annals* in the a copy of the original *Ceylon Almanack* (1833), which I have not been able to locate. Turnour republished it in his *An Epitome of the History of Ceylon, Compiled from Native Annals; And the First Twenty Chapters of the Mahāwanso* (Cotta, Ceylon: Church Mission Press, 1836); and in Jonathan Forbes, *Eleven Years in Ceylon: Comprising Sketches of the Field Sports and Natural History of That Colony, and an Account of Its History and Antiquities* (London: Richard Bentley, 1840), 2: 269–321. Forbes (1: 81–95) also seems to have been part author of Turnour's "Epitome," and Turnour wrote the introduction to Forbes's epigraphical report (2: 324ff.).

[144]Edward Upham (1776–1834), ed., *The Mahavansi, the Raja-ratnacari, and the Raja-vali, Forming the Sacred and Historical Books of Ceylon; also, a collection of tracts illustrative of the doctrines and literature of Buddhism: translated from the Sinhalese* (London: Parbury, Allen, 1833), 3 vols. In 1829, Upham, a retired British bookseller and one-time mayor of Exeter, had published an illustrated description of Kandyan Buddhism, *The History and Doctrine of Buddhism, Popularly Illustrated: With Notices of the Kappooism, or Demon Worship, and of the Bali, or Planetary Incantations, of Ceylon*. All of this information was obtained by Upham indirectly—second-hand English translations of Sinhala paraphrases of the texts in question.

[145]Tennent, *Ceylon*, 1: 316 n. 1. What really bothered Turnour was Upham's emphasis on the "mythic" portions of the Vaṃsas, which Turnour considered an embarrassment.

[146]The dates given are from P. H. L. Eggermont, "New Notes on Aśoka and His Successors" 1–4, *Persica* 2 (1965–66), 27–70; 4 (1969), 77–120; 5 (1970–71), 69–102; 8 (1979), 55–93.

the basis for reconstructing the Magadhan Prākrit in which the famous Aśokan inscriptions are composed. The problem was that the synchronism was deficient by about sixty years, yielding a date of 329 B.C. for Aśoka's coronation instead of the date later settled on, 269 or 268 B.C. Turnour and others questionably assumed that the date of the Buddha's death which Sinhalas took as the beginning of the Buddha era, equating to 543 B.C., was an accurately remembered date.[147] By the 1830s Orientalists had already determined India to be "ahistorical," repeatedly claiming that the Purāṇas, Epics, and related texts fail to provide chronological narratives that are "scientific." Indian texts were fables and myths; "true" history belonged to the West. Turnour was thus making a startling revelation when he suggested that some Indians kept accurate historical records according to a logical chronological system (based on the date of the Buddha's death). Because orientalists were so certain that South Asia lacks real history, Turnour worried about the "repulsing scepticism" with which the translation alone of such a history (that is, the *Mhv*) would be received. For that reason he proposed to the Asiatic Society that the translation be accompanied by a Romanized edition of the original Pāli text.[148]

Advance copies of Turnour's work were published the following year.[149] With them, Turnour sent the first of his many contributions to the Society's journal. Turnour pointed to the great difficulties that Professor H. H. Wilson had encountered when he attempted to translate Buddhist texts preserved in Nepal and Tibet into a chronological (empiricist) history.[150] This difficulty had been so great that Wilson was forced into wild conjecture in order to make bits of them "fit" with the Western authorities. Finally, he disparaged Buddhist chronology as even more inaccurate than Hindu chronology (he had found the Kashmiri royal chronicle *Rājataraṅgiṇī* vexing enough), and he included the Pāli Vaṃsas (on the basis of second-hand information) within that generalization. In response, Turnour suggested the possibility that only some Buddhists were inaccurate; "perhaps...some copy of this [Buddhist] history [will] be hereafter found, exempt from this minute inaccuracy, the discovery of which would fix the erratum on the transcriber."[151] In fact, later in the same article Turnour announced that "[a]s regards the Buddhistical chronology, I have it in my power to adduce *direct* evidence, independent of

[147] Based on the chronology he had worked out, Turnour thus dated Aśoka's accession to 329 B.C. and wished therefore to have Megasthenes visit his court; George Turnour, "An Examination of the Pāli Buddhistical Annals (2)," *JASB* 6.2 (September 1837), 716.

[148] James Prinsep, "Proceedings of the Asiatic Society," *JASB* 4.2 (July, 1835), 408. Turnour elicited two kinds of assistance from members of the Asiatic Society. First, he requested their critical appraisals of his work-in-progress and offered to send them advance copies of the early chapters of the *Mhv* together with his *Epitome* of 1833. Second, he made clear that the financial burden of his undertaking, borne so far by him, threatened completion of the project. When the letter was read "several Members present expressed a desire to possess Mr. Turnour's work, and 12 copies were at once subscribed for." With regard to Turnour's financial request, "the communication was referred to the Committee of Papers, to consider how the objects of the author could be best promoted."

[149] G. Turnour, tr., *An Epitome of the History of Ceylon, Compiled from Native Annals; And the First Twenty Chapters of the Mahāwanso* (Cotta, Ceylon: Church Mission Press, 1836).

[150] G. Turnour, "Examination of Some Points of Buddhist Chronology," *JASB* 5.2 (September 1836), 524–25.

[151] Turnour, "Examination of Some Points," p. 525; brackets added.

hypothetical reasoning."[152] That direct evidence was, of course, the *Mhv*, which he proceeded to describe for his readers.

This article, and the advance copies of his translation and edition of the text, the first extensive Pāli text ever published, were received with great enthusiasm in Calcutta. At the meeting of January 4, 1837, Dr. W. H. Mill presented a report of the Asiatic Society's Committee on Papers concerning Turnour's proposed publication of the *Mhv*. He concurred with Turnour's original proposition that the text and translation be published in extenso, "thus rescuing them from what is in many respects worse than total oblivion, [namely,] the confusion and misapprehension of their real testimony which a former very erroneous publication on the subject in England was calculated to produce."[153] He praised Turnour's exegetical skills and reiterated Turnour's own notion that the value of the *Mhv* "is far from being confined to the single subject of Ceylon: it extends to the whole of India: and yields in importance to nothing that has yet been produced on that most perplexed and generally unproductive subject, the history of India prior to the thousandth year of our era." Supporting Turnour's conclusion that the *Mhv* "vindicates the Buddhist authors of *Ceylon* at least, from the general censure passed on them by Professor HORACE WILSON...of being, if possible, more regardless of chronology than even the Brahmans," Mill concluded with the important statement that

> It would be undervaluing these works to suppose them to be merely a dry chronological catalogue of sovereigns and dynasties: though this is frequently all that an inquirer into ancient India is able to meet with; where, between fable on the one hand, and the strong national tendency to abstract speculation on the other, the literature of the country has so little to aid a *historical* student. These works apparently contain much that may well be deemed valuable by a philosophical inquirer into history: and the details, in particular, of the contest between the antagonist principles of Brahmanism and Buddhism, are often curiously illustrative of the genius of these two systems, which have held, and still hold, such sway over large portions of mankind.[154]

Real Indian history had finally been discovered. Prinsep added this note to Mill's "Minute": "The Society concurring entirely in the Committee's view of the value of MR. TURNOUR's intended publication, *particularly in regard to the light it throws on the early history of India*, it was resolved to advocate its patronage by the Government of India, to the fullest extent that it may have been usual for Government to subscribe to private enterprizes of similar importance in India itself."[155]

This crucial hypothesis that the *Mhv* is an historical work, and that it belongs to the whole history of India (rather than merely the history of Sri Lanka) was rapidly put to the test. Mill himself admitted that Turnour's work had led him to

---

[152]Turnour, "Examination of Some Points," p. 527

[153]That of by Edward Upham: James Prinsep, "Proceedings of the Asiatic Society," *JASB* 5.2 (December 1836), 829; my brackets.

[154]Prinsep, "Proceedings,"p. 831.

[155]Prinsep, "Proceedings," p. 832; emphasis added.

reconsider his own identification of Megasthenes' Sandracottus with Candragupta, son of Samudragupta (now dated to the 4th century) instead of Aśoka's grandfather.[156] Prinsep himself began applying his new-found knowledge of the *Mhv* to the mysterious "Feroz Shah" pillar (so named for a later Muslim ruler who had it brought to Delhi). Prinsep had piqued the curiosity of Indologists when he announced that he had deciphered the meaning of the oldest inscription on the pillar using the Pāli language of the *Mhv*.[157] Moreover, that text allowed him, rather triumphantly, to identify Piyadasi (Skt., Priyadarśī), who is named in the inscription as its author, with Devānaṃpiyatissa, king of Ceylon during the time of India's Aśoka Maurya.[158]

Turnour, meanwhile, had discovered, among a number of manuscripts brought from Thailand in 1812, the only known manuscript of another important Pāli Vaṃsa, the *Dpv*.[159] Because the *Dpv*, unlike the *Mhv*, refers to Aśoka Maurya by name as "Piyadassi," Turnour realized the mistake that Prinsep had made when he identified the author of the pillar inscription with King Devānaṃpiyatissa of Ceylon: "Piyadasi" of the inscriptions was none other than Aśoka Maurya himself. Prinsep was quick to acknowledge the blunder. To learn that the author of the inscription was from India proper reinforced his notion that the pillar symbolized a "classical age" in Indian history that the British presence had appropriated and thereby superseded.[160]

Turnour set the agenda for future study of the Pāli Vaṃsas with his full text of the *Mhv* and his detailed descriptions of it and related texts.[161] For him, authorship consisted of two problems: a document is to be treated as historical if, first, its author (or the testimony upon which he relied) was contemporaneous with the event described, and second, he was objective, without motive or bias, in recording the events witnessed (or transcribing earlier testimony).[162] The *Mhv* calls itself a

---

[156] W. H. Mill, "Restoration and Translation of the Inscription on the Bhitārī Lāt, with critical and historical remarks," *JASB* 6.1 (January 1837), 15–16 n. C.

[157] James Prinsep, "Application of the Alphabet to Other Inscriptions, Particularly Those of the Lāts of Upper India," *JASB* VI.1 (June 1837), esp. pp. 469–71.

[158] James Prinsep, "Interpretation of the Most Ancient of the Inscriptions on the Pillar called the Lāt of Feroz Shāh, near Delhi, and of the Allahabad, Radhia and Mattiah Pillar, or Lāt, Inscriptions which Agree Therewith," *JASB* 6.2 (July 1837), 566–67.

[159] Turnour initially assumed that this chronicle was the "chronicle of the ancients" that the *Mhv* names as its own source: James Prinsep, "Further Elucidation of the Lāṭ or Sīlastambha Inscriptions," *JASB* 6.2 (September 1837), 790. He later suggested that it might be the Abhayagiri chronicle referred to in the *VAP*: *JASB* 6.2 (December 1837), 1,055. The introduction to Turnour's edition and translation of the *Mhv* gives the latter hypothesis.

[160] Prinsep, "Proceedings of the Asiatic Society," *JASB* 6.2 (September 1837), 803; "Further elucidation," p. 792.

[161] Mahānāma, *The Mahāwanso in Roman Characters, with the Translation Subjoined; and an Introductory Essay on Pāli Buddhistical Literature* (Cotta, Ceylon: Church Mission Press, 1837); and George Turnour, "An Examination of the Pāli Buddhistical Annals" (1) *JASB* 6.2 (July 1837), 501–28, (2) (September 1837), 713–37; (3.1) 7.2 (August 1838), 686–701, (3.2) (September 1838), 789–817; (4) (November 1838), 919–33; (5) (Decemebr 1838), 991–1014.

[162] Turnour, "Examination (1)," 501, 504. The empiricism of Locke and Hume and the so-called Enlightenment, while rejecting the Cartesian innate ideas in favor of sense impressions as the basis of scientific knowledge, did take up its notion of source criticism: Collingwood, *The Idea of History*, pp.

poetic recension of "the Vaṃsa of the ancients" (I.1–3), and the commentary, *VAP*, states that the author of *Mhv*, called Mahānāma, compiled it on the basis of ancient records that had been kept by the residents of the Mahāvihāra, the "great monastery" near Anurādhapura, royal capital of Sri Lanka until the eleventh century (2: 687), built, it claimed, during the time of Aśoka. Turnour assumed that its residents had maintained eye-witness accounts since that time, which they appended to even earlier eye-witness descriptions of the life of Buddha and ancient Indian history, that had been brought to Sri Lanka from India. Turnour thought that Mahānāma, writing the *Mhv*, had compiled the fragments of centuries of eyewitness accounts.

The second empiricist criterion, that of objectivity, gave Turnour a bit more trouble. It was raised, indirectly, when he discovered "discrepancies" of about sixty years in the Vaṃsa chronologies. Turnour considered an empiricist epistemology to be part of human nature and so assumed it was common sense to represent the past in a chronologically consistent manner. He thus attributed these "inaccuracies" to the bad motives of the monks who compiled these otherwise "purely historical" texts: they had "designedly" created "fictional synchronisms" in the interest of proving that "certain pretended prophecies of SAKYA" had actually been realized.[163] Like many Enlightenment scholars, he simply assumed that these strange men wanted to "glorify" themselves to themselves with a "history" of lies. Turnour later argued even more strongly with regard to "those portions of the Pali Annals which treat of events of *greater antiquity than twenty-four centuries*."[164] The Pāli texts generally, and the Vaṃsas in particular, thus precede Creation itself. Their temporal scheme spans eons upon eons, with the durations of dynasties reckoned in tens of thousands of years, and through this vast expanse of time the Buddha as a Bodhisatta (Skt., *bodhisattva*) transmigrates. Knowledge of these times is obtained, Turnour's teachers at the Malvatta Vihāra in Kandy informed him, not through the senses but through the miraculous powers of Buddhist adepts who remembered their own previous lives. Turnour says of those portions that: "in an inquiry chiefly entered into for the illustration of the historical data contained in these records, the next subject for examination [following the structure of the *Mhv* itself] would have been the genealogy of the kings of India, had the chronology of the Buddhists anterior to the age of SAKYA [Buddha], exhibited the same degree of authenticity, that the portion subsequent to that era has been found to possess. In this respect, however, the Buddhistical writings are unfortunately as defective as the Brāhminical." Like the "discrepant" chronological statements posterior to the Buddha, "Both the chronology and the historical narrative prior to the advent of GOTOMO BUDDHO, are involved in *intentional perversion and mystification*; a perversion evidently had recourse to for the purpose of working out the scheme on which he [Buddha] based that wonderful dispensation, which was promulgated over Central India, during his pretended divine mission on earth

62, 71–85, 257–61. Empiricist history and its method of philological criticism became common among historians by the middle of the nineteenth century and is to be distinguished from the later positivism of Comte, with which it interacts in the latter half of the century (pp. 129–131).

[163]Turnour, "Examination (1)," pp. 716–17.

[164]Turnour, "Examination (3.1),"p. 687.

of forty-five years."[165] Although Turnour translated this material, he bracketed out of his history, which began with the death of the Buddha in 543 B.C. and ended with the accession of Devānaṃpiyatissa (which Turnour calculated at 307 B.C.), as "fabulous exaggeration" those portions of the Vaṃsas that seemed irrational to him. Turnour thus insisted that the Vaṃsa authors were common-sense historians, but did so only for select portions of each text.

Turnour's insistence was not a matter of philosophical inquiry; it was simply a presupposition. His "history" is thus more a philological than an historical reconstruction; he critically selects extracts from canonical and commentarial works, and of course from the Vaṃsas, in order to demonstrate that it all "fits" into a consistent narrative, but does not go on to reconstruct the thoughts of the agents involved. Turnour did point to the future of *Mhv* studies: the text may be inaccurate as regards India, but if someone wants to know about Sri Lanka—and these prophetic words—"Vide the *Mahāwanso*"—so ended Turnour's series of articles.[166]

Turnour had in the end submitted to Prinsep. The history of India proper was to be relinquished, in Turnour's word, to those orientalists in Bengal whose domain was the "Brahmanized Sanskrit medium"; texts in the "Buddhistical Pāli medium" would henceforth relate only to Sri Lanka.[167] A subtle change was occurring. Sri Lanka was becoming a place that *recorded* history but did not, as Mill, Prinsep and Turnour had originally thought, ever *make* history. This was consistent with Sri Lanka's supposed mission as a medieval kingdom: the preservation of early Theravāda Buddhism as an ethical religion together with its sacred Pāli texts.

The Empiricist Legacy

Turnour had formulated his philological "sift and choose" method as the primary agenda for future orientalist study of the Vaṃsas.[168] In the first generation of scholarship following Turnour, this dubious method was codified and even extended, as Turnour had hoped, to the narrative that predates the Buddha.[169] Subsequent

---

[165]Turnour, "Examination (3.1)," pp. 686, 687; emphasis added.

[166]Turnour, "Examination (5)," p. 1,014.

[167]George Turnour, "Further Notes on the Inscriptions on the Columns at Delhi, Allahabad, Betiah, &c.," *JASB* 6.2 (December 1837), 1049–50.

[168]Turnour, "Examination (2)," p. 723: "All, therefore, that I am entitled to deduce from this anachronism is that there is an undeniable and intentional perversion of historical data in the first century of the Buddhistical era. Whether this perversion can be corrected, either directly or indirectly, from other sources, is a question which those orientalists alone can answer, who have other collateral data on which they can rest their arguments."

[169]Major Jonathan Forbes, who worked with Turnour between 1827 and 1841, based much of his historical reconstruction upon Turnour's *Mhv*, which he introduced to European readers thus: "If the events be compared, *and Buddhist miracles are excluded from Cingalese history*, we shall find records of accurate detail and great antiquity commencing with Vijeya and the invasion of the Singha race, B.C. 543, and terminating in A.D. 1815, with Wickreme Singha, the last and worst of a faded dynasty and fallen nation"; *Eleven Years*, p. 69; emphasis added. Another widely read writer, missionary R. Spence Hardy, elaborated this stance in *The Legends and Theories of the Buddhists, Compared with History and Science: With Introductory Notices of the Life and System of Gotama Buddha* (London: Williams and Norgate, 1866), esp. chapter 1. Like Forbes (who tried to use the *Rāmāyaṇa* as an empiricist sourcebook on pre-Buddhist history of the island), he was more willing than Turnour to empiricize

scholars stopped talking about the "mythic" portions of the literature altogether. The most significant scholar to vindicate the historicity of the more recent narratives of the Pāli Vaṃsas was undoubtedly the German philologist Wilhelm Geiger (1856–1943), who worked after the advent of that more focused version of empiricism, positivism.[170] He pointed to "conclusive" inscriptional evidence that the sixty-year anachronism or "discrepancy" in these more recent portions, which had troubled Turnour, was the result of a change in the calculation of the Buddha era that occurred in eleventh century Sri Lanka, shifting the date of the Buddha's death from 483 (the date Indology wanted) to 543 B.C.[171] Geiger did more than assuage Turnour's sole doubt about the authenticity of the more recent narrative portions of the Pāli Vaṃsas; he went on to develop a method for reconstructing the "original" source, which would prove more "reliable" still.

In 1879 Hermann Oldenberg had argued, on the basis of statements in the *VAP*, that both the *Mhv* and the *Dpv* were based upon an earlier source entitled *Sīhalaṭṭhakathā-Mahāvaṃsa*. This was an ancient text in proto-Sinhala language, portions of which were translated into Pāli by the authors of the Vaṃsas known today. Although it is no longer extant, this ur-text was still available to the author of the tenth-century *VAP*.[172] Geiger's monumental work built up Oldenberg's hypothesis into a rigorous method for reconstructing the source-text, for sifting out all the "exaggerations" with which the Vaṃsa authors themselves supposedly had embellished this original Vaṃsa.[173] Geiger had great hopes for this method; following so clearly in Turnour's footsteps, he thought that this reconstructed original would allow us, as it were, eyewitness access to ancient South Asian history.

Another generation after Geiger, the final pieces of this puzzle were put in place when G. P. Malalasekera (1899–1973) published the critical edition of

---

portions of the Vaṃsas that predate Gotama. An insightful treatment of the appropriation of the *Mhv* for historical, and especially archeological, thought in the period directly following Turnour has been made by Pradeep Jeganathan, "Authorizing 'History'; Ordering Land: The Conquest of Anuradhapura," in Pradeep Jeganathan and Qadri Ismail, eds., *Unmaking the Nation: The Politics of Identity and History in Modern Sri Lanka* (Colombo, Sri Lanka: Social Scientists' Association, 1995), pp. 106–36.

[170]Heinz Bechert provides a detailed study of the study of the Vaṃsas up to Geiger, but it is a story of the triumphant vindication of them as "scientific" histories; *Wilhelm Geiger: His Life and Works* (Colombo: M. D. Gunasena, 1977; Tubingen: Horst Erdman Verlag, 1977), esp. pp. 84–95.

[171]Wilhelm Geiger, tr., *Mahāvaṃsa* (London: Pali Text Society, 1912), pp. xxviii–xxxi. Heinz Bechert argues against an earlier Buddha era and shows that the extant era was in use at least as early as 398 A.D.; "The Origin and Spread of the Theravāda Chronology," *The Dating of the Historical Buddha*, Abhandlungen der Akademie der Wissenschaften, Philologisch-Historische Klasse, 3, 189, (Göttingen: Vandenhoeck & Ruprecht, 1991), 1: 329–43.

[172]*Dīpavaṃsa*, pp. 1–8.

[173]*Dīpavaṃsa and Mahāvaṃsa*. The commentary on *Mhv* explains the poetic root text as a translation of the original, and in the process of commenting upon the root text makes occasional specific references to that original. Occasionally that commentator tells us that Mahānāma, the *Mhv* author, took his details about some event straight from the original *Sīhalaṭṭhakathā-Mahāvaṃsa*, which from Geiger's perspective validates the authenticity of those details; in other places the commentary itself provides the "accurate" passages by quoting the original in order to critique or elaborate upon Mahānāma's version. The *Dpv*, moreover, is taken to be an earlier translation of the same source, and so it too must be compared with the *Mhv* and *VAP* tellings of any particular event. Thornier still, Buddhaghosa's commentaries on the Buddhist canon (Tipiṭaka) quote both *Dpv* and the ur-text fairly often; these clues too must be considered before any determination is reached about the historicity of a particular event.

the *VAP*, enabling scholars to proceed, using Geiger's method. This tenth-century commentary, it will be remembered, has formed the backbone of every theory about the "historicity" of the *Mhv*. Malalasekera himself, in his scholarly introduction to that text, made many specific judgments about the "authenticity" of particular events recorded in the Vaṃsas. But his most important contribution to this project was made on the theoretical level. Within the positivist theory of knowledge, as I have already suggested, historical validity depends also upon scientific objectivity. If the ur-text contained contemporaneous eyewitness reports but the later Buddhist historians misrepresented them, then the extant Vaṃsas could not be accepted as historical documents (nor, damningly, as documents from which to reconstruct the original). Malalasekera boldly argues that almost all of the *VAP*'s "additions" to the *Mhv* are a translation of the original *Sīhalaṭṭhakathā-Mahāvaṃsa*,[174] preserving every scrap of information contained in it. And we cannot question the scientific competence of the author of the *VAP*:

> Whoever be the author of the *MT* [i.e., *VAP*] and whatever be the exact date of its compilation, it must be admitted that, for the age in which it was written, the work has been done with remarkable ability and efficiency. The author displays great critical acumen in the way in which he had handled his task. Variant readings have been noted, possible alternative explanations given, and shades of meanings in words have been distinguished with such meticulous care as any modern exponent of textual criticism may well be proud of.... His handling of his materials proves that he had a thorough and profound knowledge of the topics dealt with; nothing, however insignificant, escaped his notice.... Generally speaking, he does not allow his personal views to obtrude themselves, but, where he feels that an opinion should be expressed, he gives his decisions without any hesitation. (pp. cx–cxi)

Thus, even though Oldenberg, Geiger, and Malalasekera all claimed to be correcting Turnour's work, they were doing no more than strengthening his argument that the authors of the Pāli Vaṃsas really were protoscientific historians dressed up as medieval Sinhala Buddhist monks.[175]

Meanwhile, the separation of the histories of India and Sri Lanka solidified. Vincent Smith, the first colonial historian to provide pre-Muslim India with an empiricist history, got around the sixty-year gap in the Vaṃsas' chronology by turning away from them completely and relying instead on a Chinese "dotted

---

[174] G. P. Malalasekera, ed., *Vaṃsatthappakāsinī*, pp. lvi–lvii; lxxii.

[175] Recently, Gananath Obeyesekere has advocated a "loyal opposition" stance on this issue; denying that the Vaṃsa authors were positivist historians who told lies, Obeyesekere argues that they were "accurate" historians for whom making up dates (on the basis of a South Asian numerological predilection) was considered "legitimate fiction." Obeyesekere's insightful and colorful paper takes many steps in the direction of understanding the Vaṃsas within their own cultural context. He has verified, however, how pervasive the central thesis is, that these were scientific historians who did not always operate according to our rules; "Myth, History and Numerology in the Buddhist Chronicles," in H. Bechert, ed., *The Dating of the Historical Buddha* (Göttingen: Vandenhoeck & Ruprecht, 1991), 1: 152–82; see also his "The Myth of the Human Sacrifice: History, Story and Debate in a Buddhist Chronicle," in H. L. Seneviratne, ed., *Identity, Consciousness and the Past: The South Asian Scene*, *Social Analysis* 25 (September 1989), 78–94.

record" to establish the date of the Buddha's death at 486 B.C.[176] He also dismissed the Pāli accounts of Aśoka as "fiction," and claimed that his own knowledge of Aśoka was obtained purely from his inscriptions.[177] This claim was true to the extent that Smith refrained from simply quoting the *Mhv* for "facts" about Aśokan India, as his predecessors had done. But this position involved a bit of self-deception as well. Smith could not see *anything* in the inscriptions except through the eyes of those predecessors, for they had already determined what was "actually there" in the inscriptions—a pseudo-Pāli language, the transparent record of some beneficent act by Aśoka Maurya (complete with basic biographical details about Aśoka including lineage, date, conversion to Buddhism, etc.)—and, ironically, all of this depended upon Turnour's *Mhv*.

By the 1880s, when Smith started writing, the *Mhv* seemed irrelevant to the self-referential epigraphical studies that were now considered the hallmark of "solidly historical" work. The "hard" facts in lithic inscriptions were privileged over "soft" textual data, even though the "hard" evidence would be mere scratches in rocks except for the prior reading of the "soft" evidence. The ironic suppression of the Pāli texts has been widespread in Indology. Some historians discuss Aśoka without reference to the Vaṃsas;[178] those who do make use of literary material treat it with caution, a colorful addition to the otherwise sober "facts" that are gleaned from the inscriptions themselves.[179] In any event, the Pāli Vaṃsas have been only tangentially interesting to historians of India, for whom they have continued to provide, nonetheless, an important intellectual foundation.[180]

The Indological neglect of the Vaṃsas has more than been compensated for in the excessive use of them that historians of Sri Lanka and Theravāda Buddhism have made. Just as subsequent Indologists generally operated according to Prinsep's Sanskrit bias, later historians of Sri Lanka generally operated according to Turnour's Pāli bias. These biases participate in divisions along national (British vs. French), religious (Protestant vs. Catholic) and "sectarian" (Southern vs. Northern Buddhism) lines. But in both cases the empiricist positions and territorial divisions that Prinsep and Turnour hammered out, as well as the underlying epistemological

[176]On the basis of a supposed date in an inscription, his last edition reverted to the Sinhala date of 544/3 B.C.: *The Early History of India*, edited by S. M. Edwardes (Oxford: Clarendon, 1924), pp. 149–50.

[177]Vincent A. Smith, *Asoka: The Buddhist Emperor of India* (Oxford: Clarendon, 1909), pp. 23, 205; and his, *The Early History of India* (Oxford: Clarendon, 1904), pp. 9, 166.

[178]For example, James Merry MacPhail, *The Heritage of India: Asoka* (Calcutta: Association Press, n.d.); D. C. Sircar, *Inscriptions of Aśoka* (New Delhi: Publications Division, 1967); B. M. Barua, *Asoka and His Inscriptions* (Calcutta: New Age Publishers, 1946).

[179]P. H. L. Eggermont, *The Chronology of the Reign of Asoka Moriya* (Leiden: E. J. Brill, 1956); A. L. Basham, *The Wonder That Was India* ([1954] New York: Grove Press, 1959); R. K. Mookerji, *Asoka* (Varanasi: Motilal Banarsidass, 1962); K. A. Nilakanta Sastri, ed., *Age of the Nandas and Mauryas* (Varanasi: Motilal Banarsidass, 1967); B. G. Gokhale, *Asoka Maurya* (New York: Twayne, 1966); R. Thapar, *Aśoka and the Decline of the Mauryas* (Oxford: Oxford University Press, 1973).

[180]Ironically, the Pāli text that has been of greatest interest to historians (especially social historians) of India has been the *Jātaka* commentary, which is treated as a source for day-to-day conditions in India during the early Buddhist period, even though it was written, in Sri Lanka, approximately 1,300 years later than the period it supposedly documents.

unity of those positions, have remained virtually unaltered for one hundred and fifty years.

The legacy that these scholars have left for scholars of the present generation can be described in two ways: it is, on the one hand, a set of theoretical problems with predetermined answers and, on the other, an agenda for proceeding according to the answers that had been deduced. Ironically, the effect of the closure of the theoretical issues was to undermine the method. If the Vaṃsas are essentially historical documents, and if the translators of them (both Sri Lankan and Western) were competent, then there is little point in looking at the original texts. The more diligent historians, especially in South Asia, have been careful about using the *VAP*, the *Mhv* commentary, as a source for details not found in the *Mhv* itself, and have read the original texts in Pāli rather than English or German. But most historians, especially in the West, have bypassed the original texts altogether. They have busied themselves with the "practical" side of the positivist legacy—transforming Vaṃsa verses into narrative history—without a thought about who wrote these texts or why. The Western translations are gleaned for convenient "facts," disregarding the rigorous standards that Geiger had established for separating the "facts" from what everyone still considered the "fictions" recorded in the Vaṃsas.

The *Mhv* and related texts have thus supplied the bulk of historical detail in every work I know of that has been written on Sri Lanka and Theravāda Buddhism since 1833. Turnour's paraphrasing of the Vaṃsa genealogies is still the basis of political history in Sri Lanka (although the charts showing this chronology are more sophisticated today than they were a century and a half ago), and we should not underrate the degree to which this dynastic history project has shaped historiography there: archeological sites have been reconstructed, the authors of inscriptions have been identified and dated, and a discourse has emerged on Sri Lanka as a unified and stable polity that positions Sinhalas and Tamils as distinct (and opposed) ethnic groups.[181]

More recently, following this century's trends in historical research, historians have paraphrased the Vaṃsas more ingeniously. Thus a great deal of Sri Lankan social, cultural, and religious history has been reconstructed by taking as "authentic history" the (often minor) references to what earlier historians "left out" in their mainly political accounts.[182] Currently, historians have been concerned with "religious ideology": they reiterate the interpretive frameworks in which the Vaṃsas are written in order to elucidate a timeless "Sinhala Buddhist identity" or "ideal social order" that they believe the texts express.[183]

[181]The culmination of this project, paralleling the *History and Culture of the Indian People* and emulating the Cambridge Histories, was the multi-authored University of Ceylon's *History of Ceylon*.

[182]H. Ellawala, *Social History of Early Ceylon* (Colombo: Department of Culterel [sic] Affairs, 1969); U. D. Jayasekera, *Early History of Education in Ceylon, from Earliest Times up to Mahāsena* (Colombo: Department of Cultural Affairs, 1969); K. M. De Silva, *A History of Sri Lanka* (Berkeley and Los Angeles: University of California Press/London: C. Hurst, 1981); Walpola Rahula, *History of Buddhism in Ceylon: The Anurādhapura Period* (Colombo: Gunasena, 1956); Richard Gombrich, *Theravāda Buddhism: A Social History from Ancient Benares to Modern Colombo* (London and New York: Routledge and Kegan Paul, 1988).

[183]Smith, ed., *Religion and Legitimation of Power in Sri Lanka*; and Gananath Obeyesekere, Frank

Recently a sort of return to the empiricism of Turnour's day has occurred. At a seminar held in 1988, scholars zeroed in on the problem of the date of the Buddha's death. Heinz Bechert, in hyperpositivist mode, concluded that neither of the generally accepted dates of the "long chronology," 483 or 486, can withstand close scrutiny. Nor can the "short chronology," when based on statements that Aśoka's coronation took place one hundred years after the Buddha's death. Bechert and many others would, however, now date the Buddha's death to between 80 and 130 years before Aśoka's coronation, that is, to between 400 and 350 B.C. (based on genealogies of Buddhist adepts and revised notions about the timing of doctrinal development).[184]

Reynolds, and Bardwell Smith, eds., *The Two Wheels of Dhamma* (Chambersburg, Pa.: American Academy of Religion, 1972); Donald K. Swearer, *Buddhism and Society in Southeast Asia* (Chambersburg, Pa.: Anima, 1981); Gombrich, *Theravāda Buddhism*; Bruce Kapferer, *Legends of People, Myths of State: Violence, Intolerance, and Political Culture in Sri Lanka and Australia* (Washington, D.C.: Smithsonian Institution Press, 1988). This perspective—which misreads historically situated imperial propaganda as documents of a timeless essence, and thereby reifies violent ethnic conflict and cultural myopia as characteristic foundations of Sri Lankan polity—has already been widely disseminated in Sri Lanka, as were earlier "historical" readings of the Pāli Vaṃsas (as social history, political history, and so on.), by means direct (the use of the scholarly works under discussion) and indirect (school books, newspaper articles, radio and television programs, political speeches).

[184]"The Date of the Buddha—an Open Question of Ancient Indian History," in H. Bechert, ed., *The Dating of the Historical Buddha* (Göttingen: Vandenhoeck & Ruprecht, 1991), 1: 234–6.

4

Royal Eulogy as World History

Rethinking Copper-plate Inscriptions in Cōḻa India

Daud Ali

India: The Land with No History

The practice of inscribing words onto metal or stone has had a long history in Europe, the Middle East, and Asia—a history that has always had complicated relationships with other sorts of textual production. In addition, the reading of these inscriptions has also had a history—at least as long as that of the inscriptions themselves. I stress this because I want to contend that the way scholars read and reproduced inscriptions is today neither self-evident nor timeless. Renaissance humanists copied Roman inscriptions in order to imitate and reinvent a classical past in sixteenth-century Italy.[1] But three hundred years later, when nineteenth-century philologists collected and published classical inscriptions in the massive series *Corpus Inscriptionum Graecarum* (1828) and *Corpus Inscriptionum Latinorum* (1862)—often using the transcriptions of these earlier Italian scholars—they by no means saw themselves as the inheritors of a project begun in the Renaissance. In fact, they ignored most of the concerns of Renaissance humanists.[2] The study of inscriptions in the nineteenth century might be understood in two ways: first, as presupposing the concerns of philology, the study of languages; and second, as being a key constituent of archeology, one of the main disciplines making crucial contributions to historical positivism. As such, the study of inscriptions offers a convenient way to see how theories of language and historiography were tied together. Nineteenth-century philology took as its theoretical focus and practical concern the study of defunct, alien languages perserved in written monuments. Inscriptions, gathered together as a body, or "corpus," were dissected to produce formal linguistic laws. As Vološinov has pointed out, philology was obsessed with dead and alien languages precisely because it envisioned language itself as a hypostasized system of objective forms.[3] Integral to this will to knowledge was the presupposition, taken up by scientific linguistics, that language was a closed system of monologic utterances that humans passively understood. At the same time,

[1]F. Saxl, "The Classical Inscription in Renaissance Art and Politics," *Journal of the Warburg and Courtauld Institutes* 4 (1940–41), 19–20. John Sparrow, *Visible Words: A Study of Inscriptions in and as Books and Works of Art* (Cambridge: Cambridge University Press, 1969), pp. 10–13.

[2]Saxl, "Classical Inscription," p. 20.

[3]V. N. Vološinov, *Marxism and the Philosophy of Language* (Cambridge: Harvard University Press, 1973), pp. 67–73. Saussure's linguistic structuralism, for Vološinov, has its origin in this philological project.

moreover, the study of inscriptions in the nineteenth century was subsumed within the emerging science called archeology. Archeology sought to represent the past not for mimicry but instead for spectacle: to give the past all the qualities of an object. Archeology as a way of knowing and possessing the past—a point to which we shall return—was a science that enjoyed tremendous prestige in British India.

Unlike the other textual genres treated in this volume, inscriptions in India have not had the privilege of feeling the tremors that have shifted the ground in interpretive practices over the last hundred years in Indology and South Asian history. The reason has been that inscriptions have not actually been seen as texts; instead, they have been treated in what Dominick LaCapra has called a "documentary" fashion—as if they were simple self-disclosing objects.[4] In part, the documentary approach to inscriptions has been justified. Their functions were not the same as those of literary texts; they most often served to record property transactions. Their eulogistic preambles, however, were composed in literary style. These eulogies, which will form the subject of this paper, constituted "documentary" sources for the colonialist and nationalist reconstruction of India's past. Whereas texts like the Purāṇas have been able to move beyond the "documentary" readings of colonialist Indology, inscriptional eulogies, because of their appearance in stone and metal, have tended to remain in the empiricist framework of dynastic chronology so important at the turn of the century. This has made the study of inscriptional eulogies a particulalry underdeveloped domain in the study of South Asia history, which is ironic given their remarkable number.

The approach taken here, following LaCapra, Bakhtin, and others, will be dialogical: representational practices will be seen in an active rather than passive relationship with the world. Unlike positivist epistemology, the dialogical reading of texts will consider language and knowledge to be ontologically continuous with their contexts, within which they exist in complicated relationships (of agreement, contestation, parody, and so on). This move will require, in Dominick LaCapra's terms, a rereading of inscriptions as "works" that "supplement," rather than reflect, the world.[5]

This chapter has two goals. First, it will attempt to create a space for the rereading of post-Gupta copper plate inscriptions as the dialogical utterances of royal courts actively speaking to and positioning one another, rather than as static monological documents passively expressive of some political (or social) reality. And second, it will indicate how we might see certain inscriptional practices—namely, the deployment of royal eulogies in those copper plates—as the practice of making historical texts tied in with a world history. We need not, thus, continue to see those copper plates as merely state records tinged with irrelevant mythology and pomposity, to be culled through by the historian either for facts pertinent to the labor of reconstructing the dynastic and political chronology of ancient India or for data relating to the more recent (and productive) project of reconstructing medieval "state and society." The royal eulogies (*praśasti*) of copper plate inscriptions can

[4]Dominick LaCapra, *Rethinking Intellectual History: Texts, Contexts, Language* (Ithaca: Cornell University Press, 1983), pp. 23–71.

[5]D. LaCapra, *Rethinking*, pp. 29–35.

be read as imperial histories with which medieval agents made and remade their world in a field of highly politicized and often contestatory representations, as texts partly articulative of their contexts and partly articulated by them. The text on which I will focus, a donative order of the Cōḻa king Rājendra I (1012/14–1044) called after its findspot the "Tiruvāḷaṅgāḍu Plates," is a complex elaboration of the past. How is it that this text and others like it were shorn of this complexity and recoded as "sources"? How has India thus been denied "history," and what part have texts like these—clearly accounts of the past—played in that process?

Orientalists and Indologists for a long time have asserted that India is a land devoid of history. What they have meant by this claim is a bit more complicated than it might seem on the surface. The claims that India has had no history seem to operate on two levels. As J. E. van Lohuizen-de Leeuw says: "L'Inde n'a pas d'histoire [India has no history]. This may sound somewhat exaggerated, but whether we take it to mean that India has no single history, or that history was not produced as a branch of learning, both interpretations seem equally incontestable."[6] India possessed neither a unitary history as a state nor a tradition of historical writing. The two claims are slightly different, and it is worth distinguishing between them.

It was maintained from the very inception of Indology that India had never possessed a tradition of historical writing. James Mill wrote in his foundational history that "of this branch of literature the Hindus are totally destitute."[7] For Indologists, India's lack of an historical tradition arose from the inability of the Indian mind to represent the outside world rationally and objectively—to record what happened *as it happened.* Hegel articulated perhaps most eloquently the problem with India. In the *Philosophy of History* he argued that India's lack of history in the form of "annals" or "transactions," as they exist in the West, was due to the Hindu mind's idealism of the imagination and lack of rational self-consciousness. Hegel writes, "The Hindoos on the contrary are by birth given over to an unyielding destiny, while at the same time their Spirit is exalted to Ideality; so that their minds exhibit the contradictory processes of a dissolution of fixed rational and definite conceptions in their Ideality, and on the other side a degradation of this ideality to a multiformity of sensuous objects. This makes them incapable of writing history."[8]

For Hegel the imagination was not, as for the Romantics, a faculty commensurate with rational understanding, but instead a lower form of rationality, a sort of "prerational" and organic mode of mental activity that could only traffic in sensual images. The imagination was unable to produce a healthy opposition between spirit and nature, subject and object, symbol and referent. The failure of the Indian mind, dominated by the imagination, to keep these oppositional pairs distinct led to two extremes: either all of nature was collapsed into a spirit without rational

---

[6]J. E. van Lohuizen-de Leeuw, "India and Its Cultural Empire," in *Orientalism and History* (Cambridge: W. Heffer and Sons, 1954), p. 35.

[7]James Mill, *The History of British India* ([1817] Chicago: University of Chicago Press, 1975), p. 329.

[8]Georg Hegel, *The Philosophy of History*, translated by J. Sibree ([1899] New York: Dover, 1956), p. 162.

conceptions, or conversely, all of the spirit was confused with particular sensuous objects of nature. This is why, according to Hegel, the most abstruse idealistic monism could exist in India alongside the most vulgar idolatry. Whether due to the predominance of the imagination, as in Hegel's view, or more generally from the influence of "religion," as with the mainline empiricists and utilitarians of the nineteenth century, India could not attain the epistemological criteria for writing history. If the Indian mind was incapable of distinguishing between symbol and referent, then all objective representation was impossible. In Hegel's history of the world, it was only after the *Weltgeist* (world-spirit) passed from India and underwent further development that a continuous history was possible. India remained frozen in a perpetual stasis enthralled by Hinduism, dominated by the subjective idealism of the imagination.

For eighteenth- and nineteenth-century writers, the Hindu imagination generated wildly fantastic and rudely exaggerated reckonings of time that were cyclic and non-progressive in character. Conceptually, they were opposed to the Judeo-Christian linear conception of time that helped engender a moral purposiveness for progress and change as the basis of history. Many subsequent scholars and apologists for Western imperialism have relied on this opposition to explain the uniqueness of the West and its triumph over the world after the fifteenth century.[9] Such celebrations of the Western Enlightenment have of course provoked reactions from Romantics, Weberians, literary modernists, and others who have wished to establish a conceptual haven from modernity, a retreat from the rationalizing logic of history and its "dehumanizing" tendencies, to various forms of idealism, nihilism, and fascism. The orientalist construction of mystical India with its cyclic notion of time, undergirded by its illusionistic and world-negating philosophies, have remained a perennial source and refuge for such agendas.[10] This construction of the Indian mind, in its various disciplinary permutations, has remained a powerful orientalist assumption in writing about India.

The second ground upon which India was deemed without history by orientalists and colonial Indologists was its lack of political unity. This claim is a bit more complicated. Hegel tells us that it is the state which first presents history with its true subject matter (p. 61). The nation-state, founded on the principles of citizenship and civil society, was itself thought to be the final stage that a people or race arrived at from its origin in a kin-based tribal polity. In India, according to colonial scholars, something intervened to retard this evolution: caste. As Hegel put it, "the impulse of organization, in beginning to develop social distinctions, was immediately petrified in the merely natural classification according to castes" (p. 62). For Hegel, India's lack of political unity was in the end a result of the Indian imagination—an imagination that failed to distinguish between nature and spirit, and mistook a natural organization of labor for a divinely sanctioned society called

[9] See, for example, Daniel Boorstin, *The Discoverers* (New York: Random House, 1983), pp. 558–625.

[10] In recent scholarly circles this opposition has been most powerfully iterated by the historian of religion Mircea Eliade, who has argued that time in early India was cyclic and eternal, and sacred, as opposed to the profane linear time that has characterized modern man; Mircea Eliade, *Cosmos and History: The Myth of the Eternal Return* (New York: Pantheon, 1954).

caste. Since caste precluded the development of a unitary state, in India there could be no history as such. Although much subsequent scholarship came to presume the existence of some sort of proto-nation-state or feudal political arrangement in precolonial India, Indologists have consistently maintained that caste, village, and religion always subsumed or displaced it. This historiography has sought to deny India the triumphal history of a sovereign state.

One of the great ironies of the colonial historiography, however, is that although it denied that India had a history, it nevertheless tirelessly sought to produce a definitive chronological and historical narrative for precolonial South Asia. Indologists maintained that even if India had never enjoyed political unity, it was, nevertheless, a coherent entity. And, in this sense, the British were faced with the contradictory tasks of denying a unitary history for its subject domain but at the same time producing one for purposes of rule, as I show in the appendix to this chapter.

I have tried to show that there has been a relationship between the way inscriptions have been used as "sources" to reconstruct a positivist chronology of India and the construction of the Indian mind as incapable of representation. This chapter will attempt to develop a theoretical strategy that will change the "patients" of Indian history—"expressions" of the irrational Hindu mind and the despotic Hindu dynasty—to agents involved in articulating their own worlds.

Inscribed in Copper: Rājendracōḻa's Donative Order

Since its inception, the Archeological Survey of India has brought to light several varieties of inscriptions. Most record the gift of land, services, or other goods by kings or other agents to various institutions—Buddhist or Jaina monasteries, Vaiṣṇava or Śaiva temples, or liturgical associations of Brāhmaṇs. Others announce royal edicts, commemorate deaths, or celebrate victories. Inscriptions before the Gupta period (A.D. 320–550)—whether eulogies, edicts, or dedications—usually concerned themselves with proclaiming the deeds of only contemporary ruler(s) or agents. Perhaps most famous among these are the edicts of Aśoka (c. 268–39 B.C.), which record, in the imperial voice, the deeds of Aśoka and his commands to the people. They might be compared to certain public inscriptions—eulogies and decrees—of the Roman emperors, the most famous of which is the *Res Gestae Divi Augusti*, a long honorary inscription in the imperial voice of Augustus (27 B.C.-A.D. 14) proclaiming his achievements.[11] Examples of eulogies (*praśasti*) in Kāvya or poetry, the genre I am especially concerned with here, are also to be found in the pre-Gupta period. Inscribed in Sanskrit and Prākrit on stone at fixed locations—sculpted caves, excavated tanks, and pillars—they record the deeds of

[11]This inscription, found in the temple of Rome and Augustus at Ancyra in Galatia, among other places, is itself unusual, and its place in the elogia genre, due to its greater length, has sometimes been questioned; G. M. Rushforth, *Latin Historical Inscriptions* (Oxford: Clarendon, 1893), p. xix; P. A. Brunt and J. M. Moore, eds., *Res Gestae Divi Augusti: The Achievements of the Divine Augustus* (Oxford: Oxford University Press, 1967), pp. 2–3.

particular kings.[12] The earliest of these, dated to the first century A.D., depicts Khāravela of Kaliṅga as a paramount king. Interestingly, he claims descent from a hero of Lunar pedigree, the "royal sage" Vasu Uparicara of Cedi.[13]

After the Guptas a new sort of inscriptional text began to appear, probably at first in south India. Like their smaller ancestors, these inscriptions usually record a donation to a Brāhmaṇ. Unlike them, however, they also include eulogies of kings, usually in Sanskrit, similar to the earlier ones inscribed in stone. These copper plates go further, however, for their eulogies relate not only the deeds of the king issuing it but those of his ancestors, as well. These eulogies, most often inscribed with the details of the transaction they authorize on sheaves of copper bound together by a sealed ring, are unique, unlike anything found in Indian or European antiquity.[14] Whereas the earlier Aśokan edicts and the *Res Gestae* take on a voice of imperial immediacy, these inscriptions, with their long and elaborate Sanskrit eulogies composed not in the voice of the emperor himself but of his royal poet, are very concerned with articulating a past. As we shall see, the bards of the Rāṣṭrakūṭas, Paramāras, Cālukyas, Cōḻas, and other post-Gupta dynasties, quite explicitly look back to the world histories of the Purāṇas to tell the genealogies of their kings. Each inscription becomes much more than an imperial voice proclaiming its own magnitude; it inscribes the submission of kings to a vision of history. As such, they should not be read simply as sources that we might use to reconstruct dynastic histories, but instead as histories in and of themselves.

This chapter will focus on a particular inscription produced during the reign of king Rājendra I, which, scholars have asserted, represents the height of the Cōḻa dynasty's imperial power. The copper plates were discovered in 1905 inside the shrine of the Vāṭaraṇyeśvara temple located in the village of Tiruvāḻaṅgāḍu (in modern-day North Arcot) by K. V. Subrahmanya Ayyar, an epigraphist for the Archeological Survey of India. In a break with protocol, due to the "exceptional interest" generated by the size and content of these plates, the discovery was announced during the same year by the director general.[15] H. Krishna Sastri edited and translated the inscription sixteen years later.[16] It became the most important single "source" for reconstructing the dynastic lineage of the medieval Cōḻas, as it contains a more exhaustive list of kings than any of the three other copper plate inscriptions that had been already discovered. To date it remains one of the largest copper plate grants ever found, consisting of thirty-one sheets of copper bound together with a huge seal-ring, weighing nearly two hundred pounds and containing 816 lines of writing

---

[12]Dines Chandra Sircar, *Indian Epigraphy* (New Delhi: Motilal Banarsidass, 1965), pp. 3–5.

[13]K. P. Jayaswal, "The Hathigumpha Inscription of Kharavela," *EI* 20 (1929–30), 71–89.

[14]They tend to be much longer than their pre-Gupta counterparts, many of them considerably exceeding the length of Augustus's *Res Gestae*.

[15]*Archeological Survey of India: Annual Report 1903–04*, (Calcutta: Government Publications, 1906), p. 233.

[16]H. Krishna Sastri, ed. and tr., "The Tiruvalangadu Copper Plates of the Sixth Year of Rajendra-Chola I," *South Indian Inscriptions* (*SII*) 3 (1929), 383–439. All further references to the text of the inscription will be cited by verse (for the Sanskrit) or line (for the Tamil). Translations are mine.

Figure 4.1. Plate (on Ring) of Rājendra I's Order

(Courtesy of the State Department of Archaeology of Tamil Nadu)

(Figure 4.1).[17] The plates, we should note right away, present themselves to us as a text (Figure 4.1). In medieval India, texts were usually inscribed on palmyra leaves which were then bound with a string that fit through a hole bored through all the sheaves. The copper plates were bound similarly, indicating, as we shall see, that they themselves were the durable "hard copies" of less permanent documents kept at the palace of the king. The seal-ring that binds the sheaves of copper together, however, names the text not as the "Tiruvāḷaṅgāḍu Plates" but instead as the "Order of the King Rājendra Cōḻa" (*etadśāsanaṃ rājendracolasya*). In moving away from the idea that this text is primarily an object, it will be useful to call it instead by its own name—"order" (Skt., *śāsanaṃ*; Tamil, *tirumukam*). I will henceforth refer to the text as Rājendracōḻa's śāsanaṃ in the sixth year of his reign (*RCS–6*). The multiple donative orders inscribed during Rājendra's reign were not differentiated from one another by any strict titling practices; rather, they organize themselves only in relation to the regnal year of the king.[18]

[17] It is surpassed only by the Cōḻa Karandai Sangam grant, which consists of 55 plates and 2,500 lines of writing—weighing 246 pounds without the seal-ring.

[18] The authors of the royal eulogies that formed the introductory parts of these orders were not at-

The *RCS–6* begins with a long royal eulogy (*praśasti*) in Sanskrit, of some 272 lines (130 verses). Along with the rest of the grant, it was composed by the poet Nārāyaṇa, son of Śaṅkara and devotee of Viṣṇu, whose royal title was the "King of Tamil for the best of Cōḻas" (*uttamacoḷatamiḻataraiya*). The Sanskrit portion begins with an invocation to Pārvatī, a praise of the Cōḻa dynasty, and a request that Sarasvatī bestow the poet some supplementary letters of the alphabet in order to better describe the eminent Cōḻa dynasty. The eulogy then recounts for over 100 verses the glorious lineage of the Cōḻas, starting with the Sun and ending with Rājendra himself—detailing his conquest of the quarters (*digvijaya*) and the establishment of the famous Cōḻagaṅgam at Rājendra's capital, Gaṅgaikoṇḍacōḻapuram. Nārāyaṇa then says that Rājendra deputed his minister Jananātha, a former "ornament" of the Cālukya dynasty (*cālukyacūḍāmaṇi*) to have the village of Paḻaiyaṉūr (Skt., Purāṇagrāma), which was the ornament of Jayaṅgoṇḍacōḻamaṇḍalam, given to the god Śiva residing in the temple at Tiruvāḷaṅgāḍu. After the petitioner of the grant (*vijñāpti*), and the overseer of its implementation—its executor (*ājñāpti*)—are mentioned, the poet closes with a verse praising Rājendra.

The Tamil portion of the inscription, longer than the Sanskrit, takes up the details of how the grant of land was to be enacted. It begins in the form of a royal order issued from the department of writs at the palace of the king to the relevant local officials of Paḻaiyaṉūr-nāḍu, a district in the province of Jayangoṇḍacōḻamaṇḍalam.[19] The text then announces that a village within that district, Paḻaiyaṉūr, that was currently being enjoyed as a "gift to Brāhmaṇs," was now granted as a "temple gift"—a donation to the representation of Śiva present in the temple at Tiruvāḷaṅgāḍu.[20] After detailing the specific administrative transactions required to carry out this conversion of property, the text names the three provincial officials, all from Jayangoṇḍacōḻamaṇḍalam, who were designated to go to the village with the order and accompany a local delegation in leading a female elephant around the circumference of the village Paḻaiyaṉūr in order to mark out the boundaries of the donated land. This passage seems to be informing or assuring the local officials

---

tempting to write timeless histories. As new political acts displaced older ones, the eulogies were rewritten.

[19]The particular officials addressed included the district officials (*nāṭṭār*), the headmen of the relevant gift lands to Brāhmaṇs (*brahmadeya*), the village officials (*ūrār*), and the city officials (*nakaraṅkaḷār*).

[20]The inscription records this switch in several detailed steps. First, another gift had to be given to the Brāhmaṇ liturgical association (*agrahāram*) named Śiṅgalāntaka-caturvedimaṅgalam, which was then enjoying the village of Paḻaiyaṉūr as a "gift to Brāhmaṇs" (*brahmadeya*). Then Paḻaiyaṉūr had to be transformed to the status of "peasant-share village" (*veḷḷāṉ vakai*), the unmarked revenue-yielding class to which the majority of villages in south India belonged; Burton Stein, *Peasant State and Society in Medieval South India* (Delhi: Oxford University Press, 1980), p. 123. Concomitant to this was the reassignment of village taxes (*vari*) that had previously been enjoyed by the Brāhmaṇ association. This change, according to the text, was entered into the account books by "our executive officers," having been signed and issued by a number of officials. The grant continues two days later, and records that Paḻaiyaṉūr, now a cultivator's portion, was to be further transformed into the status of temple village (*devadāna*), whereby the tax fixed for Paḻaiyaṉūr would now be the permanently settled tax payable year after year to meet the requirements of the god Mahādeva (Śiva) residing at Tiruvāḷaṅgāḍu. This further transaction was then registered, according to the grant, into the account books by the appropriate officials.

that the formalities of the transaction have already been recorded on palm leaf (*ōlai*) in the offices at the Cōḻa captial.

The narrative voice switches in line 128 of the Tamil text from the perspective of the department of writs to the local officials. "We, the representatives of several districts" (*nāṭkīḻnāṭṭōm*), in the sixth year of Rājendra's reign, received the royal order which required "our" presence for its implementation. They deliver a shorter Tamil eulogy (*meykīrtti*) of Rājendra, and report that when they saw the order arrive, they went out and "respectfully received it and placed it on our heads and, accompanying the female elephant, walked around the hamlets (of Paḻaiyaṉūr)" (ll. 143–44).[21] The boundaries of the grant outlined by this delegation are then detailed for 280 lines. The text proceeds to enumerate the privileges (*parihāras*) secured by the temple on getting the village as a temple gift. The grant then announces that "we, the people" (*nāṭṭōm*) of Paḻaiyaṉūr "drew up" and gave the deed to Mahādeva. Finally, the signatures of the delegation are recorded.[22] The perspective then shifts back to the "central" authorities, who close the grant by listing the various officials present when the transaction, having been implemented, was finally closed in the account books. The plates conclude by naming four Vaiṣṇava Brāhmaṇs of the Hōvya family, residing in Kāñcīpuram, who engraved the plates.

It should be clear that the inscription not only recounts the history of the Cōḻa dynasty but also records its own complicated story, from its inception as a request to the king, through its performance and instantiation, and finally to its transcription onto copper. These texts encode an entire political procedure. A donation of land, even if we begin just with the king's word, was a complex procedure that involved a variety of sociopolitical agents. As the king dictated, the order was transcribed onto palm leaf, scrutinized, and checked for form by a series of officials whose title involved the word "palm leaf" (*ōlai*). It then took on the status of "edited" or "refined" (*tīṭṭu*), a status that enabled the grant to be entered into the permanent record books and/or sent in the form of a communication called an "order" (*tirumukam*) to the relevant local authorities.[23] The royal order, called in Tamil the "auspicious face" or "auspicious mouth" (*tirumukam*) of the king, was received at the locality as if it were the king himself.[24] The "men of the district" honored it by placing the order on their heads and then, mounting it on a female

[21] *nāṭṭomukkut tirumukam vara nāṭṭomun tirumukaṅ kaṇḍe tireḻuntu ceṉṟu toḻutu vāṅkit talaimel vaittu pidi cūḻntu paṭākai naṭantu/*

[22] The signatures begin with the three officials mentioned above, who were designated by authorities at the capital to supervise the drawing up of the deed. The arbitrators (*karaṇattaṉ*) of two Brāhmaṇ villages to Paḻaiyaṉūr, Śiṅgalāntaka-caturvedimaṅgalam (which had previously enjoyed the village as a gift to Brāhmaṇs) and Nittavinōda-caturvedimaṅgalam, along with the arbitrator from Paḻaiyaṉūr itself, signed the plates.

[23] K. A. Nilakanta Sastri, *The Cōḻas* (Madras: Madras University Press, 1955), pp. 468–69; K. V. Subrahmanya Ayyar, ed. and tr., "Tirumukkudal Inscription of Virarajendra" *EI* 21 (1931–32), 220–50. These accounts only articulate the process of granting land and recording it in stone/copper *after* the king had issued a royal order. Presumably, as inscriptions such as the Anbil plates intimate, there was considerable lobbying and strategizing even before the king made any proclamation.

[24] James Heitzman, "State Formation in South India, 850–1280," *The Indian Economic and Social History Review* 24.1 (1987), 43.

elephant, circumambulated the village to be donated. The plates could only be inscribed after these acts were performed.

The dates included in the inscription itself indicate the duration of time required to donate the land. The Tamil portion, although inscribed into copper at a single time, contains three dates: the sixth year, eighty-eighth day of Rājendra's reign, when the village Paḻaiyaṉūr ceased to be a gift to Brāhmaṇs; two days later, when its status was redesignated as temple village for Mahādeva at Tiruvāḷaṅgāḍu; and the seventh regnal year, 155th day, after the combined delegation had traced out the boundaries of the gift village, and the transaction closed in the account books at the "department of writs" in the capital. The plates as inscribed even at this point did not by any means constitute a totally closed text. In comparing the Sanskrit and Tamil eulogies, which emphasize different campaigns of Rājendra's world conqest, it seems that the Sanskrit eulogy was probably written, or rewritten, about ten years after the time of the Tamil portion of the *RCS–6*, and was retro-dated for consistency.[25]

The text, for all of its theological language, locates itself very carefully in its context, and is very aware of its own production. Its connection to property and state power is hardly concealed. I dare say that this is more than we usually see in our histories, which, at the level of form and notwithstanding peripheralized acknowledgments and citational markers, tend to present themselves as objective accounts located "outside" their historical situations, as decontextualized commentaries on reality simply "written down" by the inspired historian.

The textual apparatus of the RCS–6 itself raises several issues—production, use, closure, audience, property, power, performance, and complex authorship—which are often seen as irrelevant and ignored in the study of texts as we know them: the bounded, unitary expressions of a single author's mind. One might then ask, "why treat this inscription as a text at all?" This requires two responses. First, structuralists and poststructuralists over the last thirty years have gone to great lengths in showing how texts are not the unitary and rational expressions of a single human mind. Thus, it seems necessary to change our notion of what texts are. Second, this unraveling of the unitary bounded text has allowed us to enter into the realm of the textual a large body of "documents" that have hitherto stood at the periphery of textual inquiry. This is not to claim that these inscriptions can be understood as the same sort of texts as, let us say, Śāstras, Upaniṣads, or Sūtras, but that we need to interrogate both these "texts" and what have commonly been understood as "documents" as to how they are implicated as dialogical utterances in constructing the human world. If we take this text seriously on just one of its most obvious claims, that it enunciates a history, then we might raise a whole range of fruitful questions about inscriptions that have up to now been unasked. I hope to use the notion of "intertextuality" to show how in the eulogy of the *RCS–6* several different discursive practices overlap and intersect in transformative configurations, to form a coherent vision of the past. This will serve to move these "documents"

[25]Moreover, at least 150 years after the *RCS–6* was completed, another inscription was added to the remaining space on the last plate of the Sanksrit eulogy, granting a gift of land to the goddess Ammai Nācciyār, but retro-dated to the year when the original *RCS–6* was made.

in the direction of the "textual" and away from the idea that texts are hermetically sealed capsules of rational thought.

Supplementing Epic and Purāṇic Discourse

The two main approaches to reading medieval inscriptions, the older colonial and nationalist schools interested in producing the dynastic transactions of the "Hindu" states, and the more recent approach intent on discovering the structure of medieval state and society, have both tended, despite their different emphases, to read inscriptions in the same way. Apart from their "documentary" approach to texts, they have seen inscriptions as isolates, not in any crude sense but as autonomous "documents" that all bear the same relationship to the social reality that lies beyond them, like so many individual pieces of a jigsaw puzzle. "Put together" carefully, they will reflect more or less accurately the "true" dynastic chronology or the "real" state and society.

I will read inscriptions, specifically post-Gupta copper plate charters, not as so many separate "documents" that mirror political and social realities, but instead as texts that formed part of an integrated discursive practice. By reading copper plate eulogies together, we can avoid seeing them as self-contained documents or literary texts. By seeing them as discursive, we can turn our attention to how they participate in larger systems of signs that cross particular genres and textual moments. I have used the term "intertextuality" to refer to how these discourses relate to one another, and the way texts and the technologies of representation that are located within them penetrate and extend in complex ways into other discourses and texts. Foregrounding these issues will enable us to see how codes of meaning are manipulated from text to text, and text to context. We can see a continuity not only among texts but also between textual discourses and other less textual social practices. Instead of inscriptions being contextualized, contexts will be, aptly, inscribed with textuality.

At this point I should make a few disclaimers. I am wary of falling into certain structuralist and poststructuralist pitfalls in talking about discourse and sign systems. Structuralist understandings of discourse often make some of the same mistakes as the older positivist approaches to texts. For structuralists, specific texts and representations are parts of larger cultural codes, which in turn are the expressions of underlying cultural or societal themes and contradictions. All texts are collapsed into external structures and essences.[26] In some poststructuralist approaches to texts, and in certain varieties of American deconstructionism in particular, quite the opposite process occurs: all externalities, be they textual or "real," collapse into the maelstrom of a single text, in what some scholars have

[26]For a loose structuralist reading of south Indian inscriptions as myths, see David Dean Shulman, *The King and the Clown in South Indian Myth and Poetry* (Princeton: Princeton University Press, 1985), pp. 24–27.

called "pan-textualism,"the idea that all texts and realities interpenetrate with one another in the eternal free play of language.[27]

These various approaches to texts tend to ignore the historical specificities of representational practices, and sidestep the issue of human agency, instead displacing it onto underlying cultural structures or the autonomy of language itself. If the structuralist and poststructuralist interventions have helpfully destabilized the textual and authorial unity and boundedness of older textual practices by splitting the signifier from the signified, they have often failed to theorize adequately what in fact might be a new way of imagining signifier and signified. Either all signifiers come to represent a single cultural or societal signified, or they stand alone solipsistically, the realm of the signified forsaken altogether. Where we previously had the substantialized agent of the sovereign individual, we now have the bedrock of culture or language itself. Despite claims to the contrary, some poststructuralist and deconstructionist notions of language fail to arrive at a radical ontological contingency because language becomes an endless play of "floating" signifiers. Needless to say, history has figured little in either of these interpretive strategies. A theory of knowledge as articulative will attempt to return the signifier back to the signified without the identic correspondence of earlier theories of representation, building instead on the structuralist and poststructuralist critiques that have complicated authorship and textual autonomy. By using "intertextuality" as a way of understanding how textual practices interpenetrate with one another, I will not ignore the historically situated boundaries of these interwoven discourses and their relationships with historical agents.

Scholars have noticed for some time that royal genealogies in the Sanskrit eulogies issued in the copper plates of many post-Gupta dynasties have had some relationship to the Solar and Lunar dynasties elaborated in the Purāṇas.[28] The Cōḻas have been no exception here, and the *RCS–6* has been especially singled out as being Purāṇic in "idiom."[29]

One relatively recent approach to the inclusion of Purāṇic "idioms" in inscriptional eulogies has argued, along Weberian lines, that the eulogies express the inner contradiction of Hindu kingship, and indeed Indian society as a whole: a radical separation of a rationally ordered inner mental world and a chaotic outer social world. This separation has created what Heesterman and others call the "conundrum of the king's authority" in India: a tension between transcendence and immanence.[30] The "solution" that the inscriptions offer is the creation of a "ritual" sovereignty and royal "style," which kept the king seemingly powerful despite the

---

[27] Steven Best and Douglas Kellner, *Postmodern Theory: Critical Interrogations* (New York: Guilford, 1991), p. 27.

[28] J. G. de Casparis, "Inscriptions and South Asian Dynastic Traditions," in *Tradition and Politics in South Asia*, edited by R. J. Moore (Delhi: Vikas, 1979), p. 105; Hartmut Scharfe, *The State in Indian Tradition* (Leiden: E. J. Brill, 1989), p. 96.

[29] Stein, *Peasant State*, p. 362; George Spencer, "Sons of the Sun: The Solar Genealogy of a Cōḻa King," *Asian Profile* 10.1 (February 1982), 84–89.

[30] J. C. Heesterman, "The Conundrum of the King's Authority," in J. F. Richards, ed. *Kingship and Authority in South Asia*, South Asian Studies Publication Series No. 3 (Madison: University of Wisconsin South Asia Center, 1978), pp. 1–27; Spencer, "Sons," p. 94.

reality of political dispersion, decentralization, and chaos. But the royal eulogies are in the end no real help, for they themselves are symptoms of Indian kingship, and turn out to be necessary for these Weberian scholars to produce the theory of a conflicted Indian civilization. The eulogies are failed attempts to solve the problems that they themselves express.[31] Leaving aside the picture of the ancient Indian state that Weberian scholars have constructed, we should note their view of Purāṇic discourse as a transcendent, otherworldly set of myths employed by kings to legitimate their authority. In addition to assuming that kings acted disingenuously, never ascribing to the ideas they promulgated to the masses, this approach has presumed the modern antinomies of politics and religion to be inherently opposed and autonomous realms across history, "interacting" for their mutual benefit. One problem with this "interactionist" theory of religion and politics is that no religions develop in contexts that are not already implicated in political materiality and, conversely, no political action exists without metaphysical and ontological presuppositions. Although it might be true that in given historical situations—such as that of the modern nation-state—the categories of "religion" and "politics" rise like hydra heads from the same body to breath fire upon one another, this discursive opposition is not inherent, and requires historical explanation. In the medieval Cōḻa texts, "religion" (*dharma*) and "politics" (*artha*) do not form dichotomous discourses. If, however, we translate the term *dharma* as "way of life in the world," we can begin to see that it was considered in medieval India to be closer to pleasure (*kāma*) and politics (*artha*) than *mokṣa*, "liberation from life in the world," which formed the counterpoint to these three "goals of man" (*puruṣārtha*). The simple dichotomy of religion and politics, upon which much of this scholarship is based, should therefore be treated suspiciously. Consequently, it will be necessary to rethink the relationship of Purāṇic material to kingly genealogies written in stone and copper.

Instead of focusing on a single Purāṇa, as Inden has done, I will take up the issue of how the eulogies of copper plate inscriptions relate themselves to Purāṇic discourses in general. By using terms like "the Purāṇa," or "Purāṇic," I do not intend to imply that all Purāṇic discourses proceeded from a single ur-text or document, nor do I mean to imply that they all take exactly the same positions, but rather that most Purāṇic texts conceptualize time and the past in a similar language. This notion of time, like many other elements of Purāṇic knowledge, was both presupposed and transformed by new texts that emerged during the Cōḻa period.

---

[31] The circularity of this nexus is due, according to its adherents, to the contradictory nature of religious belief. George Spencer asserts that the redundancies and contradictions of inscriptional preambles simply were not apparent to Indians: "Where the non-believer sees contradiction, the believer perceives enrichment of the sacred story." George W. Spencer, "Heirs Apparent: Fiction and Function in Cōḻa Mythical Genealogies," *Indian Economic and Social History Review* 21.4 (1984), 415. Citing the authority of the anthropologist Edmund Leach, Spencer elsewhere argues that the "redundancy of such mythologies is reassuring to believers, since each alternative version of the story reinforces the basic meaning of all the others;" Spencer, "Sons," p. 82. Religion here is understood as a "subrational" form of thinking that curiously must, at the same time, constantly "rationalize" itself to its believers.

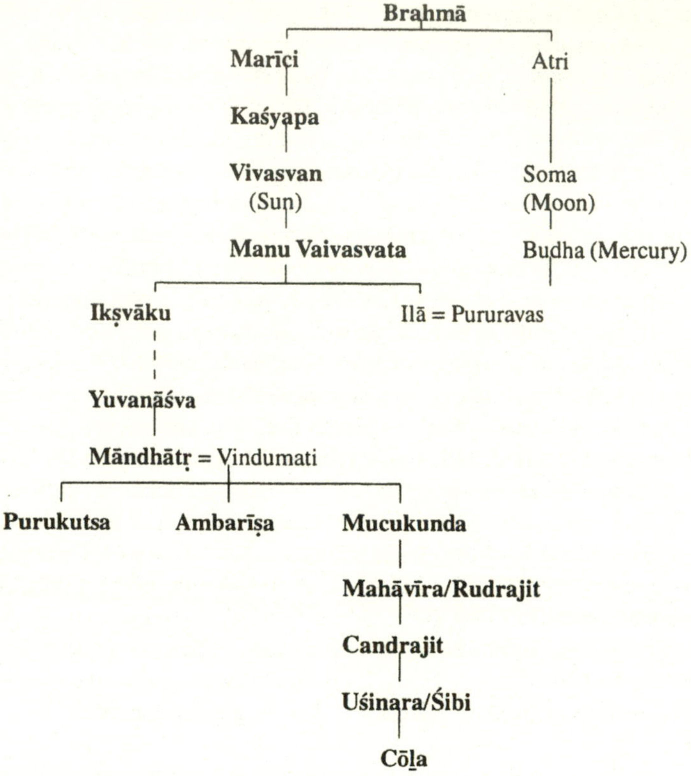

Figure 4.2. Solar Descent of the Cōḻas (bold = Cōḻa inscriptions)

The Purāṇas state that they were compiled by Vyāsa (the sage who assembled the Veda) and narrated by Sūta at the beginning of the Age of Strife. In both the Śaiva and Vaiṣṇava Purāṇas, history began with the evolution of the universe from the sleeping body of Viṣṇu. Time in Purāṇic discourses was not something in which the universe was set, nor was it an abstract object created by God. Rather, time was conceived of as a form of God himself, usually measured in terms of days and nights in the life of Brahmā, the manifestation of the supreme deity Viṣṇu or Śiva.[32] The universe, temporally and, as we shall see, spatially, was ordered into

[32] The various Purāṇas are not in agreement as to the exact enumeration of the measurements of time. For example, whereas the *Viṣṇupurāṇa* (I, 3) sees the largest division of time as the life of Brahmā, who is but an instantiation of Viṣṇu, the *Śivapurāṇa* (VII.1, 8) equates the lifetime of Brahmā as a single day in the life of Viṣṇu, whose entire existence is but a day in the life of Rudra, the lowest of Śiva's proper forms.

successive but ever inclusive tiers that resembled one another.[33] If durations of time were moments in the life of the supreme lord, then a system of equivalences could link human time to the time of the gods. In the *Viṣṇupurāṇa*, Parāśara, sage-author of the text related by Sūta, declares to his interlocutor, Maitreya: "I have already said to you, O sage, that time is a form of Viṣṇu; hear now how it is applied to measure the duration of Brahmā, and of all other sentient beings, as well as those which are unconscious, as the mountains, oceans and the like." [34] A day in the life of Brahmā consisted of an eon or cosmic formation (*kalpa*), which in turn was divided into fourteen epochs, each presided over by a progenitor of mankind, or Manu (*manvantara*). The epochs of Manu each consisted of four ages (*yugas*) wherein the world gradually declined and eventually was destroyed and reabsorbed (*pralaya*), upon which time a new epoch of Manu was initiated. This organization of time has commonly been glossed as "cosmogony"—a quaint mythological and prescientific way of understanding the beginnings of the world. I think that it makes more sense to understand the Purāṇic discourses as "universal histories" or "world histories," something on the order of what we find in Hegel's *Philosophy of History*. Hegel, who is regarded as the father of modern history, was concerned not so much with what he calls "original" or "reflective" (that is, merely empirical) history, but instead with articulating a universal and philosophical history. Significantly, the progress of the *Weltgeist*, the world-spirit that moves across and animates the history of the globe, takes the form of an evolving human life. It is ironic that much modern historiography is based on a Hegelian notion of Spirit instantiated in matter as the life of a man, while at the same time proclaiming the progress of science and the obsolescence of religion.[35] My point is that we should think of Purāṇas as world histories that were hegemonic in medieval India in the same sense that Hegelian notions of history have been for modernity; that is, they set the teleological terms to which other historical practices submitted or from which they dissented. In medieval India, inscriptional eulogies were perhaps the most important historical practice to take up and realize the world histories of the Purāṇas.

If all of time was ordered as successive moments in the life of a universal divine being, then its more minute increments here on the island continent of the earth (Jambudvīpa) might be organized by the life spans of the most preeminent of men—kings. The continuity of time would be established through a succession of these life spans, or a genealogy (*vaṃśa*). The genealogical lists, then, were conscious means of organizing polities and their histories along the lines of the larger universal histories of the Purāṇas, and not "natural" holdovers from a tribal

[33] R. Inden, "Hierarchies of Kings in Early Medieval India," in *Way of Life: King, Householder, Renouncer—Essays in Honour of Louis Dumont*, edited by T. N. Madan (New Delhi: Vikas, 1982), and *Contributions to Indian Sociology*, New Series 15 (1981), 99–125.

[34] *Viṣṇu Purāṇa*, edited H. H. Wilson ([1840] Delhi: Nag Publishers, 1980), I.3.6–7, my translation.

[35] One could cite many examples here, but perhaps the most amusing is modernization theory, which divides the globe into three worlds, all existing at the same moment but at different stages of development on the path from tradition to modernity. Developed countries, like older siblings, can see in the young a bit of their own past, and are in a perfect position to advise and admonish.

society or an earlier mode of production in the process of being tranformed into states.[36]

Purāṇic texts, thus, take as one of their main concerns the genealogical succession of kings (*vaṃśānucarita*) of the present epoch of Manu Vaivasvata (Figure 4.2).[37] Manu Vaivasvata ("born of the sun") was the manifestation of Viṣṇu who sired humanity and established order on earth at the beginning of the present epoch of Manu. He built the capital city of Ayodhyā in the Kosala country (eastern Uttar Pradesh) on the banks of the Sarayū (Ghaghara), and installed there his eldest son, Ikṣvāku, as paramount king. The descendants of Ikṣvāku became known as the Solar dynasty (*sūryavaṃśa*). Buddhists claimed that Ikṣvāku was the founder of the Śākya clan in which the Buddha was born. Manu's daughter Ilā had a son named Purūravas, whose father's father was the Moon (Soma). Manu installed his daughter's son, Purūravas, as king at Pratiṣṭhāna (Jhusi, on the left bank of the Gaṅgā, opposite Prayāga or Allahabad). His descendants, among them the Yādavas of Mathurā in the Śūrasena country and the Pauravas of the Kuru-Pañcāla country (Haryana and western Uttar Pradesh), came to be known as the Lunar dynasty (*candravaṃśa*).

The order that Manu established on earth, with the installation of Ikṣvāku as its paramount overlord (a king over other kings) and Kosala as its central country with Ayodhyā as its capital, was not a regime that would remain stable for all time. It had to be continually remade and might be challenged or reformulated at any time, since Viṣṇu privileged no one dynasty or clan as its eternal masters or beneficiaries. Viṣṇu manifested himself most fully in the king who was most prepared to support his "luminous will" (*tejas*). The days and nights into which time was divided corresponded to temporal oscillations in the lives of the beings that inhabited the universe. Consequently, there were moments of crisis and despair as well as prosperity and happiness. Viṣṇu appeared on earth at moments of instability—such as the junctures between ages—to intervene in the affairs of this world. At the end of the Age of the Trey (*tretāyuga*), he came to earth in the form of Bhārgava Rāma and rid it of the arrogant and offensive Kṣatriyas. The nearly perfect king Daśaratha of the Solar dynasty initiated the Age of the Deuce (*dvāparayuga*) with his shower bath into kingship (*rājyābhiṣeka*). Viṣṇu descended again at the end of the Age of the Deuce in the form of Kṛṣṇa and Arjuna to help the Pāṇḍavas gain victory over their rivals the Kauravas (both branches of the Pauravas). Yudhiṣṭhira, the Pāṇḍava king of the Lunar dynasty, succeeded through the great battle of Kurukṣetra (Haryana) related in the *Mahābhārata*, in capturing the paramount overlordship of Bhāratavarṣa, and initiated an order appropriate for the final Age of Strife. The center of his kingdom was Hāstinapura (near Meerut) in the Kuru country (submontane western Uttar Pradesh), which was closest to the metaphysical center of Bhāratavarṣa.[38] At his death, Yudhiṣṭhira split his kingdom, installing Parīkṣit,

---

[36]Romila Thapar, "Genealogy as a Source of Social History," in her *Ancient Indian Social History: Some Interpretations* (Delhi: Orient Longmans, 1979), pp. 326–60.

[37]A genealogical succession of kings formed one of the distinguishing marks (*lakṣaṇa*) of a Purāṇa.

[38]The geographic discourse of the Purāṇas and its relevance for the Cōḻas will be discussed later.

Arjuna's grandson, as his successor at Hāstinapura, and Vajra, great-grandson of Kṛṣṇa, and the last of the Yādavas, at Indraprastha (near Delhi).

At this point the tense of the narrative changes, for it is during the reign of king Parīkṣit that Sūta narrates a supplement to this genealogical succession of kings.[39] Vyāsa accounted for the temporal hiatus between the moment of the Purāṇas' composition and their narrator's position by casting the rest of the narrative, the elaboration of the dynasties of the Age of Strife, as Vyāsa's prediction in the future tense. This prediction begins with Parīkṣit and continues down to the time of the early Guptas, when the narrative probably became finalized.[40] The narrator prefaces his account with a clear statement that in the Age of Strife paramount kingship will come into the hands of those other than the kings of the Solar and Lunar lines, as represented by the Ikṣvākus and Pauravas. These other kings would be outsiders (*vahiścara*) and barbarians (*mleccha*). He then foretells which kings of the Solar and Lunar dynasties would rule in the Age of Strife. None of the Pauravas after Adhisīmakṛṣṇa was to regain the paramount kingship of the earth during the Age of Strife. After naming the kings of the Lunar dynasty for twenty-five generations, the sage says that "the family which was the origin of both Brāhmaṇs and Kṣatriyas, sanctified by royal sages, will meet its demise in the Age of Strife with King Kṣemaka" (IV.21.4, my translation). As for the Solar dynasty, "The family of Ikṣvāku will end with Sumitra; with this king it will meet with an end in the Age of Strife" (IV.22.3, my translation).

The sage then tells of the Bārhadratha dynasty of Magadha, but starts in the past, beginning with the princes of the dynasty who ruled during the battle of Kurukṣetra, and were contemporaries of the Pāṇḍavas. The sage recites the history of these kings down to his present and tells of their future as the paramount overlords of the earth—not simply as ordinary kings—for 723 years. Next the sage tells the history of the overlordship of the Pradyota and Nāga dynasties (ruling for 52 and 360 years, respectively), and ends a period of time. The central region from which these dynasties rule is Magadha, not Kosala, as of old. The Nāgas, who are seen as reversing the declining trend of the Age of Strife, are overthrown by the Nandas, who, descended from men of the Śūdra or servant and artisan estate, plunge the world back into dissolution for 100 years. According to the sage, the earth will then be ruled by the Mauryas (137 years), who will be followed by the Śuṅgas (112 years), the Kāṇvas (45 years), and finally by the Āndhras, who will rule for 460 years. The sage then says that kings of barbarian origin (along with the Āndhras of

---

[39]Although this is the case in the *Viṣṇupurāṇa*, in the other Purāṇas the text is narrated during the reign of Adhisīmakṛṣṇa, fourth in descent from Parīkṣit; F. E. Pargiter, *The Purāṇa Text of the Dynasties of the Kali Age* (London: Oxford University Press, 1913), pp. viii–x.

[40]The narrative of the future kings of the Age of Strife appears in several Purāṇas (*Viṣṇu, Vāyu, Bhāgavata, Matsya, Brahmāṇḍa, Garuḍa*) and a single source text has been extracted and edited with its variant versions by Pargiter. Although nearly all of the Sanskrit Purāṇas contain genealogies of ancient dynasties, some of the Śaiva Purāṇas (*Liṅgapurāṇa, Śivapurāṇa*) seem less emphatic on the elaboration of dynastic histories. They tell the history of the past, present, and future of only the Solar kings, and do not contain genealogies of the Lunar lines or future predictions concerning other kings in the Age of Strife. The Śaiva Sthalapurāṇas that helped displace them during the late Cōḷa period left all royal genealogies out, for the most part. This task was taken up by the inscriptional eulogies.

Śrīpārvata) will enjoy the paramount kingship of the earth. After about 700 years, the Vākāṭaka dynasty will recapture the overlordship from the barbarians and rule for 160 years, ruling further south from the Vindhyas. The Vākāṭakas will then slowly weaken and a king named Viśvasphūrji will appear in Magadha and change the order of things.

The Purāṇic text has maintained until now that the paramount overlordship of the world, although it might move from dynasty to dynasty, would remain in the hands of a single king. But henceforth, according to the narrative, many kings would rule simultaneously from different capitals of different kingdoms in each of the four directions—the implication being, of course, that there would be no paramount overlord. After listing these various rulers and their kingdoms (among whom are the Guptas) the narrator goes on to say that "These kings and all their contemporaries will be ruling the earth. They will continually relish falsehood and wickedness, will cause the deaths of women, children, and cows, will enjoy seizing the property of others, will have little power, will have careers that rise and fall, will have short lives, great desires, and very little piety" (IV.23.18–19, my translation). The text concludes by listing various afflictions that will arise during the last days of the Age of Strife, and predicts that when the Sun and Moon, the lunar asterism Tiṣya, and Jupiter conjoin in the same sign of the zodiac, a new Age of Completeness (*kṛtayuga*) will begin.

The narrative seems to have been composed in the political context of early Gupta India, but was hardly a text of the Gupta court. The Guptas are mentioned as one of the several insignificant dynasties that will exhibit the dissolute qualities of the late Age of Strife. There seems to be a theological point being made, namely, that entropy in the cosmos is inescapable. This narrative perhaps represents a Vedist Smārta point of view, but one must keep in mind that the text was appropriated by Purāṇic adepts and embedded in the larger Theist projects that animate Purāṇic discourses as we have them today. It is only with great effort that Pargiter was able, using principles of source criticism, to "extract" the history of the dynasties of the Age of Strife from its Śaiva and Vaiṣṇava Purāṇic environments.[41] The Purāṇas, as they have come down to us, urge Śaiva and Vaiṣṇava ways of life and co-opt Smārta texts for their own theological uses. The *Viṣṇupurāṇa* foretells, for example, that at the end of the Age of Strife a portion of Viṣṇu in the form of Kalkin would be born on earth in the family of Viṣṇuyaśas. He would gather around him those whose minds are as pure as crystal. These people would follow the ways of a new Age of Completeness to be initiated when the heavens are in the auspicious configuration mentioned above. The Solar and Lunar lines would then reappear.[42]

[41]Historians like Vincent Smith, who have otherwise been very suspicious of the Purāṇas as reliable historical sources, have at the same time, rather amazingly, based their entire dynastic chronology before the Guptas on this single extracted text.

[42]The *Viṣṇupurāṇa* mentions two kings, Devāpi and Maru, as living through all four ages in a village called Kalāpa east of the Himalayas, for the express purpose of reviving the lines at the end of the Age of Strife. The narrator of the *Śivapurāṇa* remarks that Maru, an earlier king of the Solar dynasty, was residing in a hermitage at Kapāla even during his own time, when the Solar king Bṛhadbala had been killed by Abhimanyu on the battlefield of Kurukṣetra. After the Solar dynasty died out completely in the Age of Strife, at the age's close, Maru would revive it for the next Age of Completeness.

The earliest copper plates discovered, written in Prākrit in south India during early Pallava times (fourth century), lack the long eulogies of the later Sanskrit copper plates and do not rely heavily on the Purāṇas. But the later, post-Gupta Sanskrit copper plates of dynasties such as the Paramāras, Cālukyas, Eastern Gaṅgas, Cōḻas, Pālas, and Rāṣṭrakūṭas explicitly relate themselves to the Purāṇic texts.[43] Significantly, it is where the Purāṇic text of the dynasties of the Age of Strife leaves off that the dynastic genealogies in metal and stone begin to appear in India. Down to about the eighth-century royal dynastic genealogies do not provide kings with Purāṇic ancestries. But starting then, they begin to relate themselves to the Purāṇic lists in complicated ways. Their authors had no quarrel with the Smārta notion espoused in the text of the dynasties of the Age of Strife that the present age was dissolute compared to previous ages, but not without an important qualification. They aligned themselves with the emanationist doctrines of the Śaivas and Vaiṣṇavas articulated elsewhere in the Purāṇas. If they were in the hegemonic position to do so, they constructed the king as an incarnate part of Viṣṇu born on earth with the marks of a paramount sovereign, who could initiate a new regime of moral order—one might say a new Age of Completeness. But to do this, they certainly would not construct their genealogies as extensions of the dissolute kings of the dynasties of the Age of Strife. They bypass, as we shall see, the lists of the dynasties of the Age of Strife, explicitly relating themselves to the Solar and Lunar dynasties that attained the positions of paramount overlordship in earlier times recounted by Vyāsa in Purāṇic succession of kings.

These texts do more than "presuppose" the ontology, political theology, and cosmology of the Purāṇas. They extended Purāṇic coordinates into their own present. It is useful to see these texts as "supplements" to the Purāṇas. As "supplements," the inscriptions do not divert some originary meaning of the Purāṇas, as is often claimed by scholars who see them as revisions of Purāṇic myths for political legitimation. First, this "originary" meaning has already been produced by continual "revision," as we can see in the case of the incorporation of the succession of kings into the Theist Purāṇas. But perhaps more strongly, it is impossible to approach any text from a position that would involve no supplementarity.[44] In this sense, supplementation enables texts to have ongoing historical meaning. Inscriptions as historical discourse, along with other signifying practices, helped direct the Cōḻas and their subjects as to how the Purāṇic world histories were to be read. By continuing the narrative of world history told in the Purāṇas into their present, they enabled the Cōḻas and their subject-citizens to understand the meaning of and their place in that universal Purāṇic narrative.

---

[43] Sircar, *Indian Epigraphy*, pp. 107, 131.

[44] Despite the claims of New Criticism that texts can and should be understood as autonomous entities, readers, often before they even open their texts, are thoroughly bombarded with directions and signals—in the form of reviews, genre classifications, school lectures, syllabi, marginalia, and prefatory material—on how they are to be interpreted.

Contesting Representations

Not only do the charters of the Cōḻas share a certain "intertextuality" with Purāṇic discourse, they also speak to other inscriptions. The grant portions of the copper plates, as is clear from the *RCS–6*, were themselves copies of records kept at the department of writs in Rājendra's capital. They presuppose the existence of an elaborate inventory or record of the ownership and tax status of the lands in question. The *RCS–6* records the transfer of the village of Paḻaiyaṉūr from the status of gift to Brāhmaṇs to cultivator's portion and finally to that of temple gift. The existence of a village as "gift to Brāhmaṇs" or "cultivator's share" was not a given, but required documentation. For the village to be transformed from one status to another, old documents had to be updated or removed and new ones generated, with all the relevant parties concerned being issued separate copies of these transactions. Our text informs us that the site of this complex process was the king's court at Paḻaiyāṟu.

The eulogies of Cōḻa inscriptions, especially the Tamil eulogies (*meykīrttis*), were composed by poets at the king's court who held positions specifically for this purpose. The compositions of these court poets became standardized preambles for all grants issued in that king's reign until such time as his political action required a new and more complete representation, upon which the eulogy would be supplemented.[45] These eulogies were not static representations but living narratives, continuously modified and supplemented by more complete versions. Hence it makes sense to see the *RCS–6* as a moment in a larger and continuous series of representations. Parts of the present narrative may have been abbreviated, dropped, or amplified in future eulogies, as the lordship of Rājendra became more complete. The Tamil and Sanskrit eulogies of the *RCS–6* were composed, as I have mentioned, at different times. In reading *RCS–6* I attempt to be very cognizant of how it reads in connection wih the claims of Rājendra's other inscriptions.

Tamil and Sanskrit eulogies were not "symbolic" or "functional" discourses that reflected real political relationships, but held an articulative and dialogical relationship with the kingly acts that they "represented." The acts of kings—conquests of the quarters, great gifts (*mahādānas*), and shower-baths—were themselves highly textualized articulations of and "responses" to prescriptions and ontologies located in Purāṇas, Āgamas, Śāstras, and their own previous inscriptions.

The inscriptions of Cōḻa kings were related not only to their own former self-representations and political action but also to the political representations of other kings. Medieval polities were not the "mutually repellent molecules" that Vincent Smith had imagined them to be, but instead formed complicated relation-

[45]For example, Vīrarājendra's long Sanskrit eulogy at Kanyakumari appears verbatim in the Charala plates, located in Vēṅgi north of Kāñcī; Stein, *Peasant State*, p. 355. The composition of Tamil eulogies celebrating the achievements of the reigning monarch in a single authorized account, which was modified yearly, was initiated and standardized by Rājarāja I (985–1014), replacing the "haphazard" de novo eulogies that had preceded his reign. This consecutive supplementation of a single authorized Tamil eulogy has enabled scholars like Nilakanta Sastri to reconstruct a very careful sequence of political events for subsequent Cōḻa kings; see his *Cōḷas*, pp. 4–5.

ships and hierarchies with one another. First, inscriptional representations do not confirm the Indological constructions of medieval India as consisting of a plethora of petty states, nor as being comprised of three self-sustaining and identically impotent geographical regions. They represent the world as consisting of a highly ordered hierarchy of kings, at the center of which sits a single ruler, the paramount overlord or king among kings (*cakravartin*, *rājarāja*, *rājādhirāja*, and so on.).[46] This idea perhaps has its roots in the Buddhist imperial polity of the Mauryas, and its first "theoretical" elaboration is in the oldest text on "statecraft" in India, the *Arthaśāstra*, composed at the court of Candragupta Maurya (317–293 B.C.). It is also developed in the Purāṇas, as we saw, where the paramount overlordship in previous Ages was said to pass between the various dynasties (Solar, Lunar and so forth) established by Manu Vaivasvata at the beginning of the epoch of Manu. As mentioned above, the paramount overlordship of the world was not a given. The Purāṇic succession of kings predicted that this position would be rarely attained in the dissolute Age of Strife. If achieved by a king, the paramount sovereignty had to be continually remade and rethought at every turn by both himself and his successors, for the position might be won by any king who could command the will, strength, and skill to take it. Often two or three different hierarchies might be contending for this position. The complex and contestatory claims of these kings should be understood as dialectical practices predicated on the vision of the world not as a medley of politically dispersed petty states or "natural" regions, but as a self-regulating political whole. These relationships were maintained not simply by force but also through complicated discursive acts and representations.

Eulogies and the claims made within them were signifying practices that could not be indiscriminately produced by any lord. Both lords within a polity, and other lords—rivals that might contest the integrity of that polity—were quite aware of the claims made in these texts. The positionings they articulated might be varied—including relationships of contestation, agreement, or subsumption. For example, when the Paramāra king Śīyaka II (945–973) plundered Mānyakheṭa (Malkhed, Gulbarga district), the Rāṣṭrakūṭa capital, he took copper plates from their treasury and reissued them with his own eulogy on their reverse sides.[47] The Western Gaṅga king Pṛthivīpati II Hastimalla received the Bāṇa kingdom as a "gift of grace" (*prasādam*) from his "overlord," the Cōḻa king Parāntaka I (907–954), after helping him subdue hill chiefs (*girīndra*) and the Pallavas. The subordinate relationship of Pṛthivīpati II to Parāntaka is indicated in the Udayendiram Plates by the subsumption of the Gaṅga king's lineage within what would otherwise

---

[46]Inden has developed this idea in a series of essays that have culminated in his use of the term "imperial formation," which he uses to designate the complex hierarchy of kings called a "circle of kings" in the *Arthaśāstra* and subsequent texts on polity; "Hierarchies," in *Contributions*, pp. 99–125; and Inden, *Imagining India* (Oxford: Blackwell, 1990), pp. 27–33, 228–62.

[47]G. Yazdani, ed., *Early History of the Deccan* (London: Oxford University Press, under the authority of the Government of Andhra Pradesh, 1960) 1: 297; Pratipal Bhatia, *The Paramāras: c. 800–1305 A.D.* (Delhi: Munshiram Manoharlal, 1970), p. 44; K. N. Dikshit, "Three Copper-Plate Inscriptions from Gaonri," *EI* 23 (1935–36), 101–13.

be a standard Cōḻa eulogy.[48] The placement of the history of his own polity in subordination to Parāntaka's narrative, Pṛthivīpati's assumption here of the Bāṇa king's position and title (*biruda*), his adoption elsewhere of the Cōḻa king's name in his own title as Vīracōḻa—the very articulation of his own political identity—is all explicitly dependent on his relationship of service at the "lotus-feet of the Cōḻa king."[49] It is significant that the Gaṅga king received the Bāṇa domain as a gift in the form of a "plate," which is described as the "instrument through which he obtained the kingdom."[50] I am suggesting that inscriptions were not merely representative of political relationships but in fact were the means by which a variety of lords of different domains articulated these political relationships.

To understand the discursive location of our text, the *RCS–6*, it will be necessary to explore its relationship to the political discourses that preceded it. An inscription from the middle of the sixth-century claims that a king of the Cālukyas of Bādāmi, Pulakeśin I (c. 535–566), broke away from his Kadamba overlord at Vaijayantī (Vanavāsi) in Kuntala (North Kanara, Shimoga, Dharwar, and Belgaum districts), founded the city of Vātāpī (Bādāmi), and performed a horse sacrifice (*aśvamedha*) and the golden embryo ceremony (*hiraṇyagarbha*), thereby proclaiming himself as an independent sovereign lord.[51] Since Vedic times the horse sacrifice had been the liturgical act for articulating an imperial order through combat. A king's performance of the horse sacrifice was a political challenge to other ruling kings. The golden embryo, however, was not a Vedic sacrifice but instead one of the sixteen "great gifts" elaborated in the Purāṇas.[52] Future Cālukya kings saw Pulakeśin as not only the performer of Vedic sacrifices but also as having "emerged from the golden egg."[53] The Purāṇic great gifts eventually moved from this auxiliary position in relation to the Vedic rites to one of preeminence, as the entire economy of life-transforming practices in the polity shifted from one of sacrifice (*yajña*) to giving (*dāna*).[54] These "great gifts" were included among the rites outlined in the medieval liturgical texts (Āgamas) of the Śaiva Siddhānta

[48]E. Hultzsch, "Udayendiram Plates of Prithivipati II Hastimalla" *SII* 2.5 (1916), 386–89; and Hultzsch, "The Sholinghur Rock-Inscription of Parantaka I," *EI* 4 (1896–97), 221–25.

[49]Hultzsch, "Sholinghur," p. 225. After the death of Pṛthivīpati II, the Gaṅga kingdom fell into the hands of Butuga II, who had helped the Rāṣṭrakūṭa king Kṛṣṇa III put down an usurper in his own kingdom. Owing his allegiance to the Rāṣṭrakūṭa king, Butuga II accompanied Kṛṣṇa III in his campaigns against the Cōḻas in Toṇḍaimaṇḍalam.

[50]*paṭṭamayam prasādam bāṇādhirājapadalaṃbhanasādhanaṃ*: Hultzsch, "Udayendiram," p. 384.

[51]R. S. Panchamukhi, "Badami Inscription of Calikkya Vallabhesvara," *EI* 27 (1947–48), 4–9.

[52]P. V. Kane, *History of Dharmaśāstra* (Poona: Bhandarkar Oriental Research Institute) 2.2 (1974), 869–77. Kane follows the account in the *Liṅgapurāṇa* (chapters 276–89) most closely. Inden speculates that the golden embryo performed by the Cālukyas may have been an earlier version of the great gift of the same name, which came to replace, rather than supplement, the horse sacrifice in later times; Inden, *Imagining India*, pp. 247–48.

[53]J. F. Fleet, "Mahakuta Pillar Inscription of Mangalesa," *Indian Antiquary* 19 (1890), 17. Fleet translates *hiraṇyagarbhasaṃbhūtaḥ* as "descended from the god Hiraṇyagarbha (Brahmā)."

[54]On the general change in vocabulary from sacrifice (*yajña*) to one of giving (*dāna*), see Nicholas Dirks, "Political Authority and Structural Change in Early South Indian History" *The Indian Economic and Social History Review* 13 (April-June 1976), 125–57.

disciplinary order that reformulated Śaiva Purāṇic knowledge around the temple institution.[55]

The inscriptions of Pulakeśin's successors claim him as the founder of the Cālukya line, itself descended from a son of Hāritī (a woman of the Hārita gotra) and of the Mānavya gotra.[56] They had appropriated this genealogy from their erstwhile Kadamba overlords, who had previously taken it from the Cuṭu Śātakarṇis, the "successors" in Kuntala, of the great Śātavāhana empire.[57] In the period between 600 and 750, the Cālukyas came to attain the position of "paramount overlordship" of India over and against their rivals, Harṣa Puṣpabhūti (606–647) in northern India and, closer at hand, the Pallavas of Kāñcī. The titular claims made and family name taken by the Cālukyas came to be of crucial importance for the political formations of subsequent times, being replicated by their underlords and successors in southern and western India. The Cālukyas came to conceptualize their immediate domain, Karṇāṭa (Krishna basin), overlapping with Kuntala, as the "core" of the sphere of command of a world ruler (*cakravartikṣetra*).[58] The titles articulated in their inscriptions, Great King among Kings (*mahārājādhirāja*), Paramount Overlord (*parameśvara*), Beloved of Earth and Fortune (*śrīpṛthivīvallabha*), and Worthy of the Highest Honor (*paramabhaṭṭāraka*) indicated in no uncertain terms to the kings of India that these lords of the Karṇāṭa country considered themselves rulers not simply of the Deccan but of the entire earth.

Sometime in the middle of the eighth century we find a new set of discursive practices in inscriptional representation. One of the Cālukya's ablest underlords, styled as overlord among the frontier kings (*sāmantādhipati*), Dantidurga (735–755) from the Raṭṭa country, began campaigns against his fellow underlords in Mālwa and Gujarat, thus challenging the hegemony of the Cālukyas. Dantidurga, in a direct challenge to the Cālukya king, performed the golden embryo ceremony at Ujjain after defeating the Gurjara king, whom he designated as his "doorkeeper" (*pratihāra*).[59] Since the inscriptions of the Cālukyas tell us that they themselves had performed the golden embryo ceremony to establish independence from their predecessors, Dantidurga's performance of this rite would have been seen as a direct challenge to the paramountcy of the Cālukyas. We should note that in the inscriptions of Dantidurga's successors, the great gift of the golden embryo is

---

[55]Richard Davis, *Ritual in an Oscillating Universe: Worshiping Śiva in Medieval India* (Princeton: Princeton University Press, 1991), p. 36.

[56]Yazdani, *Early History*, 1: 205. This claim was established as early as 578. Gotras were sacrificial clans to which Brāhmaṇs of the Vedic disciplinary orders belonged and to which their Kṣatriya patrons affiliated themselves.

[57]D. C. Sircar, *Successors of the Sātavāhanas in the Lower Deccan* (Calcutta: University of Calcutta, 1939), p. 222.

[58]K. V. Ramesh, "The Imperial Hegemony of the Vātāpi and Kalyāṇa Houses—A Comparative Study," in *The Cālukyas of Kalyāṇa: Seminar Papers* (Bangalore: Mythic Society, 1983), p. 28. D. C. Sircar discusses the term *cakravartikṣetra* in *Studies in the Geography of Ancient and Medieval India* (New Delhi: Motilal Banarsidass, 1971), pp. 1–16. H. C. Raychaudhuri discusses the historic variability of the terms Kuntala and Karṇāṭa: Yazdani, *Early History*, 1: 40–43.

[59]D. R. Bhandarkar, "Sanjan Plates of Amoghavarsha I: Saka-Samvat 793," *EI* 18 (1925–26), 253. For a discussion of Dantidurga's act see Yazdani, *Early History*, 1: 255; and especially Inden, *Imagining India*, pp. 246–48.

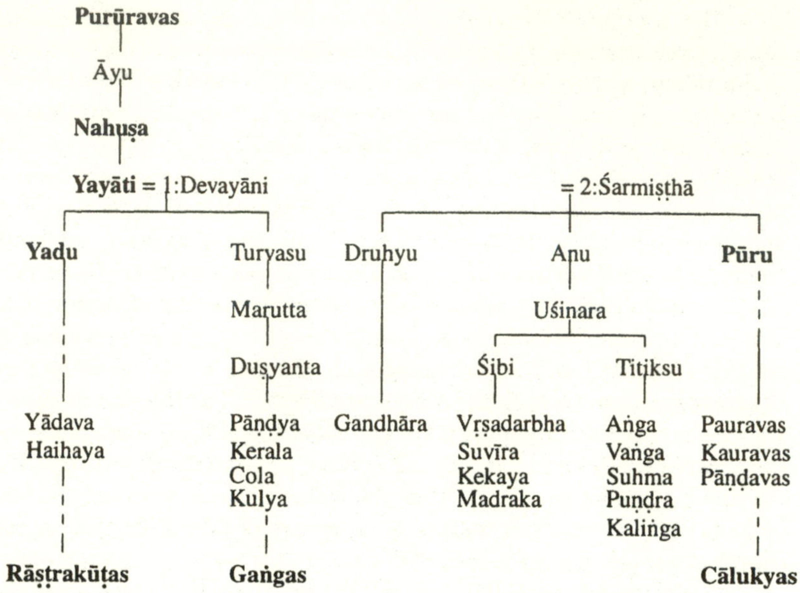

Figure 4.3. Lunar Descent of Dynasties (bold = their inscriptions)

not seen as an auxiliary rite to the horse sacrifice, as in Cālukya inscriptions, but rather comes to replace it. As medieval kings, beginning with the Rāṣṭrakūṭas and continuing with the Kalyāṇi Cālukyas, Cōḻas, Pāṇḍyas, and kings of Vijayanagara, assumed the Solar and Lunar genealogies of the Purāṇas, they also took up the Purāṇic great gifts, chief among which were the golden embryo (*hiraṇyagarbha*) and the weight in the balance ceremony (*tulābhāra*).[60]

The genealogy of these kings, who came to call themselves the Rāṣṭrakūṭas, dominated political practice in the subcontinent for nearly two hundred years.[61] The inscriptions say that after Dantidurga's eventual usurpation of the Vallabha (Cālukya) in battle, "he acquired the condition of king among kings and paramount overlord."[62] Implicit in this claim is the acknowledgment on the part of the Rāṣṭra-

[60]Inden discusses the rise of the great gift in relation to political changes in medieval India: "The Ceremony of the Great Gift (Mahādāna): Structure and Historical Context in Indian Ritual and Society," in *Asie du Sud, traditions et changements*, edited by Marc Gaborieau and Alice Thorner. Colloques Internationaux du C.N.R.S. 582 (Paris, 1979), 131–36.

[61]The Rāṣṭrakūṭas, through subordinating alliances with the Pallavas of Kāñcī and Okkākas of Sri Lanka, were able to secure overlordship of peninsular India. The Pratihāras of Kanauj and the Pālas of eastern India vied with each other for hegemony in northern India and occasionally contested the subcontinental paramountcy of the Rāṣṭrakūṭas; Yazdani, *Early History*, 1: 231.

[62]*rājādhirājaparameśvaratām avāpa:* V. S. Sukthankar, ed. and tr., "Bhandak Plates of Krishnaraja I: Saka 694," *EI* 14 (1917–18), 125.

kūṭas that the Cālukyas had been the paramount overlords of India. In filling the sandals of the Cālukyas, the Rāṣṭrakūṭas not only assumed their titles, but their dating system (Śāka era) and their banner (*pāḷidhvaja*) as well.[63]

The importance of the Rāṣṭrakūṭas for the subsequent history of the Theist polities of India cannot be overestimated. Their genealogical self-understanding represents a break with that of the Cālukyas of Bādāmi. Whereas they (and their political Others, the Pallavas) had claimed descent from sacrificial clans (*gotras*), the Rāṣṭrakūṭas began to claim descent from the Moon through the family of Yadu, into which Viṣṇu was born as Vāsudeva Kṛṣṇa. According to the Purāṇas, Yayāti, the direct, senior lineal descendant of Purūravas, the founder of the Lunar dynasty, was the most important king after him (Figure 4.3). Yadu, eldest of the two sons of Yayāti by his first wife, Devayānī, was the founder of the Yādavas. Beginning with the eulogy of Amoghavarṣa I (814–880), the Rāṣṭrakūṭas regularly asserted that they belonged to the Yādava lineage, though without giving any further genealogical details.[64] They saw themselves as the successors of the Lunar dynasty whose end had been foretold in the succession of kings of the Purāṇas. Subsequent imperial polities of south India continued the innovation of claiming Lunar or Solar descent, the Cōḻas being no exception.[65]

To make sense of the *RCS–6* and its relationship to the articulations of the Rāṣṭrakūṭa imperial formation unfortunately requires the disentanglement of the received historiography on the rise of the Cōḻas. In the seventh century, the Pallavas had defeated the Cōḻas, probably at their traditional capital in Uraiyūr, and made them their underlords.[66] Now the Rāṣṭrakūṭas, in displacing the Cālukyas, inherited their Pallava enemies. The Rāṣṭrakūṭas, according to inscriptions on both sides, consistently got the better of the Pallavas, and finally made them underlords in about 802.[67] The Cōḻas, who had long freed themselves from the yoke of the Pallavas and had caused them troubles, saw the weakening of the Pallavas as an opportunity to assert their own ambitions. So King Āditya I (871–907) apparently attacked and defeated the Pallava king Aparājita in 903.[68]

---

[63]Inden, *Imagining India*, pp. 250–51.

[64]*yādavānvaya*: Bhandarkar, "Sanjan," pp. 235–57. A. S. Altekar points out that an inscription of 808 compares Govinda III (c. 793–814) with Kṛṣṇa and the Rāṣṭrakūṭas with the Yādavas: *Rāshṭrakūṭas and Their Times* ([1934] Poona: Oriental Book Agency, 1967), p. 16. The earlier eulogy of Dantidurga's son Kṛṣṇa II (756–772), claims that Dantidurga's mother, Bhāvagaṇā, abducted by his father, Indra, was herself descended partly from the Moon on her maternal side, and the Cālukyas on her paternal (*mātṛtaḥ rājñī somānvayā tasya pitṛtaśca culukyajaḥ[sic]*); Sukthankar, "Bhandak," p. 124.

[65]J. F. Fleet noticed the use of Purāṇic genealogies, but he attributed it both to a recovery of lost knowledge (the process in which he was engaged) and to social climbing, with which every English gentleman, whether in India or not, was familiar; "Spurious Sudi Copper-plate Grant Purporting to Have Been Issued by Butuga in Saka-Samvat 860," *EI* 3 (1894–95), 154–84.

[66]E. Hultzsch, ed. and tr., "A Pallava Grant from Kūram," *SII* 1 (1890), 152, and Hultzsch, "Two Cave Inscriptions from the Triśirapaḷḷi Rock," *SII* 1 (1890), 28–30.

[67]The Rāṣṭrakūṭa king, Govinda III, defeated them at Kāñcī and received the allegiance of Dantivarman and his successors. The bond was sealed by intermarriage; K. A. Nilakanta Sastri, *A History of South India from Prehistoric Times to the Fall of Vijayanagar* (Delhi: Oxford University Press, 1966), pp. 159–60.

[68]Hultzsch, "Udayendiram," p. 388. Scholars have interpreted this battle as the Cōḻa bid for the regional mastery of south India. They have therefore assumed the Cōḻas to be the "successors" of the

Indian historiography has consistently interpreted the rise of the Cōḻas as a chapter in the history of south India or Tamilnadu, as distinct from the Deccan. Colonial historiography plotted medieval Indian history onto the three "natural" geographic regions of north, south, and Deccan to fit this history into the well-worn garments of a more familiar body politic, that of "medieval" Europe. If "ancient" history in India, as in the West, was characterized by the rise of the great unifying empires (Greek/Mauryan, Roman/Gupta) then the subsequent epoch of Indian history had to conform with the political fragmentation of Europe in the Middle Ages. Colonial historiography was able to generate the requisite political fragmentation by building into its narrative structure the three regions before any of the medieval history itself unfolds.[69] An unfortunate casualty of this historiography, the Cōḻas have been seen as inheriting the dominion of south India from its previous rulers, the Pallavas (and Pāṇḍyas).[70]

But the inscriptions indicate that the Pallavas at this time were themselves subordinate to the Rāṣṭrakūṭas. By seeing the connections between these polities, we can begin to interrupt the tidy genealogies of "south India" and the Deccan that claim the Pallavas and Rāṣṭrakūṭas, respectively, as their patients. The Cōḻa attack on the Pallava king Aparājita, like the Rāṣṭrakūṭa attack on the Pratihāra and Cālukya kings nearly two centuries before, was seen by the overlord of this lesser king as a direct challenge to his hegemonic political position. Parāntaka's defeat of the Pallava monarch was not only an appropriation of the Pallava's own domain, but an assault on his Rāṣṭrakūṭa overlord.[71] Meanwhile, Parāntaka's forces attacked Madurai and sent the Pāṇḍyan king Rājasiṃha fleeing to Sri Lanka to deposit his regalia, where the Cōḻas pursued him. The Cōḻas claimed several victories over the combined forces of the Sinhalas and Pāṇḍyas, who were intermittent underlords of the Rāṣṭrakūṭas. As if these were not enough, Parāntaka performed the ceremony of the golden embryo (*hiraṇyagarbha*) and the ceremony of the weight in the balance (*tulābhāra*), signifying a challenge to the Rāṣṭrakūṭas in the very same manner that they themselves had challenged the Cālukyas nearly two centuries earlier.[72]

Pallavas as the new rulers of south India. The problem with this reasoning is that the Pallavas were not the autonomous sovereigns of south India, but the underlords of a larger imperial formation that stretched far to the north. We shall see that the Cōḻas came to see themselves as the successors not of the Pallavas—who get very scant mention in their inscriptions (their defeat is cursorily mentioned alongside the conquest of hill chiefs)—but of those glorious overlords of the world, the Rāṣṭrakūṭas.

[69]Never mind that the inscriptions of the "ancient" Mauryan "empire" do not claim hegemony over the "far south," and that the inscriptions of the "petty medieval kingdoms" of the Rāṣṭrakūṭas, Cōḻas, and Cālukyas make pan-Indian imperial claims.

[70]Post-independence Indian historians have tended to read the history of these three regions as the unfolding narrative of the linguistic regions or states of modern India. The Tamilnadu state government, heir to colonial constructions of Indian history, has named its three major bus systems after these dynasties: Pallavaṉ, Pāṇḍyaṉ, and Colaṉ.

[71]K. V. Subrahmanya Ayyar, ed. and tr., "Takkolam Inscription of Rajakesarivarman (Aditya I)," *EI* 19 (1927–28), 81–88.

[72]The Udayendiram Plates claim that Parāntaka, along with giving gifts to Brāhmaṇs and building temples for the gods, performed these important great gifts: Hultzsch, "Udayendiram," p. 383. The Velañjeri Plates of Parāntaka claim that he performed the weight in the balance ceremony three times—at Rameśvaram, Kanyākumarī, and Śrīraṅgam; R. Nagaswamy, *Thiruttani and Velanjeri Copper Plates* (Madras: State Department of Archeology, 1979), no pagination.

Parāntaka also made claims to a descent that countered their predecessors and rivals. The earlier Pallavas had claimed descent from Brahmā and a succession of six sages, the last of whom sired Pallava.[73] Later Pallavas (such as Nandivarman II Pallavamalla, c. 731–796, and Nandivarman III, 846–869) add Viṣṇu as the progenitor of Brahmā.[74] Parāntaka and his successor, Sundara, continued the practice of claiming descent from Brahmā and of representing him as born of Viṣṇu.[75] They also continued their genealogy with a claim to descent from sages, but here they name the sage Marīci, eldest of the seven mental sons of Brahmā, and then his son, the sage Kaśyapa. Then, instead of continuing with sages, the inscriptions name Aryaman or Sūrya, synonyms for Vivasvan, the Sun, just as the Purāṇas do when beginning the Solar dynasty. Here, however, the Cōḻas hesitate. Instead of naming Manu Vaivasvata, the founder of humankind and his eldest son, Ikṣvāku, founder of the Solar dynasty, the inscriptions give a succession of three or five warriors (Figure 4.2). The first two or three of these (Mahāvīra and/or Rudrajit and Candrajit) are, in Purāṇic terms, indeterminable. The last one or two, Uśīnara, and/or his son, Śibi, who begets Cōḻa, are identifiable. The latter is known for saving a pigeon attacked by a hawk through offering an equal weight of his own flesh in its stead. Early texts apparently considered the Cōḻas descended to be from Śibi, a hero in the Purāṇas and the Buddhist Jātakas, and that is why the Cōḻas include him even though the Purāṇas classed him as being descended from the Moon.[76] The omission of Manu and Ikṣvāku from the early Cōḻa genealogies might well have been a response to the claims of their rivals in Sri Lanka. Although they did not claim Solar or Lunar descent, Sri Lankan kings did claim to be the only extant Okkākas or Ikṣvākus, that is, descendants of the ancestor of Gautama Buddha, and also claimed, thereby, to be the only extant linear successors of Mahāsammata, the Buddhist equivalent of Manu Vaivasvata, and royal founders of the present epoch (see Chapter 3).

The Cōḻas were, nonetheless, making enough trouble for themselves by challenging the Rāṣṭrakūṭas. The Rāṣṭrakūṭa forces of King Kṛṣṇa III, accompanied by contingents from his underlords, the Gaṅgas and Nolambas, converged on the Cōḻa armies and defeated them decisively at Takkōlam, where the crown prince Rājāditya was killed by the Gaṅga feudatory Butuga II.[77] The Karhad plates of Kṛṣṇa III and the Sudi plates of Butuga II proclaim that after destroying Rājāditya,

[73]Aṅgiras, Bṛhaspati (Devaguru), Bhāradvaja, Droṇa, and Aśvatthāman (Drauṇi). The descent of Bṛhaspati from Aṅgiras and of Bharadvāja from Bṛhaspati are attested to in several texts. Aṅgiras was one of the seven mental sons of Brahmā. Droṇa was a Brāhmaṇ fathered by Bharadvāja in a bucket (*droṇa*). He was military preceptor of both the Kauravas and Pāṇḍavas; afterward, he became king of Pañcāla and general of the Kauravas, husband of Kṛpī and father of Aśvatthāman.

[74]T. V. Mahalingam, *Inscriptions of the Pallavas* (New Delhi: Indian Council of Historical Research, 1988), pp. 314–20, 372–79, 439–50.

[75]One inscription of Sundaracōḻa begins with obeisance to Viṣṇu (vv. 1–2), to Śiva (v. 3) and Brahmā (v. 4). Then the text asks for the succession of Cōḻas, "whose root," it proclaims, "is the glorious light that has originated in the eye of Mukunda (Viṣṇu)," and "the abode of Viṣṇu," to protect the world; T. A. Gopinatha Rao, "Anbil Plates of Sundara-Chola: The 4th Year," *EI* 15 (1919–20), 44–72.

[76]Nilakanta Sastri, *Cōlas*, pp. 19–20.

[77]Subrahmanya Ayyar, "Takkolam," pp. 82–83. For a full account of Kṛṣṇa's campaigns, see Nilakanta Sastri, *Cōḷas*, pp. 129–32.

the Rāṣṭrakūṭa monarch went on to conquer the city Tañjāvūr and extract great wealth and tribute from various southern kings. The Karhad grant, issued from the victory camp of Kṛṣṇa III, king among kings, at Mēlpāḍi, claims that after conquering the Cōḻas he distributed their lands to his own dependents, made the Pāṇḍyas, Ceras, and Sinhalas his underlords, and erected a pillar of victory at Rameśvaram.[78] This defeat proved ruinous, and in the thirty years following the death of Parāntaka in 955 until the accession of Rājarāja in 985, the Cōḻa "field" (*kṣetra*) was severely diminished.[79]

Not surprisingly, we find scant mention of conquests and great gifts in the inscriptions of Parāntaka's successors. During the reign of Parāntaka's sons Gaṇḍarāditya (949–956) and Ariñjaya (956–57), and the latter's son Sundaracōḻa (957–973), the Cōḻas not only lived under the shadow of the Rāṣṭrakūṭas in the north, but experienced difficulty from the south at the hands of the Sinhalas. Sundaracōḻa's general, Iruṅgōḷār Śiṟiyavēḷār, was killed in Sri Lanka, and Cōḻa troops were made to withdraw from the south.[80] As Walters shows, the Sinhala kings themselves were articulating their own imperial project with the monks at the Mahāvihāra. The dominance over the south enjoyed by the Cōḻas slipped away.

But the Rāṣṭrakūṭas were soon to experience problems themselves. The Paramāra king Śīyaka II (945–972), who had founded in Mālwā a tributary kingdom located in the interstices of Rāṣṭrakūṭa and Pratihāra domains, attacked the Rāṣṭrakūṭa king Khoṭṭigadeva (967–972) and sacked his capital, Mānyakheṭa, in 972. This defeat signalled to the kings of India that the Rāṣṭrakūṭa king no longer commanded the paramount overlordship of India. After the fall of the Rāṣṭrakūṭas, four royal courts attempted to appropriate their position. To their north, the Paramāra king Vākpati Muñja (974–c. 997), who succeeded his father Śīyaka II just two years after the sack of Mānyakheṭa, claimed the titles Beloved of Fortune and Earth, King among Kings, and Paramount Overlord—epithets indicating that he had displaced the Rāṣṭrakūṭa and was the rightful claimant to the paramount overlordship of India.[81] Śīyaka II, who "equalling the Garuḍa in fierceness, took in battle the splendour of king Khoṭṭigadeva," also appropriated the Garuḍa emblem, which became the future mark of the Paramāras.[82] In Sri Lanka, the Okkāka king, Mahinda IV (956–972), who died the year that Mānyakheṭa was sacked, had signaled his attempt to constitute himself as paramount overlord by defeating Cōḻa forces in Sri Lanka and south India and forging alliances with Pāṇḍyas, Kaliṅgas, and Buddhist kings in Śrī Vijaya. The Sinhala challenge in the closing years of the Rāṣṭrakūṭas was the first bid for paramount overlordship to which the Cōḻas responded. Sinhala genealogical claims, as we shall see, had great implications for the Cōḻa understanding of their own past. Meanwhile, another southern underlord of the Rāṣṭrakūṭas, a

---

[78] R. G. Bhandarkar, ed. and tr., "Karhad Plates of Krishna III: Saka Samvat 880," *EI* 4 (1896–97), 278–90.

[79] Nilakanta Sastri, *Cōḷas*, pp. 140–61.

[80] E. Hultzsch, ed. and tr., "Inscriptions of Rajakesarivarman Sundara-Chola Parantaka II," *SII* 3 (1920), 255; Nilakanta Sastri, *Cōḷas*, pp. 153–56.

[81] Nilakantha Janardan Kirtane, ed. and tr., "On three Mālwa Inscriptions," *Indian Antiquary* 6 (1877), 52; Bhatia, *Paramāras*, p. 46.

[82] Bhatia, *Paramāras*, p. 44.

"high lord among frontier kings" (*mahāsāmantādhipati*), Taila II (973–997) of the Cālukya family, defeated the last Rāṣṭrakūṭa king, Karka, and occupied his capital from 973 to the end of the tenth century. Taila II also took the titles of his erstwhile overlord, calling himself the Beloved of Earth, King among Kings, Paramount Overlord, and Worthy of the Highest Honor. One inscription explicitly states that Taila, "after obtaining the fortune of the glorious Rāṣṭrakūṭa kings, sun-like heroes though they were, has ruled the earth as sovereign lord, without rival."[83]

The Cōḻa kings of this period were battling or consolidating alliances with Kṛṣṇa's underlords in Toṇḍaimaṇḍalam.[84] But in the inscriptions of Rājakesari Aruṇmoḷivarmaṉ, who acceded in 985—nearly ten years after the Rāṣṭrakūṭa capital had been sacked—we see for the first time a claim made to the Rāṣṭrakūṭa imperium. Aruṇmoḻivarmaṉ calls himself King among Kings. But in doing so, he had to answer to the other kings who were trying to claim this position. He signified his challenge by embarking on the conquest of the quarters.[85] So these four vying polities, the Paramāra, the Cālukya, the Cōḻa, and the Okkāka or Sinhala, all in contact with one another and aware of each other's claims to the overlordship of Bhāratavarṣa, constituted the shifting imperial formation of India from 975 to 1200.

Remaking the Solar Dynasty

Our text, the *RCS–6*, was composed during the reign of Rājarāja's son, Rājendra (1012/14–1044). The text presupposes that the "domain" Rājendra had inherited from his father, a domain that he, acting as crown prince (*yuvarāja*), had helped constitute, was the expanding polity of a world ruler (*cakravartikṣetra*). The eulogy of Rājendra, composed by his court poet Nārāyaṇa, takes the form of a proclamation from a preeminent standpoint, praising Rājendra's ongoing articulation of this polity.

The introduction of the *RCS–6*, it should be noted, is a eulogy praising the Cōḻa dynasty, and in particular king Rājendra. It takes the form of a genealogical narrative of the Cōḻa dynasty from the birth of Manu, the first king, from the Sun, to the accession and reign of its main protagonist, the world ruler Rājendra. Nārāyaṇa ends his narrative with that king among kings, Rājendra, seated at court, having performed the act of paramount sovereignty, the triumph over the quarters. It is from his court at Mudikoṇḍacōḻapuram, or Paḻaiyāṟu, that Rājendra authorizes the grant as well as commissions this eulogy. The eulogy was received by an audience not only in the village of Paḻaiyaṉūr and at the temple of Śiva at Tiruvāḷaṅgāḍu but also at Rājendra's court, where emissaries from other kingdoms must have visited.

The eulogy frames its narrative with several invocatory and miscellaneous verses, three of which fall at its beginning and eight at its end. One verse invokes the blessings of Pārvatī on the texts' listeners, and another asks the goddess Sarasvatī

[83]F. Kielhorn, ed. and tr., "Nilgund Inscription of Taila II: Saka-samvat 904," *EI* 4 (1896–97), 207.

[84]Nilakanta Sastri, *Cōlas*, p. 152–54.

[85]Not surprisingly, he was the first Cōḻa king to perform it, since he was the first king in a position to take the Rāṣṭrakūṭas' titles.

to bestow on the poet all the extra letters of the alphabet necessary to describe the illustrious clan of the Cōḻas. A final verse praises the Cōḻa family as the sole caravan leader of pilgrims on the two routes that might be taken in this world: the route on which travelers see the fruits of their actions; and the route, less traveled, where travelers do not see the results of their efforts. The poet here puts Rājendra at the center of both the pursuit of the three worldly goals of Theist life—wealth, pleasure, and righteousness (*artha, kāma, dharma*)—as well as the pursuit of the transcendent goal of release from life in the world (*mokṣa*). This construction of the king flies directly in the face of Weberian understandings of Hindu kingship, which see the king as master of an external, "real" world that is in fundamental opposition to the transcendent, ideal role of the priestly class in India. It will serve us well to keep this in mind to avoid pitfalls when thinking about the king's "divinity" in the text. The final verses of the Sanskrit eulogy give the details of the grant, name its petitioner (*vijñāpti*), executor (*ājñāpti*), the author of the grant, and praise Rājendra himself.

In taking up the Purāṇic histories, the text makes certain claims about the "divinity" of the king that will be likely to cause confusion among those of us who have been tutored in the Indological constructions of Hinduism. First, the Cōḻa kings are consistently identified in this inscription, as well as other imperial texts after Rājarāja, with Viṣṇu. This claim in itself should not surprise us, since it was common for medieval kings all over India to claim some ontological connection with Viṣṇu—either as receptacles of a small portion of his being or more strongly as full incarnations of him. But it is well known that the Cōḻa kings were devout worshipers of Śiva. In fact, Rājarāja, who is identified in our text as a "veritable Viṣṇu" (Murāri), also has the title Śivapādaśekhara, "the highest among those at Śiva's feet." There has been a will in Indological scholarship to see the king either as a gentle secular monarch who, despite his own sectarian leanings, patronizes and placates all faiths, or as a "fanatic" who tries to stamp out practices other than his own. These accounts fail to recognize the dialogical positions that not only kings but the Theist texts and "rituals" themselves took with regard to contesting ways of life. Viṣṇu, in the language of early medieval Śaivism, was god of this world, while Śiva was lord over the next. According to the *Śivapurāṇa*, Viṣṇu was produced by Śiva so that he could create, protect, and dissolve the world, while Śiva would roam as he pleased, keeping instead the prerogative of conferring release (*mokṣa*).[86] It is Viṣṇu who is responsible for intervening in the everyday world when things go awry (II.1.10.2–4). In the succession of kings as told by the *Śivapurāṇa*, Viṣṇu is the main actor in history, incarnating himself in various kings to save the world. But Viṣṇu is also Śiva's chief devotee. If we look at the claims of Cōḻa kings in this light, we can see that they were by no means being inconsistent in their claims to be infused with a portion of Viṣṇu and yet to be ardent devotees of the great Parameśvara. This accommodation of Viṣṇu, of course, could allow Vaiṣṇavas to be positioned strategically within the polity as receiving great honor, but in the

[86] *Śivapurāṇa* II.1.6.33–34. Here Śiva replaces the Vaiṣṇavas' Nārāyaṇa, who sleeps while Vāsudeva Kṛṣṇa acts.

end being subordinated to the preeminent recipients of the king's generosity, the Śaivas. The writing of the Cōḻa lineage by the king's court poet, then, was an act that would best be taken up by a Vaiṣṇava. Indeed, Nārāyaṇa, the poet of both Rājarāja's and Rājendra's Sanskrit eulogies, is described as a devotee of Viṣṇu (*bhaktena muravidviṣaḥ*, 134). The key position of royal preceptor (*rājaguru*) of the Cōḻa king, however, was held by Śaivas.

Elaborating the Past: Mucukunda's Sons

After invoking Pārvatī and Sarasvatī, the eulogy begins its history of the Cōḻa dynasty, following the Purāṇic succession of kings (*vaṃśānucarita*).[87] The narrative does not concern itself with the life of every king in the family's genealogy. Often the poet places ellipses in the genealogy, stating that a particular king was born "in the family" of the previous king rather than as his son. This allows him to telescope large periods of time into just a few verses. Starting with the Sun and Manu Vaivasvata, the *RCS–6* narrates the genealogy of the Solar dynasty as articulated in the Purāṇas from Ikṣvāku, its founder, down to King Māndhātṛ, who was born from his father Yuvanāśva's side and suckled by Indra, lord of the gods (Figure 4.2). Māndhātṛ was a king among kings and had three sons through his wife Vindumati: Purukutsa, Ambarīṣa, and Mucukunda. The Purāṇic list of kings mentions the descendants of Māndhātṛ's second son, Ambarīṣa, for three generations, and then return to the account of the Solar line as it continued through Māndhātṛ's first son, Purukutsa, into whom Viṣṇu descends in order to win back the treasures of the Nāgas from the Mauneyas.

It is from Mucukunda, the third son of Māndhātṛ, that the author of the eulogy sutures the lineage of the Cōḻas into the Solar dynasty.[88] As in our inscription, Mucukunda is mentioned in the Purāṇas as the Solar king who woke from sleep to destroy the king Kālayavana, who, intent on vanquishing the Yādavas of Mathurā, was pursuing Kṛṣṇa.[89] The Purāṇas, however, do not trace the descent of the Cōḻas from Mucukunda, to whom they give no heirs, nor from any other Solar king. On the contrary, they mention the Cōḻas as among the barbarians conquered by the famous Solar king Sāgara, son of Bāhu.

---

[87]The account tallies with that listed in several Purāṇas, but since the eulogist was a devotee of Viṣṇu, it may have been taken from the *Viṣṇupurāṇa* or *Bhāgavatapurāṇa*.

[88]Three other Sanskrit eulogies composed during the reign of Rājendra I are extant: the Essālam Plates, 25th year; the Karandai Tamil Sangam Plates, 8th year; and the Larger Leiden Plates. The eulogy of the last was composed in Rājendra's reign by the poet Nārāyaṇa, who composed the others mentioned above; Subrahmanya Ayyar, ed. and tr., "The Larger Leiden Plates of Rajaraja I," *EI* 22 (1933–34), 222. Although they vary in their lists of the Solar kings down to Mucukunda, all relate the descent of the Cōḻas from this last son of Mandhātṛ. There are also Tamil court poems that give this genealogy: K. V. Kanakasabhai Pillai, "Tamil Historical Texts (2): The Kalingattu Parani," *Indian Antiquary* 19 (1890), 329–45; Ottakūṭṭar, *Mūvarulā*, edited by U. V. Caminataiyar ([1946] Madras: U. V. Caminataiyar Nul Nilaiyam, 1992). Although Tamil Sthalapurāṇas generally do not contain kingly genealogies, some mention Mucukunda as the Cōḻa king who brought down from heaven the famous Tyāgarāja-Śiva at Tiruvārūr; Shulman, *The King and the Clown*, pp. 241–46.

[89]*Viṣṇupurāṇa* V.23–24; *Bhāgavatapurāṇa* X.51.

Suturing the Cōḻas to the Solar dynasty was not, however, without difficulties. Elsewhere the Purāṇas name the Cōḻas as descendants of the Lunar dynasty (Figure 4.3). The texts list Cōḻa, along with Pāṇḍya, Kerala, and Kulya, as the descendants of Turvaśu, the second son of Yayāti, and as founders of countries (in south India). The earlier genealogies in the Cōḻa inscriptions, however, traced their descent not to Turvaśu but to Śibi, son of Uśīnara whom the Purāṇas represent as a younger half-brother of Turvaśu.[90] The later genealogies continue to derive the Cōḻas from Śibi, but they do so through Marutta and his son, Duṣyanta, whom the Purāṇas name as descendants of Turvaśu, and Bharata who, in the Purāṇas, is the son of another Duṣyanta, a descendant of Puru, son of Santurodha, married to Śakuntalā.[91] In other words, they claim descent from the best-known collaterals descended from Yayāti, Yadu apart.

The *RCS–6*, having done its best to ameliorate these inconsistencies, continues the history of the Cōḻavaṃśa through the end of the Age of Completeness. The text introduces in the Age of the Trey the eponymous king Cōḻa, "after whom the Solar family prospered on the earth" (v. 28).[92] Only three kings is mentioned during the Age of the Deuce, two of the Lunar dynasty, according to the Purāṇas. As we might expect, when we come to the Age of Strife, none of the Solar kings that Vyāsa predicted would rule during the Age of Strife are mentioned—for we are presumably hearing the history of a hitherto unknown Solar lineage. Beginning in the Age of Strife the laud lists some kings that are mentioned in Tamil Sangam and Bhakti literature—Perunatkiḷḷi, Karikāla, Kocceṅgaṇṇaṉ—and, finally, lists the Cōḻa kings from Vijayālaya with increasingly greater detail, finally ending with the poet's own lord, Rājendra I.

The Purāṇic succession of kings, if we remember, predicted that both the Lunar and Solar dynasty would come to an inglorious end in the Age of Strife, and the paramount overlordship of the earth would pass into the hands of barbarians. Finally, world sovereignty itself would become unattainable, as churlish kings fighting among themselves would forget the laws of *dharma*. These worsening conditions themselves were signs of the ongoing regress of the Age of Strife. The dynasties of the so-called "medieval" period, beginning with the Rāṣṭrakūṭas, however, saw themselves as the descendants of the supposedly defunct Solar and Lunar dynasties. Their inscriptions proclaim that not only had these dynasties continued into the Age of Strife but the paramount overlordship of the world was still possible late in that age. The *RCS–6* and other Cōḻa inscriptions are no exception here, and this is worth noting, since the increasing fortune and splendor of the Solar dynasty during the dark and wicked Age of Strife is perhaps the most persistent theme of our text. Not only do the fortunes of the Solar clan increase with the advent of the Cōḻas but many of the Cōḻa kings, according to the eulogy, attain to the position of

[90]He was the son of Anu, the second of three sons of Yayāti by a second wife, Śarmiṣṭhā Āsurī, the eldest of whom was Druhyu and the youngest, Pūru. Śibi had fours sons, Vṛṣadarbha, Suvīra, Kekaya, and Madraka, each the founder of a country (in northwest India). The brother of Śibi, Titikṣu, sired Aṅga, Vaṅga, Suhma, Puṇḍra, and Kaliṅga, each, again, the founder of a country (in eastern India).

[91]This Marutta is to be distinguished from an Āvikṣita Marutta, a paramount king of the Solar dynasty.

[92]*yannāmataḥ prathitamarkkakulam pṛthvyām*/

paramount overlordship. In speaking of Sundaracōḻa, the grandfather of Rājendra, the text declares that he was thought by his subjects to be "Manu, arrived on earth once again to reestablish his law that had fallen away as a result of the power of the Age of Strife" (v. 57).[93] His descendants, Rājarāja and Rājendra, also reverse the decline of the Age of Strife. The shower bath into kingship of Rājarāja is likened to a cleansing of the earth, which was dirtied by the wicked ways of the Age of Strife. The point of these references is quite clear. The rise of the Cōḻa family was a signal of the closing Age of Strife. The political theology of this implication was, as we shall see, that a line of kings would rise that would be the vessels of Viṣṇu's grace and establish righteousness on earth at the end of the Age of Strife.

Conquering the Quarters: Articulating a Polity

As the narrative approaches its present, we become aware not only of its "vertical" descent through time but of an increasing "horizontal" movement. Each successive king in the Cōḻa family is given more narrative attention than his predecessor. The eulogy mentions only in passing several kings in the Cōḻa family as it moves toward its real concern: narrating the careers of Rājarāja and his son Rājendra. Nearly half the eulogy is devoted to elaborating the acts of these two kings. The text organizes the accounts of these kings through the act that established them as paramount overlords, the conquest of the quarters. This complex act, which sometimes took several years to perform, was the process whereby a king traversed all the directions of the earth and, through conquest, negotiation, and displays of will, brought its rulers into a single imperial formation. Endemic internecine war is the picture that Indology has left us for the medieval period. Undoubtedly medieval polities spent much of their time at war, but often within the discursive parameters of performing or interrupting the conquest of the quarters.

Nārāyaṇa tells us that after his shower bath into kingship, Aruṇmoḻivarmaṉ (Rājarāja's birth name) performs one of the great gifts, the weight in the balance ceremony (*tulābhāra*). In this Theist rite enjoined by Purāṇic texts, the king ascended one side of a balance scale and gold was placed on the other. This gold was in turn given to officiating priests and pious Brāhmaṇs. [94] In the case of Aruṇmoḻivarmaṉ, the poet says, no amount of gold seemed to balance the scale, he being "unequalled" (*atula*) (v. 75).[95] This ceremony initiated the continuing process of acts of giving (*dāna*) by which the king distributed and redistributed the movable and immovable wealth of his expanding domain. It is only then that Aruṇmoḻivarmaṉ begins his conquest of the quarters with a campaign in the direction of the south (*triśaṅku*), and proceeds in each direction in the proper order (v. 76). The text then narrates the highlights of this royal progress, starting with the

[93]*kalerbalāt praskhalitaṃ svaśāstraṃ punar vyavasthāpayituṃ pṛthvyām prāptuṃ manuṃ janaughaḥ/*

[94]Kane, *History of Dharmaśāstra* 2.2 (1974), 870–2.

[95]This trope no doubt indicates a connection between the king's greatness and how much wealth he was able to bestow, in gold and often other forms, to Brāhmaṇs as householder liturgical adepts of some Vedist or Theist disciplinary order or temple.

south, where Aruṇmoḻivarmaṉ defeats the Pāṇḍya and Sinhala kings allied against him, taking command of the Pāṇḍya country and the northern domains of Sri Lanka (see Chapter 3).[96] He then moves to the north and attacks Satyāśraya (997–c. 1008) of the Western Cālukya family and a king Jaṭā Cōḍa Bhīma (973–999) ruling from Vēṅgi, who was probably his underlord, having usurped the throne of the Eastern Cālukya king Śaktivarman (1000–1011) (pp. 180–82). If the Cōḻas claimed to be manifestations of Viṣṇu in the Solar dynasty, the question was, who did so in the Lunar dynasty? The answer was, the Cālukyas of Veṅgī, but not in quite the way their rivals, the Cālukyas of Kalyāṇi, might have wished. The restored Cālukyas of Veṅgī make a full claim to Lunar descent more elaborate and Purāṇic in its specificity than even the Cōḻas'. Vimalāditya (1011–1018), contemporary of both Rājarāja I (whose daughter Kundavai he accepted in marriage) and Rājendra I, ruled as a Cōḻa underlord. He represents the Cālukyas as the descendants of no less than the Pāṇḍavas, the heroes of the Bhārata war (Figures 4.2, 4.3). Just as in the Purāṇas, his inscription of 1018 represents that genealogy as descending from Brahmā: the gaze of the sage Atri, one of the mental sons of Brahmā; Soma, the Moon; Budha, the planet Mercury; and the human founder of the Lunar dynasty, Purūravas.[97] Together, then, the Cōḻa and his protégé, the Cālukya of Veṅgī, represented themselves as the present-day manifestations of Viṣṇu—the one in the Solar dynasty, the other in its supplement, the Lunar.

To continue, the Cōḻa then turns to the west and conquers Kerala, the birthplace of the fearful sage Bhārgava Rāma, an earlier emanation of Viṣṇu that had destroyed all the men of the Kṣatriyas (warrior estate) of the world. The poet then summarizes the other kings whom Aruṇmoḻivarmaṉ defeated and subjugated—Gaṅga, Kaliṅga, Vaṅga, Magadha, Āraṭṭa (Rāḍha), Oḍra, Saurāṣṭra, and Cālukya.[98] The poet then calls him the king among kings, and proclaims that he "ruled the earth" (v. 84). Even though, as we shall see, the Cōḻa king Aruṇmoḻivarmaṉ is imagined from his birth by the poet as more than ordinary, it is only after his conquest of the quarters that he is said to "rule the earth." Paramount overlordship was not a position that was simply "received," but a sovereignty that had to be "made" by each king who aspired to it.

After describing his conquest of the quarters, the text turns to the birth of Rājarāja's son, whose limbs had all the distinguishing marks of being lord of the earth," named Madhurāntaka, "destroyer of Madurai," capital of the Pāṇḍya kingdom (v. 85).[99] Madhurāntaka, wanting to accrue merit by properly giving and distributing "wealth acquired by his own arm," commenced his own conquest of the quarters (v. 89). The text then describes the military exploits of Madhurāntaka's progress, beginning again with the south, where the Pāṇḍya king is again defeated

---

[96]Nilakanta Sastri, *Cōḻas*, pp. 169–83. The author reconstructs a detailed chronology of Rājarāja's campaigns using his successive Tamil eulogies.

[97]Descent is traced to Pūru, the youngest son of Yayāti by a second wife, Śarmiṣṭhā Āsurī, and founder of the Pauravas, Nahuṣa, his father, and Āyu, Nahuṣa's father, back to Purūravas; V. Venkayya, "Raṇastipūṇḍi Grant of Vimalāditya Dated in the Eighth Year," *EI* 6 (1900–1901), 347–61.

[98]This list, Saurāṣṭra and Cālukya apart, seems to anticipate Rājendra's northern campaign (see below), rather than record any action of Rājarāja.

[99]*kṣitipatilakṣaṇalakṣitākhilāṅga/*

and made to retreat to the hills of Kerala. Although the Sanskrit eulogy of the *RCS–6* does not mention Rājendra's battles in Sri Lanka, the Tamil eulogy of the text lingers proudly on Rājendra's campaign on the island. Earlier the text had compared Rājarāja's victory over Sri Lanka to the conquest of the island by a more famous king in his own Ikṣvāku lineage, Rāma Daśarathi (v. 80). Rājendra's defeat of the Okkāka king, Mahinda V (982–1029), proved that the Cō̱la and not the Sinhala king was the true descendant of Ikṣvāku, and enabled the Cō̱la to name that ancestor in his orders. Rājendra's primary purpose in his campaign to the island that his father had for the most part conquered was to obtain the regalia of not only the Sri Lankan king but of the Pāṇḍya, who had earlier deposited it there for safekeeping: "He took, with his great fierce army the crown of the war-like king of Ī̱lam [Sri Lanka] on the sea, the exceedingly beautiful crown of the queen of that king, the beautiful crown and the pearl necklace of Indra which the Pāṇḍyan had previously deposited with that king, and the entirety of Ī̱la-maṇḍalam on the heaving sea (ll. 135–39, 141)."[100] Having obtained this famous pearl necklace called the "Garland of Indra," and these crowns, thereby appropriating the splendor and wealth of these kings, Madhurāntaka establishes his son as "Cō̱lapāṇḍya," ruler of Madurai (v. 93). He then moves west to Kerala, where he conquers several kings in a pitched battle, and according to the Tamil eulogy, takes various dynastic treasures. After these engagements, Madhurāntaka returns to his capital.

The king next ventures in the direction of Kubera (north). Declaring that king Jayasiṃha II (1015–1042) of the Cālukya family, who was ruling in the Raṭṭa kingdom (formerly the domains of the Rāṣṭrakūṭas), was "king of the Age of Strife," Madhurāntaka, styled by the poet as "reverser of the Age of Strife" (*kalikālakālaḥ*) set out to destroy him (v. 100). The Cālukyas formed the chief political rivals of the Cō̱las in the Deccan. Along with the Paramāras of Mālwā in northern India and the Okkākas in Sri Lanka, they were the chief contenders with the Cō̱las for the paramount overlordship of India left vacant by the Rāṣṭrakūṭas. The next eight verses are dedicated to the description of Rājendra's campaign in Raṭṭa country, ending in the eventual defeat of Jayasiṃha II and the appropriation of his title, Beloved (*vallabha*). This term, positioning the king as the "beloved" of the spouses of Viṣṇu, Bhū (Earth) and Śrī (Fortune), was the distinctive title of the earlier Cālukyas of Bādāmi and had been appropriated by the Rāṣṭrakūṭas. The Cālukyas of Kalyāṇi, in articulating themselves as the successors of the Rāṣṭrakūṭas, took for themselves these appropriated titles as well as the lineage of the earlier Cālukyas and invested themselves with an extended pedigree that strongly hinted at Solar descent.[101] The claims being made by the Cālukyas were quite clear to the Cō̱las.

---

[100] *poru kaṭal ī̱lattaraicar tam muṭiyum āṅkavar teviyaroṅke̱lil muṭiyum mu̱ṉnavar pakkal te̱ṉnavar vaitta cuntaramuṭiyum intira̱nāramum teṇṭiraiy ī̱lamaṇṭala mu̱luvatum...mā poru taṇṭāḷ koṇṭu*. The Sanskrit eulogy of the Karandai plates, in addition to the looting of these items, also mentions the capture of a Sri Lankan queen and princess: K. G. Krishnan, *Karandai Tamil Sangam Plates of Rajendrachola I*, Memoirs of the Archeological Survey of India, 79 (New Delhi: Archeological Survey of India, 1984), p. 199.

[101] The elder brother of Jayasiṃha II (mentioned in the *RCS–6*), Vikramāditya V (1008–1014), had claimed that the Cālukya family ruled in Ayodhyā for fifty-nine generations before moving southward to the Deccan (*dakṣiṇāpatha*), where their rule was interrupted twice before being finally restored by Taila

The Cōḻas preempted the desire to make this a strong invocation on the battlefield. The Karandai plates, composed at about the same time as our text, mention that Rājendra's father, Rājarāja, had taken a vow to destroy Mānyakheṭa, the former capital of the Rāṣṭrakūṭas, newly occupied by the Cālukyas. Rājendra, who finally fulfilled this vow, burnt the city, "which was the residence of Cālukyas as well as the Yadus who have adorned the quarters by their spotless fame and which, like the celestial city, was unassailable even in mind by their enemies."[102] The Cōḻas clearly recognized not only that the Rāṣṭrakūṭas were of Lunar descent (from the family of the Yadus), but also that the Cālukyas had attempted to reoccupy the Rāṣṭrakūṭa's position by residing in their old capital. In driving the Cālukyas from Mānyakheṭa and burning the city, Rājendra effectively supplanted the Cālukya claim to the former Rāṣṭrakūṭa imperium and took it for himself, signifying this new sovereignty with the title Beloved.

Having defeated the major contenders for the paramount overlordship of India, Rājendra returned to his capital, and prepared for a campaign that would without a doubt make manifest to the kings of India that he was the new ruler of the earth. Rājendra ordered his generals to move again northward to capture the Gaṅgā. In their campaign northward, the Cōḻa generals, in alliance with a Paramāra force from Mālwā, defeated the Oḍra (Utkala, Orissa), Kaliṅga (coastal Andhra) and Somavaṃśi kings (of South Kosala), who were underlords of the Kalyāṇi Cālukya.[103] They defeat as well Dharmapāla of Daṇḍabhukti (Tāmralipti, Midna-

II, whom historians have dubbed the founder of the Later Cālukyas of Kalyāṇi; J. F. Fleet, "Kauthem Plates of Vikramaditya V, Saka-samvat 930," *Indian Antiquary* 16 (1887), 17. As Sheldon Pollock notes, intimations of this linkage with the past occur as early as 982 in the old-Kannaḍa text *Gadāyuddham* of Ranna written in honor of the heir apparent, Cālukya king Satyāśraya I (997–1008): "Making History: Kalyāṇi A.D. 1008," in *Śrī Nāgābhinandanam: Dr. M. S. Nagaraja Rao Festschrift* (Bangalore: M. S. Nagaraja Rao Felicitation Committee, 1995), p. 569. Ayodhyā was, it will be recalled, the capital of Ikṣvāku, founder of the Solar dynasty and of other famous kings of that line such as Rāma. So although it does not say so explicitly, the text seems strongly to evoke Solar descent. Later, Vikramāditya VI (1076–1126), who twice seized Veṅgī from the Cōḻas and built an empire that clearly rivaled theirs, began to represent the Western Cālukyas as having Lunar ancestry, but without providing a Purāṇic genealogy, as their collaterals in Andhra had done: Fleet, "Taila II," *Indian Antiquary* 21 (1892), 167–68, refers to two inscriptions, from Gadag and Kalige, that assert their descent from Soma, born from the eye of Atri, son of Brahmā. Historians have been too ready to reduce these differing representations to an essential Cālukya one and have therefore glossed over the shift from vague Solar to definitely Lunar: Krishna Murari, *The Cālukyas of Kalyāṇi (from Circa 973 A.D. to 1200 A.D.)* (Delhi: Concept Publishing Company, 1977), pp. 2–28; B. V. Krishnarao, "The Origin and the Original Home of the Cālukyas," *Proceedings of the Indian History Congress* 3 (1939), 390–91.

[102] Krishnan, *Karandai*, pp. 4–5.

[103] The Paramāras, it will be recalled, also appropriated the crest and titles of the Rāṣṭrakūṭas, and they remain conspicuously absent from most Cōḻa eulogies. Rājendra formed an alliance with the Paramāra king Bhoja (1011–1055), most likely through their shared enmity toward the Cālukya kings of Kalyāṇi, and their underlords in Orissa. It has been surmised that Rājendra's campaign northward was acccompanied by a Paramāra push southward, putting pressure on the Cālukya domains in between. In their inscriptions, both Rājendra and Bhoja claim to have defeated the Somavaṃśi king Indraratha of Ādinagara. This king was probably Nahuṣa Mahābhavagupta III (c. 1020–1025) of Yayātinagara, the Somavaṃśi capital; *HCIP* 5 (1957), 209–10. In our text, the Kaliṅga and Oḍra kings are described as following the orders of the "king of the Kali age," earlier identified as the Cālukya Jayasiṃha II. An inscription from Cālukya domains probably refers to these battles fought in lower Orissa, where it is stated that Jayasiṃha fought the Cōḻas, Paramāras, and Gaṅgeyas together; Lionel Barnett, ed. and tr.,

Figure 4.4. Seal (on Ring) of Rājendra I's Order

(Courtesy of the State Department of Archaeology of Tamil Nadu)

pur district), Raṇaśūra of Rāḍha (western Bengal), and Govindacandra of Vaṅga (eastern Bengal), all probably underlords of the powerful Pāla monarch Mahīpāla (c. 988–c. 1038).[104] After this campaign, Rājendra turns his attention eastward, conquering Kaṭāha (on the modern Malay peninsula), a part of the Śrī Vijaya empire under the Śailendra king Saṅgrāmavijayottuṅgavarman.[105] As we know from the "Larger Leiden Plates," this king's predecessors had built, in conjunction with Rājarāja and his son, the heir apparent, a Buddhist monastery (*vihāra*) at the coastal town of Nāgapaṭṭana (Nagapattinam), not far from Tañjāvūr. The Cōḻas, in helping to build this monastery, had attempted to position themselves as the allies of Buddhist polities across the eastern seas, probably in league against the Sri Lankan Buddhist polity to its south.[106] During the reign of Rājendra, however, cause seems to have arisen for an expedition to subdue the islands. Although the campaign is

---

"Kulenur Inscription of the Reign of Jayasimha II: Saka 950" *EI* 15 (1919–20), 333; Nilakanta Sastri, *Cōḻas*, p. 206. For the relations of the Paramāras, Cōḻas, Cālukyas, and Orissan dynasties, see Mahesh Singh, *Bhoja Paramāra and His Times* (Delhi: Bharatiya Vidya Prakashan, 1984), pp. 65, 88; Bhatia, *Paramāras*, pp.77–78; *HCIP* 5 (1957), 66–67. For a detailed account of the ongoing wars between the Paramāras and the Cālukyas of Kalyāṇi, see Yazdani, *Early History* I, 319–49.

[104]For a detailed reconstruction of these conflicts, based mostly on Rājendra's Tamil inscriptions, see Nilakanta Sastri, *Cōḻas*, pp. 208–34.

[105]On the identification, location, and invasion of Kaṭāha, Śrī Vijaya, and other locales in the Malay archipelago, see K. A. Nilakanta Sastri, *History of Sri Vijaya* (Madras: University of Madras, 1949), pp. 1–26, 75–85; George Spencer, *The Politics of Expansion: The Cōḻa Conquest of Sri Lanka and Sri Vijaya* (Madras: New Era, 1983), pp. 100–37.

[106]As Walters has noted, the name of the monastery, Cuḍāmaṇivihāra, signified in Buddhist texts the residence of the Buddha when he visited Indra's heaven.

only briefly mentioned in the *RCS–6*, in Rājendra's Tamil inscriptions, especially at Tañjāvūr, we find an elaborate description of the conquest.[107]

Returning to his kingdom, Rājendra, using water brought earlier from the Gaṅgā, erected a "victory pillar" (*jayastambha*) in his new capital (v. 123). The narrative then closes: Rājendra has performed his triumph over the quarters, obtained the Cālukya's title, Paramount Overlord, and sits ruling the earth from his palace at Paḻaiyāṟu, from where he issues this order.

According to the text, Rājendra had more truly fulfilled the requirements of the paramount overlordship of the world than any other king. This position was predicated on a vision of the kings of Bhāratavarṣa forming a single polity. The seal of our inscription and others like it also participated in the articulation of the Cōḻa king as imperial sovereign. All the seals of the Cōḻas represent the images of two fish, and a tiger sitting on a bow—the three emblems of the Pāṇḍyas, Cōḻas, and Ceras, respectively—flanked by whisks, lampstands, flags, and weapons (Figure 4.4). The juxtaposition of the fish, tiger, and bow had come down to the Cōḻas from an earlier tripartite polity developed during what is sometimes called the Caṅkam period.[108] In the seals of the Cōḻas, however, we can see that an imperial parasol (*chatra*; Tamil, *kavikai*) hangs above all these figures. The parasol was an emblem that not only shaded the world but shone brilliantly in and of itself—an indication of "valour, invincibility and victory." As such it shed "a cool lustre on all the subjects of the king."[109] The umbrella indicated the paramount king's suzerainty. Under it all other kings sought protection. Speaking of Rājarāja, the inscription says that the ocean itself, which surrounded the island continent of the world (Jambudvīpa) became his parasol, implying that all the world had been brought under the sway of that universal king. Rājendra's seal is an iconic representation of this idea. What is new with the seals of Rājendra is the appearance below the bowstring of the famous crest of the Cālukya family, the boar, along with other auspicious objects perhaps associated with the Cālukya king.[110] The placement of the Cālukya crest, itself appropriated by the Kalyāṇi Cālukyas from their Bādāmi ancestors, below the Cōḻa/Pāṇḍya/Cera signs indicated the hierarchical relationship between the Cōḻa king and the defeated Raṭṭa monarch.

The Sanksrit verse that circumscribes the seal reads: "Hail, Prosperity! This order of Parakesarivarman Rājendra Cōḻa is to rest on the jewels in rows on the crests of [other] kings."[111] This language is more than metaphoric. The Tamil portion of

[107]By the time of Kulōttuṅka I, the Cōḻas had again subdued and reinstalled the Śailendra kings. We find a new request for exemptions for the Buddhist monastery at Nagapattinam on behalf of a Śailendra king; Subrahmanya Ayyar, ed. and tr., "The Smaller Leiden Plates (of Kulottunga I)," *EI* 22 (1933–34), 267–81; R. C. Majumdar, "Note on the Sailendra Kings Mentioned in the Leiden Plates," *EI* 22 (1933–34) 284.

[108]R. Nagaswamy, *Studies in Ancient Tamil Law and Society* (Madras: Government of Tamilnadu, 1978), pp. 51–55.

[109]N. Subrahmanian, *Śangam Polity: The Administration and Social Life of the Śangam Tamils* (Bombay: Asia, 1966), p. 72.

[110]See Krishnan, *Karandai*, pp. 4–5.

[111]*svasti śrī| rājadrājanyamakuṭaśreṇiratneṣu śāsanaṃ| etadrājendracolasya parakesarivarmmaṇaḥ||* my translation; *Archeological Survey of India, Annual Report 1903–4* (Calcutta: Office of the Superin-

the text tells us how the officials at Tiruvāḷaṅgāḍu received the order: "Seeing the royal order, we, the chief men of the district, went out, reverenced it and placed [it] on our heads" (ll. 143–44). The seal implies that not only local officials but kings as well received the orders of the Rājendra by bowing and touching the orders to their heads. The text of the inscription asserts that after Rājarāja conquered Kerala, his orders (*śāsanam*) were made to shine, being placed on the rows of diadems of these rulers. Perhaps one of the most common tropes of our text is the arrangement of other king's crowns below, or at the feet of, the Cōḻa monarch. These actions of honor were part of the ongoing practices at the court of the Cōḻa overlord that ordered the relationships of his imperial polity. The king must have been seated on his throne above his underlords, whose crowns "crowded about his feet" as they bowed before him. Rājendra's underlords received his orders, often issued on plates (*paṭṭa*), by the respectful act of touching them to their heads.

Gathering and Emitting Light

The accumulation and display of fame (*kīrti*) in the form of visible luster or light was essential to the paramount king's sovereignty. Consequently, we find images of light and luminosity to be the most consistently used metaphors of the text. According to the Purāṇas, the abstract force that gave everything in the cosmos the power to realize its destiny was luminosity (*tejas*).[112] It was this luminosity from which the king's fame arose. In fact, this ordering luminosity found its chief earthly receptacle in the paramount sovereign. The paramount king was a repository of light, drawn from above, that illumined the world (v. 56). For it was no mistake that the two major Purāṇic lineages proceeded from the two luminaries that ordered time in the world: the sun and moon. But luminosity and its fulfillment in the person of the paramount sovereign would be in abeyance during the Age of Strife.[113] Our text speaks of the "blinding darkness of the Age of Strife" (v. 69). But this dissolution, according to the Purāṇas, was not without one caveat. At the end of the Age of Strife a resplendent being would appear who, with the kings of the renewed Solar and Lunar dynasties, would reverse its entropic process and gather the people who would form the pure souls of those to be born in the next Age of Completeness:

> When the Vedic knowledges (*śrauta*, *smārta*, *dharma*) have met with utter disaster and when the course of the Age of Strife is at an end, a portion of the Lord Vāsudeva, creator of the entire world, lord over the movable and immovable, who in his own form is the beginning, end, and everything, and is Brahmā, will be born [emanate] here on earth in the form of Kalkin, possessed of the eight felicitous qualities, in the house of Viṣṇuyaśas, the chief Brāhmaṇ in Sambhalagrāma, and having incredible and eternal strength, will cause

tendent of Government Printing, 1906), p. 234.

[112]Luminosity (*tejas*) itself depended on the favorable ordering of the three constituent forces (*gunas*) of the universe. Inden, *Imagining India*, pp. 235–38.

[113]Ideally, goodness (*sattva*) and activity (*rajas*) would predominate over darkness (*tamas*), but in the Age of Strife, darkness and activity were dominant over goodness, and divine luminosity faded. (pp. 235–8).

> destruction for all the barbarians, enemies, people of wicked behavior, and the rest of them. His greatness and might will be unobstructed. He will again establish virtue on earth, and when the Age of Strife will completely close, the remaining people will be awakened and their minds will be as pure as crystal. There will be issue from all those men, transformed as a result of those times, who will be the seeds for future beings. And their progeny will follow the laws of the Age of Completeness. As it is said, "when the sun, the moon, the lunar asterism Tiṣya, and the planet Jupiter are in one mansion then there will be another Age of Completeness.[114]

This is the future horizon or the "social imaginary" of the Purāṇic world history under which theist polities labored. They might shine luminously in the entropic darkness of the Age of Strife. This is precisely how our narrative portrays the genealogy of the Cōḻas. As the narrative nears the present, there is an acute awareness of the onset of dark and wicked times, but at the same time a consistent emphasis on the brilliant luminosity of the Cōḻa kings. Perhaps the most common epitaph taken by the kings of our text is crest-jewel or head-ornament (*tilaka*, *śikhāmaṇi*, *cūḍāmaṇi*) of the Solar dynasty (*ravivaṃśi*). In fact, the eulogy presents us with a genealogy that is arranged like a glittering string of jewels. And the fortunes of the Cōḻa family in our text increase as the narrative moves toward its present. But this progress was not a given. The Age of Strife even had its effects on the Cōḻa line. When the Cōḻa king Sundara died, he left two sons. The elder ruled until he died, and then a cousin, Uttamacōḻa, stepped in, after some dispute, to take the throne. This was an unprecedented break in the dynastic line. But the poet assures us that it had been accounted for through an intervention of Viṣṇu, who infused the younger son with a particle of his being: "His son Aruṇmoḻivarmaṉ was born a Murāri (Viṣṇu), with his hands bearing the auspicious marks of the conch (*śaṇkha*) and wheel (*cakra*), and his arms, long like the javelin (*prāsa*), holding the goddess Śrī, who embraced tightly his whole body" (v. 61).[115] Born with the appropriate bodily marks, and with the first of Viṣṇu's consorts, Śrī, in his arms, Rājarāja was clearly considered to be an emanation of Viṣṇu and a world ruler. His uncle Uttamacōḻa, who was improperly enjoying the paramount kingship, immediately installed him as crown prince instead of his own son when he saw the marks on Aruṇmoḻivarmaṉ's body, indicating that the child was Viṣṇu born on earth (70). In a possible reference to Uttamacōḻa, Nārāyaṇa proclaims that Aruṇmoḻivarmaṉ's shower bath into kingship, the rite that further imbued him with divine energy, removed the stain that the Age of Strife had left upon the earth (72).

But Aruṇmoḻivarmaṉ's luminosity as a world ruler was continually enunciated to the people by other signs of his glory and fame. The king's glory was constituted partly by the wealth that he continually won at war and redistributed properly in his kingdom. Fame (*kīrti*) was not only the quality that accrued to the

---

[114]*Viṣṇupurāṇa* IV.24.26–30, my translation. The *Śivapurāṇa*, although not mentioning this figure, does name the king Maru, living in a hermitage in the Himalayas during the time of its composition, who would restart the Solar dynasty for the next Age of Completeness: *Śivapurāṇa* V.39.28–29.

[115]*ajani bhujayugena prāsadīrghena dīptasriyam akhilasarīrāśleṣinīm ādaghānaḥ/ adhikaram atharekhārūpinau śaṅkhacakrau dadhadaruṇmoḻivarmmā tasya sūnurmurāri//*

king for his generous and heroic actions but "the thing that speaks or glorified him."[116] So not only his reputation but the monuments he built and institutions he endowed to establish that reputation were part of the king's glory. As such, the eulogy itself was a part of the king's fame. This goes some way to explain the deferential treatment that the inscription itself was bestowed when it was received at the village of Paḻaiyaṉūr. As we have noted above, local officials understood the order, as its Tamil nomination implies, as the "auspicious face" (*tirumukam*) of the king. It was treated as an extension of the king himself and, as such, was infused with divine luminosity.

The king's triumph over the quarters was a process that involved the appropriation of the fame and luminosity of other kings. The tropes of light, fame, and wealth converge in the descriptions of the fabulous jewels that Rājendra, Aruṇmoḻivarmaṉ's son, collected from rival kings. Our text states that "the son of Rājarāja, skilled in leadership, took the spotless and lustrous pearls that were like the seeds of the untarnished reputation of the Pāṇḍya king" (v. 92).[117] Not only were jewels invested with fame, but fame itself sparkled like jewels (*maṇi*). By defeating the Somavaṃśi king Indraratha, Rājendra deprived the Lunar dynasty of its jewel, and hence its fame and splendor. The chief minister of Rājendra, Jananātha, formerly a minister of the Cālukyas, is represented as a "crest-jewel" captured from the Cālukyas (*cālukyacūḍāmaṇi*) (v. 127). As the king of kings progressed through the quarters, he appropriated the splendor of other kings, increasing the glory of his own family.

To understand this language as merely a theological justification for the amassing of wealth would be to miss its crucial importance in medieval polities. It is true that the capability of extracting and redistributing tribute from lesser lords in the form of services and resources was integral to bringing together the domain of a world ruler. But we must be careful not to assume that the gaining of this tribute, often in the form of precious, lustrous objects, was some symbolic or superfluous activity in relation to the nitty-gritty of surplus extraction and real economic exploitation. These tributes themselves, often transacted in an economy of lustrous objects and glowing light, were significations that constituted a polity.[118] The crowns and crest-jewels of other kings, for example, are valued not only for their precious metal (although this is sometimes the case) but also for their ability to light up the feet of the Cōḻa king (v. 41). The crowns of other kings, when placed before the Cōḻa king as he sat upon his raised throne at court, do much more work than their weight in gold: they articulate a relationship between the paramount sovereign and his loyal underlords.

---

[116] D. C. Sircar, *Indian Epigraphical Glossary* (Delhi: Motilal Banarsidass, 1966), p. 156; also Sircar, *Indian Epigraphy*, p. 3 n. 5.

[117] *pāṇḍyarājayaśaśāṃ vimalānām bījatāmiva gatāni lasanti/ rājarājatanayo nayavedī mauktikāni jagṛhe vimalāni//*

[118] For an interesting reading, against the grain, of this "exchange" of valuable icons and objects in medieval Indian polities, see Richard Davis, *The Lives of Indian Images* (Princeton: Princeton University Press, 1998).

Remaking the Sphere of a World Ruler

If the Cōḻas articulated their sovereignty by supplementing Purāṇic notions of time and cosmology, they also constructed their domain as a supplement to the cosmographic representations of the Purāṇas. Indeed, perhaps Rājendra's most famous act aimed at supplementing the world geography of the Purāṇas.

The complex agents who composed the earlier Purāṇas saw the world as consisting of a series of six ring-continents, at the center of which was the preeminent one, an island continent called Jambudvīpa. At the center of Jambudvīpa stood the cosmic mountain-pillar called Meru, encircled by the river of the gods. On top of Meru was the palace of the cosmic overlord, Śiva or Viṣṇu, in the form of Brahmā.

The southern section of this huge island continent was termed "Bhāratavarṣa." As with sovereignty, the geography of the Purāṇas was laid out in hierarchically successive and inclusive spheres, so that larger parts contained smaller parts and smaller parts often mirrored the structure of larger parts. Just as Jambudvīpa as a whole had a preeminent center, and mountain, around which circled the river of the gods, so each lesser region had a "middle" or "central" region, with a preeminent mountain and river. The ruling societies and knowledges of early India had construed the 'preeminent "middle region" of the southern portion of Jambudvīpa to be what is today north India, a region they designated, metonymically, as Bhāratavarṣa. Being homologous to the center of Jambudvīpa itself, Bhāratavarṣa possessed a central mountain and a preeminent river. Located in the Himalayas was Mount Kailāsa. Near it, the river Gaṅgā descended from the heavens, where it had circled the palace of Brahmā at Meru.

Each of the peripheral regions of Bhāratavarṣa had its own Gaṅgā and Himalaya, but they were all subordinate to the preeminent middle region. All rivers, for example, were said to have their source in the Gaṅgā. This hierarchization had political and soteriological implications. At the world's creation, Bhāratavarṣa was created from its preeminent portion, its middle region—and it is here that the souls who would be the seeds for the beings recreated in the next epoch of Manu (*manvantara*) would take refuge. The foremost pilgrimage places of the Vaiṣṇavas and Śaivas were located at Kailāsa, and here Viṣṇu and Śiva were said to reside in their omniscient forms. The middle region was the soteriological and ontological center of the world.[119] The "middle region" was the political center of the world, as well, the point from which the paramount king "enjoyed the earth." According to the Purāṇas, the Solar and Lunar dynasties had in previous ages resided in the splendid kingdoms of Kosala and Kuru-Pañcāla, which together constituted the chief kingdoms of the "middle region" of India.

This geography, like paramount overlordship itself, was not a static, natural condition, but one that continually had to be made over again, and one that might shift if any king could muster the strength and fame to do so. This is precisely what dynasties such as the Pallavas, Rāṣṭrakūṭas, and Cōḻas attempted to do as part of their claims to world sovereignty. The world ruler, after all, ruled from

[119]Inden, *Imagining India*, p. 257.

the "middle region" of Bhāratavarṣa. His paradigmatic political act, the conquest of the quarters, presupposed a "center" from which the king moved. Integral to articulating his polity, then, was making his domain the new center of Bhāratavarṣa. In doing so, he made a strong case that the Purāṇic world history would culminate in his own kingdom.

Moving Rivers and Mountains, Embracing the Earth

Rājendra, if he was to fulfill the position of world ruler that the Rāṣṭrakūṭa king had held, not only needed to articulate his sovereignty by accumulating the tribute and fame of other kings, but he also had to convince the royal courts of India that his was the new "middle region" of Bhāratavarṣa. The eulogy of the *RCS–6* certainly took part in this process. After introducing the eponymous king Cōḻa, who made the Solar race famous on the earth, the text tells us that the lustrous riches of the Cōḻa country humbled the abode of the gods (v. 29). Four generations later, king Citradhanvan, "thinking of the fact that the river of the gods was caused to descend at the wish of king Bhagīratha in penance, this king, wanting fame, caused her to descend to his own land as [with the name] Kaverakanyākā" (v. 35).[120] The "river of the gods" (*surasarit*) of this verse is clearly the celestial Gaṅgā noted in the famous Bhagīratha story. Crucial, however, is the way the Gaṅgā is envisaged. The river is not conceived of as a fixed and reified geographical entity, but instead as a river that could be "won" by the greatness of any king. The possessor of this river (not to mention his kingdom) would be invested with fame and prosperity. The text explains that Citradhanvan brings the river to the Cōḻa domain in the form of the goddess Kāverī. The Kāverī River had long watered the fertile plains of the Cōḻa kingdom, whose ancient capital Uṟaiyūr sat on its banks near the great temple of Śrīraṅgam. In the *RCS–6*, the Kāverī is introduced as the celestial Gaṅgā, descended into the Cōḻa's land. Soon after, the text mentions the Cōḻa king Karikāla, known from earlier literature, who earned his fame by constructing embankments on the river.

But possessing the river of the gods within the Cōḻa kingdom in the form of the Kāverī was not enough. There were other representations and practices that had to be addressed. The most important act of Rājendra's triumph over the quarters, mentioned in all his inscriptions, was his famous trip to the Gaṅgā.[121] In the standard Tamil introductions to his inscriptions, we only hear that Rājendra conquered, among other places, "the Gaṅgā, whose waters dashed against banks filled with

---

[120] *surasaridavatāriteti matvā tapasi ratena bhagīrathena rājñā/ narapatir avatārayan yaśortthī nijabhuvi tām sa kaverkanyākākhyām//*

[121] The purpose and nature of this expedition has generated an ongoing debate in the study of Cōḻa history. George Spencer, in his monograph on the subject, questions the veracity of the conquest of the Gaṅgā based on the "confused" geography the inscriptions present. He finally concludes that the event probably did take place, describing it as a "dramatic gesture" of Oedipal envy, the desperate attempt of Rājendra to outdo his father. He reads the claims of the eulogies as legitmating masks for "plunder…a type of compulsive behavior dictated by the needs of statecraft" that "partook of an element of fantasy." Spencer, *The Politics of Expansion*, pp. 5, 43.

fragrant flowers."[122] But the Sanskrit accounts, as found in the Tiruvāḷaṅgāḍu, Karandai, and Essalam plates, along with the Sanskrit eulogies of his sons, make much of this act, no doubt because they were addressed to an all-India "audience" of imperial and would-be imperial kings.

The *RCS–6*, after noting that Rājendra was born with "with the marks of a king of the entire earth" (v. 86) describes his triumphal conquest of the quarters. Rājendra makes a series of campaigns in the southern and western directions before moving north, where he defeats the Cālukya king Jayasiṃha II decisively at Musangi.[123] Returning to his capital, Rājendra, "light of the solar lineage, laughing at Bhagīratha who had brought down the Gaṅgā to the earth from heaven with the power of his austerities, wished to brighten his own country with the water of the Gaṅgā carried back through the strength of his own arm" (v. 109).[124] As in the case of Citradhanvan, Rājendra is likened to Bhagīratha. But he laughs, intending to make a mockery out of Bhagīratha's deed through bringing the Gaṅgā to his country by his own hand. But this would be no easy task, for the Gaṅgā's location in north India was not a "natural" reality, but one that had been produced and maintained through complex political relationships. In displacing this geography, Rājendra had to answer to the kings and lords who held it preeminent. Rājendra ordered his armies northward "to subdue the kings occupying the banks of that river" (v. 110). Their campaign northward, as mentioned before, was probably facilitated by an alliance with Bhoja of Mālwā and his Kalacuri underlord, King Gaṅgeyadeva (c. 1018–1035). Together they defeated a confederation of kings allied with Jayasiṃha II. The kings that were currently in possession and command of the banks of the Gaṅgā were in a sense its interlocutors, the spokesmen to the polities of India, for the geography that placed that river as preeminent. This is why their recognition of Cōḻa imperial claims was so crucial. Only by their conscious subordination could a new geographical center of India be effected. This is precisely how the *RCS–6* constructs the event: "The general (*daṇḍanāyaka*) then immediately caused to be brought to his own master Madhurāntaka the most cleansing waters of that [Gaṅgā River] by the defeated kings [living] on its banks" (v. 117).[125] These kings were made to recognize the new "middle region" of India in a profound way: they publicly handed over their Gaṅgā to its new earthly possessor, and assumed a "tributary" role in the new imperial formation. The Kānyakumārī inscription of Vīrarājendra not only claims that the armies of Rājendra subjugated these kings, but that the banks of the river itself were "trampled by his [Rājendra's] own roaring troop of elephants."[126] For the Cōḻas, the northern Gaṅgā had been

[122]The Tamil (*veṟimalarttīrat teṟipuṉaṟ kaṅkaiyum*) varies very little in Rājendra's Tamil eulogies. E. Hultzsch, ed. and tr., "Tirukkalar Plate of Rajendra-Chola I," *SII* 3 (1929), 467 and n. The claim is not made in the Tamil eulogy of the *RCS–6* because it long preceded the campaign, after which the Sanskrit portion was composed.

[123]Nilakanta Sastri, *Cōḷas*, p. 204.

[124]*tapaḥprabhāvādavatīrnnagaṅgam bhagīratham bāhubalāddhasan saḥ/ gaṅgājalaiḥ pāvayituṃ svakīyāmiyeṣa pṛthvīṃ ravivaṃśadīpa//*

[125]*vijitaistadīyataṭbhūmināyakais salilantadīyamatha pāvanaṃ paraṃ/ nijanāyakāya madhurāntakāya tat samanīnayat sapadi daṇḍanāyakaḥ//*

[126]Subrahmanya Ayyar, ed. and tr., "Kanyakumari Inscription of Virarajendra," *Travancore Archae-*

successfully displaced—its banks destroyed and its waters handed over. To display his achievement at every place where his returning army camped in Cōḻanāḍu on the way to his capital, Rājendra had a hall for the conquered Gaṅgā (*gaṅgaikoṇḍa-maṇḍapam*) constructed in its temple.[127] These actions were more than simply attempts to "sacralize" his plundering expedition. Cōḻa kingship was much more intimately connected with temple practices. Just as Rājendra's actions in our text were a continuation of Purāṇic world sovereignty, the temples he constructed and supported, whose architecture and liturgical practices were so carefully described in the Āgamas, were themselves updates of Purāṇic knowledge. Thus it is not surprising that Rājendra installed these "halls for the Gaṅgā" in temples, for in the Śaiva Siddhānta Āgamas that rearticulated Purāṇic knowledge the temple became the chief site of soteriological practice.

Meeting his general at the Godāvarī River, Rājendra bathed there, as the poet Kālidāsa had represented the hero Raghu to have done during his conquest of the quarters, making the lord of rivers jealous (v. 118). The Godāvarī was the preeminent river of his rival, the Cālukya. Mānyakheṭa and Kalyāṇi were both situated up that river. By bathing in this river, Rājendra indicated that being master of the Gaṅgā made him master of all the other rivers (and their attendant domains). Returning to his capital, which was given the name Gaṅgaikoṇḍacōḻapuram ("city of the Cōḻa who conquered the Gaṅgā"), Rājendra turned his attention to the eastern direction. The Cōḻa kingdom being already situated on the eastern boundary of the land, where would the king go? Rājendra crossed the ocean and conquered the king of Kaṭāha (v. 123), who had previously been an ally.[128] The clear implication of the text is that while returning from this campaign, Rājendra had performed the conquest of the quarters more completely than any other Cōḻa monarch—he had indeed conquered all the directions. The poet then writes that after arriving in his capital, "that lord established in his own region a pillar of victory consisting of the waters of the Gaṅgā known by the name Cōḻagaṅgam" (v. 124).[129] With this, the eulogy turns to the details of the grant. "Erecting" a pillar of victory in the Cōḻa land composed of the Gaṅgā water brought from the campaign, to the north was the culmination of Rājendra's conquest of the quarters. The waters were poured into a large artificial lake nearly five kilometers in length, called the Gaṅgā of the Cōḻas in the inscription. This lake was filled partly through channels from the Veḷḷār and Koḷḷidam rivers.[130] The Koḷḷidam River was itself a branch of the Kāverī so that

ological Series 3: 146, my translation. Note the importance placed on destroying the banks of the displaced river—concomitant with the importance of maintaining the banks of the new one.

[127]C. Sivaramamurti, *Royal Conquests and Cultural Migrations in South India and the Deccan* (Calcutta: Indian Museum, 1955), p. 22.

[128]Whereas Rājarāja I had been on friendly terms with rulers in Kaṭāha, granting the village of Āṉaimaṅgalam to the Buddhist monastery that king Cūḍāmaṇivarman had built in the Cōḻa coastal port Nāgapaṭṭana, his son Rājendra transformed them into underlords. During his reign the privileges enjoyed by the Cūḍāmaṇi monastery must have been revoked, for another copper plate grant during the reign of king Kulottuṅka I, Rājendra's distant grandson, reinstates them; Subrahmanya Ayyar, "The Smaller Leiden Plates of Kulottunga I."

[129]*cōḻagaṅgamiti khyātyā prathitan nijamaṇḍale/ gaṅgājalamayandevo jayastambhaṃ vyadhatta sah//*

[130]Nilakanta Sastri, *Cōḻas*, pp. 234–35; S. R. Balasubrahmanyam, *Middle Chola Temples: Rajaraja to*

here in this tank the waters of the two rivers were one. Rājendra made it clear that he now possessed the Gaṅgā, the river of the gods, which resided at the center of the human world.

Along with the river Gaṅgā, Rājendra also made Mount Kailāsa appear in the Cōḻa land in at least two places. Flanking the north and south sides of the main temple he completed at the capital, "Lord of the Cōḻa who conquered the Gaṅgā" (Gaṅgaikoṇḍacōḻeśvaram), are two smaller Śiva temples denoting the great Mount Kailāsa, called Southern Kailāsa (*teṅkailāsam*) and Northern Kailāsa (*vaṭakailāsam*).[131] Just as the Rāṣṭrakūṭas had represented the rivers Gaṅgā and Yamunā on either side of the entrance of their "new Kailāsa" temple at Ellora, the Cōḻas placed the shrines Southern Kailāsa and Northern Kailāsa on either side of the temple dedicated to the Śiva who was lord of the Cōḻa at the city that housed the Gaṅgā of the Cōḻas.[132] Perhaps just as important, however, were the modifications that Rājendra made to a temple up the river at Tiruvayāṟu, or "the place of five rivers." On both sides of a Śiva shrine dedicated to "the lord of five rivers," Pañcanadīśvaram, are two shrines, one built by Rājendra's mother and the other an earlier shrine renovated by Rājendra, both of which he renamed, respectively, Northern Kailāsa and Southern Kailāsa.[133] On the Southern Kailāsa shrine (where the saint Appar is said to have been granted a vision of Śiva and Pārvatī after searching tirelessly for Mount Kailāsa) is inscribed the full regnal title of Rājendra in Sanskrit, as it is found on the seal of the *RCS–6*. The topography that the Cōḻas constructed, proclaimed in the *RCS–6*, was not a permanent configuration, and would eventually be displaced by their successors, the rulers of the Vijayanagar imperium of the fourteenth and fifteenth centuries. At the time, however, this remarking of the earth was crucial to the Cōḻa project of winning "her" over.

The terms for earth (*bhū*, *pṛthivī*) and fortune (*śrī*, *lakṣmī*), ubiquitous in our narrative, name not simply things but also goddesses, the consorts of Viṣṇu.[134] If the Cōḻa kings contained portions of Viṣṇu, then they bore the same relationship to Viṣṇu's consorts—Earth and Fortune—as Viṣṇu himself. The possession of Viṣṇu's first consort, Śrī, allowed the king to redistribute the movable resources of his domain, while the courtship of Viṣṇu's other consort, Bhū, bestowed mastery over the immovable resources of his kingdom. Consequently, one of the chief tropes in our text is the ongoing and sometimes tenuous relationship that the Cōḻa kings have with these goddesses. At first, the mere concept of a "feminine" land seems to

Kulottunga I (Faridabad: Thomson, 1975), p. 254.

[131] Balasubrahmanyam, *Middle Chola Temples*, pp. 252–53. These refer not to north and south India, but north and south of the main shrine.

[132] Inden analyzes the Rāṣṭrakūṭa supplementation of Purāṇic geography in *Imagining India*, pp. 256–60.

[133] S. R. Balasubrahmanyam, *Four Chola Temples* (Bombay: N. M. Tripathi, 1963), pp. 39, 44–45.

[134] In speaking of goddesses, I am not interested in determining the significance of goddesses or some feminine principle for the whole of Indian civilization, but only the status of Viṣṇu's consorts in the imperial practices of Śaiva and Vaiṣṇava kings in medieval India. Madeleine Biardeau offers a structuralist interpretation of Indian civilization that, in moving away from the evolutionist and racialist paradigms of earlier theories of Indian religion, proposes a single interpretation of all Indian history and culture based on the interacting principles of Viṣṇu, Śiva, and the Goddess in *Hinduism: The Anthropology of a Civilization* ([1981] New Delhi: Oxford University Press, 1989), pp. 1–15; 128–42.

foreshadow Bankimchandra's "richly. -watered, richly fruited" "Mother," taken up by later Indian nationalists.[135] But the relationship in our text between sovereign and Earth is one not of filial love but rather of amorous desire. The "Mother" in nationalist discourse signifies the nascent state itself, a mother who will claim sacrifice and duty from her sons. The feminine Earth in the discourse of our eulogy is not the site where duties to the state are performed but instead the site where a complex political erotics are elaborated—an erotics not simply between king and Earth but between the subjects and the king. The Earth as an object of the sovereign's desire, and the king as object of his subjects' desire, would indeed seem strange to the nationalist project.

In an important sense, the eulogy of our text might be read as the Cōḻa family's long courtship of the Earth. Since only a king among kings could be the beloved of the entire Earth and the chief consort of Fortune, the king's relationship to these goddesses was by no means a given. It had to be "won" and then maintained. For, as Kālidāsa tells us, the goddess was notoriously fickle, and frolicked about with any king who might be strong enough to attract her.[136] The Cōḻa king Kulōttuṅka I (1070–1125), when he took the throne in 1070, was said to have stopped the "commonness" (*potumai*) of the goddess Fortune.[137] Mother India, however, is by no means fickle. In nationalist discourse, Mother India remains truly devoted to her faithful sons who must protect her virtue from the violation of foreigners. The sons of the soil guard and protect against those outside the family.[138] The boundary-drawing exclusionary practices of the modern nation state are forged through this language of kinship. Medieval Indian polities did not organize political place as a feminine presence that could only be protected by those tied to her by blood. The king had an erotic relationship to these feminine goddesses, rather than a filial one. The king had to compete with other suitors to gain the affection of the Earth. The *RCS–6* describes the Cōḻa king Āditya's victory over the Pallava Aparājita as a cuckolding. Āditya woos or enchants the Earth, who was formerly the beloved of the Pallava (v. 49).[139] The cuckold, we might note, is not transformed into a "foreign other" but instead is incorporated into the imperial formation as a king who may enjoy the Earth only through submission to her foremost suitor. As for the Earth's most beloved, he might enjoy her fruit, with his subjects and underlords following behind him, only as long as he pleased her by ruling properly.

The text often describes the Earth as taking enjoyment or refuge on the body of the world-ruling king. The king is repeatedly called "bearer of the Earth" (*bhūdhara*). But he bears the Earth not through the muscular strain of Atlas but

---

135 From "Vande Mātaram," as quoted in Subodh Chandra Sengupta, *Bankimchandra Chatterjee* (New Delhi: Sahitya Akademi, 1977), pp. 57–58; The Tamil poet Subrahmania Bharati's own version of Bankim's poem, also entitled "Vande Mataram," was published in 1907.

136 Kālidāsa, *Raghuvaṃśa*, edited with Mallinātha's commentary and translated by C. R. Devadhar and N. G. Suru (Poona: C. R. Devadhar, 1934) XVII.46.

137 E. Hultzsch, "Inscriptions of Kulottunga-Chola I" No. 68 "Inscription in the Pandava-Perumal Temple," *SII* 3, 141.

138 Perhaps it is modern nationalism rather than medieval polities that rests its sovereignty on metaphors of kinship.

139 *dayitāmapi tasya medinīṃ svavaṃśīkṛtya/*

instead in loving embrace. Vijayālaya wears the Earth, brilliant with the garment of the four oceans, like a garland (v. 47). The poet, in describing Aruṇmoḻivarmaṉ's body at birth, notes the presence of Śrī, who clung to him. Praising Madhurāntaka's virtuous devotion to Śiva, his generosity, temple construction, and frequent performance of processions, the poet remarks that the king "even bore the Earth on his mighty arms" (v. 71).[140]

The conquest of the quarters, which forms the organizing structure for the most important sections of our text, partakes of an erotics as well. Again, this conquest requires both Rājarāja and Rājendra to win Bhū from her other suitors. The Rāṣṭrakūṭas had earlier signified their paramount overlordship with the title Beloved of the Earth and Fortune (*śrīpṛthivīvallabha*). This title, of course, was taken up by the Cālukyas of Kalyāṇi in their claim to the Rāṣṭrakūṭa imperium. When Rājendra defeats the Cālukyas, in our inscription, the poet calls him "beloved" (v. 106), indicating not only that the king had defeated the Cālukya and appropriated his title but that Rājendra was the new beloved of Prosperity and the Earth, the paramount sovereign. The king's conquest of the Earth cuckolds not only the kings of the Earth but certain gods themselves. In a passage that harks back to the *Raghuvaṃśa*, the *RCS–6* tells us how Rājendra, waiting for his generals on the banks of the Godāvarī, played in her waters. The cosmetics from his body, washing off, gave the river Rājendra's scent, causing her lord, the ocean, to become suspicious (v. 118).

But the king is not simply the subject of desire in our text. For Fortune and Earth will not resort to simply any king. He must be physically beautiful. As such, he constitutes an object of desire for not only Earth and Fortune but his subjects as well. The eulogy frequently marvels at the beauty and splendor of the king's body. Sundaracōḻa, Aruṇmoḻivarmaṉ's father, was born with an "incomparable body from Kāma" (*vapuranupamam kamāt*, v. 56). The beauty of Rājarāja and Rājendra constantly pleases not only the consorts of Viṣṇu but their subjects as well. Aruṇmoḻivarmaṉ's body was enjoyed by the eyes of the people (v. 62). The king's body in the Cōḻa polity required constant attention, not only from his subjects but on his own part, as well. The king's daily bathing and adornment were highly discursive acts, specially attended to by servant communities called *vēḻams*, probably composed of women captured during his campaigns.[141] Although I do not have the space here to pursue this issue, I would like to stress that medieval Vaiṣṇava and Śaiva kings articulated their sovereignty, at least in part, through a complex erotics. Our text offers us a glimpse of this discourse.

Conquering the Purāṇas: Articulating an Imperial Canon

Inden shows how modified versions of the Purāṇas became the prevalent guides to Vaiṣṇava and Śaiva traditions in the seventh to ninth centuries. Medieval Śaiva orders rearticulated the theological knowledge of the Purāṇas in a variety of other types of texts beginning in the ninth century. The monks of Śaiva Siddhānta, one

[140] *kṣitimapi bhuje bhūyasi dadhe/*
[141] Nilakanta Sastri, *Cōḻas*, p. 450.

of the contending orders of medieval Śaivism in the ninth and tenth centuries, founded their practice upon the texts called Āgamas, which while drawing on the Śaiva Purāṇas, focused their concerns very firmly around the institution and practices of the temple.[142]

Placing the Cōḻas in the history of Indian Śaivism is a task that has been complicated both by the shifting history of Śaivism on the subcontinent and the more recent discursive "regionalization" of south India. The received historiography of the dominant Śaiva disciplinary order in Tamilnadu, known as Śaiva Siddhānta, sketches a seamless continuity from the wandering Śaiva saints (*nāyaṉmār*) of the late Pallava period down to the present. Scholars as early as G. U. Pope argued that Śaiva Siddhānta was distinctively "Tamil." But the copious Sanskrit Āgama literature, forming the basis of liturgies in Śaiva temples all over south India, indicates a more complicated history, and a much wider circuit for Śaiva Siddhānta knowledge. Recent work by Richard Davis has forcefully argued that Śaiva Siddhānta during the early tenth and eleventh centuries was not "Tamil Śaivism," but a pan-continental disciplinary order that had emerged sometime in the mid-ninth century.[143]

Śaiva Siddhānta monks, who took new names at initiation (*dīkṣā*) ending in *śiva* or *śambhu*, were linked among themselves through lineages (*vaṃśa*, *anvaya*) and sublineages (*santati*, *santāna*) associated with particular monasteries (*maṭhas*).[144] The famous Śaiva Siddhānta *maṭhas* of medieval India—Āmarda, Mattamayūra, Gōlaka—should be seen as "emanating centers and portable affiliations" rather than fixed locales. Between the tenth and thirteenth centuries Śaiva gurus and ascetics identifying themselves with these monasteries took up preeminent positions, often including that of royal preceptor (*rājaguru*), in several polities across the subcontinent. During the eleventh century, the Cōḻas, the Paramāras, and the Kalacuris, who united together against the Kalyāṇi Cālukyas, were all initiated by Śaiva Siddhānta gurus. The Mattamayūra monk Lambakarṇa initiated Sīyaka II (945–973), the first independent Paramāra sovereign.[145] Yuvarājadeva (915–945), the first Kalacuri king to assume titles of independence, brought the renowned Mattamayūra monk Prabhāvaśiva to his kingdom from the Madhumati region.[146] The first clear indication of Śaiva Siddhānta presence at the Cōḻa court

[142]Other Śaiva orders emphasized different texts. The Pāśupātas, for example, relied on the *Pāśupātasūtras*.

[143]Richard Davis, "Aghoraśiva's Background," *Journal of Oriental Research* 56-62 (1986–92), 367–78; Davis, *Ritual*, pp. 14–19.

[144]The Śaiva Siddhānta *dīkṣā* names distinguish them from their contemporaries, the Kālamukhas, prevalent in Western Cālukya domains, whose *dīkṣā* names end with the suffix *rāśi* or *śakti*, or begin with the prefix *bhava*; J. Van Troy, "The Social Structure of Śaiva Siddhāntika Ascetics," *Indica* 11 (1974), 77–86. Richard Davis notes that *kaṇṭha* was a common *dīkṣā* name of Śaiva Siddhāntins dominant in Kashmir during the period when Abhinavagupta and Kṣemarāja, proponents of the burgeoning nondualist orders (Trika), were writing; Davis, "Aghoraśiva's Background," pp. 370–72; Alexis Sanderson, "Śaivism: Śaivism in Kashmir," *Encyclopedia of Religion*, edited by Mircea Eliade (New York: Macmillan, 1987), 13: 16.

[145]Davis, "Aghoraśiva's Background," pp. 375–76.

[146]V. V. Mirashi, "The Śaiva Ācāryas of the Mattamayūra Clan," *Indian Historical Quarterly* 26 (1950), 1–16; *Inscriptions of the Kalachuri-Chedi Era* vol. 4 of *Corpus Inscriptionum Indicarum* (Ootacamund: Government Epigraphist for India, 1955), cli–clix.

also occurs during the reign of a king who took on a title with ambitious imperial overtones: Rājarāja I (985–1014). It is clear from the initiation names of the royal preceptor (*rājaguru*) and temple officials during the reign of Rājarāja that the Śaiva Siddhāntins finally gained the upper hand over other Śaiva orders in the Cōḻa domains such as the Kālamukhas and Pāśupatas.[147] Īśānaśiva, royal preceptor of Rājarāja and presiding priest of his royal temple at Tañjāvūr, Rājarājeśvara, was undoubtedly a Śaiva Siddhāntin. He authored the liturgical manual *Īśānaśivagurudevapaddhati*, and probably spent the first years of his career at the Āmarda monastery in north India before arriving in the Cōḻa kingdom.[148] Īśānaśiva's successor, Śarvaśiva, also a Śaiva Siddhāntin, was the royal preceptor of Rājendra, the king of our grant. The Essālam Plates of Rājendra I call him "master of all Āgamas" (*sakalāgamapaṇḍitaḥ*) and a Māheśvara, the generic term used by Śaṅkarācārya and others to denote dualist Śaiva monks.[149] The initiation of the king by a Śaiva Siddhānta *rājaguru* had important consequences. Rājarāja and his son Rājendra both built massive imperial temples presided over by Śaiva Siddhānta priests. It also insured the widespread mobilization of labor and resources, often initiated from the royal court in the form of gifts to images of Śiva in temples whose liturgical practices were governed by the Āgamas, thereby proliferating the knowledge of Śaiva Siddhānta.[150]

During the eleventh century, at the height of Cōḻa power, Śaiva Siddhānta monks from all over India arrived in the kingdom. In 1031 Rājendra ordered that 2,000 "dry measures" (*kalam*) of paddy (about 12,000 cubic feet) be awarded to his lord, the Śaivācārya Śarvaśiva, and to those worthy among his students and their

---

[147]The singers of the *tirupatiyam* (the hymns of the *nāyaṉmār*) at Rājarāja's royal temple at Tañjāvūr, for example, all have characteristically Śaiva Siddhānta *dīkṣā* names, ending with the suffix *śiva*; E. Hultzsch, "Inscription of Rājarāja on the Outside of the North Enclosure," *SII* 2.3 (1916), 252–59. For notices of other Śaiva disciplinary orders in the Cōḻa imperium, see Nilakanta Sastri, *Cōḻas*, pp. 647–51. Swamy argues that the Śaiva Siddhāntins who gained prominence in the Cōḻa polity were linked to the Gōlaki lineage founded, according to the thirteenth-century Malkāpuram inscription, by the Kalacuri king Yuvarājadeva. In the south these lineages took the titles Bhikṣāmaṭhasantāna, Lakṣādhyāyisantāna, and Jñānāmṛtācāryasantāna; B. G. L. Swamy, "The Golaki School of Śaivism in the Tamil Country," *Journal of Indian History* 53 (1975), 167–220. Although Swamy amasses an impressive array of evidence for his claim, his rather hasty assumption that the suffix *-śiva* indicates Gōlaki affiliation alone has been rightly questioned by some; Cynthia Talbot, "Golaki Matha Inscriptions from Andhra Pradesh: A Study of a Śaiva Monastic Lineage," in A. M. Shastri, R. K. Sharma, and Agam prasad, eds., *Vājapeya: Essays on Evolution of Indian Art and Culture* (Delhi: Agam Kala Prakashan, 1987), p. 133. What does emerge forcefully from Swamy's study, however, is the intimate relationship between Śaiva Siddhāntins and the Cōḻa kings of the eleventh and twelfth centuries, as well as the continuing connections that late medieval Tamil Śaivism had with the monasteries to the north.

[148]The identification of Īśānaśiva, the royal preceptor of the Cōḻa king Rājarāja, with the Āgamic commentator of the same name is probable but not conclusive; B. G. L. Swamy, "The Golaki School," pp. 192, 197. The original location of the Āmarda monastery is unknown.

[149]R. Nagaswamy, "Archeological Finds in South India: Essalam Bronzes and Copper Plates," *Bulletin de l'École Français d'Extrême-Orient* 76 (1989), 32; Nilakanta Sastri provides other notices of the Cōḻa *rājagurus* in *Cōḻas*, p. 452.

[150]The architectural manual *Mayamata*, which bears a characteristic Śaiva Siddhānta inflection, was probably composed in the Cōḻa kingdom during the tenth or eleventh century; *Mayamata: An Indian Treatise on Housing, Architecture and Iconography*, edited by Bruno Dagens (New Delhi: Sitaram Bhartia Institute of Scientific Research, 1985), pp. i–viii.

students (*śiṣyarum praśiṣyarum*) from Āryadeśa, Madhyadeśa, and Gauḍadeśa.[151] The Śaiva Siddhānta monastic lineages (sustained by relationships of preceptor and pupil) present at the Cō̱ḻa court stretched far beyond the boundaries of modern Tamilnadu, just as did the imperial ambitions of the Cōḻas themselves.

But in the late twelfth and thirteenth centuries, when the Kalacuri and Cōḻa kingdoms were beset with difficulties, gurus from both of these kingdoms associated with the famous Gōlaka *maṭha* sought refuge in the Kākatīya polity. The Gōlaki monk Dharmaśiva spent the early part of his life in the Kalacuri kingdom, but when it was attacked by the Candellas and Yādavas, he fled southward to the Kākatīya kingdom, where he quickly became royal preceptor to King Gaṇapati (1199–1262), no doubt due to his Gōlaki affiliation. His disciple, Viśveśvaraśiva, who had been residing in the Cōḻa kingdom at a monastery near Triśirapaḷḷi during the reign of the Cōḻa king Rājarāja III (1216–1253), soon joined him there, where the Gōlaki Śaiva Siddhāntins held prominence for nearly sixty years.[152] This strategic regrouping, which prompted some influential monks to move away from the collapsing Cōḻa imperium, was only part of a more general reconfiguration that Śaiva Siddhānta was undergoing during the thirteenth century.

The rise and hegemony of Islamic polities in north India during the thirteenth century disrupted the pan-continental circuits of the Śaiva Siddhānta order.[153] The Śaiva Siddāntins were hurt more than the peripatetic sects by the shift in power away from dynasties that supported temples and monasteries. As a result, Śaiva Siddhānta soon disappeared as a distinctly identifiable order in north India, surviving only in the south. But even there it suffered setbacks. In Āndhra, the Gōlaki Śaiva Siddhāntins were eventually displaced by the Vīraśaivas in the early fourteenth century.[154] The early kings of the Vijayanagara imperial formation, founded in the fourteenth century, took as their royal preceptor the monist Śaiva Kriyāśakti from Kashmir, and gave their support to the Advaita Daśanāmis at Śṛṅgeri. The triumph of the Advaita position in this major imperial formation also had consequences for Śaiva Siddhāntins living further south, where underlords (*nāyakas*) of the Vijayanagar kings altered preexisting cultural formations. The Nārpatteṇṇāyira Maṭha, a Śaiva Siddhānta monastery at Tiruvanaikka that was established during Cōḻa times, for example, was appropriated by Advaitins who obtained grants from seventeenth century Nāyaka kings.[155]

---

151 E. Hultzsch, "Inscription of Rājendra-Chōla I on the South Wall, First and Second Tiers," *SII* 2.1 (1892), 105–9.

152 K. R. Srinivasa Aiyar, *Inscriptions in the Pudukottai State* (Pudukottai: Sri Brihadamba States Press, 1941), no. 196. The Malkāpuram inscription acknowledges both the Paramāra and Cōḻa kings as disciples of Viśveśvaraśiva; *SII* 10 (1948), 205–9. On the relationship between the Gōlakis and the Kākatīya kings of Wāraṅgal, see Cynthia Talbot, "Golaki Matha Inscriptions," pp. 133–46.

153 Davis, *Ritual*, pp. 17–19.

154 Cynthia Talbot shows the gradual displacement of Gōlaki Śaiva Siddhāntins from Śrīśailam by Vīraśaivas. She notes that the very name of the Vīraśaiva monastery at Śrīśailam, Bhikṣāvṛtti, is a vestige of Gōlaki affiliation, through a reference to the original donation of three *lakhs* of villages that the Kalacuri king gave to the monks at Gōlaka called *bhikṣā*; Cynthia Talbot, "Golaki Matha Inscriptions," pp. 140–41.

155 C. R. Srinivasan, "Two Inscriptions for Tiruvanaikka," in *Svasti Śrī: Dr. B. Ch. Chhabra Felicitation Volume*, edited by K. V. Ramesh (Delhi: Agam Kala Prakashan, 1984) pp. 157–59.

In the faltering Cōḻa domains, Śaiva Siddhānta was rearticulated by a new lineage of teachers, beginning with monk Meykaṇṭār, author of the *Civajñāṉapotam* (c. 1221).[156] Temple liturgy, although still governed by the Sanskrit Āgamas, became less important in spiritual attainment, and Tamil became a language not simply of praise but of Śāstra and theology. At the same time, the priests and ascetics of Meykaṇṭār's lineage drew connections between their own rearticulations of Śaiva Siddhānta theology and the older *bhakti* hymns of the Tamil "saints" (*nāyaṉmār*). During the height of Cōḻa power in the eleventh century, these hymns (*tirupaṭiyam*) formed an important but secondary role in temple liturgy. Known in Sanskrit texts as Drāviḍastotra, the hymns were to be recited by the pure among the serving estate, the Satśūdras, who, although they could receive initiation, were required to stand behind the image of Nandi situated in front of the main shrine.[157] During the eleventh and twelfth centuries these hymns were organized through hagiographical traditions, culminating in a text, the *Periyapurāṇam*, which recounted the lives of the sixty-three *nāyaṉmārs*. Later in the fourteenth century, probably during the life of Umāpati Civācāryar, they were combined with a variety of other Śaiva writings in Tamil to form a canon called the *Tirumuṟai*.[158] Śaiva Siddhānta became localized in the far south, and after the Cōḻa period its theology and religious practice came to rely more and more on these hymns. Thus it is that Śaiva Siddhānta was transformed from a pan-Indian phenomenon in the tenth and eleventh centuries to the distinctively Tamil phenomenon it is today.

But how does our text, a eulogy composed by a Vaiṣṇava court poet, fit into this history? How did inscriptional eulogies, which presuppose Purāṇic genealogies, articulate with the Āgamas, which had largely displaced the Purāṇas as authorative texts for medieval Śaivas? Although the Āgamas do occasionally reiterate the cosmology and temporal notions of the Purāṇas, they focus much more closely on the theology and liturgy of worshiping Śiva. They do not significantly extend the narrative and genealogical portions of the Purāṇas. Cosmology and genealogy were concerns taken up by other sorts of texts in Cōḻa India.

Toward the end of the eleventh century we see the emergence of new texts called Sthalapurāṇas and Māhātmyas, which recast Purāṇic stories around particular temples. With the accession in 1070 of the Veṅgī-born prince Kulōttuṅka I, Śaiva priests attempted to constitute Cidambaram as the soteriological center of

---

[156]Karen Pechilis takes up the reconfiguration of Śaiva Siddhānta as a more Tamil-centered practice beginning in the twelfth century; Karen Pechilis, "Bhakti through Poetry, Polity and Philosophy: On the Work of Culture"; Ph.D. dissertation, University of Chicago, 1993, pp. 158–285.

[157]The *Jātinirnayapūrvakālayapraveśavidhi*, attributed to Rāmakaṇṭha, provides us with this valuable information. For a translation of the text, see Pierre Sylvain Filliozat, "Le Droit d'entrer dans les temples de Śiva au XIe siècle," *Journal Asiatique* 263.1–2 (1975), 103–117; Davis, *Ritual*, pp. 69–72; Karen Pechilis, "Bhakti through Poetry," pp. 196–201.

[158]Daud Ali, "Buddhist Footprints and Śaiva Wanderers: Religion and History in Cōḻa India" (unpublished paper, 1990), pp. 16–17. Pechilis has argued, from the appearance of the term *Tirumuṟai* in an inscription datable to Rājarāja's reign and in the twelfth-century *Periyapurāṇam*, that there were probably two redactions of the *Tirumurai*: the first during the middle Cōḻa period, that included just the hymns; and a larger more inclusive redaction, during the fourteenth century: Pechilis, "Bhakti Through Poetry," pp. 224–8.

the Cōḻa imperium through the composition of *Cidambaramahātmya*.[159] Later, the court poet Cēkkiḻār composed the first Tamil Purāṇa, entitled *Tirutoṇṭarpurāṇam*, the Purāṇa of the Prosperous Servants or, as it came to be known, *Periyapurāṇam*, the Great Purāṇa, to "please the court of Kulōttuṅka II" (1133–1150).[160]

These texts, and the numerous Mahātmyas and Sthalapurāṇas that followed them, marked an important transformation of the earlier Purāṇic knowledges. They seem so different from their earlier namesakes that at face value they warrant no connection. But their nomenclature cannot be dismissed so easily. Sthalapurāṇas related certain aspects of Purāṇic narrative, especially the history of Śiva's escapades in this world and the stories of his devotees, as entwined with history of a specific site (*sthala*). By framing Purāṇic knowledge in this way, they complemented the importance that the Āgamas had placed on the temple as the premier site of spiritual transformation. In other words, framing the history of particular shrines within the larger Theist cosmology, first articulated in the Purāṇas, had itself been made possible by the Āgamic rearticulation of the Purāṇas. As the pan-continental connections of Śaiva Siddhānta fragmented in the thirteenth century, Sthalapurāṇas, by then spread through many kingdoms south of the Vindhyas, became very important in the restructuring of local discplinary orders.

Although they often contain sections praising the excellence of a particular land (*tirunāṭṭuciṟappu*) and city (*tirunakaraciṟappu*), the Sthalapurāṇas do not consistently take up the royal genealogies of the Sanskrit Purāṇas. The *Periyapurāṇa*, for example, connects itself explicitly with the Cōḻa court and sings the glories of the Cōḻa domain (*nāṭu*), but contains no genealogy of the Cōḻa family. Instead, it was the *praśasti*, *meykīrtti*, and other courtly genres that met the task of extending Purāṇic royal genealogies into the present. As Śaiva Siddhāntins, the Cōḻa kings sought to represent themselves as portions and emanations of Viṣṇu, the custodian of the earth according to Śaiva texts. It is in this way that Vaiṣṇavas were incoporated into the Cōḻa imperium, in a profoundly dialectical fashion. Royal genealogy was the Vaiṣṇava niche in the Śaiva polity. Scholars of the Cōḻa period have not worried enough about how the Āgamas, Sthalapurāṇas, and eulogies might have articulated with one another. I would like to suggest that if we read the Sthalapurāṇas, Āgamas, and royal eulogies together we can see that they form parts of single textual configuration during the tenth through twelfth centuries that positioned the Cōḻas, led by their Śaiva Siddhāntins, as heirs to the world knowledges of the Purāṇas.

Eulogy as History

I have argued in this chapter, through an examination of the *RCS- 6*, that the eulogies of post-Gupta copper plates were in fact complicated elaborations of the

[159]Hermann Kulke, "Functional Interpretation of a South Indian Māhātmya: The Legend of Hiraṇyavarman and the Life of King Kulottuṅga I," in Hermann Kulke, *Kings and Cults: State Formation and Legitimation in India and Southeast Asia* (Delhi: Manohar, 1993), pp. 192–207.

[160]*Periyapurāṇam* I.8; Cēkkiḻār's own biography, the *Cēkkiḻārnāyaṉārpurāṇam*, written by Umāpati in 1313, claims that he diverted the king's pleasure from the Jaina work *Cīvakacintāmaṇi*.

past, crucially involved in articulating the polities of medieval India. In concluding, I return to the issue of history, and sort out some preliminary questions raised in reconsidering these medieval texts as visions of the past. Colonial knowledge, as I have mentioned, argued for the lack of historical writing in India by recourse to two arguments: the overbearing presence of a sensual or imaginative faculty in the Hindu mind, and India's lack of political unity. This appraisal, to a large extent inherited by nationalist, Marxist, and post-independence Anglo-American and European historians, is still very much with us today.

The latter claim, that India had never sustained a strong political unity and therefore had no proper object for historical inquiry, formed the foil against which nationalist historiography arose. Colonialists helped secure their own position in India by asserting that the medieval Indian state was dispersed, fragmentary and, except during European-inspired moments of unity, ultimately epiphenomenal to the eternal verities of caste, village, and tribe. In response, nationalists envisioned the ancient and, to a lesser extent the medieval Indian state as a sovereign, unitary, centrally administered polity that expressed a fundamental "Indian" (or "regional") character.[161] Ancient India became, as Gyan Prakash has noted, one of the major sites where nationalist thought began to assert the sovereignty of the Indian nation.[162] As recent work on Indian nationalist thought has made clear, nationalists, like orientalists, assumed that India was an undivided entity ontologically prior to, and expressed in, history.[163] Whereas the British constructed that essence as politically fragmented, the nationalists attributed to it a sovereign unitary will.

The other argument claimed that the accurate and objective representation of reality necessary for a genuine historical tradition was absent in India because of the Hindu mind's imaginative or religious affinities. It is on this basis that inscriptions, to the extent that they harked back to what were deemed the religious texts of the Purāṇas, could not constitute a genuine historical discourse. With few exceptions, orientalists and nationalists alike have seen inscriptional eulogies not as histories in themselves but as "sources" from which histories might be constructed. Like colonial scholars, post-Independence historians denied the existence of historical writing in precolonial India, while at the same time busying themselves in producing just such a history.[164] Some have taken a sort of ameliorated view, seeing the

---

[161]For discussions of how the colonial views of the medieval Indian state and society changed with the transformations of British rule, see Bernard Cohn, "African Models and Indian Histories," *An Anthropologist among the Historians and Other Essays* (Delhi: Oxford University Press, 1990), pp. 200–23; Inden *Imagining India*, pp. 162–212. For a nationalist science of the Indian polity, see A. S. Altekar, *State and Government in Ancient India* (Delhi: Motilal Banarsidass, 1958). On regional states in ancient India, see Romila Thapar, "The Scope and Significance of Regional History," in her *Ancient Indian Social History: Some Interpretations* (Delhi: Orient Longman, 1978), pp. 361–76.

[162]Gyan Prakash, "Writing Post-Orientalist Histories of the Third World: Perspectives from Indian Historiography," *Comparative Studies in Society and History* 32.2 (April 1990), 388.

[163]Partha Chatterjee, *Nationalist Thought and the Colonial World: A Derivative Discourse* ([1986] Minneapolis: Minnesota University Press, 1993), pp. 36–53.

[164]The nationalist historians remained somewhat vindicated in this project through their elevation of the "object" of history, the ancient Indian state. R. C. Majumdar, ed., *History and Culture of the Indian People*, vol. 1, *The Vedic Age* (London: George Allen and Unwin, 1951), 47, 52–56; Nilakanta Sastri, *Cōḷas*, p. 5; Altekar, *State and Government*, p. 24.

inscriptional eulogies as a sort of proto-historical genre still struggling to emerge from the long stretches of their religious pedigree.[165]

Religion preempted any historical consciousness in at least three ways. First, it "encrusted" ancient Indian writing with fantastic legends and fables that seemed patently absurd to modern historians. Religion generated cosmological, mythic, and in the case of India "cyclic" time—all of which functioned to hold India in stasis. Second, it attributed human agency to the divine world.[166] And finally, Brahmanical religion represented the priestly urge to fabricate outlandish theologies in order to secure the position of both themselves and their kingly patrons through duping the massses into a blind acceptance of their lot.[167]

It is not difficult to see how this characterization of religion has formed the necessary prehistory for the emergence of an enlightened and scientific notion of history. But since the turn of the century, the objectivist claims of scientific history have themselves been repeatedly called into question, as various challenges to postivist historiography have emerged. These criticisms have shown how modernist scientific history is "mythic," essentialist, and complicit with modes of domination—all the indictments consistently directed against religion. There is no need to rehearse these critiques here. The neat dichotomy between cyclical and linear time, for example, has proved useless for the careful scrutiny of conceptions of time and history in various societies.[168] But even for much of the scholarship that has atttempted to problematize modernity and history, often in the context of nationalism, the premodern period remains a conceptual stumbling block. Scholars such as Benedict Anderson and Partha Chatterjee have continued to characterize premodern conceptions with the very modernist teleology that they seek to problematize. Partha Chatterjee, for example, has insightfully illuminated the major

---

[165]Romila Thapar argues that the Itihāsa-Purāṇa tradition constituted an historical consciousness out of which later emerged a tradition of historical writing (biographies/inscriptions) in the post-Gupta period. Although she raises the important issue of historical consciousness and its relation to state formation, she retains the dichotomy of myth and reality—with the Itihāsa-Purāṇa tradition being predominantly the former and post-Gupta historical writing the latter; Romila Thapar, "The Tradition of Historical Writing in Early India," in her *Ancient Indian Social History: Some Interpretations* (Delhi: Orient Longman, 1979), pp. 268–93. More recently, Thapar has distinguished cyclic from linear notions of time within single textual strata, associating the former with cosmology and the latter with historical thinking, the latter of which "goes beyond," rather than supplements, the former; Romila Thapar, *Time as a Metaphor of History: Early India* (Delhi: Oxford University Press, 1996), p. 37.

[166]On the "false consciousness" of the peasant during colonial times and his estrangement from his own actions as a result of the semi-feudal religious ideology he inherited, which attributed his own actions to anothers' will, see Ranajit Guha, *Elementary Aspects of Peasant Insurgency* (Delhi: Oxford University Press, 1983), p. 277; and Guha, "Dominance without Hegemony and Its Historiography," *Subaltern Studies 6* (Delhi: Oxford University Press, 1989), 210–309.

[167]These views, articulated eloquently by James Mill, have continued through the scholarship of some Marxist historians. It has recently been argued that the ever-present Vedic ideology, with its transcendent claims, functioned to supress history; Sheldon Pollock, "Mīmāṃsā and the Problem of History in Traditional India," *Journal of the American Oriental Society* 109.4 (1989), 603–10.

[168]Romila Thapar makes this valuable point. She argues that the Purāṇas contain both linear and cyclical notions of time, wherein "fragmentary arcs within the cycle...take on the role of linear time the dichotomy becoming increasingly vague"; Thapar, *Time as a Metaphor of History*, p. 31. Although she questions the clarity of any distinction between the two, Thapar nevertheless retains cyclical and linear as legitimate theoretical concepts for understanding medieval Indian genres concerning the past.

ruptures in Indian thinking about the past during the colonial period. He argues that the older Purāṇic and Mughal court histories underwent a fundamental change in historical consciousness with the long birth of the modern Indian nation. In an important sense, then, the history of the "nation of India" is something absent in ancient and medieval texts. As Chatterjee argues, the terms through which the past is articulated move from the succession of kings to the eternalities of land and people.[169] Although the term "Bhārat" seems to resonate with earlier Purāṇic discourses, its signifying domain was greatly transformed and reduced in nationalist historiography. The history of "Bhārat," for example, does not find itself within a Purāṇic geography that includes Kailāsa, Meru, and Jambudvīpa. Despite noting the appropriation of premodern ideologies by nationalist history, Chatterjee nevertheless tends to understand these texts within a rationalist framework that would place them within the telos of the modern nation. Although he subtly points out the discursive shifts in conceptions of the past that emerged in the nineteenth century, he contrasts this new nationalist history with a Purāṇic account that in the end reproduces standard modernist dichotomies of myth versus history and divine will versus human action. He argues that the Purāṇic accounts of the past mix history and myth freely, and that major actors in these accounts are gods, not men.[170] Myth and religion themselves have not been problematized in these accounts. Any historicization of rationality or modernity that leaves medieval myth and religion intact only goes half the journey. Far from existing since time immemorial, the terms "religion" and "myth," as we know them today, gained their meanings only during the Enlightenment, when they were constituted as foils against a newly emergent "rationality."[171] If we recognize the fact that modernity has to a large extent generated its own prehistory by re-inflecting certain practices, then we can see that precolonial texts did not anticipate modern political rationality, in any "regional," "mythic," or fragmentary sense. They signified something different.

Some scholars, as part of their critique of modernity, have argued that history itself is profoundly modern.[172] From this perspective, the attempt to see the *RCS–6* and other precolonial discourses as forming "histories" is at best an apologetic attempt to bestow modern European rationality upon precolonial India. This argument might be easily sustained if historical writing had been invented in the nineteenth century, or if "our" notion of history were singular and stable. But to do so would reoccupy the very apocalyptic claims that characterize much of modernist thought. We have to think about what we mean by "history" and its various discursive positions—for Kant's universal history, the medieval monk's *historiarum*, and the positivist's social history are radically different enterprises.[173] The

[169]Partha Chatterjee, *The Nation and Its Fragments: Colonial and Post-Colonial Histories* (Princeton: Princeton University Press, 1993), p. 95.

[170]Chatterjee, *The Nation and Its Fragments*, p. 80.

[171]For an insightful meditation on the emergence of the concept of religion, see Talal Asad, *Genealogies of Religion: Discipline and Reasons of Power in Christianity and Islam* (Baltimore: Johns Hopkins University Press, 1993), pp. 27–54.

[172]Nicholas Dirks, "History as a Sign of the Modern," *Public Culture* 2.2 (Spring 1990), 25–32.

[173]Sheldon Pollock has suggested that we reconsider the "long-held view concerning the absence of historical understanding in India...on the basis of recent scholarship on the notion of history itself."

inscriptional eulogies and Purāṇas clearly do not present a conception of the past identical to the nineteenth-century positivist notion of history. Nor does the *RCS–6* presuppose a foundational geographical or national space that somehow precedes the actions of its narrative agents. Even if we admit, taking a nominalist approach, that the modern word "history" has no exact equivalent in medieval India, then it would be equally anachronistic to apply the word "myth" or "legend" to these texts, as many scholars do. How, then, shall we place conceptions of the past within the discursive terrain of "Middle India"?

Conceptions of the past in early medieval India arose from two distinct types of discourse: Purāṇa and Kāvya. Kāvya, writing marked by its capacity to give pleasure through ornament or mood, included a variety of genres in both prose and verse. Only certain genres of Kāvya, like the eulogy, concerned themselves exclusively with the elaboration of kingly genealogies, although many others located their narratives within temporal frames articulated in the Purāṇas. Purāṇas, texts in prose or verse concerned with the universal knowledge about the world appropriate for the Age of Strife, were, on the other hand, usually seen as distinct from Kāvya, coming instead to supplement or displace the revealed literature, Veda, and normative treatises, Śāstra.[174]

Some sholars have seen inscriptional eulogies as quite distinct from other forms of Kāvya. As Sheldon Pollock has noted, virtually none of the authors we know from the corpus of lithic eulogies can be found as authors of "textual" literary Kāvyas.[175] Moreover, other scholars have made sharp distinctions between panegyrists and poets (*kavis*) proper. We do indeed find that the authors we know from Cōḻa inscriptional eulogies, like Narāyaṇa of the *RCS–6*, did not compose the longer works known from the period. There was undoubtedly a complex division of poetic labor across genres and languages at the Cōḻa court, which remains to be fully excavated. The poet Nārāyaṇa's title, as we have mentioned above, was "Lord of Tamil for the Best of Cōḻas" (*uttamacōḻatamiḻataraiya*), whereas Kambaṉ, author of the Tamil *Irāmavatāram*, the epic of the Solar dynasty the Cōḻas claimed ancestry from, was dubbed "Paramount Overlord among Poets" (*kaviccakravarti*). A complex relationship between courtly position and poetic mastery is borne out by these titles, indicating that the organization of poets mirrored the hierarchy of the lords whom they served. This is not surprising, since poets often held imperial office or were even kings themselves. It is likely, however, that the office of imperial

He nevertheless maintains that "the absence of a historical-referential dimension of Sanskrit discourse remains a serious problem," concluding that "history, seems not so much to be unknown in Sanskritic India as to be denied"; Pollock, "Mīmāṃsā," p. 603. More recently, Pollock has shifted this view, arguing that the medieval kings of Karnataka employed an all-too-familiar species of historian—"what else shall we call a person who examines ancient documents and possesses the necessary philological and paleographic skills to do so?"; "Making History," p. 573. What seems clear, despite his subtle considerations of the recent debates on "history" as such, is that history still remains a system of "dating," and that the historian remains a fact finder.

[174]For the relationship of the Purāṇas to other varieties of Sanskrit literature, see Maurice Winternitz, *History of Indian Literature* (Calcutta: University of Calcutta, 1927), 1: 517–30; Ludo Rocher, *The Purāṇas* (Weisbaden: Otto Harrassowitz, 1986), pp. 80–94. The *Bhāgavatapurāṇa*, however, was written as a *mahākāvya*.

[175]Pollock, "Making History," p. 561.

eulogist, author of the Sanskrit and Tamil eulogies that formed the introductions of the king's orders, was a position distinct from those of other poets at the king's court. This division of labor, however, does not mark a radical separation in mode of composition. Imperial eulogies are composed in ornate Kāvya style and use meters and adornments familiar to us from "textual" poetry. Furthermore, many longer works in both Sanskrit and Tamil contain the genealogical eulogies of kings we are accustomed to finding in inscriptional eulogies.[176] Medieval Tamil grammars treat the royal eulogy (*meykīrtti*) no differently from the myriad other compositions that poetic form could take.[177] Kāvya as a discursive form, whether in its eulogistic or more narrative forms, was indissociably linked, from its very inception, with the courts of kings, making Sanskrit Kāvya, in the apt words of Sheldon Pollock, a "public political language."[178]

The poetic genre of our text, the Eulogy, meaning literally "praise," actually marks a general theme of Kāvya. As David Smith has argued, royal eulogy forms one of the truly integral aspects of Kāvya.[179] Medieval Tamil grammars name many genres that take up aspects of royal eulogy: the celebration of the ten aspects of polity (*tacāṅkam*), the naming of the eight auspicious things to be seen by the king (*aṭṭamaṅkalam*), the description of the king's procession (*ulā*), the song on the king's birthday (*perumaṅkalam*), and the praise of the king's childhood (*piḷḷaitamiḻ*).[180] Many of these genres were simultaneously deployed to praise Śiva or Viṣṇu. For, just as the lordship of king and deity were continuous, so were the discourses that celebrated this lordship.[181] Moreover, Kāvya, through its ornament and mood, was meant to give aesthetic pleasure to its royal audience. Pleasing a lord through the narration of his past deeds was itself one of the main practices in Theist ways of life, and preoccupies countless medieval liturgical practices as well as "religious" compositions that describe the sports and escapades of Śiva or Viṣṇu while giving them praise.[182] Thus, the genealogical eulogies that connected

[176]The *Rājarājavijayam*, a Sanskrit *kāvya* describing the victories of Rājarāja I referred to in epigraphy but no longer extant, undoubtedly contained a genealogy of the Cōḻa family. The early twelfth-century Sanskrit *Vikramāṅkadevacarita*, describing the life of Cālukya king Vikramāditya VI (1076–1126), begins with a genealogical eulogy. The long Tamil poem *Kaliṅkattuparaṇi*, describing Kulōttuṅka I's war against the king of Kaliṅga, contains two books devoted to the elaboration of the Cōḻa king's genealogy and deeds. The *ulā* genre, four examples of which have survived from the Cōḻa period, begins with a full genealogical eulogy of the king.

[177]For example, the twelfth century *Paṉṉiruppāṭṭiyal*; *Paṉṉiruppāṭṭiyal* with commentary of K. R. Kōvintarāca Mutāliyār ([1943] Tinnevelly: South India Saiva Siddhanta Works, 1963), v. 197.

[178]Sheldon Pollock, "The Sanskrit Cosmopolis, 300–1300: Transculturation, Vernacularization and the Question of Ideology," in Jan Houben, ed., *Ideology and the Status of Sanskrit: Contributions to the History of the Sanskrit Language* (Leiden: E. J. Brill, 1996), pp. 197–247.

[179]David Smith, *Ratnākara's Haravijaya: An Introduction to the Sanskrit Court Epic* (Delhi: Oxford University Press, 1985), pp. 55–102.

[180]An exhaustive list of medieval genres (*pirapantam*) is provided in K. Zvelebil, *Tamil Literature* (Wiesbaden: Otto Harrassowitz, 1974), pp. 193–230.

[181]For the "courtly" organization of temple ritual, see Saskia Kersenboom-Story, *Nityasumaṅgalī: The Devadasi Tradition of South India* (Delhi: Motlilal Banarsidass, 1987), pp. 99–128.

[182]Certain medieval bhakti poetry works within a much more severe economy of pleasure that disdains the ornamentation characteristic of Kāvya.

medieval kings with the dynasties of previous ages at the same time linked the lives of these kings to Theist ways of life.

This Theist knowledge presupposed by the Kāvya texts held that time, which stretched infinitely into both the past and the future, was ordered into the successive days and nights of the worlds's most preeminent beings. These moments constituted together the progression of Brahmā's life, which was in turn framed as a moment in the life of an even higher lord, Viṣṇu or Śiva.[183] If the movement of time was the unfolding and succession of divine lives, on a smaller scale it could also be seen as the unfolding and succession of human lives—the genealogies of sages or kings, both of which are taken up in the Purāṇas, and elaborated further in the Kāvya texts.

The passing of Brahmā's days and nights, the oscillations in his existence, had great repercussions for the rest of the world, because they also constituted the innumerable millennia in which the world was repeatedly created (*sṛṣṭi*) and destroyed (*pralaya*). Each successive age (*yuga*) of the four that were to constitute an epoch of Manu (*manvantara*) saw a steady decline in the completeness of Brahmā's creation, culminating in the fourth and dissolute Age of Strife, when lifespans and fortunes would diminish, the practices of the Vedas (as reformualted in the Sūtras) would cease, and kings abuse their subjects. Finally, as I have mentioned, there would be born an instantiation of Viṣṇu, who, along with seeds of the Lunar and Solar lines that had been incubating in hermitages near Kailāsa, would initiate a new epoch of Manu and a new Age of Completeness (*Kṛtayuga*).[184] According to the Purāṇas, as time traversed the reaches of the island continent (*Jambudvīpa*) wherein resided the world's lesser beings, it always signified this universal history.

The Purāṇic vision leaves a peculiar sort of agency for the characters in its drama, quite unlike modern history. To understand this agency, we must remember that in medieval India, thinking about the past was not, as in modern times, an intellectual method that might be applied to a diverse field of phenomena, producing autonomous and varied results in each. The Purāṇic histories tell, instead, the history of a world wherein the lives of gods and ghosts, kings and sages, lords and subjects—of every inert and living being—were caught in the same stream.[185] Similar notions of history in premodern Europe, Foucault argued, were displaced as each of the new human sciences emerged with its own historicity.[186] It is in the modern episteme, according to Foucault, that literature, economy, and society all

---

[183]The *Viṣṇupurāṇa* (I.3.6–7) says that one of the four aspects of Viṣṇu is time itself. Viṣṇu as time is applied to measure the life of Brahmā. The *Śivapurāṇa* (VII.1.7.9) places Śiva beyond the control of time. But his lesser forms (VII.1.8.2–28) are used to measure it; so that one lifetime of Brahmā is equivalent to one day in the life of Viṣṇu, whereas one life of Viṣṇu is equal to one day in the life of Rudra, and so on.

[184]Although the Purāṇas say that the dissolution occurs at the end of the day of Brahmā, (*Viṣṇupurāṇa*, I.3.22–23) or Parameśvara (*Śivapurāṇa*, VII.1.8.28), they also imply that it would be destroyed at the end of the present Age of Strife, located in the seventh epoch of Manu, which was by no means at the end of a day of Brahmā (*Śivapurāṇa*, V.39.28–29; *Viṣṇupurāṇa*, IV.24.26–30).

[185]I do not mean to imply that there was no contestation. The Sri Lankan Pāli chronicles discussed in Jon Walters' chapter in this volume provide one major alternative to the Purāṇic history of the Cōḻas.

[186]Michel Foucault, *The Order of Things: An Archeology of the Human Sciences* (New York: Vintage, 1973), pp. 367–69.

came to have their own autonomous historicity.[187] "Man" exists in this scheme as both an ahistoricity and the unwritten subject of all histories. "Man" has no such transparent transcendence in medieval Indian conceptions of the past.

If the Purāṇic world does not contain "man" as a sovereign being, the master of his own history, neither should we conclude that the actions of medieval peasants, kings, and priests were all displaced onto some distant and immutable force. Despite the presence of the divine in this vision of history, it was profoundly actionist. In order to grasp this, we must remember that Śaiva and Vaiṣṇava conceptions of divinity are radically immanent, to borrow a phrase from Protestant theology—where it seems diluted in comparison. One can hardly claim that divinity displaces human agency when medieval agents could claim divine agency as their own. Our text characterizes the king's action as "doubly agentive"—as the action of both a paramount sovereign and Viṣṇu himself.[188] The sphere of the world ruler was not simply bestowed by Viṣṇu but had to be made and remade. Inscriptional eulogies acknowledge that paramount overlordship could switch from one polity to another, based at one and the same time upon divine favor and a king's ability to supplant an earlier order and articulate a sovereignty worthy of that favor.

The seeming determinacy of the Purāṇic world vision did not, as our inscription patently illustrates, close off thinking about the past. It instead provided a frame for its unfolding—a frame that gave scope for continual elaboration. Although the Purāṇas place their own narration soon after the Mahābhārata war on the eve of the Age of Strife, the species of Kāvya that concerns itself with kingly genealogy understood its present as the decadent Age of Strife. These texts did not simply resign themselves, however, to its dissolute conditions. They saw the kings at whose courts the texts were composed as vessels of light in the surrounding darkness. Their royal histories are the shining completions of the Purāṇic narratives. They celebrated their kings as the successors of the extinct Solar and Lunar dynasties that would be resuscitated, it was foretold, at the end of the Age of Strife. The royal texts of medieval Indian courts represented the reigns of their kings, if they were able to do so, as the reestablishment of paramount overlordship in the Age of Strife and the heralding of a new Age of Completeness. We have seen that the *RCS–6* articulated this claim by linking the Cōḻa kings to the age-old Solar dynasty at a moment when a series of mutually conflicting claims were made by other powerful dynasties.

The eulogies that made these claims traveled far beyond their point of origin. They proliferated the king's fame across the locales of his kingdom, where they prefaced the appearance of his "auspicious face" (*tirumukam*), and thus authorized the mobilization of labor and resources. I have not in this chapter taken up the

[187] Total history differs from the universal medieval history in that it remains in the end an aggregation of these narrower histories under a single topos.

[188] If a complex polity that claims such a dubious entity as god as one of its constituent agents seems strange to us, we might inquire into the ontological status of that somewhat intractable constituent of the modern polity, "the people." Baudrillard puts it well: "The whole chaotic constellation of the social revolves around that spongy referent, that opaque but equally translucent reality, that nothingness: the masses." Jean Baudrillard, *In the Shadow of the Silent Majorities, or the End of the Social and Other Essays* (New York: Semiotexte, 1983), p. 1.

issue of what the medieval Indian polity might have looked like. But if, as Hegel says, history is integral to the "very progress of its [the state's] own being,"[189] then these eulogies conceived as histories would be a useful point of departure to rethink the medieval Indian polity. I have made only a few suggestions in that direction. Rereading the *RCS–6* as an articulative history of the Cōḻa polity, not as an "historical source" reflecting Hindu society, may help us to rethink our received images of medieval India. And in doing so, the horizons of modernity may look quite different.

Appendix: Archeology and the History of India

The subjugation of large parts of Asia and Africa by the Anglo-French imperial powers during the eighteenth and nineteenth centuries entailed complicated methods of mastery, chief among which was the "invention" of a certain sort of history and civilization for colonized territories. Massive surveys undertaken by the British in nineteenth-century India brought together a whole range of "facts" that became the tools integral to the technology of British rulership.[190] Orientalism and Indology as disciplines have their roots in the complicated discursive process of producing and mastering the other—"inventing" the history and civilization of the subject peoples.[191] By using the term "invention," I do not imply that the British fabricated *ex nihilo* the history and culture of an entire civilization, but rather stress their appropriation and transformation of a large variety of preexisting knowledges and practices, while claiming merely to represent them as they were. India as "invented" by orientalists was an entity with "natural" boundaries and essential traits. The claims about the Indian mind were part of this process of producing the colonial subject. So, on the one hand, some unitary entity had to be posited that was to be the ongoing "patient" of British rule. But on the other hand, the claim was made that this "entity" was actually incapable of unifying itself, and hence needed the guiding hand of the British empire. Orientalist histories are situated at this precarious nexus. The most important formulation that resolved this difficulty was the claim made by Indologists and historians that the unity of India lay not in a continuous political history but in the "cultural" and "societal" sphere.[192] This process involved depoliticizing a number of Indian textual and institutional practices and reframing them within the domain of "society" or "religion." Political history became fragmentary, and ultimately epiphenomenal in the constructs of India. As the British assumed political control over India, they theorized that the Indian state and its rulers did not form the "natural leadership" of India—instead this role was

[189] Hegel, *Philosophy*, p. 61.

[190] Shahid Amin, ed., "Introduction," in *A Glossary of North Indian Peasant Life* by William Crooke ([1879] Delhi: Oxford University Press, 1989), xviii–xlii.

[191] The groundbreaking work that located orientalist knowledge as part of the ongoing political domination of its object, the Orient, was Edward Said's *Orientalism* (New York: Pantheon, 1978).

[192] On the origin of this bifurcation of the domain of the human and social sciences into "political" and "social" during the latter half of the nineteenth century, see Eric Wolf, *Europe and the People without History* (Berkeley and Los Angeles: University of California Press, 1982), pp. 7- 19.

assumed by the age-old village economy and the caste system.[193] Indologists figured that the ever-changing political history of petty states did not matter in the "real" lives of Indians.

The role of the British "self" in all of its discourse on the "other" is complex. The colonial scholars reasoned that because the state was weak in India, invasion was endemic to Indian history. In fact, the narrative of Indian political history was largely organized around the trope of invasion and empire—beginning with Alexander the Great and ending with the British. Not surprisingly, it was these invasions, according to Indologists, that constituted the brief chapters of political unity in the subcontinent.[194] Historians saw the British presence in India as necessary for the maintenance of political order. As Vincent Smith wrote in his hegemonic history of ancient India, "Harsha's death loosened the bonds which restrained the disruptive forces always ready to operate in India, and allowed them to produce their natural result, a medley of petty states, with ever varying boundaries, and engaged in unceasing internecine war.... The history, told in the next chapters, serves to give the reader a notion of what India always has been when released from the control of a supreme authority, and what she would be again, if the hand of the benevolent power which now safeguards her boundaries, should be withdrawn."[195] This is the moral lesson of Smith's history: the British presence in India was necessary to prevent political chaos. One of the paradoxes of his text is that he is able to tell the political history of a land whose natural condition is political chaos. What moves the narrative along, consequently, are the multiple invasions of India, beginning with the most important, that of Alexander the Great. The unwritten denouement of this narrative, of course, is the British arrival in India—presumably the most comprehensive and final foreign hand to unify India.

Thus the British positioned themselves in this discourse not only as the political heirs of a fragmentary, politically dispersed Hindu nation(s), but also as the authoritative and final arbiters or interlocutors of Indian history. The claims that India had no history did not mean that India's past was without events, but that, due to its lack of political unity and, perhaps more importantly, the irrationality of the Hindu mind, India had no way of knowing its own true history save by the rational methods of Western science. Preeminent among these sciences was archeology.[196]

Because it lacked unified states and their histories, early Indologists lamented the difficulty in reconstructing a history for ancient India. But at the same time scholars and bureaucrats had discovered, quite accidentally, numerous free-standing

---

[193]Cohn, "African Models and Indian Histories," pp. 211–15.

[194]But then again, these invaders, operating on the superficial realm of politics, never had any effect on the eternal stasis of Indian society. This perhaps justified turning away from the rhetoric of "improvement" after the Mutiny, when the British assumed complete sovereignty over India; Ranajit Guha, "Dominance without Hegemony."

[195]Vincent Smith, *The Early History of India from 600 B.C. to the Muhammadan Conquest* ([1904] Oxford: Clarendon, 1924), pp. 370, 372.

[196]For an analysis of Indian archeology and its relation to colonial and nationalist ideologies along lines somewhat different from those pursued here, see Tapati Guha-Thakurta, "Monuments and Lost Histories: Archaeology in the Colonial and Nationalist Imagination," in Giles Tillotson, ed., *Towards an Indian Aesthetics* (London: Curzon, 1997), pp. 29–63.)

pillars, stupas, temples, stones, and copper plates whose surfaces were covered with inscriptions that seemed to open up India's past. Notices of archeological artifacts, particularly stone and copper plate inscriptions, began to appear, albeit in an unsystematic fashion, as early as 1837 in periodicals like *Asiatic Researches*, *Journal of the Asiatic Society*, *Indian Antiquary*, and *Madras Journal of Literature and Science*.[197] The creation of the post "Archeological Surveyor of India" in 1861, and ten years later in 1871 of the "Archeological Survey of India," marked a turning point in this trend, and massive amounts of material began to be collected from all over India. Epigraphy, the study of inscriptions, began to achieve autonomy as a discipline distinct from its parent, archeology, with the publication in 1877 and 1888 of the two important volumes of the series *Corpus Inscriptionum Indicarum*, that collected the inscriptions of Aśoka and the Gupta kings. By 1887, the Government of Madras was publishing notices of the numerous inscriptions examined by its officers in a series that came to be called the *Annual Report on South Indian Epigraphy*. The appearance of two series devoted solely to the publication and translation of stone and copper plate inscriptions—*Epigraphia Indica* in 1889 under the direction of J. Burgess, and *South Indian Inscriptions* a year later under the direction of E. Hultzsch—officially inaugurated the epigraphical industry, which was to become the foundation of the historiographical quest for the chronology of ancient India. Vincent Smith, whose text (1904) was to inherit the hegemonic position among colonialist histories from James Mill, begins by stating that as a result of "immense progress...made during the last forty years" it was now possible "to exhibit the results of antiquarian studies in the shape of a connected relation."[198]

In the 150 years since Mill's *History*, the definitive chronologies of India before the Muslim conquests have been constructed largely on the basis of the interpretation of stone and copper-plate inscriptions. The narrative of ancient and medieval Indian history has, of course, relied heavily on the discipline of archeology. Jonathan Faithfull Fleet (1847–1917) officially explained the role that archeology should assume in historical research.

> Rich as have been their bequests to us in other lines, the Hindus have not transmitted to us any historical works which can be accepted as reliable for any early times. And it is almost entirely from a patient examination of the inscriptions, the start of which was made more than a century ago, that our knowledge of the ancient history of India has been derived. But we are also ultimately dependent on the inscriptions in every other line of Indian research. Hardly any definite dates and identifications can be established except from them. And they regulate everything we can learn from tradition, literature, coins, art, architecture, or any other source.[199]

This passage articulates quite well what one might call the epistemological regime of the archeology. Literature and art, as valuable as they were in throwing light on the Hindu mind, were of little value for reconstructing the history of India.

---

[197] Sircar, *Indian Epigraphy*, p. 8.

[198] Smith, *Early History*, pp. 1–2.

[199] J. F. Fleet, *The Imperial Gazetteer of India*, vol. 2 (Oxford: Clarendon, 1909), 3.

Sure knowledge of events and dates in Indian history could be extracted only from inscriptions. Inscriptions more clearly than any other source could "represent" the Indian past. I use the word "regime" to indicate the preeminent or controlling status that these objects have continually been given over other "sources" that were available from ancient India. Inscriptions have been used as anchors to establish dates in the chronology of ancient India. Various phenomena—architecture, religious institutions, literature—have been placed within this chronological narrative. Hence, inscriptions have had a "regulating" effect on these other domains of inquiry.[200]

On one level, these "discoveries" profoundly disturbed colonial historiographies of India. They seemed to call for a reappraisal of the colonialist claim that India's past before the coming of the Muslims was totally devoid of all historical writing. However, by no means did they absolve India from Hegel's condemnation. Although Fleet declared inscriptions to be the most important documents for historians of India, he did not consider them to be histories in themselves. They exhibited no "true historical sense." Rather, he saw them as more or less flawed "sources" for the reconstruction of Indian history: "While however they contain the historical and other information we seek, they were written...not with the object of presenting that information, but for other purposes...and it is only incidentally...that they record the details which are so valuable to us."[201] It turns out that these "other purposes" were primarily "religious." So inscriptions were not only enabling for the Indologist, but irritating as well. The historical circumstances of the authors of inscriptions were always distorted by the imagination of the Hindu mind; "facts" were freely mixed with "myths." D. C. Sircar, the eminent Indian epigraphist, warns that "history is often shadowed in them by poetical or eulogistic and conventional elements."[202] The job of the archeologist or historian, then, was to sift through the overblown language of inscriptions for useful facts with which they might reconstruct the dates of kings.

The colonialist and early nationalist historians saw the careers of kings and dynasties as the "stuff" of Indian history that the inscriptions revealed. India's past was the story of the rise and fall of countless dispersed and regional empires ruled by petty tyrannical despots fruitlessly vying for territorial hegemony. Inscriptions were used by these older schools of history to establish successions of regnal regimes and interstate relationships. These complicated dynastic histories of petty medieval empires formed a tedious history, indeed. The mainstream of Indology held that the real continuity of India lies not in the political but in the eternalities of caste and religion. Consequently, the dynastic narratives constructed from inscriptions have held a peripheral locale in the hegemonic constructs of India.

---

200 The regulatory value of inscriptions that Fleet proclaimed nearly eighty years ago seems to have been heard of only recently by art historians; *Indian Epigraphy and Its Bearing on the History of Art*, edited by Frederick M. Asher and G. S. Gai (New Delhi: American Institute of Indian Studies, 1985). Art historians, with the help of epigraphical sources, can now recover substantial information on the creators of monuments, so that "eventually it might be possible to treat the corpus of a certain artist as it is done for a Mughal painting," and to trace the "stylistic evolution of temples" with a "greater precision than ever before" (p. v).

201 Fleet, *Imperial Gazetteer*, pp. 4–5.

202 Sircar, *Indian Epigraphy*, p. 23.

They merely form a weak but expedient frame for the studies of caste and religion. The famous Indologist A. L. Basham, introducing the nine-page treatment of seven hundred years of medieval Indian political history in his five hundred-page book *The Wonder That Was India*, states, "The history of the succeeding dynasties is a rather drab story of endemic warfare between rival dynasties. It can be followed in some detail, thanks to numerous inscriptions and copper plate charters, but the detail is monotonous and uninteresting to all but the specialist."[203] More recently, scholars of medieval south India have used the copious inscriptions associated with the Cō̱la empire to produce what might be called the "history of state and society."[204] Burton Stein, probably the preeminent spokesman of this new approach, wrote in 1977 that while inscriptions could be used as "control evidence" for economic and social transactions "historians have seldom used inscriptions for this purpose."[205] Instead, according to Stein, they had concentrated on their eulogistic introductions—their "ideological content." In contrast Stein and others have been concerned with theorizing the structure of "state and society" supposedly mirrored in epigraphy. In the histories of south Indian "state and society," several important correctives have been made over the older dynastic reading of inscriptions. Several provocative and potentially fruitful questions were asked: How do inscriptions function and what do they do? Who signed and endorsed them? What governing bodies and social institutions are reflected in them? These questions have allowed historians to theorize Cō̱la history with greater sophistication than ever before. But in doing so, these historians have relegated the theological and political claims of the inscriptions to the Weberian model of "legitimation"—the generic religious justification of authority. Within such frameworks, it has been impossible to understand the actual ideological programs, discursive strategies, ideas of sovereignty, and conceptions of time—past and present—current in the royal courts from which these inscriptions emerged.

---

[203] A. L. Basham, *The Wonder That Was India* ([1954] London: Sidgwick and Jackson, 1967), pp. 69–70. This book deals with the "more interesting" topic of "culture" in ancient India.

[204] See Y. Subbarayalu, *The Political Geography of the Chola Country* (Madras: Tamilnadu State Department of Archeology, 1973); Noburu Karashima, Y. Subbarayalu, and T. Matsui, *A Concordance to the Names in the Cōla Inscriptions* (Madurai: Sarvodya Ilakkiya Pannai, 1978); Noburu Karashima, *South Indian History and Society: A.D. 850–1300* (Delhi: Oxford University Press, 1984); Burton Stein, *Peasant State and Society in Medieval South India* (Delhi: Oxford University Press, 1980).

[205] Burton Stein, "Circulation and the Historical Geography of the Tamil Country," *Journal of Asian Studies* 37.1 (November 1977), 17.

Index

SOAS LIBRARY

Lightning Source UK Ltd.
Milton Keynes UK
UKOW01n0138170817
307439UK00004B/35/P

9 780195 124309